The Law of God

Studies in Reformed Theology

Editor-in-chief

Eddy Van der Borght (*Vrije Universiteit Amsterdam*)

Editorial Board
Abraham van de Beek (*Vrije Universiteit Amsterdam*)
Martien Brinkman (*Vrije Universiteit Amsterdam*)
Dirk van Keulen (*Theological University, Kampen*)
Daniel Migliore (*Princeton Theological Seminary*)
Richard Mouw (*Fuller Theological Seminary, Pasadena*)
Emanuel Gerrit Singgih (*Duta Wacana Christian University, Yogjakarta*)
Pieter Vos (*Protestant Theological University, Amsterdam*)
Conrad Wethmar (*University of Pretoria*)

VOLUME 28

The titles published in this series are listed at *brill.com/srt*

The Law of God

Exploring God and Civilization

Edited by

Pieter Vos and Onno Zijlstra

BRILL

LEIDEN | BOSTON

Cover illustration: Courtesy of the Uffizi Gallery, Florence.

Library of Congress Cataloging-in-Publication Data

The law of God : exploring God and civilization / edited by Pieter Vos and Onno Zijlstra.
　　pages cm. -- (Studies in Reformed theology, ISSN 1571-4799 ; VOLUME 28)
　Includes index.
　ISBN 978-90-04-28183-7 (hardback : alk. paper) -- ISBN 978-90-04-28184-4 (e-book) 1. Religion and civilization. 2. God. I. Vos, Pieter, 1970- editor.

BL55.L28 2014
201'.7--dc23

2014028945

This publication has been typeset in the multilingual 'Brill' typeface. With over 5,100 characters covering Latin, IPA, Greek, and Cyrillic, this typeface is especially suitable for use in the humanities. For more information, please see brill.com/brill-typeface.

ISSN 1571-4799
ISBN 978-90-04-28183-7 (paperback)
ISBN 978-90-04-28184-4 (e-book)

Copyright 2014 by Koninklijke Brill NV, Leiden, The Netherlands.
Koninklijke Brill NV incorporates the imprints Brill, Brill Nijhoff, Global Oriental, Hotei Publishing.
All rights reserved. No part of this publication may be reproduced, translated, stored in a retrieval system, or transmitted in any form or by any means, electronic, mechanical, photocopying, recording or otherwise, without prior written permission from the publisher.
Authorization to photocopy items for internal or personal use is granted by Koninklijke Brill NV provided that the appropriate fees are paid directly to The Copyright Clearance Center, 222 Rosewood Drive, Suite 910, Danvers, MA 01923, USA. Fees are subject to change.

This book is printed on acid-free paper.

Printed by Printforce, the Netherlands

Contents

Introduction 1
    Pieter Vos and Onno Zijlstra

PART 1
Secularity

The Law of God in a Secular State
    Claiming Space in the Public Domain 23
        Gé Speelman

Multiculturalism, Religion and Public Justice 44
    Jonathan Chaplin

The Natural Law and Liberal Traditions
    Heritage (and Hope?) of Western Civilization 64
        David VanDrunen

The Empire and the Desert
    Eastern Orthodox Theologians about Church and Civilization 84
        Alfons Brüning

Whose Civilization is Europe Today?
    Encounters between Hungarian Reformed Faith and Secular Worldviews 105
        Ábrahám Kovács

PART 2
Monotheism

The Aniconic God in Isaiah 43:10 and the Contemporary Discourse on Monotheism 135
    Emanuel Gerrit Singgih

Is Christ Among Us?
Mystical Christology from the Perspective of Pseudo-Dionysius and Taoism 151
    Jaeseung Cha

A Violent God?
Philosophical Reflections on Monotheism and Genesis 22 173
    Renée van Riessen

The Irreducibility of Religious Faith
Kierkegaard on Civilization and the Aqedah 194
    Pieter Vos

PART 3
Transformation

Civic Integration
A Mission to Civilize Religious Believers? 217
    Mechteld Jansen

Prophecy and Democracy?
Some Arguments in Favor of Prophetic Discourse in Civilizing Democratic Societies 239
    Nico Koopman

Mapping the Christian Character
Calvin and Schleiermacher on Virtue, Law and Sanctification 256
    Heleen Zorgdrager

In Defense of Authenticity
On Art, Religion and the Authentic Self 282
    Onno Zijlstra

Religious Transformations within Modernity
Religion and the Modern Discourse about Human Dignity and Human Rights 300
    Wilhelm Gräb

List of Contributors 319
Index 323

Introduction

Pieter Vos and Onno Zijlstra

The theme of God and civilization is both fascinating and complicated. Without doubt religion has been a major factor in the cultural development of humanity. Western culture, for instance, is unthinkable without Christianity. Through the ages religion has contributed to the good life and to living well together. Adherence to God has motivated believers to contribute to the improvement of education, care, community formation, good citizenship, equal regard of women and men, black and white, homosexuals and heterosexuals, in short to what many regard as principal characteristics of civilized society. On the other hand, the combination 'God and civilization' immediately prompts severe criticism of religion. From a post-colonial perspective, for instance, the idea of Christian mission as a civilization project has been seriously contested because of its destructive and oppressive effects. The same holds for those civilizing projects in which Christian faith was uncritically identified with decent moral behavior as the outcome of disciplining and oppressive conduct towards children, strangers, lunatics and prisoners. Some critics consider monotheistic belief itself to be inherently repressive and violent, and in conflict with what is seen as humane and good. Against this contradictory background, one may ask if it is still possible to connect 'God' and 'civilization' in a fruitful way.

The present volume takes up this question as a theological challenge. It contains a collection of contributions (doubly peer-reviewed) that all focus on clashes and disclosures of 'God' and 'civilization.' The initial investigations of the theme took place in a group of theologians and philosophers of the research group 'Beliefs' at the Protestant Theological University (Amsterdam/Groningen). During the project the scope was broadened by inviting scholars from other European countries and other continents to offer their reflections on the theme from their own contexts and perspectives. Most of the final drafts were presented at an international conference that took place from 19 till 21 May 2014 at the Protestant Theological University in Amsterdam.

Conceptualization

In today's 'secular' society, a positive relation between God and civilization is by no means evident. In the West, religion is seen by many as a threat to civilization. Religious believers, wanting to live their lives in accordance with God's will, the divine law, are often considered to be a threat to Western civilization. From this point of view some admit for instance that the 'Jewish-Christian tradition' was foundational for Western civilization, but maintain that this tradition has been overcome in modern times. Against this standpoint others hold that religion remains a necessary or at least desirable element in any culture that highly regards values like love and righteousness, or that civilization is in need of some form of transcendence to keep it open to others and the future. "If Christianity goes, the whole of our culture goes" (T.S. Eliot).[1] In this volume we hold that both ways of reasoning are too monolithic. On the one hand religion may offer a positive contribution to civilization, e.g. by providing the moral underpinnings of a society, and civilization may create free space for religiousness. On the other hand religious convictions may prove to be a threat to what is generally seen as civilized.

Whether the concept of civilization is put forward as a disciplinary project of Christian mission aimed at transforming people into true believers or as an argument against the 'barbarism of religion' in general, in each case 'civilization' is used as a *normative* concept that serves to distinguish the civilized and the barbarian, the cultured and the uncivilized.

Historically, the concept of civilization goes back to eighteenth-century thinkers who developed the idea of civilization as the opposite of barbarism. During that age the word *civilisation* was coined both in France and in England—by Mirabeau in 1757 and Ferguson in 1767—to designate the practice of good morals and the modernization of legislation. Being civilized meant to strive for a high standard of morality. In Germany *Bildung* initially had a meaning parallel to *civilisation*, designating the inner formation of *Kultur*. While German *Bildung* stressed the inner, spiritual formation of a person, and French *civilité* the societal qualities, Dutch *beschaving* had a meaning somewhere in between, uniting the concept of inner refinement as well as *politesse* or *politeness* as part of the individual's behavior, and the notion of *civilisation* as characterizing the process of society as a whole.[2]

---

1 T.S. Eliot, "Notes Towards the Definition of Culture," in T.S. Eliot, *Christianity and Culture* (San Diego: HBJ Book, 1976), 200.
2 Pim den Boer, "Vergelijkende begripsgeschiedenis" (Comparative History of Concepts), in Pim den Boer (ed.), *Beschaving: Een geschiedenis van de begrippen hoofsheid, heusheid, beschaving en cultuur* (*Civilization: A History of the Concepts of Courtliness, Courtesy, Civilization and Culture*) (Amsterdam: Amsterdam University Press, 2001), 9, 28; Cf. Remieg A.M. Aerts & W.E. Krul, "Van hoge beschaving naar brede cultuur, 1780–1940" (From High Civilization towards Broad Culture), in Den Boer, *Beschaving*, 213–254: 216. Cf. Theo Boer & Rinse Reeling

In *theological* discourse the concept of civilization functioned as a self-characterization of Christendom. 'Civilization' was conceived as a secular synonym for Christendom.[3] Modern theologians spoke of civilization as an ongoing process of true enlightenment, stressing the Christian contribution to this process as the best guarantee for progress, but without claiming the inherent Christian nature of this civilization process. Part of civilization was the notion of formation or training, which had a religious form in *disciplina* as the expression of rebirth or spiritual renewal.[4]

Around 1850 the meaning and interpretation of the concept altered. Civilization was generally used to distinguish settled, urban and literate societies from primitive societies. Throughout the nineteenth century European intellectuals developed criteria by which non-European societies could be judged as more or less 'civilized.' Whereas civilization initially was regarded as a *process* rather than as a given totality,[5] concepts like *civilisation*, *Kultur* and *Bildung* were now objectified and defined in terms of *results* rather than processes. Hence, theologians too regarded civilization as the result of historical formation, and Christianity as the definite power that transformed human civilization and culture.[6] Moreover, people began to speak of civilizations in the plural, assuming that there were many civilizations, each of which was civilized in its own way. Western people saw their own civilization as better and more civilized than other civilizations. The world had to be civilized in the direction of Western Christian civilization.

Against this background, German thinkers like Oswald Spengler drew a sharp distinction between *Zivilization*, which involves technology and material factors, and *Kultur*, which involves values, ideals and the higher intellectual and moral qualities of a society. *Zivilization* was not only seen as the final stage of *Kultur* but also as its downfall (*Untergang*). However, more important than the various distinctions between the terms is the fact that up to the twentieth

---

Brouwer, "Herstel voor de relatie tussen God en civilisatie" (Restoring the Relation between God and Civilization), *Theologisch debat* 8:3 (2011), 25–32: 26.

3 Den Boer, "Vergelijkende begripsgeschiedenis," 21.

4 Joris van Eijnatten, "Protestantse schrijvers over beschaving en cultuur" (Protestant Writers on Civilization and Culture), in Den Boer, *Beschaving*, 258–273, describes this way of thinking in the Netherlands from Hieronymus van Alphen to Hofstede de Groot. Cf. also Den Boer, *Beschaving*, 265; Boer & Reeling Brouwer, "Herstel," 26.

5 Words like *beschaving* (civilization), *verlichting* (enlightenment), *vorming* (formation), *opvoeding* (upbringing) were construed with the suffix '-ing,' demonstrating the process nature of these concepts.

6 Den Boer, *Beschaving*, 218–225.

century the concept of civilization (or culture) was defined in terms of a normative ideal.[7]

Nowadays the normative meaning is still active in expressions like 'the clash of civilizations' in so far as this clash is supposed to result from conflicting normative claims: conflicts between civilizations which Samuel Huntington predicted would dominate the future of world politics, conflicts between religions leading to eruptions of violence and destruction excluding rather than including others, and conflicts between religion and secularity, i.e. between what the Law of God demands and what is generally seen as normative in a secular state.

Aim

Against the backdrop of the present discourse on clashes and conflicts, the central question of this volume is whether it is possible to think of both God and civilization in a more open, space-giving way. Our aim is to explore 'God' and 'civilization' as terms that both connect and disconnect with the cultures and religions in which we participate. In doing so we propose a less antithetical use of the term 'civilization,' but without ignoring its inherent normative meaning. Hence, we use civilization basically in the singular instead of the plural. This does not mean that we opt for a universal world civilization, but it does mean that 'civilization' is a common interest of which no one can say that he has realized it absolutely. As a dis/connecting term, *civilization* comes to mean that we do not have an entire commitment to our own culture, but that we always keep an openness to what is different, strange, i.e. to 'the other.' Likewise, from a Protestant point of view, *God* is seen as the One who prevents us from making any absolute claim for a relative reality, including our own religion and culture.

A conceptualization like this is reflected in various voices in the Reformed tradition. Paul Tillich formulated as the core "Protestant principle" both the divine and the human protest against any absolute claim made for a relative reality, even if this claim is made by a 'Reformed church,' a culture of 'Protestantism' or a 'Christian civilization.' The Protestant principle

> is the theological expression of the true relation between the unconditional and the conditioned or, religiously speaking, between God and

---

7 Samuel Huntington, *The Clash of Civilizations and the Remaking of World Order* (London: The Free Press, 2002), 41.

man. As such, it is concerned with what theology calls 'faith,' namely, the state of mind in which we are grasped by the power of something unconditional which manifests itself to us as the ground and judge of our existence.[8]

These formulas are helpful in drawing attention to the meaning of a core Protestant notion: the human being's relation to God as the Sovereign and the Calvinist conception of life *coram Deo*, i.e. the human being in his thoughts and actions as standing before God. Responsibility for the other is conceived as one's responsibility towards God and participation in culture and society is *coram Deo*. From this perspective, God is not just a motivational power in building a civilization, but first and foremost a guarantee for a critical distinction towards what humans may label as holy, sacred or willed by God. In this vocabulary, civilization can never be the last word, because the last word is never on our side—it has to be God's word.

This does not mean that God and civilization should be seen as completely disconnected. Interestingly, the twentieth century saw the development of a Reformed theological discourse on 'Christ and Culture,' in which the 'Protestant principle' was, so to speak, applied in the idea of a qualitative transformation. Neo-Calvinists like Herman Bavinck, Abraham Kuyper, Herman Dooyeweerd, H. Richard Niebuhr and others emphasized the transforming power of Christianity, using terms like reformation, transformation, recreation, rebirth, sanctification and vivification. Divine grace transforms human nature and the Christian gospel provides us with basic normative principles qualitatively transforming human culture (or 'world' in New Testament vocabulary).[9] However, these thinkers avoided speaking of 'Christian civilization' or 'Christian culture.'

This volume is a collection of explorations of the multifaceted relation between God and civilization, especially from Reformed theological and philosophical perspectives, but also from other points of view. The theme is viewed from characteristically Reformed articulations of the good life in terms of the law of God, including discussions of natural law, divine command ethics and the so-called 'third use of the law,' as well as from the perspectives of Eastern Orthodoxy, Islamic political thought, human rights and recent investigations of monotheism, secularity and the culture of authenticity. Moreover, the volume includes, within the outlined framework, Reformed theological contributions from different contexts, varying from reflections on religious violence in

---

8　Paul Tillich, *The Protestant Era* (Chicago: University of Chicago Press, 1948), 163.
9　Van Eijnatten, "Protestantse schrijvers," 273–285.

Indonesia and interpretations of incarnation in relation to Taoism to historical accounts of the Hungarian Church in a post-communist culture and the prophetic task of the church in post-apartheid South Africa. Some contributions take their point of departure in the tension between religion and civilization. Others seek mutual disclosures of God and civilization in thinking through the meaning of multiculturalism, liberal democracy and human dignity.

The clashes and disclosures of 'the law of God' and 'civilization' are explored via the following three key concepts in contemporary philosophical and theological discourse: secularity, monotheism and transformation.

Secularity

The first part of this volume is centered around the concept of secularity as the dominant background of current reflections on God and civilization. In *The Law of God in a Secular State: Claiming Space in the Public Domain*, Gé Speelman opens this part with the observation that in modern Western societies Muslim communities are not often sought out as participants in debates on the good life in society. More often, Muslim communities and their spokespersons are in focus when the majority consensus is offended by religiously inspired practices. For their part, many Muslims fear that the secular state will expand. Against this backdrop, it is relevant how the British anthropologist Talal Asad criticizes the attempts by Muslim thinkers to develop the idea of an Islamic State. According to Asad, this idea is derived from Western concepts of the nation state that are alien to Islam, because for a Muslim, only God can demand absolute loyalty from His creatures. Human constructs like *Shari'a* take the position that only God can take. Asad, however, does not discuss what other form of state organization is preferable. Should a state be based on the secular idea of neutrality with regard to the different religious convictions of its citizens, as the Sudanese-American Abdullahi an-Na'im argues? In a recent debate with an-Na'im, Asad expressed doubt: there is no state that is in this sense truly 'secular.' In fact, *secularism*—as distinguished from the secular—often functions as a doctrine that works in a quasi-religious way, judging the religious views and practices of its citizens. Speelman detects as the core question: how may we safeguard true religious freedom and find ways in which Muslims, Christians and Jews can live under the 'law of God' in a secular nation state? In the final part of her contribution, she discusses John Milbank's notion of 'Gothic Space' as a possible answer. She concludes that the state should not presume to take on a transcendental hue, but should instead be seen as a mediator between different communities, albeit that the political middle often will appear to be a 'broken middle.'

In *Multiculturalism, Religion and Public Justice*, Jonathan Chaplin takes up the argument in exploring the principle of 'public justice' in Reformational thought, rooted in the political theology of Abraham Kuyper and his neo-Calvinist associates, and developed in the Christian philosophy of Herman Dooyeweerd. Chaplin points out that the central task of the state is not to protect 'national core values' but to establish justice in the public relationships of a society. Plural religious and other orientations should be accorded equitable treatment in law and public policy under the norm of public justice. This does not involve the imposition of a blueprint, but rather the taking up of a dynamic, ongoing struggle to justly balance the many legitimate jural interests rising up within a complex society. Because the state is essentially a politico-legal rather than a cultural or religious institution, it is not the task of the state to directly create moral virtues in its citizens, nor to protect something as amorphous as 'national culture.' The state should protect the 'public good,' which is a more precise notion than that of national culture. Chaplin explains how the Reformational idea of 'legal sphere sovereignty' offers an adequate principle of public justice. The state establishes societal space and infrastructural conditions within which individuals, associations, institutions and other agents can pursue their own distinctive vocations and pursuits, and also restrains acts which violate the capacity of such agents to do these things. Chaplin demonstrates how this principle is helpful in thinking about cultural and religious diversity and how it constructively and critically contributes to current debates on multiculturalism. Against the categorical and unqualified priority of secular law over any claims arising from culture or religion, Chaplin makes a plea to respect the complexities of the multi-sided relationships between religion, culture and politics. He applies the principle of public justice in weighing up various multicultural policies and actual debates, such as the social and political integration of immigrants.

After this insightful neo-Calvinistic perspective on public justice, it is relevant to broaden the perspective to two other great Western traditions that have shaped contemporary socio-political life: natural law and liberalism. In *The Natural Law and Liberal Traditions: Heritage (and Hope?) of Western Civilization* David VanDrunen observes that both these traditions continue to have their staunch defenders as well as severe critics. Many wage intellectual battles *within* each tradition: What is natural law? What is liberalism? Others wage battles *between* these traditions: does the hope of Western civilization lie in recovering the natural law tradition *or* in renewing and advancing liberalism? Many participants in these latter battles share Alasdair MacIntyre's verdict that the two traditions present competing and incompatible visions of social life. Natural law theory, it is often thought, rests upon a shared conception of the common good, while liberalism allows the autonomous individual to choose his/her own good. Natural law theory, it is claimed, presumes a theocratic ideal and is based upon a religious worldview, while liberalism leads to a secular ideal and is inherently skeptical toward religion. VanDrunen, however, is with those scholars who argue that the two traditions have much in common and that the best hope of a peaceful and productive future for Western civilization (and beyond) lies in their rapprochement. He argues that much of this debate is shaped by what one thinks lies at the heart of liberalism, on the one hand, and at the heart of natural law, on the other. Some versions of each are indeed hostile to one another and probably beyond hope of reconciliation. According to VanDrunen, a Reformed version of natural law theory, which finds its theological foundation in the Noahic covenant (Gen. 8:20–9:17), offers prospects for rapprochement with certain versions of liberalism: a moderate liberalism allied to a modest theory of natural law. Such an alliance, he claims, can capture strengths of both traditions while guarding against both the moral/religious exclusivism characteristic of much of the natural law tradition and the moral/religious skepticism that has often plagued liberalism.

After these explorations in Islamic and Western political and theological thought, we turn to discussions in Eastern Orthodox theology. In *The Empire and the Desert: Eastern Orthodox Theologians about Church and Civilization* Alfons Brüning points out how in the actual search for religious identity in Russia the concept of civilization is used in the plural. 'Orthodox civilization' is made into one of the global spheres of influence in the world. This reflects a train of thought borrowed from global theorists like Oswald Spengler, Arnold Toynbee, and Samuel Huntington. Brüning argues that the initial semantics of 'civilization' (in the singular)—civilization as superior to not being civilized—remains active behind the scenes and has consequences for how one understands an encounter between 'civilizations' in the plural. Throughout the twentieth century, Orthodox theologians like Georges Florovsky and Aleksandr Shmemann, working in Western emigration centers of Orthodoxy around the middle of the 20th century, opposed such a narrow-minded political and cultural ideology, or were at least more ambivalent, emphasizing the universalism of the Christian message. In the situation of an Orthodox diaspora, Florovsky turned to the early times of Byzantium, in which a creative combination of "Empire and desert" was achieved: the movement of the desert fathers occurred at the same time that Christendom gained increasing significance among the elites of the Roman Empire. Brüning concludes that Florovsky's program 'back to the fathers' reflects an ambiguity of universalism and ecumenism on the one hand,

and civilizational particularism and fundamentalism on the other. Shmemann, one of Florovsky's followers, takes a somewhat different approach; he analyzes what it means to be a believer under the circumstances of the present, 'civilized' world, and discusses whether a high level of culture may possibly erode the roots of true Christian belief. Having left behind the theoretical problems of 'civilizations' in world history and their relation to faith, Schmemann operates with the concept of 'civilization' only in the singular. Despite different accents, both authors raise the question whether there has to be a 'barbarian' element in Christian faith that counters the threat of a weakened and domesticated Christendom, reduced to either merely bourgeois lifestyles or narrow-minded ideology.

In the final contribution to this part of the volume Ábrahám Kovács highlights how theologians and church leaders in Hungary needed and still need to apply God's law in very different forms of social orders. By sketching the political, social and ecclesiastical contexts in constitutional monarchy (1867–1918), communist totalitarian dictatorship (1948–1989) and neoliberalism (1990–2014), Kovács offers a picture of the kinds of challenges presented by each of these 'secular' worldviews. Each historical era posed questions for Reformed Hungarians who sought to find contemporary answers to the problem of living in accordance with God's commandments. First, in the era of constitutional monarchy, the debate was about whether true Calvinism should be seen as aristocratic or democratic. Whereas Béla Kenessey represented a conservative position which sided with the current state order and supported aristocratic Calvinism, Zoltán Jánosi defended a more progressive interpretation of Calvinism in terms of social-liberalism and democracy. Second, Kovács explores the pitfalls of the 'servant theology,' a vision developed by bishops who wished to justify the place of the Christian church in a communist state. The author demonstrates the failure of this harmonizing attempt and shows how this theological concept was a servant of the state's ideology, which detested religion and severely restricted religious freedom. Finally, Kovács offers a reflection on topical issues concerning the relationship of the Reformed Church of Hungary with a secular state and society today. He defends a self-critical stance as well as a humble prophetic voice based on God's commandments and in full respect of the other's otherness as essential for a Christian contribution to civilization.

Monotheism

The explorations of the theme so far have highlighted that in religion and theology we seriously have to consider the secular outlook of modernity. At the same time, it is clear that (mono)theistic religions have been of great importance in the development of liberalism and democracy as important secular features of modernity. Nowadays, however, monotheism is being criticized by many 'secular' thinkers, because of its alleged violent characteristics, justified in a so-called Divine Command Theory that finds the objective, universal and stable foundation of morality in God's commands. The classic example of such an ethics is supposed to be found in the father of the three monotheistic religions: Abraham, who proved to be the father of faith through his willingness to obey the divine command to kill his only son Isaac (Gen. 22).

The second part of this volume is dedicated to an examination of monotheism, its sources and actual meaning, and of Divine Command Theory and its biblical roots. Is monotheism repressive and inherently violent? Does monotheism imply certain forms of violence, resulting from a Divine Ruler who does not only exclude other divinities but also commands his people to obey his will, even if this would violate what is generally seen as humane, morally right and good? Or is it possible to think of monotheism in another way? In order to find answers to these questions, it is worthwhile to trace back the origins of monotheism and to rethink the nature of monotheism. Notwithstanding the violent potential of monotheism, one could say that belief in God as the One who is worth worshipping may empower us both to associate with others (because the one God is the God of all people) and to criticize what is wrongly identified as godly or absolute.

Recent debate on the origins of monotheism is often centered on Jan Assmann's *Moses the Egyptian* and its sequel, *The Price of Monotheism*. Assmann's work can be seen as a reconsideration of Sigmund Freud's *Moses and Monotheism*, which tries to locate the beginnings of Israel's monotheism in a concrete historical event, namely the monotheistic religious reformation in Egypt under king Amenophis or Amenhotpe IV. Emanuel Gerrit Singgih confronts Assmann's thesis with a close reading of the text of Is. 43:10 ("Before me no God was formed") in the context of Deutero-Isaiah. This reading suggests that monotheism may arise out of Israel's need for self-identification in the exilic period (587/6 538 BC). Singgih agrees with Assmann that monotheism in Scripture does not mean that there is one god and no other, but that alongside the True One God there are only false gods, whom it is forbidden to worship. However, the exegesis of Is. 43:10 teaches us that this text not only *forbids* the worship of other gods, but also *denies* their existence. As such Deutero-Isaiah refers to monotheism pure and proper. Singgih deploys his exegesis in the present situation in Indonesia, where attacks on religious statues, either in the public domain or in areas of worship, are increasing. He argues that Christians should be truthful to their belief in a monotheistic God and at the same time should fully respect the cultural iconic heritage of Indonesia, mindful of the dark side of monotheism, i.e. the violent exclusion of those who held different views.

The critical concern that the monotheistic God may be violent and even a threat to human civilization is also the starting point of Jaeseung Cha's contribution. He addresses this question in an examination of the apophatic tradition, especially of Pseudo-Dionysius, as part of the Christian understanding of God, in comparison with another tradition, Taoism. In Dionysius' view God is hidden, not fully revealed. God is the inscrutable and inexpressible One to whom we must not dare to apply words or conceptions. God transcends "one and oneness" even beyond being and non-being. At the same time, God is present to all and is everywhere. Likewise, the Tao cannot be known and is beyond the distinction between being and non-being, and is present in its profound identification with all things. Cha approaches both traditions from a Reformed theological perspective. In Scripture, God is both ontologically and epistemologically beyond us. The deepest mystery of Christianity, however, is to be found in the incarnated God, Jesus Christ, who shares and bears humanity in his incarnation, crucifixion, and resurrection. Cha criticizes Dionysius' mysticism because it lacks the crucial reflection of Christ's suffering on the cross and thereby its substantial relevance to human suffering from violence. Taoistic mysticism has a similar problem, as it does not fully embrace the substantial limitation of human sufferings and miseries, even though it has a profound concept of sacrifice. According to Cha, the concrete presence of the divine being in history and human civilization is itself a critical challenge to both Western and Eastern ideas of the divinity. That the Christian God in Christ is both transcendent and immanent suggests a third way between a violently monotheistic god and a mystically apophatic god.

Renée van Riessen also takes up the theme of monotheism and the threat of (religious) violence associated with it, including sexism and homophobia, in her contribution *A Violent God? Philosophical Reflections on Monotheism and Genesis 22*. In views that emphasize the violent nature of monotheism, God is often seen as an almighty sovereign who wishes His will to be the universal law. Van Riessen takes this criticism as the starting point of her exploration. One of the results of Paul Cliteur's research into monotheism is that religions like Judaism, Islam and Christianity are ultimately based on some form of Divine Command Theory, a position in ethics that seems to leave no room for independent human agency. Equally critical towards monotheism, although for different reasons, is Peter Sloterdijk in *God's Zeal*. According to Sloterdijk, the main problem is the capacity of monotheist religion to kindle religious zeal in its supporters. For Christians, Jews and Muslims, such interpretations are often confronting, and therefore the tendency to emphasize historical and exegetical misunderstandings in these and comparable studies is understandable. Van Riessen demonstrates that it can nevertheless be fruitful to discuss such 'misinterpretations' in a more positive way. Gen. 22 *is* indeed a cruel and violent story, and the history of the three monotheist religions *has been* so full of tensions and conflicts as to undercut their self-presentation as being directed to mercy, love and mutual understanding and respect. The author approaches the positions of Cliteur and Sloterdijk as a horizon from which to ask about the image of God in the public domain. Referring to theological and philosophical interpretations of Gen. 22, especially Assmann's and Kierkegaard's, she discusses Abraham's story as a reflection of different representations of God. The aim is not to defend one image of God and to reject another, but rather to show how different (even conflicting) images of God can be interdependent. Awareness of the interdependence of different images could promote a more appropriate context for hospitality and tolerance towards groups with different (religious) opinions. Van Riessen concludes, with Kierkegaard, that Gen. 22 should not be considered a story about the violence of the divine commandment, but rather a story that confronts the reader with the difficult question of how to communicate faith. Faith should be considered a phenomenon that deserves respect in its own right.

In *The Irreducibility of Religious Faith: Kierkegaard on Civilization and the Aqedah*, Pieter Vos continues this line of thought in a discussion of Gen. 22, especially as interpreted in Kierkegaard's *Fear and Trembling*. Like Van Riessen, Vos takes as the starting point of his reflection Cliteur's promotion of an autonomous morality in secularism against religious (mono)theism and its supposed divine command ethics. He offers an in-depth interpretation of Kierkegaard's book as one of the most evocative interpretations of the *Aqedah*, the Binding of Isaac. Kierkegaard presents the divine command to offer one's son as a real dilemma, a *horror religiosus*, between the law of God and 'civilized' morality. The question Vos addresses is: can ethics ever be legitimately suspended out of deference to a religious command? He investigates several interpretations of the relationship between religion and ethics, divine command and human morality, especially in *Fear and Trembling*, in dialogue with modern thinkers like Kant and Hegel, with a focus on issues of civilization and *Bildung*. In Kierkegaard's use of the Danish word *Dannelse* (formation, civilization) the two concepts of civilization and *Bildung* are brought together. Vos concludes that Kierkegaard helps us to understand that religion should not be reduced to what it contributes to *Dannelse*, nor should it be seen as only a private matter with no consequences for the public domain. Religion first of all disengages us from a given social, cultural, and moral background and this 'movement to the absolute,' to God, opens up the possibility of critique without making our own stance absolute.

In these interpretations of monotheism, adherence to God allows room both for a positive connection to civilization and for an open, critical distance to what is wrongly identified as 'absolute.' That God does not 'belong' to the natural world—this seems to be a core conviction of monotheism and is expressed in Tillich's Protestant principle—implies that believers belong to civilization, but should not have an absolute commitment to it.

Transformation

Emphasis on the irreducibility of religious faith should not conceal that a process of training and discipline has always been involved in religion. Faith is not just a matter of a specific stance toward the world, but includes certain transformative practices and thus 'materializes' in one way or another into a sociocultural outlook. Therefore, the Protestant principle should not lead to a negation of the social and material implications of faith in practice, which traditionally is described in terms of discipline, conversion, formation, transformation, and sanctification. Something similar may hold for people who adhere to other religious or non-religious worldviews and ways of life.

A focus on these aspects brings religion again in a close relation to the theme of civilization. For 'civilization' too implies the idea of training, formation (*Bildung*), transformation and discipline. In civilizing projects discipline has been an important aspect of transforming people into useful civilians. Moreover, religions have played important roles in disciplining and civilizing programs. The third and final set of contributions looks at how religion and culture, God and civilization are related constructively. The focus here is on the mutual transformative influence of religion (especially Christian faith) and civilization.

On the one hand, religion has contributed to the valuation of human dignity, the human rights discourse, the recognition of the individual as an authentic self *coram Deo* and the cultivation of good character and openness toward the other. Christianity has contributed to many civilizing developments, though the outcome has sometimes been contrary to it. T.S. Eliot phrases the significance of Christianity and Christian culture in the development of science, art, and thought of the West as follows:

> It is the common tradition of Christianity which has made Europe what it is. ... It is in Christianity that our arts have developed; it is in Christianity that the laws of Europe have—until recently—been rooted. It is against a background of Christianity that all our thought has significance. An individual European may not believe that the Christian Faith is true, and yet what he says, and makes, and does, will all spring out of his heritage of Christian culture and depend upon that culture for its meaning. Only a Christian culture could have produced a Voltaire or a Nietzsche.[10]

From this perspective the question is: how are modern core concepts of what it means to be civilized historically and systematically tied up with their religious underpinnings?

On the other hand, processes of modernization, including their civilizing aims, have led to transformations of religions in general and Christianity in particular.

One could say that the values of human dignity, authenticity, democracy and human rights have themselves religious aspects, as in the end they ask for an ultimate consent, for commitment and dedication that go beyond argumentative foundation. As such, values like human dignity, human rights and authenticity can be conceived as manifestations of a transformed religion, motivated by belief in God or not.

At the same time, these core values of modernity are not uncontested. In contexts of immigration, globalization and post-colonialism, questions arise about their actual meaning. How do secularized values relate to individuals and communities who want to live by religious convictions that do not support them? Or, to put it critically, are human dignity, equal regard, non-discrimination and tolerance, as part of modern secular 'civilization,' actually still respected in relation to people from other backgrounds? In *Civilizing Believers: Making Modern People out of Immigrants* Mechteld Jansen observes that recent immigration and naturalization programs for immigrants can be seen as a renewal of the cultural process of disciplining. A comparison of integration programs in the EU shows that integration is increasingly viewed as a one-way process of adaptation to the receiving country, with responsibilities and duties exclusively placed on the immigrants' side. Behind this view of integration lies the idea of an already-integrated, united 'civilization,' of which the newcomer

---

10   Eliot, *Christianity and Culture*, 200.

can strive to become a part. Jansen points out that civic integration programs assume that secularism is the gateway to integration and the only basis for creating a critical attitude to dogmatism, fanaticism, and violence. Religious immigrants have to turn to secularism. Jansen juxtaposes efforts by Christian missionaries to civilize non-Europeans and the new heralding of liberal secularism and suggests that they work with analogous concepts of civilizing 'the other.' She argues that the current debates about the 'amount of religion' that can be tolerated in a democratic society pit religious and non-religious worldviews against each other in an atmosphere of political negotiation. However, the language of negotiation, of give and take, of winning some and losing some is unsuited to the sphere of religions and worldviews. This sphere of convictions, traditions, practices, and beliefs—many of which are non-negotiable in the eyes of believers—requires a language of solidarity in hope. Moreover, the language of negotiation assumes that religions and non-religious worldviews are fixed packages of beliefs, whereas in real life people are constantly making up their life stories, which contain complex patterns of multiple modernities, religious affiliations, and secularisms. A language of solidarity in hope means strengthening one another's hope for a peaceful and just society. Jansen concludes that such language can be spoken between adherents of different religions and between religious and secularist groups in society as long as both recognize that no other language is more pure, holy, mature or sensible. Hope, kept alive by religions, is desperately needed in societies that want to tackle extremist and violent absolutisms of secular and religious nature alike.

From a different perspective, Nico Koopman makes a strong case for a prophetic revaluation of dignity, freedom and justice for all. In the context of an increasing number of Christians on the continent of Africa, his question is whether Christianity honors God in a way that advances and actualizes these goods for all. In *Prophecy and Democracy?* Koopman argues for a prophetic presence of Christian faith in democracies that is crucial for the quest of democratic societies to build a life of civility and justice. He joins pleas, both outside and inside the churches in South Africa, that the prophetic voice of churches be heard as clearly as in apartheid South Africa. So-called postliberation societies that have struggled against oppression, but do not yet fulfill the vision of an alternative society, are in need of a renewed prophetic voice that contributes to the building of a new and civilized society that is not demarcated against others who are placed outside. Koopman develops a concept of five modes of prophetic speaking: prophetic vision, criticism, narrative, analysis and policymaking. An awareness of the plurality of prophetic discourse might help to overcome the reduction of prophetic discourse to mere criticism. Following James Gustafson, Koopman emphasizes that prophets are first of all visionaries who portray an alluring vision of the future, in which the strife and suffering that we currently experience are overcome. Prophetic criticism also entails self-criticism of the church. In South Africa the mainly white Dutch Reformed Churches are still divided racially and socio-economically, whereas the mainly black Uniting Reformed Church in Southern Africa shows an inability to fulfill the wonderful prophetic vision of the Confession of Belhar (1986). In dealing with the prophetic practice of storytelling Koopman points out that the conviction of God's special identification with the poor and the marginalized also has origins in the experience of oppression in the era of the Reformation, though this has subsequently been neglected. Prophecy that impacts public life requires concise ethical analysis as well as policymaking as a way of acting under particular conditions.

In the next contribution, Heleen Zorgdrager explores and assesses the remarkable quest for a Christian character in Western post-secular society as a manifestation of what traditionally is defined as sanctification. She discusses various contemporary authors who are convinced that embodying Christian religion in the public domain should be a matter of cultivating Christian character by practicing specific virtues. At the rise of modernity, it was Friedrich Schleiermacher who already offered a conception of a set of virtues that should structure the life and daily worship of a Christian. The notion of a Christian character intends to portray human life in the power of the Spirit, while avoiding the extremes of a legalistic attitude ('keeping the rules') and individual libertarianism ('because I feel it this way'). The 'turn to a Christian character' in theology corresponds to contemporary moral philosophy's turn to virtue ethics. It is also strongly reminiscent of the Byzantine notion of *theosis* (deification) with its focus on discipline and cultivation of virtues. Zorgdrager develops a preliminary idea of the formation of a Christian character that may offer a constructive way of valuing the continuing relevance to Western post-secular civilization of early Christian notions like discipline, ascetical practices and character formation.

Whereas Zorgdrager takes an internal Christian perspective as the starting point of her explorations, Onno Zijlstra's *In Defense of Authenticity* is dedicated to the notion of authenticity, which has become a core value in the West. In the seventies of the twentieth century, authenticity became a criterion for judging people, their products and institutions. In the nineties, however, it was increasingly held that 'authenticity' is a subjectivist and egocentric ideal and that its requirement has led to the moral crisis we find ourselves in today. Zijlstra argues that the critics certainly do have a point, but tend to underestimate the importance of authenticity because of the factual derailment of the ideal in 'the culture of narcissism,' consumer society and culture of greed. He supports those thinkers who have worked at consolidation and repair of the ideal. Through 'authenticity' attention is paid to everyone's unique individuality. The moral crisis we find ourselves in may well point to a loss of self and a lack of authenticity, rather than to an overestimation of their value. On this point Zijlstra follows Charles Taylor in his defense of 'authenticity' in relation to religion, but also in the importance he attaches to the arts. Søren Kierkegaard, especially his book *Fear and Trembling*, features as a source of ideas on (religious) authenticity. At the end of Zijlstra's contribution Kierkegaard's oeuvre as a whole is brought forward as an instance of religious art in a culture of authenticity.

In the closing essay of this volume Wilhelm Gräb observes that interpreters of religion are continuously updating and modifying secularization theory. Charles Taylor proclaims a 'Secular Age,' Jürgen Habermas speaks of a post-secular society and Hans Joas describes Christian belief as one option for individual life interpretation. For many prominent interpreters, religion is definitely not a constitutive factor of modernity that has normative influence on human development. Gräb argues for a different approach with regard to religious development in modernity. Referring to human rights discourse he demonstrates that the theory of secular differentiation is untenable. In no way has modernity led to a depreciation of religion, and religion is not only alive in fundamental, aggressive anti-modernist movements. Rather it is precisely modernity's own modes of power—the separation of religion from politics, progress in science and technology, the all-determining authority of economy and mass media—that are the productive forces of religion today. In order to recognize not only religion in modernity, but the modernity of religion as well, Gräb also considers the transformations religion has undergone in modernity. In his opinion this is the lasting achievement of the Enlightenment's critical analysis of religion. The human rights discourse that emerges from this analysis contributes to the presence and liveliness of religions today. By analyzing the human-religious substrate of human rights, religion is seen to be an important factor of human civilization and a normative power for humanity's self-preservation.

Epilogue

This theological study reflects the multifaceted nature of the theme. It brings to the fore political and juridical aspects as well as cultural-philosophical and historical facets. It discusses both Christianity and Islam in modern Western secularized culture as well as the role of religion in other parts of the world.

The concept of civilization is analyzed both in the sense of a normative ideal of good conduct (in the singular) and as a set of cultural values and patterns, as distinguished from or opposed to other such sets (in the plural). Particular attention is paid to religious adherence to the law of God as conflicting or not with what is generally seen as civilized.

As a whole this volume relativizes absolute aspirations in applying 'the law of God.' The law always remains above all factual applications. In the same way, 'civilization' is always a norm for all civilizations and civilizing processes. Moreover, 'law' and 'civilization' are too interwoven to be played off against each other. This also goes for cultures of liberalism, democracy and tolerance. Each of the contributions underlines the central idea that God and civilization do not, in principle, have to be placed in opposition to each other nor identified with each other. Civilization, as given and as ideal, and God are interrelated in a multiplicity of often subtle ways.

The first set of contributions shows that secularity is not only a determining condition of modernity but also in many respects part of the Christian faith itself. Ideas of secularity are to a great extent formed from and informed by the three monotheistic traditions. On the other hand, adherence to God as the One and absolute prompts the question whether this conviction is not inherently violent to other conceptions of the absolute. The contributions grouped under the heading of monotheism tend toward the conclusion that monotheistic belief should always give space to others because to exclude others would be to make one's own conviction absolute again. Finally, faith is not just a matter of a specific stance toward the world, but includes certain transformative practices that influence this world. In the final set of contributions it becomes clear how God may have positive civilizing meaning and effect in various cultural contexts.

This study does not pretend to be exhaustive in its analyses and conclusions. Much remains to be discussed. Three clusters of questions in particular could be explored further. First, questions remain about the meaning of civilization in multicultural and multi-religious societies. How do non-Western conceptions of civilization and their religious claims relate to a conception of 'civilization' as norm for all civilizations and civilizing projects, as proposed in this study? How can the positive, civilizing contribution of non-Christian believers (immigrants) be made fruitful in (Western) secularized culture and a democratic state?

A second theme that asks for further exploration is the applicability of the law of God. If the divine law remains above all factual applications, does this prevent us and others from ever saying that something is God's command? To put it differently, how does the law of God in its critical meaning relate to its constructive meaning as providing prescripts for the moral life?

A third cluster concerns questions about how faith contributes to civilization. What is the relation between sanctification as a state before God (and its significance in 'the communion of the saints') on the one hand and its meaning in society and the world on the other? Is, for instance, Protestantism in need of correction or completion from the direction of Eastern Orthodox theologies that conceive sanctification in a deeply universal sense, as an elusive perspective of participation of each created being in God?

Bibliography

Aerts, Remieg A.M. & W.E. Krul, "Van hoge beschaving naar brede cultuur, 1780–1940" (From High Civilization towards Broad Culture), in Pim den Boer (ed.), *Beschaving: Een geschiedenis van de begrippen hoofsheid, heusheid, beschaving en cultuur (Civilization: A History of the Concepts of Courtliness, Courtesy, Civilization and Culture)* (Amsterdam: Amsterdam University Press, 2001), 213–254.

Boer, Theo & Rinse Reeling Brouwer, "Herstel voor de relatie tussen God en civilisatie" (Restoring the Relation between God and Civilization), *Theologisch debat* 8:3 (2011), 25–32.

Boer, Pim den, "Vergelijkende begripsgeschiedenis" (Comparative History of Concepts), in Pim den Boer (ed.), *Beschaving: Een geschiedenis van de begrippen hoofsheid, heusheid, beschaving en cultuur (Civilization: A History of the Concepts of Courtliness, Courtesy, Civilization and Culture)* (Amsterdam: Amsterdam University Press, 2001), 9–28.

Eliot, T.S., "Notes Towards the Definition of Culture," in T.S. Eliot, *Christianity and Culture* (San Diego: HBJ Book, 1976).

Eijnatten, Joris van, "Protestantse schrijvers over beschaving en cultuur" (Protestant Writers on Civilization and Culture), in Pim den Boer (ed.), *Beschaving: Een geschiedenis van de begrippen hoofsheid, heusheid, beschaving en cultuur (Civilization: A History of the Concepts of Courtliness, Courtesy, Civilization and Culture)* (Amsterdam: Amsterdam University Press, 2001), 258–273.

Huntington, Samuel, *The Clash of Civilizations and the Remaking of World Order* (London: The Free Press, 2002).

Tillich, Paul, *The Protestant Era* (Chicago: University of Chicago Press, 1948).

PART 1

Secularity

∴

The Law of God in a Secular State
Claiming Space in the Public Domain

Gé Speelman

On November 21, 2013, Rasit Bal, president of the Dutch Contact Organ for Muslims and Government (CMO),[1] gave a lecture for local interreligious dialogue groups on 'The Agenda for the Future.'[2] According to Bal, closed communities are met with distrust in our society and are framed as a potential threat. The public space is expanding, and it is becoming increasingly difficult to solve problems within one's own circle. The public space does not allow norms or values to be justified by an appeal to authoritative sources or traditions. "The state has won the battle and religious traditions should adapt," Bal says.[3] All religious communities are minorities, and religious believers, according to Bal, should be committed to society as a whole and participate in the debate on what is good for society—but not from a privileged position. They are "co-owners" of public space and should refrain from attempts to dominate it. Bal observes that society needs religious communities to create social cohesion, but such cohesion is also being threatened as communities struggle with a growing internal diversity when it comes to the interpretations of traditional norms and values. While some believers tend to uphold tradition, others seek, in Bal's terms, "authentic" and "liberating" norms that fit in with their experiences as members of modern society.[4]

The interpretation that a community leader like Bal gives of the position of Muslim communities and their members in Dutch society is familiar. What is striking, however, is an unresolved tension he addresses in his speech. He speaks of twin fears: on the one hand the fear—implicit in his description—that many Muslims have of an expanding state and of a public space in which nothing remains hidden from the public gaze, and, on the other, the fear in modern society of religious communities, given the distrust he describes.

Bal is involved in a platform of Jewish, Christian, and Muslim religious leaders debating social issues. But the Muslim community is not often sought out as a participant that could make a valuable contribution to ideas of the good

---

[1] http://www.cmoweb.nl.
[2] Rasit Bal, "De agenda van de toekomst" (The Agenda for the Future), http://www.raadvankerken.nl/fman/5038.pdf.
[3] Bal, "Agenda," 3 (my translation, GS).
[4] Bal, "Agenda," 5

life in society. More often, it is Muslim communities and their spokespersons that are held to account when the majority consensus is offended by certain religiously inspired practices, as we will see below.

Modern secular nation states present themselves as open access societies. No particular cultural or religious community is privileged in the public domain, which therefore becomes a neutral ground where every individual citizen has an equal say. Problems arise, however, when citizens claim space for the religious or cultural practices that are seen in their community as the 'law of God.'[5] Norms for behavior must be legitimized by a generally shared view of the good life in the public domain, not by an appeal to religious authority. For many, this implies that religiously based behavior should not have a place in the public arena. This is especially clear when the debate focuses on migrant religious communities and even more so when these are Muslim communities. For religious people who want to follow the 'law of God' in their daily lives, this creates problems. What exclusions lie behind such a common-sense representation of what it means to be 'religious' in a 'modern' and 'secular' context? What place could the 'law of God' have in the public domain?

In this article, I will start by pointing out some of the tensions that arise from marking the boundaries between the public domain and the space claimed by religious communities in modern Dutch society. I will then turn to Talal Asad's analysis of 'secularism' as a disciplinary system that, in effect, excludes religion from the public space. Asad attempts to read the various meanings of secularism, secularity, and the secular state into different Western modern contexts and so presents a view from outside that can help us discover unspoken assumptions behind these terms. Then I will discuss the ways in which the Shari'a—for Muslims the 'law of God'—could function in public space in modern nation states, comparing the approach of Asad with that of another Muslim thinker, Abdullahi Ahmed an-Na'im. I will conclude with a brief exploration of the concept of 'middle space.'

---

5   Pieter Dronkers has elegantly summed up the different approaches to the tension between political and religious loyalty in liberal political theory, see Pieter Dronkers, *Faithful Citizens: Civic Allegiance and Religious Loyalty in a Globalized Society. A Dutch Case Study*, doctoral thesis (Amsterdam/Groningen: Protestant Theological University, 2012).

The Dutch Debate: Religion as an Individual Opinion

In recent years, Dutch politicians have contributed to the debate on religion in the public domain. One of them is Jeanine Hennes Plasschaert, a leading MP for the Liberal Party, the VVD, at the time of the interview I quote from (March 15, 2011) and now the Dutch Defense Minister. She declares: "Look how France is doing it; there the headscarf is forbidden in public schools. The debate, when do you wear a headscarf?—that's what I want to conduct."[6] Hennes Plasschaert would like to prohibit civil servants working behind the counters in municipal offices from wearing headscarves and other religious symbols.

> All religions are equal for me in that respect. Universities, schools, I would like a debate about them too.[7] But the Christian parties see this immediately as an infringement of the freedom of religion. That's nonsense as freedom of religion is covered in so many other articles: freedom of assembly, freedom of opinion. In fact, the article about religious freedom is superfluous. We talk a lot about the separation of church and state, but, in fact, the church has encroached upon the state substantially. Look at confessional schools, the organization of public broadcasting, and—a sensitive issue—this also goes for ritual slaughter.[8]

Hennes Plasschaert is not the only one urging that Article 6 in the Dutch Constitution on the freedom of religion be abolished. At the other end of the Dutch political spectrum, a member of the Socialist Labor Party (PvdA), Paul de Beer, writes that the article on freedom of religion has on several occasions forced the state or legal authorities to evaluate the content of religious convictions. Thus, servants of the neutral, secular state had to formulate theological judgments.

To prevent such an infringement of state neutrality in the religious field, freedom of religion should not be used as an argument in public debate, says de Beer.[9] De Beer is aware that many believers see their religion not merely as

---

6   Kustaw Bessems, "Religieus symbool niet achter de balie" (Religious Symbols Not at the Counter), *De Pers* (20 March 2011), http://www.depers.nl/UserFiles/File/De%20Pers%20dinsdag%2015%20maart%202011.pdf (my translation, GS).

7   I.e., on the existence of ideologically based schools and universities; see Bessems, "Religieus symbool," 1.

8   Bessems, "Religieus symbool," 1 (my translation, GS).

9   Paul de Beer, "De paradox van de godsdienstvrijheid" (The Paradox of the Freedom of Religion), in H.M.A.E. van Ooijen, L.F. Egmond, Q.A.M. Eijkman, F. Olujic & O.P.G. Vos (eds.), *Godsdienstvrijheid: Afschaffen of beschermen?* (*Freedom of Religion: Should It be*

an opinion but as a way of life that prescribes certain forms of behavior. An example he gives is that of a Muslim street coach who refuses to shake hands with women, not because he does not respect women but because his religion forbids him to do so.[10]

De Beer points out that a state that defends the rights of its citizens to choose their own religion and therefore freedom of individual choice becomes problematical if these individuals subsequently appeal to a collective, the religious community, that determines their actions. Although the choice to belong to a religious community means far more to the adherents of a particular religion than, say, the choice of a holiday destination or brand of cell phone, a judge can do nothing else but treat the appeal to the law of God as another individual opinion.

> A street coach ... who *is not allowed* to shake hands with females ... becomes a *contradictio in terminis*. If religion is a free choice, one can no longer say that one's religion *does not allow* one to shake hands with females. What you mean by saying this is that you *do not want* to shake hands with a female because of your religion. If religion is a free choice, then any behavior and any utterance originating from that religion is inevitably a personal, free choice. And then there is no justification to judge that behavior or utterance legally in another way than you would if they did not originate in a religious conviction.[11]

De Beer makes it clear that the consequence of the idea of a secular state is that public law can protect the individual but not a religious community that prescribes a certain set of rules for its followers. A consequence of the necessary constraints on the lawgiver's scope to interpret the law of God is that article 6 of the Dutch Constitution should be expunged, de Beer argues.

De Beer's article makes it clear that in late modernity, secular public space is a place where free individual citizens and not religious communities are seen as agents. Individual citizens decide together what norms and rules are acceptable for all, creating a public law. The traditional concept of freedom of religion may be at odds with this principle.

      Abolished or Protected?) (Leiden: Stichting NJCM-Boekerij, 2008), 5–9. Cf. Paul de Beer, "Waarom vrijheid van godsdienst uit de grondwet kan" (Why Freedom of Religion Can Be Removed from the Constitution), *Socialisme & Democratie* 64 (2007), 18–24.

10   De Beer, "Paradox," 6.

11   De Beer, "Paradox," 9 (my translation, GS).

In many religious communities, people want to live their lives according to how they believe God wants them to live, according to the 'law of God.' For Muslims, for instance, the Shari'a prescribes the way they pray, fast, what they may eat and drink (and what not), how children should behave toward their parents, how marriage ceremonies are conducted, how money is lent. In late modern secular states, the room for such collective religious precepts is limited. Only if they do not infringe on public laws and do not offend public morality, there may be space for the 'law of God.' In practice, this may mean that if religious precepts clash with certain majority norms, they should be forbidden by public law.

This is not only a problem for Muslims. Recent debates in the Dutch media have shown the tension between secular society and religious people who live according to religious rules. For instance, the secular legal system has to deal with religious communities that do not admit women to the pulpit or the altar, or with religious schools that refuse homosexual teachers. Recent debates also concern the practice of circumcising small boys, thereby violating the integrity of their bodies.

Legally, as de Beer points out, the lawgiver and judge cannot see religion as anything but an opinion, a set of ideas. De Beer could also have appealed to the Dutch Constitution here. Article 6.1 says: "Everyone shall have the right to profess freely his religion or belief, either individually or in community with others, without prejudice to his responsibility under the law."[12] What Dutch law protects when it protects 'freedom of religion' is the freedom to *confess* a religion or philosophy of life. And confession implies a set of convictions that are chosen by a believer to be his or her guidelines in life. The article does not speak about behavior or actions connected to that choice. In this light, the argument for abolishing Article 6 becomes understandable. After all, a confession may be just another, more formal description of a set of opinions, a view of life that one subscribes to.

Behind the debate about curtailing the freedom to follow religious precepts in guiding one's behavior lies a certain approach to what 'religion' actually *is*. If religion is indeed a set of ideas, then religious practices are not protected by the Constitution. If, on the other hand, religion can be approached as a disciplinary system, then the article on religious freedom would create more room for religious communities to follow practices that diverge from majority customs than the articles on freedom of opinion and expression do. I will

---

12   http://www.st-ab.nl/wetgrondwet.htm#h1, 6–1 (translation: http://legislationline.org/documents/section/constitutions/country/12, consulted March 28 2014).

therefore turn to the debate about the meaning of the word 'religion' in order to expose alternative views on the place of religion in the public space.

'Religion' versus 'the Secular'

The question of what 'religion' is and is not has become a hot topic, both in the political arena (the debate on freedom of religion) and in the field of religious and cultural studies (the distinction between 'religion' and 'culture').[13] In this debate, critical thinkers point out the close connection between the definitions that are given of religion and secularity. One of the first observers of this connection between views on religion and secularity was the anthropologist Talal Asad. In his book *Genealogies of Religion*, Asad deconstructs modern essentialist definitions of religion that "separate religion conceptually from the domain of power."[14] Taking his starting point in the definition supplied by the anthropologist Clifford Geertz,[15] Asad traces the genealogy of this view, with its separation between the 'meaning' of symbols and the social and historical disciplines of power and knowledge in which they function, back to seventeenth-century debates on 'natural religion.'[16]

> Thus, what appears to anthropologists today to be self-evident, namely that religion is essentially a matter of symbolic meanings linked to ideas of a general order (expressed through either or both rite and doctrine), that it has generic functions/features, and that it must not be confused with any of its particular historical or cultural forms, is in fact a view that has a specific Christian history. From being a concrete set of practical rules attached to specific processes of power and knowledge, religion has come to be abstracted and universalized.[17]

---

13 Kim Knott, *The Location of Religion: A Spatial Analysis* (Durham: Acumen (Equinox 2005), 2013), 66. Cf. Richard King, *Orientalism and Religion: Postcolonial Theory, India and 'The Mystic East'* (London & New York: Routledge, 1999), 36.

14 Talal Asad, *Genealogies of Religion: Disciplines and Reasons of Power in Christianity and Islam* (Baltimore and London: Johns Hopkins Press, 1993), 29.

15 Asad, *Genealogies*, 29 f: "Religion is a system of symbols which acts to establish powerful, pervasive, and long-lasting moods and motivations in men by formulating conceptions of a general order of existence and clothing these conceptions with such an aura of factuality that the moods and motivations seem uniquely realistic."

16 Asad, *Genealogies*, 32–39.

17 Asad, *Genealogies*, 42.

For the lawgiver in secular Dutch society, as we saw, 'religion' is indeed a set of meanings linked to ideas of general order, ideas that one can affirm by subscribing to a confession of faith. Such a view paves the way for politicians who reason that religion in the public domain is basically an opinion, not unlike a political or aesthetic opinion, an opinion that every individual is free to develop on his or her own.

Asad contrasts this with a view that was operative in earlier periods in the Christian world when both 'autonomy' and 'choice' were seen as the result of disciplining practices. As Augustine taught, an act of choice, though spontaneous, must be prepared by a long process of teaching (*eruditio*), and warning (*admonitio*), in which there might even be an element of fear and punishment: "Let constraint be found outside; it is inside that the will is born."[18]

In the religious world of earlier Christians, as well as that of Muslims, Jews, and others, religion was not a matter of 'faith' as an autonomous a priori choice of a set of symbols giving meaning to life, but of certain practices that were approved by religious authorities as 'correct.' Most believers followed these disciplines without engaging in theological discourse or having clear-cut "conceptions of a general order of existence."[19] Thus, what Asad wants to contest is the idea that there is a natural, self-evident connection between the modern categorization of the religious field as being essentially about ideas and the way Muslims or Christians lived their lives before God in other times and places.[20] The historically and culturally located view on 'religion' is closely bound up with the secular societies of the West.

In his book *Formations of the Secular*, Asad discusses the relationship between 'the secular' as an epistemic category, 'secularism' as a political doctrine, and 'secularization' as a process that transforms social, cultural, and religious forms of life.[21]

The separation of religion from other institutions ('church' from 'state') is not confined to modernity. It can be found in medieval Christendom and in the Islamic world, as well as elsewhere.[22] As a political doctrine, however, this separation found its full-fledged formulation in early modern Europe.

---

18   Asad, *Genealogies*, 34.
19   Asad, *Genealogies*, 36.
20   As Asad explains in a later publication, in traditional Islamic Shari'a there is no distinction between 'law' and 'morality,' Talal Asad, *Formations of the Secular: Christianity, Islam, Modernity* (Stanford: Stanford University Press, 2003), 241.
21   Asad, *Formations*, 16.
22   Asad, *Formations*, 1.

As a political doctrine, secularism arose in Europe after the religious wars in the seventeenth century. It is often presented as the only possible system for creating a political ethics independent of religious convictions, thereby guaranteeing religious peace and the accessibility of all inhabitants of the nation state to the political process. To do so, however, there must be some starting point on which all participants agree. John Rawls has introduced the concept of "overlapping consensus" as such a starting point.[23] The citizens of a secular nation state may come from very different religious backgrounds and may not agree on all points about what exactly 'justice' is or what normative codes of behavior they have to follow. But they can find agreement on certain principles of justice (for instance, that one should deal with one's neighbor in a fair and just way). Such principles are foreground political principles. For a secular state to function, citizens do not need to agree about their background justifications (we do not need to agree *why* we should be fair to our neighbors), but they do need to have a basic consensus about the foreground political principles.

Drawing on an article by Charles Taylor,[24] Asad analyzes the workings of this concept of overlapping consensus. Taylor argues that there must be more space between the foreground political principles of citizens than Rawls maintains. He paints a picture of constant debate and negotiation between different groups in secular society, not only on the norms and values themselves but also on the question of which norms and values count as political principles and which are background justifications. It is not difficult to connect this picture of constant debate and negotiation with the practice in Dutch society, where ethical questions like same-sex marriage, the treatment of animals, or euthanasia are subjects of an ongoing debate.

Asad comments that Taylor is too optimistic about the outcomes this process has for minorities.

> Consider what happens when the parties to a dispute are unwilling to compromise on what for them is a matter of principle (a principle that is justifiable by statements of belief). If citizens are not reasoned around in a matter deemed nationally important by the government and the majority that supports it, the threat of legal action (and the violence this implies) may be used. In that situation, negotiation simply amounts to

---

23 John Rawls, *A Theory of Justice* (revised ed.) (Harvard: Harvard University Press, 1999 (1971)), 340.

24 Charles Taylor, "Modes of Secularism," in Rajeev Bhargava (ed.), *Secularism and its Critics* (Delhi: Oxford University Press, 1998), 138–163, quoted by Asad, *Formations*, 2.

the exchange of unequal concessions in situations where the weaker party has no choice.[25]

The possibility of legal action mentioned by Asad is not a theoretical one for religious minorities in the Dutch nation state. It was invoked when some Christian civil servants appealed to their freedom of conscience when they were asked to conduct marriage ceremonies between same-sex partners. A law was recently passed in Parliament stating that it would be impossible for such conscientious objectors to be appointed as wedding registrars.[26] A law forbidding ritual slaughter was passed by Parliament but did not reach consensus in the Senate,[27] and another law obligating general practitioners to refer patients requesting euthanasia to a colleague has passed preliminary hearings in Parliament.[28] A law banning headscarves for government employees has been a topic of debate in Parliament but was rejected by a large majority.[29] In these instances, it is not so much the "conceptions of a general order of existence" of certain Christians, Muslims, and Jews that are at stake but the actions that result from them. And it is difficult to see how this could be otherwise in present-day Dutch society. If some acts that offend the majority norms and values should be allowed in the public domain, this would create inequality before the law and therefore go against one of the most sacred values of modern secularist societies. Also, on a more practical level, allowing such differences in practice would lead to a further segmentation and fragmentation of the nation state.

Minorities for whom 'religion' is not so much a worldview as a system of knowledge and power that also entails certain forms of action or behavior cannot go their own way unchecked by the majority consensus on the good life. If they nevertheless want to live by 'the law of God,' what alternatives to the modern secular nation state could be found? A recent study showed that one of the alternatives that appeal to many Muslims is a country where democracy is combined with an Islamic state based on Shari'a. In other words, in situations where the majority of the population is Muslim, a Shari'a-based state is, in the

---

25 Asad, *Genealogies*, 6.
26 http://www.nrc.nl/nieuws/2013/06/11/grote-kamermeerderheid-maakt-einde-aan-weigerambtenaar/.
27 http://www.nrc.nl/nieuws/2012/06/19/eerste-kamer-stemt-tegen-verbod-op-onverdoofd-ritueel-slachten/.
28 https://www.d66.nl/actueel/initiatiefwet-verwijsrecht-euthanasie-ingediend/.
29 http://www.volkskrant.nl/vk/nl/2824/Politiek/article/detail/707588/2004/03/18/Kamer-wijst-hoofddoekverbod-ambtenaren-af.dhtml.

eyes of many Muslims, a viable alternative to a secular state.[30] But can such a state be truly 'Islamic'?

The Impossibility of a Modern Shari'a-based State

In a lecture given in Saudi Arabia, Talal Asad addressed the intellectual legacy of his father, Muhammad Asad.[31] Muhammad Asad (1900–1992; formerly Leopold Weiss) was a Jewish convert to Islam who was actively involved in the debates on the foundation of the Islamic state of Pakistan. Muhammad Asad laid down his ideas about the Islamic state in his book *Principles of State and Government in Islam*.[32] He argues that unanimity about right and wrong is essential for any community, and only religion can provide a permanent and absolute moral basis for such an agreement. For Talal Asad, the concept of the Islamic state his father proposes is highly problematic. One of the reasons why he disagrees with his father in this respect is that religious minorities could not fully participate in the political life of such a state.[33] But Talal Asad's more deeply rooted objection rests on the theological basis of the idea of a Shari'a-based Islamic state. Modern nation states are sovereign and claim absolute loyalty from their subjects. This is a completely new phenomenon for many traditional Muslim societies, as this type of nation state is the offspring of modernity. For a Muslim, only God can demand absolute loyalty from His creatures.[34] The whole idea of a modern nation state is therefore problematic for Muslims who want to live in accordance with the Islamic *shahada*. Defenders of the idea of a Shari'a-based Islamic state often refer to the Qur'anic precept that Muslims should "enjoin what is right and forbid what is wrong" (*amr bi al-maruf wa-nahy 'an al-munkar*).[35] This important doctrine, Asad argues, does not require a *state* that decides what is 'wrong' and 'right.' Indeed, he tells his Saudi audience, it would be intolerable if the modern nation state would as-

---

30 http://www.pewforum.org/2013/04/30/the-worlds-muslims-religion-politics-society exec/.
31 Talal Asad, "Muhammad Asad Between Religion and Politics," *Insan ve Toplum* 1:2 (2012), 155–165, http://www.interactive.net.in/content/muhammad-asad-between-religion-and-politics, accessed Jan 29, 2014.
32 Muhammad Asad, *The Principles of State and Government in Islam* (Berkeley: State University of California Press, 1961).
33 Asad, "Muhammad Asad," 159.
34 Asad, "Muhammad Asad," 160.
35 Cf. Michael Cook, *Commanding Right and Forbidding Wrong in Islamic Thought* (Cambridge: Cambridge University Press, 2000).

sume a theological role. As strict monotheists, Muslims cannot subscribe to a political theology in which the state makes decisions about "the morality of a national population."[36]

The philosopher of law Abdullahi Ahmed an-Na'im, of Sudanese descent, also argues against the application of Shari'a law as the codified law of nation states with a Muslim majority population. An-Na'im points out that, traditionally, Shari'a (a theological concept) and its application in *fiqh* (more a collection of case-law decisions than a law code) belonged traditionally to the domain of religious scholars and jurists, not to the state.[37] By nature, actual rulings based on Shari'a law are diffuse, ambiguous, and contradictory and therefore liable to manipulation by elites.[38] An-Na'im might agree with Asad that the problem is not the 'law of God' in itself but the present-day context in which it is brought into the political process: it is precisely because Shari'a has been made into something that it had not been hitherto (a law code, applied by a sovereign nation state) that Shari'a was perverted into something encroaching on the freedom that is essential to religious Muslims in their relationship with God.

> Muslims everywhere, whether minorities or majorities, are bound to observe Shari'a as a matter of religious obligation, and ... this can best be achieved when the state is neutral regarding all religious doctrines and does not enforce Shari'a principles as state policy or legislation.[39]

According to An-Na'im, only constitutionalism, based on human rights, in a secular state is able to ensure the right relationship between God and human beings as it guarantees the complete freedom of religious choices made by Muslims. If an individual is not free in his or her decision to follow the path of God, then his or her faith cannot be sincere.[40]

In a modern sovereign nation state, therefore, Muslims, as well as others, need to be protected in their rights, not by a modern adaptation of Shari'a law, however modified, but by a secular constitution. To prevent pressure groups from taking over the apparatus of the state, constitutionalism, human rights, and free access to public debate, together with the free exchange of ideas, are

---

36   Asad, "Muhammad Asad," 162.
37   Abdullahi Ahmad an-Na'im, *Islam and the Secular State: Negotiating the Future of Shari'a* (Cambridge: Harvard University Press, 2009), 65.
38   An-Na'im, *Secular State*, 108.
39   An-Na'im, *Secular State*, 3.
40   An-Na'im, *Secular State*, 137.

necessary.[41] An-Na'im points out that the advocates of a state based on Shari'a law invariably present a distorted picture of what Shari'a actually is. He gives the example of Pakistani Islamist Abu al-A'la Mawdudi, who explicitly advocated a totalitarian state along the lines of a fascist/Soviet model.[42]

If a Shari'a-based modern national state is a barrier to the right relation between a Muslim and God, and if he or she experiences resistance when following Shari'a precepts as a minority in the West, then the question is how a Muslim today can live according to the 'law of God.'

Re-defining the Public Domain: Complex Space?

In his lecture on Muhammad Asad, Talal Asad briefly addresses the way Islam may be brought into the public debate:

> It therefore seems to me that for Muslims the possibilities of 'political Islam' may lie not in the aspiration to acquire state power and to apply divinely authorized law through it but in the practice of public argument—in a struggle guided by deep religious commitments that are both narrower and wider than the nation state. Politics in this sense is not party politics, it is not a duel between pre-established partial interests: it is about values in the process of being discovered (or rediscovered) and formed (or reformed) within complex traditions. It presupposes openness and readiness to take risks in confronting the modern state that the state (and party politics) cannot tolerate. This politics may confront the liberal state by opposing particular policies through civil disobedience, or even by rising up against an entire political order.[43]

For Asad, it is the modern sovereign nation state, the guarantor of a political order that thrives on greed and growing militarization, that Muslims should oppose and confront—in both Western and so-called Islamic states. In this struggle they should form alliances with non-Muslims, accepting that the heterogeneity and diversity of different communities are here to stay. Does this form of 'public argument' help us find ways in which Muslims, Christians, and Jews can live under the 'law of God' in a secular nation state?

---

41   An-Na'im, *Secular State*, 92.
42   An-Na'im, *Secular State*, 292.
43   Asad, "Muhammad Asad," 162.

An-Na'im gives a more optimistic view of the possibilities for religious communities to be engaged politically in the secular public space. Although some Western nation states do promote "a hegemonic idea of national culture" in the moral domain,[44] the state should ideally leave a maximum of space for associations of citizens to debate moral issues. For the state can never be the final source for morality. Secularization can be effective only if the state itself has limited moral claims to make and does not operate as an arbiter in situations of disagreement. Citizens should be able to enter into the debate on policy and legislation on the basis of what An-Na'im calls "civic reason." This is a reasoning that the large majority of citizens in the state can accept or reject. "Civic reason and reasoning, and not personal motivations, are necessary, whether Muslims constitute the majority or the minority of the population of a state."[45]

'Civic reason' resembles what Rawls calls "public reason,"[46] but An-Na'im shares Habermas' criticism of how Rawls sets up an impermeable boundary between the private and the public domains of social life.[47] For Rawls, politics are confined to the public domain. Habermas points out that, in actual fact, other spaces than the public domain, like the arenas offered by NGOs, trade unions, or churches, can be important places of debate on the order and direction of society.[48] They are not institutions of the state but active partners in the political debate. An-Na'im distinguishes between the state and politics. The state has to do with the exercise of power, with legal punishment and warfare. Politics, on the other hand, is a continuing public struggle between various contenders. For An-Na'im, public space is the place where people from different backgrounds try to explain to one another what the common good is. Muslims can do this, using their own Shari'a precepts but translating them into a common 'language.' According to Shari'a law, for instance, demanding interest on loans is *haram*. Muslims are free to follow the precepts against requiring interest. They could, for instance, create an interest-free banking system. However, if they want to persuade others that an interest-free economy should be the object of public policy or legislation, they need to give other arguments

---

44 The French banning of headscarves in public schools "illustrates how secularism can be invoked as a hegemonic idea of national culture to the exclusion of other identities ..." (An-Na'im, *Secular State*, 41).
45 An-Na'im, *Secular State*, 8.
46 John Rawls, *Political Liberalism* (expanded ed. New York: Colombia University Press, 2003), 441.
47 Jürgen Habermas, "Reconciliation through the Public Use of Reason: Remarks on Rawls' Political Liberalism," *Journal of Philosophy* 92 (1995), 109–131.
48 An-Na'im, *Secular State*, 101.

than "Interest is not permitted by our religion."[49] So, the Muslim participants in the debate on the common good should try to reach common ground with others, and, in doing so, they have to translate the principles of Shari'a into a common language.[50] But An-Na'im does have an important proviso in his argument for a form of public space that allows minorities to live according to the 'law of God': human rights should provide the framework for civic reason. He addresses the tension that may arise from this: some rulings of the traditional Shari'a are not compatible with important human rights like equality between men and women or that of non-Muslims and Muslims.[51] He is optimistic, however, about the possibility of overcoming these tensions. He points out that the traditional interpretations of Shari'a are human, not divine, and that there has always been the possibility of an ongoing process of re-interpretation and adjustment of Shari'a precepts.[52]

An-Na'im wants to uphold the universality of human rights, although he points out that, like Shari'a law, human rights are the outcome of human efforts and struggle and therefore not unchangeable. The original charter of human rights was laid down by Western nation states, and these rights can become universal norms only through a global consensus-building process in which different participants within as well as among cultures have their say.[53] If one were to treat either Shari'a or human rights as solid blocks, the acceptance of either one or the other would suffer in our modern pluralistic nation states. Only by concentrating on the difficult and dynamic process of negotiation and interpretation can we resolve the dilemmas of diversity.

We can conclude that An-Na'im, like Asad, questions the secular liberal notion that the introduction of religious and moral questions into the public arena would result in chaos and that in a secular state people can engage in political debate only by leaving their religion at home. For An-Na'im, civic reason compels Muslims to enter into the debate on the good life with others. They need to use terms and arguments in that debate that are understandable and acceptable to others. But Muslims should not be asked *not* to talk about Shari'a in the public arena or not to follow it either in their private lives or in the public domain. In other words: space should be made for Muslims to use Islamic banking systems, to eat and drink what is permitted by Shari'a, or to create Islamic forms of mediation for Muslims with marital problems. Ideally,

---

49   An-Na'im, *Secular State*, 93.
50   An Na'im, *Secular State*, 95.
51   An Na'im, *Secular State*, 109.
52   An Na'im, *Secular State*, 112.
53   An Na'im, *Secular State*, 114.

in modern Western states, this should not pose a problem. In a secular state, Muslims and other believers have free access to the public debate, and the state is neutral in regard to the religious practices, the law of God they want to follow, either in their private lives or in the public arena. In reality, however, the individual European countries react very differently to the emergence of elements of Shari'a in European public space. This is partly so because there is no consensus about what 'public space' really is.

Kim Knott points out that, whereas 'public space' in political theory is perceived as neutral, homogeneous, and passive, in reality it is fragmented, powerful, active, and dynamic.[54] She also states that there are many images of what 'public space' should be in a secular state. If we trace the debate about the neutrality of public space back to the time of the great religious wars in Europe in the 17th century, we can distinguish two different ways of stating its neutrality. Knott calls the first a 'common ground' strategy: in spite of religious differences, there is a sort of neutral common ground where the communities can meet and negotiate about society as a whole. In this view, religious communities each have a space of their own that is neither completely public nor completely private, and the secular public space is the space between these communities. The second strategy sets up a secular public space as an *alternative* to religion as such: the 'independent political ethic' strategy (Grotius, Hobbes).[55] Here, the public space of secularism is qualitatively different from the (private) spaces of religious communities. The only way to obtain peace between rival religious systems is to leave the public space as empty of religion as possible. There has always been a mix of both views in the different European countries. The way this mix is constructed differs from one country to another. In France, with its system of *laïcité*, more stress is laid on the 'independent political ethic' strategy, whereas in England, with the strong role granted to the Anglican Church, the state creates more space for religious communities in the public debate. The Netherlands has traditionally had a model that verges toward that of overlapping consensus. Recently, however, the representation of the ideal public space as empty of intermediate organizations of citizens and the ensuing erosion of the tolerance of different/deviant behavior is increasingly influential. This creates problems for religious people who want to live their lives in line with the law of God. Therefore, a strong 'independent political ethic' strategy is less desirable if religious people are to give full expression to their citizenship in secular society. Is the 'common ground' strategy the line one should follow, then?

---

54 Knott, *Location*, 43.
55 Knott, *Location*, 66.

In fact, the actual public space in many modern European nation states in the past has often been a 'common ground' type of area. The Netherlands, for instance, had the 'pillar' system: the Protestant, Roman Catholic, Socialist, and Liberal communities were each seen as a different pillar, together supporting the building of society but from separate starting points. The leaders of the pillars would meet in the middle space and reach consensus. This model gave space to religious and other communities to participate in the public debate *as* communities, a middle space between 'public' and 'private.' The pillar system no longer works, however. People no longer feel a strong commitment to their religious or ideological community. Leaders of the communities have to deal with growing internal diversity, and this gives increasing power to the state, which acts on behalf of the greatest common denominator of the population. The 'common ground' strategy works best when there are strong interest groups many people can identify with. In the postmodern era, with its many transient communities, this is not likely to occur. Advocates of secular public space as a kind of middle space between the state and individuals must find other means than the traditional pillar system to achieve this space.

An example of such a renewed plea for a middle space is a lecture by the former archbishop of the Anglican Church, Rowan Williams, in 2008. Williams drew attention to the possibilities of implementing elements of Shari'a family law on a voluntary basis as a supplement to secular family law.[56] In an article on the controversy that arose about this proposition, Vincent Lloyd states that Rowan Williams and other critics of secular liberal forms of political theology, like John Milbank and Gillian Rose, argue for a 'politics of the middle.' In such a politics, it is not the sovereign (secular, liberal) state that is the center of theological deliberations—deliberations that either offer a theological basis for that sovereignty or deconstruct such attempts:

> Rather than affirming the sovereignty of the secular liberal state, offering a genealogy of that sovereignty, or offering an alternative conception of sovereignty, a politics of the middle does away with the concept of sovereignty altogether. Instead of focusing on a secular liberal subject in relation to an all-powerful state, or a Muslim subject in relation to all powerful Allah, a politics of the middle focuses on the myriad intermediary associations between the individual and some higher power.[57]

---

[56] Vincent Lloyd, "Complex Space or Broken Middle? Milbank, Rose, and the Sharia Controversy," *Political Theology* 10:2 (2009), 225–245.

[57] Lloyd, "Complex Space," 226.

In this conception, the state should not assume a transcendental role but should instead be seen as a mediator between different communities.

Lloyd points out that for some theologians of the middle space, public space is not an empty market square but a complex building full of structures under construction. The theologian John Milbank uses the image of a Gothic cathedral.[58] Different groups of workmen and architects are constructing their own chapels and belfries in nooks and crannies, often in competition with other groups. Their work is never quite finished: the complex space they add to is fragmentary, and there is no a priori harmony in their attempts. What is the role of the state in such a building-in-process? Lloyd suggests that the state may have to step in as an arbiter whenever major disagreements arise between groups working from different premises. In this image, the state fulfills the role of a nexus of master artists, advising local workmen how to harmonize their efforts with the whole. The image of public space as 'gothic space' is attractive. It differs from the previous image of communities as different 'countries' negotiating in a no-man's-land because it makes more allowance for the dynamics involved. The Dutch pillar system provided religious communities with a place in the political debate—but at the cost of immobilizing them. Traditions became static, and religious communities concurred with their leadership. If religious communities could be seen as groups of builders rather than as teams of negotiating diplomats, there would be more room for change and movement.

Yet Milbank's 'gothic space' is a rather optimistic and harmonious picture of the political middle, as Lloyd comments. More often, the middle ground between public and private space is a "broken middle": "The broken middle focuses on intermediary institutions that are always getting it wrong, that are always in tension with those that compose them, with each other, and with those other organizations of which they are components."[59] There is a difference, for instance, between the officially professed beliefs of religious communities and the way these are lived out by their members.[60] Instead of happily contributing to the cathedral, the workers are engaged in struggles within and between their communities. Communities are often not built solidly but are makeshift constructions. This brings to mind the proviso An-Na'im made about the contingent nature of formulations of 'the law of God' in the Muslim community. The Shari'a was developed during centuries of negotiation and reinterpretation. Up till now, the community of religious and legal scholars was

---

58 Cf. Asad, *Genealogies*, 179.
59 Lloyd, "Complex Space," 239. The term 'broken middle' comes from Gillian Rose.
60 Lloyd, "Complex Space," 241.

responsible for its development, but, lately, new voices can be heard urging new interpretations—the voice of female scholars, for instance. If we accept the strategy of the middle space as a solution for the problems religious people have to live according to the law of God in the secular public space, we should not try to view religious communities as happy harmonious wholes but as struggling and constantly evolving entities, debating and negotiating both internally and externally. These debates are not only about conceptions and ideas but also (and for the most part) about practices in everyday life. Allowing space for these debates in the public domain would not lead to harmony and social peace.

If one looks at the principle of freedom of religion from the perspective of the 'middle space' interpretation of secularism, 'religion' could mean more than "conceptions of a general order of existence." There might be more space for members of Muslim communities in Europe to practice the precepts of Shari'a (in its various interpretations) in their daily lives, as well as for Roman Catholics to use elements of canon law, or for Jews to apply precepts from the Shulkhan Arukh. This would certainly not result in a lessening of tensions in society, and in that respect the middle space is always a broken middle. Some precepts of 'the law of God' might, for instance, be in contradiction with the publicly approved and applied norms about the equality of men and women. Moreover, which members of the community have the authority to decide how 'the law of God' of a particular community should be applied? There is great internal diversity in Muslim, Jewish, and Roman Catholic communities.

Hence, there must be some provisos in the ground plan of the cathedral. One can only allow forms of 'the law of God' in secular nation states if adherence is be absolutely voluntary and if any member can always opt out of her or his community. Individuals can opt out of or into different jurisdictions—a difficult choice—thus combining their ability to choose with the discipline and commitment that group membership requires. The groups in turn must be in a continuous state of negotiation between their traditions and the requirements of their members, a process that could ultimately be benevolent as it calls for a process of "transformative accommodation."[61] Why should this difficult road toward a broken middle space be preferred to a 'laicist' option? Because this model offers the opportunity to all citizens in modern nation states to truly combine their rights and duties as citizens of nation states characterized by diversity with their calling to follow what they hold most sacred, for some the law of God.

---

[61] Ayelet Sachar, *Multicultural Jurisdictions: Cultural Difference and Women's Rights* (Cambridge: Cambridge University Press, 2001).

Conclusion

Starting with the struggle of a Dutch Muslim community leader, Rashid Bal, with the tensions his community experiences in the public space, we looked at different approaches to 'religion,' 'the secular' and the differentiation between them. If religion is defined in an essentialist way as 'a symbolic system' giving meaning to the world, then this definition excludes approaches to religion that allow for the importance of religious practice. For many believers, religion is a 'way of life' that is closely connected to forms of behavior determined by other fora than the forum of public debate. They want to follow the 'law of God' that is given and interpreted in their religious community in their daily lives. I have shown how two Muslim thinkers, Asad and An-Na'im, argue that 'the law of God' should not be conflated with a modern nation state using Shari'a rulings as basis for public law because in that case a modern nation state assumes transcendent power. The 'law of God' does, however, require the active engagement of Muslims in the political process. If these Muslims are living in a minority situation in the West, they, like members of other communities, should try to open up the public space to religiously based arguments. Even more so, they should claim space (the middle space) for the exercise in public of relevant religious practices, seeing the public arena not as an empty square but as a building to which each community is actively contributing. But communities engaged in the collective building up of public space cannot remain static. They need to engage in continuous internal negotiation within their religious communities, negotiating between transmitted traditions and authoritative interpretations and the requirements of their members in the present context, between their views on society and those of others, between the freedom to apply their own disciplines and a 'transformative accommodation' to the norms of society, knowing that the space in which the law of God operates is, on this earth, always a broken middle space.

Maybe this is what Rasit Bal too means when he concludes his lecture on the participation of Muslim communities in Dutch society. In his final words, he discusses the possibilities of co-operation between the Muslim, Christian, and Jewish groups in which he is involved:

> Two topics are at the center: how should we relate to each other, and what does it mean for our own identity if we travel together? We constantly do this on account of a concrete societal problem, and we strive for a common approach, interpretation and statement. The second perspective that is a point of focus is how we as religious traditions can relate to politics, the state and public space. How can we be present in public

space and contribute in a meaningful way? I can see that the people involved connect their norms to this, all the while putting them in perspective, working within this framework and reinterpreting them. That is very promising.[62]

Bibliography

An-Na'im, Abdullahi Ahmad, *Islam and the Secular State: Negotiating the Future of Shari'a* (Cambridge: Harvard University Press, 2009).

Asad, Muhammad, *The Principles of State and Government in Islam* (Berkeley: State University of California Press, 1961).

Asad, Talal, *Formations of the Secular: Christianity, Islam, Modernity* (Stanford: Stanford University Press, 2003).

Asad, Talal, *Genealogies of Religion: Disciplines and Reasons of Power in Christianity and Islam* (Baltimore and London: Johns Hopkins Press, 1993).

———, "Muhammad Asad Between Religion and Politics," *Insan ve Toplum* 1:2 (2012), 155–165.

Bal, Rasit, "De agenda van de toekomst" (The Agenda for the Future), http://www.raadvankerken.nl/fman/5038.pdf.

Beer, Paul de, "De paradox van de godsdienstvrijheid" (The Paradox of the Freedom of Religion), in H.M.A.E. van Ooijen, L.F. Egmond, Q.A.M. Eijkman, F. Olujic & O.P.G. Vos (eds.), *Godsdienstvrijheid: Afschaffen of beschermen? (Freedom of Religion: Should It be Abolished or Protected?)* (Leiden: Stichting NJCM-Boekerij, 2008), 5–9.

———, "Waarom vrijheid van godsdienst uit de grondwet kan" (Why Freedom of Religion Can Be Removed from the Constitution), *Socialisme & Democratie* 64 (2007), 18–24.

Bessems, Kustaw, "Religieus symbool niet achter de balie" (Religious Symbols Not at the Counter), *De Pers* (20 March 2011), http://www.depers.nl/UserFiles/File/De%20Pers%20dinsdag%2015%20maart%202011.pdf.

Cook, Michael, *Commanding Right and Forbidding Wrong in Islamic Thought* (Cambridge: Cambridge University Press, 2000).

Dronkers, Pieter, *Faithful Citizens: Civic Allegiance and Religious Loyalty in a Globalized Society. A Dutch Case Study*, doctoral thesis (Amsterdam/Groningen: Protestant Theological University, 2012).

Habermas, Jürgen, "Reconciliation through the Public Use of Reason: Remarks on Rawls' Political Liberalism," *Journal of Philosophy* 92 (1995), 109–131.

---

62   Bal, "Agenda," 5 (my translation, GS).

King, Richard, *Orientalism and Religion: Postcolonial Theory, India and 'The Mystic East'* (London & New York: Routledge, 1999).

Knott, Kim, *The Location of Religion: A Spatial Analysis* (Durham: Acumen (Equinox 2005), 2013).

Lloyd, Vincent, "Complex Space or Broken Middle? Milbank, Rose, and the Sharia Controversy," *Political Theology* 10:2 (2009), 225–245.

Rawls, John, *A Theory of Justice* (revised ed.) (Harvard: Harvard University Press, 1999 (1971)).

———, *Political Liberalism*, expanded ed. (New York: Colombia University Press, 2003).

Sachar, Ayelet, *Multicultural Jurisdictions: Cultural Difference and Women's Rights* (Cambridge: Cambridge University Press, 2001).

Taylor, Charles, "Modes of Secularism," in Rajeev Bhargava (ed.), *Secularism and its Critics* (Delhi: Oxford University Press, 1998), 138–163.

Multiculturalism, Religion and Public Justice[1]

Jonathan Chaplin

This is how Jonathan Sacks, prominent British Jewish intellectual and former Chief Rabbi, opens an important book on the future of British society, *The Home We Build Together*:

> Multiculturalism has run its course, and it is time to move on. It was a fine, even noble idea in its time. It was designed to make ethnic and religious minorities feel more at home in society ... It affirmed their culture. It gave dignity to difference. And in many ways it achieved its aims ... But there has been a price to pay, and it grows year by year. [It] has led not to integration but to segregation ... It was intended to promote tolerance. Instead, the result has been ... societies more abrasive, fractured and intolerant than they once were.[2]

While in an earlier book, *The Dignity of Difference*, Sacks argued for the public recognition of cultural and religious difference,[3] in this book he warns that the public realm is in danger of falling apart. Multiculturalism has created for us not a 'home' where we belong but a mere 'hotel' in which residents co-habit but share no common purposes.

British debates about multiculturalism parallel those occurring in the Netherlands and across much of Europe, although the shape and intensity of these debates differ significantly across diverse national contexts.[4] Everywhere leading commentators from across the political spectrum, and not just the popular media, are urging us to move 'beyond multiculturalism' and reaffirm the importance of social cohesion, political integration, national identity and shared values. Among the numerous statements appearing across Europe from prom-

---

[1] This chapter is a revised and abridged version of "Beyond Multiculturalism—but to where? Public Justice and Cultural Diversity," *Philosophia Reformata* 73:2 (2008), 190–209. We are grateful to the board of the Foundation for Christian Philosophy and to the editors of *Philosophia Reformata* who gave permission to use this material.
[2] Jonathan Sacks, *The Home We Build Together: Recreating Society* (London: Continuum, 2007), 7.
[3] Jonathan Sacks, *The Dignity of Difference: How to Avoid the Clash of Civilizations* (London: Continuum, 2003).
[4] See, e.g., Steven Vertovec & Susanne Wessendorf (eds.), *The Multiculturalism Backlash: European Discourses, Policies and Practices* (London: Routledge, 2010).

inent public figures over the last decade or so, here are two from the UK. First, in 2006 British Prime Minister Tony Blair made a significant speech, evidently prompted by the London bombings of July 2005, called "The Duty to Integrate: Shared British Values." In it, while continuing to affirm multiculturalism, he asserted:

> Obedience to the rule of law, to democratic decision-making about who governs us, to freedom from violence and discrimination are not optional for British citizens. They are what being British is about. Being British carries rights. It also carries duties. And those duties take clear precedence over any cultural or religious practice.[5]

Second, *Daily Telegraph* journalist Janet Daley, evidently speaking for many among British political and cultural elites, responded to Archbishop Rowan Williams' controversial (and widely misunderstood) 2008 lecture on sharia law and English law with the emphatic declaration that, "In the contest between the principles of modern democracy and doctrines of faith, democracy and the rule of secular law must always win."[6]

These statements sharply disclose the widely perceived anxiety to which this book addresses itself, namely that religion may once again be becoming a threat to the Western way of life—that 'the law of God' might undermine 'civilization' and that those appealing to such law need to be 'disciplined' when acting in the public realm so that their religious claims do not disrupt or subvert societal stability or corrode commonly accepted norms and values. What is striking in such statements is the categorical nature of their assertion of the unqualified priority of secular law over any claims arising from culture or religion. Now everyone will immediately recognize that certain extreme political claims, or violent actions, must be restrained by the rule of law irrespective of a putative religious or cultural justification. But it is remarkable that such utterances can be issued by leading public figures without any awareness of the complexities of the multi-sided relationships between religion, culture and politics. They imply that the claims of the (secular) state can trump any possible appeal either to the protection of minority cultural identities not shared by the majority of the *demos*, or, even more troublingly, to a transcendent authority or purpose not derived from the state itself. Citizens of a modern secular state, it seems, are expected to show an absolute commitment to their

---

5 Tony Blair, "The Duty to Integrate: Shared British Values," 8 December 2006, http://news.bbc.co.uk/1/hi/uk_politics/6219626.stm.
6 Janet Daley, *Daily Telegraph*, 11 February 2008.

'civilization,' allowing no possibility that a conviction about divine authority might properly fund a critical counter narrative to a state that sees its laws as self-evident.

I will respond to this debate from the standpoint of a core principle of Reformed political thought: the principle of 'public justice.' With roots in the political theology of Abraham Kuyper and his neo-Calvinist associates, the principle was first precisely formulated by the legal philosopher Herman Dooyeweerd in the 1930s.[7] Since then the term has been frequently invoked by Protestant political parties in the Netherlands, and since 1980, also by the ecumenical *Christen-Democratisch Appèl* (Christian-Democratic Appeal) (CDA)—although the stream of thought associated with Kuyper and Dooyeweerd has only ever been one of several in the CDA itself and today plays at best only a subsidiary role.[8] The principle has been widely applied to many areas of public policy in the Netherlands in reports of the party's research institute, the *Wetenschappelijke Instituut voor het CDA* (Research Institute for the CDA). Yet there has been surprisingly little scholarly reflection on how it might apply specifically to multiculturalism.

Since there are so many diverse meanings attached to this term let me make clear that what I have in mind in this chapter is multiculturalism as a *public policy objective* adopted in certain liberal democratic states. Tariq Modood defines this sense as "the political accommodation of minorities formed by immigration to western countries."[9] Since the 1960s several European (and other) states have adopted at least some such policies pursuant to this goal. These have been pursued most consistently, albeit in diverse ways, in the Netherlands, Britain and Canada. Their intended objective has been to move away

---

7   Herman Dooyeweerd, *A New Critique of Theoretical Thought*, Vol. 3 (Philadelphia: Presbyterian and Reformed Pub. Co., 1953–8), 445 f. This is a revised and expanded translation of a Dutch work published in the 1930s. See Jonathan Chaplin, *Herman Dooyeweerd: Christian Philosopher of State and Civil Society* (Notre Dame: University of Notre Dame Press, 2011), 219 ff.

8   Wetenschappelijk Instituut voor het CDA, *Publieke gerechtigheid: Een christen-democratische visie op de rol van de overheid in de samenleving* (*Public Justice: A Christian-Democratic Vision on the Role of the Government in Society*) (Houten: Bohn Stafleu van Loghum, 1990).

9   Tariq Modood, *Multiculturalism: A Civic Idea* (London: Polity, 2007), 5. I will not address political philosophies of multiculturalism developed by thinkers such as Charles Taylor, Bikhu Parekh, Seyla Benhabib or Pierre Bourdieu. Nor will I address the populist usage according to which the term serves, pejoratively, merely as a synonym for ethnic segregation or societal fragmentation. See for a critique Jonathan Chaplin, *Multiculturalism: A Christian Retrieval* (London: Theos, 2011).

from models of cultural *assimilation* (in which cultural differences are dissolved) towards societal *integration* (in which such differences are protected). A wide range of policies has been introduced pursuant to this goal, and some are noted below.

Cultural and Religious Diversity and Public Justice

Christian political thought in the strand of the Reformed tradition on which I am drawing has devoted much attention to the way in which plural religious orientations should be accorded equitable treatment in law and public policy under the norm of public justice.[10] American political thinker James Skillen, among others, has stated this as the principle of 'principled pluralism' (or 'confessional pluralism,' or 'equitable public pluralism').[11] But relatively little attention has been paid to the question of whether the norm of public justice can also be applied in a parallel way to cultural and ethnic minorities within western states. Hans-Martien ten Napel rightly argues that the notion of a 'pluriform democracy,' long associated with Christian political thought, be complemented by that of a 'multicultural democracy.'[12] Ten Napel identifies five broad purposes typically advanced by multicultural policies worldwide: political participation to secure power-sharing; access to justice, especially customary law; protection of minority languages; socio-economic policies to redress inter-cultural inequalities; and securing religious liberty. These entail supplementing a principled equitable treatment of religious plurality with the same treatment of cultural plurality. There remains much work to do to flesh out precisely what this might mean. This chapter hopes to offer a few pointers.

The central idea of 'public justice' is that the task of the state is the *establishment of justice in the public relationships of a society*.[13] This involves not the

---

10   I will not here set out the various biblical or theological foundations offered in support of the notion of public justice or of the positive affirmation of culture(s) on which my own argument depends. See, e.g., James W. Skillen, *The Good of Politics: A Biblical, Historical, and Contemporary Introduction* (Grand Rapids: Baker Academic, 2014).

11   James W. Skillen, *Recharging the American Experiment* (Grand Rapids: Baker Books, 1994). See also Richard Mouw & Sander Griffioen, *Pluralisms and Horizons* (Grand Rapids: Eerdmans, 1993); Jonathan Chaplin, "Rejecting Neutrality, Respecting Diversity: From 'Liberal Pluralism' to 'Christian Pluralism,'" *Christian Scholar's Review* 35 (2006), 143–176.

12   Hans-Martien ten Napel, "The Concept of Multicultural Democracy: A Preliminary Christian-Philosophical Appraisal," *Philosophia Reformata* 71 (2006), 145–153.

13   For a technical exposition of Herman Dooyeweerd's sense of this term see Jonathan Chaplin, "Public Justice as a Critical Political Norm," *Philosophia Reformata* 72 (2007),

imposition of a fixed blueprint, but rather the taking up of a dynamic, ongoing struggle to justly balance the many legitimate jural interests rising up within a complex society at any time. By 'jural interests' I mean valid claims to just treatment in law and public policy, and this may be realized by the state and its organs in a wide variety of ways. These interests are many and varied, but many of the most important ones can be grouped under three heads: those attaching to or benefiting individual persons; those possessed by associations or institutions; and those arising from the wider demands of the 'public good.' I briefly comment on each below.

On this conception of public justice, the state is to pursue its highly complex jural balancing task by means of (substantively just) law. The state is essentially a politico-legal rather than a cultural or religious institution, and this specification has several important implications of which I here mention two. First, while law necessarily reflects underlying moral commitments and is never morally neutral, it is not the task of the state to directly create moral virtue in its citizens (though just laws and policies will help do so). Second, nor is it the state's task to protect (still less define) something as amorphous as 'national culture' (just laws and policies may sustain it, though they may also correct it). The state should protect the 'public good,' but this is a more precise notion than that of national culture. Protection of particular components of national culture (for example, language or significant objects of historical patrimony) can, however, legitimately be seen as part of the public good.

The task of the state, then, is to establish relationships of societal justice by means of just frameworks of law and public policy. By so doing, the state establishes societal space and infrastructural conditions within which individuals, associations, institutions and other agents can freely and responsibly pursue their own distinctive vocations and pursuits, and also restrains acts which violate or damage the capacity of such agents to do these things. Such, at least, is a summary of how public justice has been understood in the strand of Reformed political thought on which I am drawing. Obviously, it must immediately be acknowledged that what both 'justice' and 'public' (and 'public good') actually mean will be fiercely contested in a plural society. Supporters of the principle will have their own distinctive views of their meanings, and their view will have to be commended to fellow citizens amidst the noisy and unpredictable processes of a deliberative democracy, in which no one conception of the role of the state will prevail entirely.

131–150. For a popular account, see Jonathan Chaplin, "Defining Public Justice in a Plural Society: Probing a Key Neo-Calvinist Insight," *Pro Rege* (March 1994), 1–11 (http://www.dordt.edu/publications/pro_rege/crcpi/115667.pdf).

What, then, what might *cultural* public justice look like? What types of claims to just treatment on the part of the state might properly arise from cultural membership or identity? We can put the question more precisely: who or what may be the bearer of cultural rights or duties, or the holder of cultural responsibilities? Obviously no comprehensive answer can be given here. I address this question illustratively in relation to three specific areas of application: individual cultural rights; associational cultural rights; and what is technically termed 'legal pluralism.' I shall also introduce here a consideration of religious rights. Notwithstanding certain similarities with cultural rights for the purpose of law and public policy, religious rights should not be conflated with them. While my opening definition of multiculturalism was *cultural* in focus, it is clearly the case that for many cultural minorities religious affiliation looms large in their cultural identities, and also that in popular debate 'multiculturalism' is often seen as inseparable from religion.[14]

First, however, let me pre-empt a possible misunderstanding. I suggest that it is not meaningful to speak of the legal rights or duties of entire cultural, ethnic or religious communities, such as 'the Black community,' 'the German Turkish community,' or 'British Muslims.' To exercise legal rights and duties it is necessary to possess legal agency, but cultural and religious communities lack this. Thus, in *Pluralisms and Horizons* Mouw and Griffioen correctly deny that what they call "cultural contexts" exist as organized communities with the capacity to act. A culture is, they propose, rather a *unique configuration or patterning of associational and religious practices*.[15] In similar terms, David Koyzis defines an ethnic nation as "an aggregating or non-totalizing community that may or may not coincide with the political nation," and "a non-purposive network of interrelated individuals, institutions and associations bound together by a common culture, however this may be defined."[16] Amorphous groups like 'the Polish community'—as distinct to a 'Polish Community *Centre*'—lack defined structure, clear purposes and centers of decision-making and so cannot be bearers of legal rights or duties (though they are indeed deserving of 'public respect' in a looser, but no less important, sense).

---

14   Thus, Ralph Grillo speaks of the expansion of multicultural discourse beyond its original focus on race, ethnicity and culture into what is today increasingly a "faith-based multiculturalism", see "British and others: From 'race' to 'faith,'" in Vertovec & Wessendorf, *Multiculturalism Backlash*, 50–71.
15   Mouw & Griffioen, *Pluralisms and Horizons*, 153.
16   David T. Koyzis, *Political Visions and Illusions* (Downers Grove: Inter-Varsity Press, 2003), 117.

These cautions about the ontology of cultural communities reflect the pluralistic, anti-totalizing social theory of Herman Dooyeweerd. Dooyeweerd held that complex macro-social phenomena like 'the city' and 'society' are not discrete entities like families, schools or states but rather complex networks of "enkaptic interlacements" (a species of normative interconnection, existing between many independent social structures).[17] Dooyeweerd's concern is to resist the dangerous proposal that societies are determinate social structures, for such would imply an erroneous "whole-part" conception of society which carries "totalitarian" tendencies. For Dooyeweerd, amorphous phenomena like cultures, ethnic nations or societies have no "structural principle" and so lack independent agency.[18] Like societies, cultural communities do not *do* anything themselves; they are enabling and formative contexts in which things are done.

Individual Cultural and Religious Rights

Let us now turn to the three areas of application of cultural and religious public justice. The first area is *individual cultural rights*.[19] This point is strongly emphasized within liberal multicultural theory. The leading Canadian multicultural theorist Will Kymlicka, for instance, proposes to add a selection of cultural rights to the standard list of individual civil and political rights currently established in western liberal democracies; he terms them 'polyethnic rights.'[20] It seems to me that certain individual cultural rights can indeed be seen as legitimate on the basis of the concept of public justice. Where a person's inherited or adopted cultural or religious affiliation is experienced as profoundly important to their social identity and standing—to the public face they desire to present to society or at least have society respect—and where it is vulnerable to hostility or corrosion, then arguably the state may (and in some cases must) need to respond positively to identity-based claims. We can discern here the possibility of a legitimate jural interest. At least, one can argue that this should be the state's *prima facie* stance—even though such identity claims cannot simply trump all other considerations.

Consider cultural rights. No one can claim a right to be *given* a cultural identity by the state or to have it protected *at any cost*. But where cultural identity

---

17 Dooyeweerd, *New Critique*, Vol. 3, 582.
18 Dooyeweerd, *New Critique*, Vol. 3, 163, 167, 196.
19 We could also speak of certain cultural and religious *duties* but I shall not comment on that notion here.
20 Will Kymlicka, *Multicultural Citizenship* (Oxford: Oxford University Press, 1995).

is already established (usually in common with others) and is an important marker of an individual citizen's public standing, then the state may acquire a duty to protect it by granting some individual cultural or religious rights, such as a right to speak one's own language in certain official public *fora* such as courts (or to have access to a translator); a right to receive minority language instruction in public schools for one's children; a right to have cultural festivals recognized in schools or other public settings; a right to adopt certain kinds of culturally normative dress in certain public contexts; and so on.

The category of individual *religious* rights, such as the right to freedom of religion, or to join or leave a religious association, or to change one's religion, must be kept distinct and not assimilated to cultural rights. Claims for legal recognition or protection may be even stronger here since for many citizens religious identity—deriving from a powerful apprehension of transcendent authority—is more fundamental than cultural or ethnic identity. Of course, some citizens may not wish to, or be able to, draw bright lines between their religious and cultural identities, so that it may not be easy for the state to determine which is really at stake in any recognition-claim arising from a particular identity (and it is not for the state to force its own determinations on unwilling citizens). But increasingly the clarity and primacy of the religious identities of some citizens, notably, but not only, for Christians and Muslims, are becoming more evident to them as they engage with a secular and plural society seemingly less and less hospitable to their ways of life.

The protection of individual religious rights, it might be thought, presents few problems to a liberal society priding itself on its strong and longstanding affirmations and protections of religious freedom. Certainly, Reformed political thought concurs strongly with professed liberal principles on this point. Yet across Europe there is evidence of a growing clash between a certain class of religious rights, such as the right to have one's individual religious conscience accommodated in certain areas (such as participation in abortions, or in actions that might commit one to affirming the moral legitimacy of same-sex relationships) and particular imperatives of public policy, notably those arising from equality and anti-discrimination laws. The clash has become dramatized in a number of high profile national and supra-national court cases where individuals have been driven to appeal to the European Court of Human Rights to secure their 'right to manifest' their religious belief in public settings, against restrictive national (or EU) legislation. The clash is emerging because of the simultaneous *expansion of the scope of equality law* (some of it emerging from what is really judicial legislation at national and European levels) and a *constriction of the scope of religious conscience* as perceived by legislators and judges. The resultant squeezing of the claims of individual religious conscience may lead to a growing number of religiously-motivated citizens experiencing marginalization from political and legal fora. It may also have the further effects of, first, weakening the capacities of religious communities to inculcate valuable social and civic virtues in their members (eroding their internal resources of 'self-discipline') and, second, muting their abilities to engage in constructive, critical political dissent. In both senses, liberal democracy (perhaps even 'civilization') could be the loser.

Yet having acknowledged that worrying development, it remains the case that, as with any putative rights-claim, the concrete implications of individual cultural and religious rights need to be defined carefully with an eye on particular circumstances, and balanced against and limited by other rights; no legal rights are absolute. Not just any claim to a supposed individual cultural or religious right can be allowed to stand. Consider this example. Claims by parents to a right to practice cliteridectomy on their daughters must be clearly resisted because they breach our societies' conviction (shared also by the great majority of religious citizens) that bodily integrity is a fundamental human right. Consider a more extreme case. In some American court cases (and more recently also in British ones), perpetrators of serious crimes such as rape or even murder (so-called 'honor killings') have tried to invoke 'cultural defense' arguments (which can be crudely summed up as 'my culture made me do it'). Such claims must be dismissed even more robustly. By contrast, the cases of culturally or religiously sanctioned polygamy or arranged marriage (as distinct to *forced* marriage) involve more complex considerations. Like any broad normative political principle, the principle of public justice does not instruct us on precisely where such lines should be drawn. As noted, it is not a blueprint but a dynamic assignment involving subtle, demanding and inescapably controversial judgments of many particulars.

Associational Cultural and Religious Rights

So much, then, for the implications of public justice for individual cultural and religious rights. I turn, secondly, to *associational cultural and religious rights*. Under cultural rights, we can draw a technical distinction between cultural rights attaching to independent associations per se (e.g., the right of a representative of a Wallonian trade union to speak French in public fora), and rights attaching to associations pursuing specifically cultural purposes (e.g., a Polish community center). In either case, it seems clear that associations can be bearers of cultural rights. Equally, religious associations—by which I mean not only churches, mosques, temples, etc., but a wide range of faith-based social organizations engaged in education, health, welfare (even commerce)—possess a *prima facie* right to govern their internal affairs according to their own convictions. This requires that state legislation should impinge upon those convictions only where there is (to use American jurisprudential language) a 'compelling state interest.' When the British government compelled Catholic adoption agencies either to provide adoption services for same-sex couples in breach of the Church's longstanding moral theology, or to close down, it failed to meet that condition. Here we meet the associational parallel to the conflict just noted earlier between individual religious rights and the recent demands of equality legislation, instances of which are finding their way into national and European courts with increasing frequency. The genuine force of legitimate cultural and religious identity claims—their capacity to generate legitimate jural interests—should lead us to resist what American political scientist Nancy Rosenblum has called the "logic of congruence" whereby states progressively seek, through law and policy, to bring the norms and values of non-state associations into increasing conformity with those of the state itself, thereby undercutting the autonomy of civil society institutions and sapping their ability to embody alternative forms of life than that promoted by the state.[21]

It is vital to note that the position of cultural and religious associations should be regarded in principle as essentially akin to that of any other non-governmental association which may claim some public legal protection or benefit, and not construed (or presented) as special pleading. Indeed the robust protection of associational rights in general serves as a vital contributor to inter-cultural and inter-religious justice. A strong civil society is an institutional precondition for a vibrant multicultural and religiously plural society.

The question then arises whether the state should go beyond the mere legal protection of associational autonomy of cultural or religious groups and actively support the cultural or religious purposes they pursue, for example by granting them public funds or access to fora of public consultation and representation. It would seem that the same broad principles should apply here as apply to all non-governmental associations. While there can be no assumption of automatic entitlement to public funds, such funds are often provided to a range of such organizations insofar as they are deemed to be making some significant contribution to the public good. This contribution does not have to be pursuant to the *state's* own purposes. If the state only supports groups that advance social purposes of which it approves ideologically, then civil society will be damagingly politicized and its capacity to serve as a platform for critical

---

21   Nancy Rosenblum (ed.), *Obligations of Citizenship and Demands of Faith: Religious Accommodation in Pluralist Democracies* (Princeton: Princeton University Press, 2000), 187.

dissent weakened. For the purposes of qualifying for public funds, or access to representation, it should be enough that groups make some tangible contribution to the welfare of some section of society. Such contributions need not be precisely measurable, nor must they be made to conform to the imperatives of any sitting government. What is implied here is a cooperationist model of church-state relationships rather than a separationist model represented by states such as France, Turkey or the USA.

As with individual cultural or religious rights, there will also need to be legal limits set to the scope of cultural or religious associational activities. For example, public funds should not go to support a community center or school where there is credible evidence that it openly or tacitly harbors or supports illegal activities, or engages in activities likely to create civil disorder of feed serious prejudice (e.g., the British Islamic school found to be using textbooks containing anti-Semitic propaganda). Setting such limits today is both urgent and controversial and delicate prudential judgments will need to be made in specific cases.

Cultural and religious associations will also need to work within the wider framework of public policy, whereby the state properly sets constraints or encourages actions pursuant to protecting the public good, itself a bearer of its own legitimate jural interests. It is impossible to specify the full range of such interests, but they include such matters as public health and safety, essential transport infrastructure and the fundamentals of economic stability. But the public good is a necessarily contested and slippery term often invoked by states for dubious purposes. For example, following a recent change in British law, if a cultural or religious community group wants to avail itself of charitable status, it will have to demonstrate that its activities meet a so-called 'public benefit' criterion. This may not be a bad development in itself, but everything depends on how the criterion of 'public benefit' comes to be defined, and the concern of some is that the definition will be construed so narrowly as to compromise the cultural or religious integrity of such groups (their experienced 'authenticity'). The further requirement that such groups must now show how they are contributing to 'social cohesion' could also prove to be quite burdensome if this term is defined too restrictively. For example, must an Islamic community center be able to demonstrate that it is engaged in inter-faith activities in order to qualify for charitable status? Many Christian groups would object to such an imposition, even if they actually wanted to engage in such dialogues.

A Special Case of Associational Rights: 'Legal Pluralism'

The sense of the term 'legal pluralism' I am using here must be distinguished from that more familiar in Christian political thought, which Reformed thinkers have referred to as 'legal sphere sovereignty'—the idea that there exist many distinct original sources of valid (positive) law, not only the state. Here I have in mind instead arrangements in which certain religious associations, or the tribunals or councils representing or governing them, are granted public legal standing and authority over their members in certain limited aspects of civil law, such as family or property law (referred to by Ten Napel as "access to customary law"). Such systems exist in a number of jurisdictions across the world such as India, Israel and Indonesia.[22] They often evoke strong opposition, since the rulings of such tribunals sometimes conflict with the plain requirements of individual civil rights established in the same legal system.

Such legal pluralism can best be described as a system of 'religious corporatism,' where 'corporatism' is understood as the conferral of public legal authority on a private body. Reformed thinkers have expressed negative views of corporatism in the sphere of political economy, regarding it as an illegitimate blurring of the boundary between the public jurisdiction of the state and the private jurisdictions of non-state economic organizations. On its face, the same critique seems applicable in the area of family and property law. Dooyeweerd, for example, holds that the principles of civil-legal equality and freedom are crucial to protecting a sphere of publicly-authorized equal individual legal rights for all citizens irrespective of their (private) kinship, cultural or religious associations.[23] Legal pluralism certainly seems to render the civil rights of some members of the recognized cultural or religious associations (especially women and children) vulnerable to unjustified restriction. This is so, for example, if such an association delivered differential, publicly enforceable rights to divorce between male and female members of the group.

I offer two remarks about legal pluralism. First, it has proven historically necessary, in India for instance, to allow such arrangements to exist, at least for a transitional period, in order to accommodate powerful or threatened minority groups and to enlist them in support of the state. This may be troubling, but the notion of public justice could perhaps accommodate this possibility in virtue of its commitment to a public good which is wider than the sum of individual and associational rights. In saying that public justice is not a blueprint,

---

22 For a description of such systems, see Ayelet Shachar, *Multicultural Jurisdictions* (Cambridge: Cambridge University Press, 2001).
23 Herman Dooyeweerd, *Roots of Western Culture* (Toronto: Wedge, 1979), 186.

we also say that it involves achieving the most just arrangements compatible with current historical possibilities. We readily recognize this in, for example, the case of economic equity, so there seems no *a priori* reason why we may not recognize it in the case of certain civil or political rights, which are also historical achievements. This is not to say, however, that systems of legal pluralism should be introduced in contemporary western states where they do not exist.

The second remark is to draw a distinction between what I have called religious corporatism and private religious arbitration. In recent years, many 'Sharia Councils' have been set up in various towns in the UK with significant Muslim populations. These councils do not have official public standing *per se* but they are not illegal. They make rulings between (supposedly) consenting individuals on the application of limited aspects of sharia law to cases involving family and property matters, utilizing provisions available to all citizens for the private settlement of disputes. They can function as a form of Alternative Dispute Resolution. Individual Muslims can decide to have their differences arbitrated in such a way, instead of simply going to the civil courts, a route which is more expensive, time-consuming and often publicly shaming. The civil courts can enforce their decisions under contract law, although parties can appeal against a council's ruling if they think it is manifestly unjust. Now, the legal status of such councils is similar to any private tribunal recognized under British law of the kind used by all kinds of people for many purposes. The entitlement to avail oneself of such a private tribunal is a general right available to all UK citizens, and there are as yet no legal grounds for disallowing such councils to operate freely—so long as the parties using them genuinely consent to doing so. Some Muslim women's groups argue, however, that Muslim women in fact are subtly coerced into accepting them. This was one of the fears unleashed by the Archbishop of Canterbury's lecture on sharia law to which I alluded earlier.[24] The issue merits careful investigation and looks set to be one of the most contested cases of multicultural policy in the UK in the years to come.

These, then, are a few implications of one Christian political orientation for weighing up various multicultural policies. I have suggested that at least some such policies can indeed be offered critical support by the principle of public

---

24   Rowan Williams, "Civil and Religious Law in England: A Religious Perspective," 7 February 2008 (http://rowanwilliams.archbishopofcanterbury.org/articles.php/1137). For a response to this lecture see Jonathan Chaplin, "Legal Monism and Religious Pluralism: Rowan Williams on Religion, Loyalty and Law," *International Journal of Public Theology* 2:4 (2008), 418–441.

justice. If so, then we should not seek to move 'beyond multiculturalism' where such policies really do advance cultural or religious public justice.

Multiculturalism and Citizenship

Finally, I will address the question whether the duties of citizenship place additional limits around multicultural claims beyond those already mentioned. Let me allude here to an important distinction drawn by Hendrik Woldring between "social cohesion" and "societal integration" although I will express it in my own way.[25] The notion of social cohesion, Woldring says, refers to the need for internalized *affective or moral bonds*, which will hold diverse citizens together in their social interactions in spite of all their other differences. Minimal norms such as trust, truthfulness and toleration are what make social intercourse possible at all, and every society needs to find ways to cultivate and sustain these basic norms of sociality. I do not think the state should take the lead in this process but rather it must defer to, and support, other associations far better equipped to do so: families, schools, neighborhoods, the media and other institutions of civil society. By contrast, societal integration refers to *participation* in various social institutions and relationships: employment, education, neighborhood, voluntary bodies, and so forth. Woldring quotes the definition of integration developed by the Dutch Commission for Research on Integration Policy: "A person is integrated into Dutch society when they enjoy equality under law, participate equally in socio-economic life, have knowledge of the Dutch language, and respect current values, norms and behavior patterns."[26] These are all desirable goals, but it is important to note that many institutions and persons share the responsibility to advance them. Realizing equal legal status is uniquely a task of the state, but the other three goals cannot simply be realized by the state alone. Indeed I suggest that the primary duty to achieve these belongs to individuals and non-government institutions. The state's role here is facilitative rather than directive. For example, in the case of 'equal participation in socio-economic life' a typical task of the state is to remove unjust barriers to participation. This may involve legal action (e.g., anti-discrimination legislation), and structural action (e.g., policies aimed at relieving those trapped in poverty in segregated or deprived neighborhoods).

---

25 Hendrik Woldring, *Pluralisme, Integratie en Cohesie* (*Pluralism, Integration, and Cohesion*) (Budel: Damon, 2006).
26 Woldring, *Pluralisme*, 76 (my translation, JC).

We should not have utopian expectation for societal integration. We may need to accept a considerable degree of social distance between certain communities where they choose to (rather than being forced to) live comparatively separate lives. No public blame should be attached to living apart from the mainstream where this does not harm a clearly identifiable feature of the public good (as distinct, for example, to merely evoking social disapproval or discomfort). Here we will confront a complex spectrum of possibilities, each meriting attention on its own terms and in its own contexts. At one end, for example, many members of the Chinese community in Toronto (especially older ones) make few efforts to integrate closely with non-Chinese inhabitants living right next to them. This does not in itself create any social problems. At the other end, for example, certain Islamist-influenced groups in the London borough of Tower Hamlets have taken to patrolling their neighborhoods in search of 'un-Islamic' behavior (alcohol consumption, inappropriate dress, etc.), claiming these areas as 'Muslim territory.' The latter example is clearly an unacceptable violation of the civil liberties of every British citizen; or, where the offending behavior is actually illegal, is a usurpation of the role of the police or local government.

Yet while the state (and, where appropriate, other agencies) must act against such extreme examples of separatism, it should avoid setting the threshold of social integration too high. Where precisely it should be set may depend on circumstances such as population density (an obvious issue for countries like the Netherlands or cities like London), or the capacity of certain ethnic groups (including 'white majority' populations) to accommodate challenging behavioral diversity in their midst. In some circumstances, absence of social conflict may be all that can be realistically expected. We must work to protect individuals and communities from public harm but resist frog-marching them into fraternity. Nonetheless the state and many other agencies can do much to foster the conditions for greater cooperation and partnership across cultural and religious communities that are at risk of lapsing into balkanization.

Let me turn now specifically to *political* integration, which is but one sectorial dimension of societal integration. By 'political integration' I mean the appropriate relationships between people in their capacity as citizens, and between them and the state. What duties may the state properly lay upon its citizens? I suggest the proper way to approach this question is to explore further what it means to define the central norm of the state as public justice. Citizenship is membership in the political community, a community existing to realize public justice, a goal to be pursued both by government and citizens. In a democracy, citizens are co-responsible with government for the discernment and realization of public justice. This implies a positive calling to active political participation in many ways, as far as the capacities and opportunities of individual citizens and their associations allow. Such participation should not be compelled (and in liberal democracies cannot be, apart from rare exceptions such as compulsory voting as in Australia), though the state may legitimately encourage other institutions to promote it by various means, for example, by giving incentives to schools to include civic education in their curricula. The state can certainly create proper channels for political participation but it may not make participation into a legal obligation.

Mere Citizens and Virtuous Citizens

It may be helpful here to introduce a distinction between the 'mere citizen' and the 'virtuous citizen.'[27] The *legal* obligations of citizenship should, I suggest, be tailored to the mere citizen, while the state may seek to nurture virtuous citizenship only *indirectly* by supporting other institutions. What, then, might the minimal legal duties of citizenship be? Obviously the answer to this question will differ from country to country, but we might consider four: law-abidingness; payment of taxes; knowledge of the host language; willingness to engage in jury service or military service (or comparable public duties in other jurisdictions).

This may strike some as a disappointingly minimal list, but consider, for example, what the first implies. The duty to abide by the law is actually very far-reaching. It is not simply adherence to the formal principle of legality, for law is impregnated with normative commitments. It embraces, for example, the acceptance of the outcomes of constitutional democratic government and a respect for the fundamental constitutional rights and freedoms for all citizens, including those we may vigorously disagree with politically. (This does not mean that it should be illegal to campaign for changes to such basic constitutional provisions, so long as the existing law is adhered to in the process. But it may, perhaps, be desirable to entrench some parts of the constitution in order to prevent future ephemeral majorities dismantling them.) It also includes the acceptance of the state's discretion to determine the level and types of taxation, and the uses to which public spending is put, for example, on public welfare, education, health, housing, defense, and so forth. A 'mere' citizen must abide by public policies in all these areas, even though they may campaign against them politically. Further, tax evasion or welfare benefit fraud obviously violate the duties of the mere citizen.

---

27 See for an elaboration of this distinction: Chaplin, *Multiculturalism*, ch. 6.

Over the last decade or so some countries (e.g., the UK and the Netherlands) have added to this list of the duties of a mere citizen a requirement to learn the host language and, for new citizens, to pass a citizenship test including knowledge of national history or even 'national values.' Consider language first. Learning the language is obviously highly important to societal integration, and ignorance of it will obstruct advancement in many contexts. Imposing this requirement as a condition for certain types of employment is certainly legitimate. Those who decline or are out of reach of opportunities to learn the language must accept the consequence that this will diminish their social and economic opportunities. On the other hand, there may be some citizens (vulnerable women in patriarchal communities, for instance) who are effectively prevented from learning the language through family constraints. That presents a difficult dilemma for the state in deciding whether and if so how to intervene in such communities to promote equality of opportunity for these citizens without breaching the integrity and autonomy of families. The state can certainly support other institutions, such as schools or community centers, in their distinctive task of teaching a host language.

Yet the demands of only *societal* integration seem insufficient to warrant a *legal* duty to learn the host language. Consider the case of elderly recent immigrants who do not need to (or are not equipped to) work, lack the ability for language education, but are adequately cared for by their families. Must they nevertheless be coerced into learning the language as a condition of permanent residence? By contrast, the demands of *political* integration, and especially the acquisition of the specific legal status of citizenship and the rights to political participation attached to it, do indeed seem to justify an obligation to master the host language.

Now consider a supposed duty to learn or even profess 'national values.' This seems inherently problematic. Who determines what these values are? And how would 'learning outcomes' be assessed? As it happens, such assessment is attempted! The UK Citizenship Test requires aspiring citizens to memorize a range of facts about British history and society in order to reach a minimum score. But whether this indicates the genuine adoption of 'British national values' is extremely doubtful. Most indigenous UK citizens would in any case fail the test without considerable preparation; and they get on fine for most of their lives without such knowledge. The idea that citizens should be compelled to be exposed to or even publicly profess something as essentially contestable as a set of 'national values,' or some 'national narrative,' seems at best ineffective and at worst potentially oppressive. The articulation and transmission of such values surely belongs to institutions other than the state, such as families, schools and universities, trades unions, NGOs, churches and the media.

My claim is that the state should focus on the task of specifying and then legally enforcing that narrow but highly important set of duties I suggest is entailed under mere citizenship. But it can and must also support many other institutions in their distinctive roles both of fostering an ethos of social cohesion, and of encouraging and empowering people to move beyond mere citizenship and towards what I am calling virtuous citizenship. In the first instance, this might well also involve a role in defining and advancing basic norms of *political* morality (which is far from the whole of public morality), i.e., norms vital to the sustainability of a society's capacity to generate responsible (mere) citizens as well as healthy political institutions and practices. Such norms might include: adherence to the rule of law; tolerance of political disagreement; acceptance of established deliberative procedures; respect for fellow citizens in public space; commitment to essential public policies of social solidarity; and so forth. These will not best be advanced by politicians posing as public preachers or moralists but rather by, for example, measured articulations, in contexts like parliamentary sessions, party policy debates, or media discussions, of core principles of public morality that the state presupposes if it is to fulfill its own distinctive task. Such principles could even be formulated in official documents (preferably with sitting governments kept well away from the drafting process), so long as the content steers well clear of anything like a 'civil religion.' Politicians are not their citizens' moral guardians but they do have a role in giving leadership in upholding and improving the necessary principles of specifically political morality.

Let me conclude with some further remarks on the responsibilities of virtuous citizenship—often termed the practices of 'civic virtue.' These will exceed the duties of mere citizenship, and the more citizens aspire to fulfill them the more robust a polity and society will be over the long term. Today there are powerful forces at work eroding a sense of such duties, such as consumerism and individualism but what government can do to combat these needs to be very carefully specified. Essentially, virtuous citizenship involves active participation in political life: not mere periodic voting but regular and informed engagement in public discussion in civic fora and elsewhere, promoting political education, working in political organizations or parties, campaigning on public issues, and, for those so equipped, a readiness to hold public office. Those so inclined will likely already be actively engaged in other spheres of public life, whether business, education, civil society associations, community development, and so on. The latter often serve as 'schools of civic virtue,' as civil society theorists do not tire of reminding us (rightly so). But I would emphasize again the distinction between these forms of *societal* participation, and *political* participation. Involvement in non-state institutions should not be classified as a form of political activity or a mode of *citizenship*. There are, of course, powerful reasons in both Christian and secular traditions for enthusiastically encouraging these forms of societal participation, but there is no need to do so by packaging them as examples of *political* participation. Citizenship is enormously important, but it is only one of the many roles humans are called to fulfill in contributing to the flourishing of society. For that, we must look beyond politics to the (re)generative forces of culture and religion, while also, of course, resisting their degenerative potentials.

Bibliography

Blair, Tony, "The Duty to Integrate: Shared British Values," 8 December 2006, http://news.bbc.co.uk/1/hi/uk_politics/6219626.stm.

Chaplin, Jonathan, "Beyond Multiculturalism—but to where? Public Justice and Cultural Diversity," *Philosophia Reformata* 73:2 (2008), 190–209.

———, "Defining Public Justice in a Plural Society: Probing a Key Neo-Calvinist Insight," *Pro Rege* (March 1994), 1–11.

———, *Herman Dooyeweerd: Christian Philosopher of State and Civil Society* (Notre Dame: University of Notre Dame Press, 2011).

———, "Legal Monism and Religious Pluralism: Rowan Williams on Religion, Loyalty and Law," *International Journal of Public Theology* 2:4 (2008), 418–441.

———, *Multiculturalism: A Christian Retrieval* (London: Theos, 2011).

———, "Public Justice as a Critical Political Norm," *Philosophia Reformata* 72 (2007), 131–150.

———, "Rejecting Neutrality, Respecting Diversity: From 'Liberal Pluralism' to 'Christian Pluralism,'" *Christian Scholar's Review* 35 (2006), 143–176.

Dooyeweerd, Herman, *A New Critique of Theoretical Thought*, 4 Vols. (Philadelphia: Presbyterian and Reformed Pub. Co., 1953–8).

———, *Roots of Western Culture* (Toronto: Wedge, 1979).

Daley, Janet, in *Daily Telegraph*, 11 February 2008.

Grillo, Ralph, "British and others: From 'race' to 'faith,'" in Vertovec, Steven & Susanne Wessendorf (eds.), *The Multiculturalism Backlash: European Discourses, Policies and Practices* (London: Routledge, 2010), 50–71.

Koyzis, David T., *Political Visions and Illusions* (Downers Grove: Inter-Varsity Press, 2003).

Kymlicka, Will, *Multicultural Citizenship* (Oxford: Oxford University Press, 1995).

Modood, Tariq, *Multiculturalism: A Civic Idea* (London: Polity, 2007).

Mouw, Richard & Sander Griffioen, *Pluralisms and Horizons* (Grand Rapids: Eerdmans, 1993).

Napel, Hans-Martien ten, "The Concept of Multicultural Democracy: A Preliminary Christian-Philosophical Appraisal," *Philosophia Reformata* 71 (2006), 145–153.

Rosenblum, Nancy (ed.), *Obligations of Citizenship and Demands of Faith: Religious Accommodation in Pluralist Democracies* (Princeton: Princeton University Press, 2000).

Sacks, Jonathan, *The Dignity of Difference: How to Avoid the Clash of Civilizations* (London: Continuum, 2003).

——, *The Home We Build Together: Recreating Society* (London: Continuum, 2007).

Shachar, Ayelet, *Multicultural Jurisdictions* (Cambridge: Cambridge University Press, 2001).

Skillen, James W., *Recharging the American Experiment* (Grand Rapids: Baker Books, 1994).

——, *The Good of Politics: A Biblical, Historical, and Contemporary Introduction* (Grand Rapids: Baker Academic, 2014).

Vertovec, Steven & Susanne Wessendorf (eds.), *The Multiculturalism Backlash: European Discourses, Policies and Practices* (London: Routledge, 2010).

Wetenschappelijk Instituut voor het CDA, *Publieke gerechtigheid: Een christen-democratische visie op de rol van de overheid in de samenleving* (*Public Justice: A Christian-Democratic Vision on the Role of the Government in Society*) (Houten: Bohn Stafleu van Loghum, 1990).

Williams, Rowan, "Civil and Religious Law in England: A Religious Perspective," 7 February 2008 (http://rowanwilliams.archbishopofcanterbury.org/articles.php/1137).

Woldring, Hendrik, *Pluralisme, Integratie en Cohesie* (*Pluralism, Integration, and Cohesion*) (Budel: Damon, 2006).

The Natural Law and Liberal Traditions
Heritage (and Hope?) of Western Civilization

David VanDrunen

The natural law and liberal traditions must play a major role in any account of the complex story of the development of Western civilization. In discussions about the disputed place of religion in the present and future of the West, these two traditions often have center stage: liberalism is taken to represent indifference or even hostility toward religion in public life while natural law is understood to reflect a deep respect for religion and the transcendent underpinnings of a well-ordered human society. Yet there are many exceptions to this general sentiment. Many deeply religious people are skeptical about the notion of natural law and other religious people believe that the rise of liberalism over the past few centuries has brought more benefit than harm to Western civilization. Christian theologians pondering the future of Western civilization cannot avoid confronting and evaluating these two traditions.

The natural law and liberal traditions are ordinarily viewed as competing visions of the organization of human society. While this opinion has much to commend it, certain features of *both* traditions are attractive to many people. I think especially of liberalism's goal of ordering intractably pluralistic societies in peaceful ways and the natural law tradition's attempt to provide a moral, and not simply pragmatic, basis for our fundamental obligations toward one another. The questions I wish to pose in this essay are whether Scripture and Reformed theology provide good reason to appreciate these aspects of both traditions and also whether they explain how these traditions can be embraced simultaneously, despite prevailing sentiment about their mutual hostility. I answer these questions in the affirmative, pointing especially to the covenant with Noah recorded in Gen. 8:20–9:17, understood in the broader context of Reformed covenant theology. I argue that a proper understanding of this biblical covenant provides a theological foundation for affirming both a version of natural law theory and a version of liberalism. This Noahic foundation suggests that a modest natural law liberalism, while offering no hope of any utopian future, is a faithful Christian—and perhaps even the best available—approach to the exigencies of social life in this present age.

To argue this case I first offer some broad discussion of the natural law and liberal traditions. Then I discuss the covenant with Noah in Genesis and explain why it provides reasons for Christian theology to affirm versions of both natural law and liberalism. Finally, I describe how this natural law liberalism can answer certain longstanding objections to these traditions from Christians and other thoughtful critics.

The Natural Law and Liberal Traditions: Friends or Foes?

An initial problem is identifying precisely what is meant by liberalism and natural law. With respect to the liberal tradition, some writers describe liberalism in a way that makes it, almost by definition, antagonistic to historic Christianity,[1] while others characterize it with benign features that most Christians would find generally attractive.[2] Defining liberalism is perhaps especially difficult in my own American context. America was founded as a religion-friendly liberal polity, exhibiting not only the broad freedoms inscribed in the Bill of Rights but also an enterprise economy. Yet contemporary Americans supportive of this original American liberalism are usually called 'conservatives,' while today's American 'liberals' are generally more skeptical about the enterprise economy and religion.[3] Such use of conservative and liberal may be puzzling to Continental Europeans, and readers of this chapter ought to be aware of a possible bias in my understanding of liberalism that reflects this American context: I am inclined to think of liberalism in its traditional (conservative) American version, which tends to be less radical and also more religion-friendly than many continental European and contemporary American versions.[4]

---

1   For example, Patrick J. Deneen claims that while many things often thought to be liberalism's main features were also characteristic of medieval thought, liberalism itself is "constituted by a pair of deeper anthropological assumptions that give liberal institutions a particular orientation and cast: 1) anthropological individualism and the voluntarist conception of choice, and 2) human separation from and opposition to nature." See "Unsustainable Liberalism," *First Things* (August/September 2012), 25–31: 26.
2   E.g., Christopher Wolfe identifies the following five principles as the core of liberalism: the foundation of human dignity rooted in equality, political rule requiring consent, the purpose of government as the protection of rights, the need for a strong but limited government, and the rule of law. See *Natural Law Liberalism* (Cambridge: Cambridge University Press, 2006), 144 f.
3   On liberalism as, in a sense, the American conservative tradition, see e.g. Alexander M. Bickel, *The Morality of Consent* (New Haven: Yale University Press, 1975), 118; and Friedrich A. Hayek, *The Constitution of Liberty* (Chicago: University of Chicago Press, 1960), 397.
4   For relevant observations, see e.g. Wolfe, *Natural Law Liberalism*, 137, who comments on the anti-clerical character of French liberalism and the emphasis on autonomy in Kant's. Striking to me as an American was seeing in James Bratt's recent biography of Abraham Kuyper how

I believe that the following description of the origin of liberal thinking, in distinction from predominant classical and medieval perspectives, is generally accurate:

> That a diversity of rival and incompatible conceptions of the good should obtain the allegiance of a variety of contending parties was from now on increasingly to be taken for granted. The practical question became rather: what kind of principles can require and secure allegiance in and to a form of social order in which individuals who are pursuing diverse and often incompatible conceptions of the good can live together without the disruptions of rebellion and internal war?[5]

While liberalism can take many specific forms, I will take liberalism in general to represent the abandonment of the quest to build political society on a moral-metaphysical-religious unity among its citizens, in favor of seeking to build political society as an ordered community that acknowledges broad liberties for individuals, families, and voluntary associations to pursue their own goods and goals derived from their particular moral-metaphysical-religious convictions. I am thus primarily taking liberalism as a kind of polity, or political-social arrangement, not as a kind of philosophical theory.

Defining natural law is hardly any easier than defining liberalism. Unlike liberalism, natural law has a long history as a standard feature of Western Christian theology and ethics, not only in its medieval versions but also throughout most of the history of the Reformed and Lutheran traditions. But even if a standard feature, natural law has taken different forms within different theological streams, whether in competing Thomistic and voluntarist

---

strongly Kuyper and his Anti-Revolutionary Party opposed the rival liberal party, and vice versa, despite Kuyper's support for free (non-state) churches, democratic government, and other seemingly liberal sentiments; see *Abraham Kuyper: Modern Calvinist, Christian Democrat* (Grand Rapids: Eerdmans, 2013), 65 f, 71–77, 115, 117, 224 ff, 298–301, 304 f. Also relevant may be Peter G. Klein's description of the "two kinds of liberalism" to which Hayek often referred: "the continental rationalist or utilitarian tradition, which emphasizes reason and man's ability to shape his surroundings, and the English common-law tradition, which stresses the limits to reason and the spontaneous forces of evolution." See "Introduction," in F.A. Hayek, *The Fortunes of Liberalism: Essays on Austrian Economics and the Ideal of Freedom*, ed. Peter G. Klein (Chicago: University of Chicago Press, 1992), 12. The latter of the two liberalisms, of course, has most deeply shaped the historic American liberal tradition.

5 Alasdair MacIntyre, *Whose Justice? Which Rationality?* (Notre Dame: University of Notre Dame Press, 1988), 210. For similar remarks, see John Rawls, *Political Liberalism* (New York: Columbia University Press, 1993), xvi ff.

versions in the Middle Ages, in the modification of natural law ideas within Reformed, Lutheran, and Roman Catholic theologies after the Reformation, or even in debates over the new natural law theory in the fragmented world of contemporary Roman Catholic thought. Furthermore, in the past century much of the Protestant world took a decidedly negative posture toward natural law theory, particularly under pressure from Barthian (and to some degree neo-Calvinist) theology.[6] Various attempts to resurrect constructive Protestant theologies of natural law are emerging, but they are following different paths and there is no broad consensus that such attempts are even a good idea at all.[7]

The general idea of natural law that I utilize here is that all human beings know their basic moral obligations through their natural faculties, apart from biblical revelation. To put it a bit more broadly, I take natural law to represent a natural moral order that impresses obligations upon all human beings, known through apprehension of their own nature and the nature of the broader cosmos that God has structured in the way he has.

As even this initial discussion may hint, the natural law and liberal traditions are often interpreted as competing traditions whose core convictions lie in stark contrast to one another. The basic reason why is fairly simple. The natural law tradition, at least in its most prominent line, the Aristotelian-Thomistic, typically identifies a range of human goods to be achieved in community, especially in the political community whose citizens are united in their moral-metaphysical-religious perspective.[8] The liberal tradition, conversely, envisions political society as composed of a broad conglomeration of individuals,

---

[6] See discussions in Stephen J. Grabill, *Rediscovering the Natural Law in Reformed Theological Ethics* (Grand Rapids: Eerdmans, 2006), chap. 1; and David VanDrunen, *Natural Law and the Two Kingdoms: A Study in the Development of Reformed Social Thought* (Grand Rapids: Eerdmans, 2010), ch. 8–9.

[7] Two recent collections of essays discussing Protestant re-explorations of natural law illustrate the diverse opinions on the issue: Robert C. Baker & Roland Cap Ehlke (eds.), *Natural Law: A Lutheran Reappraisal* (St. Louis: Concordia, 2011); and Jesse Covington, Bryan McGraw & Micah Watson (eds.), *Natural Law and Evangelical Political Thought* (Lanham: Lexington, 2012). For other recent Protestant attempts to develop constructive theories of natural law, see also Thomas K. Johnson, *Natural Law Ethics: An Evangelical Proposal* (Bonn: Verlag für Kultur und Wissenschaft, 2005); J. Daryl Charles, *Retrieving the Natural Law: A Return to Moral First Things* (Grand Rapids: Eerdmans, 2008); and David VanDrunen, *Divine Covenants and Moral Order: A Biblical Theology of Natural Law* (Grand Rapids: Eerdmans, 2014).

[8] While the Aristotelian vision saw the *polis* as the highest community, the Thomistic vision looked to the church as providing resources for achieving virtues higher than those achievable in a political community.

who live peacefully and collaboratively with each other but do not share a common notion of the ultimate human good.

Advocates of both traditions highlight this antagonism. From the Aristotelian-Thomistic side, perhaps no one in the English-speaking world has contrasted this perspective with the liberal perspective more sharply or insistently in recent decades than Alasdair MacIntyre. MacIntyre describes Aristotle's account of the good in terms of an integrated form of life, embodied in a *polis*, and Thomas's account of the best political regime as the one that conduces to education into the virtues, in the interest of the good of all. In contrast, claims MacIntyre, the modern liberal conception of government seeks to secure a minimal order such that individuals may pursue their own freely chosen ends.[9] From a similar but somewhat different angle, Patrick Deneen has portrayed liberalism as rejecting the premodern conviction—exemplified by Aristotle and Thomas—that human creatures are part of a comprehensive natural order, and thus as repudiating the idea of human nature altogether and, with it, a sense of human self-limitation.[10]

From the other side, many contemporary proponents of liberalism paint a similar antithesis between the two traditions. John Rawls, for example, asks how to determine the "fair terms of cooperation" that define his famous "justice as fairness," and explains that these terms are not laid down "by God's law," known through an "independent moral order," or recognized as a requirement of "natural law." Instead, they are determined by *agreement* among "free and equal citizens."[11] Similarly, although Bruce Ackerman does not polemicize against natural law theory explicitly, his requirements for the liberal state demand rejection of the Aristotelian-Thomistic notion of grounding political society in a shared conception of naturally ordered human goods. For Ackerman, *neutrality* toward different visions of the good is a hallmark of the liberal state. No political authority can be justified, he claims, "by asserting a privileged

---

9   See e.g. MacIntyre, *Whose Justice?*, 90, 201. MacIntyre, I note, has not been a proponent of natural law per se. For relevant discussions, see Lawrence S. Cunningham (ed.), *Intractable Disputes About the Natural Law: Alasdair MacIntyre and Critics* (Notre Dame: University of Notre Dame Press, 2009).

10 Deneen, "Unsustainable Liberalism," 27. For another Aristotelian-Thomistic attempt to contrast natural law theory and liberalism, see also Robert P. George, *Making Men Moral: Civil Liberties and Public Morality* (Oxford: Clarendon, 1993).

11 Rawls, *Political Liberalism*, 22 f. Later he asserts that his liberal theory does not seek to refute a natural law perspective so much as remain agnostic about its claims: "justice as fairness is a political conception of justice, and while of course a moral conception, it is not an instance of a natural law doctrine. It neither denies nor asserts any such view." See Rawls, *Political Liberalism*, 406.

insight into the moral universe"; no assertion of right or power can legitimately rest upon a claim that one's "conception of the good is better than that asserted by any of his fellow citizens."[12] As he puts it elsewhere,

> I cannot define the terms of political conversation in a way that disparages my fellow's right to express his ideals *in the words that make most sense to him*. I cannot force him to argue his claims ... in terms that require him to deny the validity of his own answer to the question of life's meaning.[13]

From the perspective of proponents of both natural law and liberalism, therefore, these two traditions represent exceedingly different visions for the organization of political life.

Not all contemporary observers agree that the lines between the natural law and liberal traditions ought to be drawn so sharply, however. In fact, some Christian thinkers of diverse provenance have proposed a convergence of these traditions as a fruitful way forward. Christopher Wolfe, for example, adopts a broadly Thomistic version of natural law—shorn of a few of its traditional characteristics he believes are non-essential, such as its curtailment of religious liberty—and seeks to carry on a debate within what he sees as a broad tradition of liberalism marked by five key principles.[14] From a rather different perspective, Nicholas Wolterstorff has recently defended liberal democracy from an explicitly natural rights standpoint that is, I believe, a version of natural law theory.[15] He understands liberal democracy not as a theory per se, but

---

12 Bruce A. Ackerman, *Social Justice in the Liberal State* (New Haven: Yale University Press, 1980), 10 f.
13 Ackerman, *Social Justice*, 54 (italics his).
14 See generally Wolfe, *Natural Law Liberalism*. See note 2 above for Wolfe's five principles. See also Daniel J. Mahoney's response to the essay of Deneen cited above. Mahoney, like Wolfe and Deneen a Roman Catholic, agrees with Deneen about "philosophical liberalism's" opposition to the notion of a natural order, but believes "he goes too far in assuming that our political and social order is simply an embodiment and reflection of these modern philosophical assumptions. Liberalism in theory and in practice is far more variegated than he suggests." See "The Art of Liberty," *First Things* (August/September 2012), 33–35: 33.
15 See generally Nicholas Wolterstorff, *The Mighty and the Almighty: An Essay in Political Theology* (Cambridge: Cambridge University Press, 2012); and *Understanding Liberal Democracy: Essays in Political Philosophy*, ed. Terrence Cuneo (Oxford: Oxford University Press, 2012). I cannot explain here why I take his natural rights theory to be a kind of natural law theory, but see e.g. his *Justice: Rights and Wrongs* (Princeton: Princeton University Press, 2008), 82–87, where he pursues an argument that he admits would ordinar-

as a kind of polity that guarantees its citizens their equal natural rights, and which correspondingly entails a protectionist rather than perfectionist view of the state.[16] Wolterstorff, therefore, presents a strong conception of natural rights (natural law) as constitutive of the liberal polity he seeks to defend, and he thereby refutes the accusation that liberal democracy lacks a moral basis. From yet a third perspective I might mention Michael McConnell, who defends liberalism (denoting a political arrangement that protects people's essential liberties rather than promotes a particular conception of the good life) as the political arrangement most compatible with Christianity. He argues that liberalism is grounded in important respects in the Reformation notion of the two kingdoms, a doctrine organically linked to natural law in much historic Protestant thought.[17]

The terms of discussion are certainly not simple. It does seem that a full-fledged Aristotelian-Thomistic natural law theory is fundamentally incompatible with contemporary versions of liberalism that seek neutrality with respect to public reason and conceptions of the good. And yet, with a modified understanding of what natural law and liberalism essentially entail, some diverse but serious Christian thinkers have argued for what we might call a natural law liberalism.[18] In what follows I wish to pursue such an idea, but to do so in a distinctive way that draws from a particular text of Scripture and reflects my Reformed theological convictions.

The Noahic Covenant (Gen. 8:20–9:17)

Gen. 8:20–9:17 describes a covenant God made with Noah and, through him, with all of creation after the great flood. Reformed Christianity has traditionally looked to the biblical covenants as a major organizing feature of its

---

ily be considered under the rubric of natural law (though he explains why he avoids this terminology).

16 See e.g. Wolterstorff, *Understanding Liberal Democracy*, 1 f, 135; and *The Mighty and the Almighty*, 101 f. I explain and discuss the protectionist vs. perfectionist views below.

17 Michael W. McConnell, "Old Liberalism, New Liberalism, and People of Faith," in Michael W. McConnell, Robert F. Cochran, Jr. & Angela C. Carmella (eds.), *Christian Perspectives on Legal Thought* (New Haven: Yale University Press, 2001), 5–24. On the organic relationship of natural law and the two kingdoms in historic Protestant thought, see VanDrunen, *Natural Law and the Two Kingdoms*, especially ch. 2 and 4.

18 A very interesting question that may arise at this point is: what about John Locke? This father of liberalism was also a natural law thinker, and may be the first proponent of a natural law liberalism. Unfortunately, I cannot evaluate Locke's work here.

theology.[19] It has given the post-diluvian Noahic covenant relatively little attention, however, as has contemporary biblical scholarship, despite its considerable interest in the biblical covenants generally.[20] Though many Reformed theologians have treated the Noahic covenant as an administration of the broader covenant of grace continuing and developing through the later covenants with Abraham, Israel, and the New Testament church, I follow another stream of Reformed thought that sees the post-diluvian Noahic covenant as a distinct divine work, perhaps best described as a covenant of *common grace*.[21] Understood along these lines, as I believe the biblical text demands, I claim that the Noahic covenant provides a Reformed theological foundation for affirming versions of natural law and liberalism, and in such a way that envisions them as organically linked to one another.

To begin this discussion I first identify three prominent features of this covenant, all of which are highly pertinent for considerations of natural law and liberalism.[22] First, Gen. 8:20–9:17 describes a divine covenant that is truly *universal*. God makes this covenant not only with Noah, but also with his "offspring" after him (9:9), and indeed with "every living creature of all flesh that is on the earth" (9:16; cf. 9:10, 11, 12, 15, 17).[23] This includes "the birds, the livestock, and ... every beast of the earth" (9:10) as well as all human beings. It also extends to the broader natural order, as God promises the ceaseless regularity of "seedtime and harvest, cold and heat, summer and winter, day and night" (8:22).

Second, Gen. 8:20–9:17 describes divine promises. God's basic commitment to all alike is wonderful, but is perhaps surprisingly modest: God promises *preservation*. Elsewhere Scripture promises much more—the forgiveness of sins, reconciliation with God, a new age of everlasting peace—but we find no such promises here. Instead God commits himself, for as long as the present

---

19   See e.g. Geerhardus Vos, "The Doctrine of the Covenant in Reformed Theology," in Richard B. Graffin Jr. (ed.), *Redemptive History and Biblical Interpretation: The Shorter Writings of Geerhardus Vos* (Phillipsburg: Presbyterian and Reformed, 1980), 234–267.

20   See e.g. the comments in James Barr, "Reflections on the Covenant with Noah," in A.D.H. Mayes & R.B. Salters (eds.), *Covenant as Context: Essays in Honour of E.W. Nicholson* (Oxford: Oxford University Press, 2003), 11; and Katharine J. Dell, "Covenant and Creation in Relationship," in *Covenant as Context*, 111.

21   For bibliographic details see VanDrunen, *Divine Covenants and Moral Order*, 99 note 4.

22   For more detailed defense of this exegesis of Gen. 8:20–9:17, as well as its relation to natural law, see VanDrunen, *Divine Covenants and Moral Order*, ch. 2.

23   Scripture quotations are from The Holy Bible, English Standard Version® (ESV®), copyright © 2001 by Crossway Bibles, a publishing ministry of Good News Publishers. Used by permission. All rights reserved.

earth remains, to sustain the regular cycles of nature (8:22), to prevent mass destruction through another great flood (8:21; 9:11, 15), to keep wild animals from overrunning the human race (9:2), and so forth. The text speaks not of God abolishing evil, but of managing it by keeping it within certain constraints. Such promises are far from meaningless, but the picture is decidedly non-utopian.

Third, Gen. 8:20–9:17 describes human responsibilities in this world. These responsibilities are remarkably few and basic. First, God twice commissions the human race to be fruitful, multiply, and fill the earth (9:1, 7); second, he gives them plants and animals to eat but forbids the eating of flesh with its lifeblood still in it (9:3–4); finally, God appoints human beings to administer retributive justice against their fellow human beings who violently harm other human beings: "Whoever sheds the blood of man, by man shall his blood be shed, for God made man in his own image" (9:6). That is it. The requirements are few, but they are basic and foundational. If the human race is to survive (which is the main point of this covenant), then at a minimum it must procreate, eat, and constrain violence. Of course, some other human activities are highly conducive—perhaps even necessary—to the effective accomplishment of these three tasks. Being fruitful and multiplying suggests the need for family institutions; eating plants and animals requires rules about property and economic activity; and inflicting equitable punishment upon those who harm others prompts establishment of formal legal systems. And once families, economic structures, and legal systems are put in place, a great many possibilities for productive activity beyond the three minimal requirements open up for the human race. Thus, while this covenant with Noah does not constrict the arena of human endeavor to just a few things, it does establish a basic foundation, without which the development of latent human potentialities and complex civil societies are impossible.

Each of these three characteristics of the Noahic covenant in Gen. 8:20–9:17 has direct bearing on the issue of natural law. First, with respect to universality, theories of natural law traditionally entail some conception of a stable and objectively meaningful natural order, and this text provides an etiology of such an order. Furthermore, natural law theories affirm that there is a moral order in this world known to *all* human beings. This text speaks in such a universal vein. Neither Christian nor Jewish readers can find any special privileges for themselves in this covenant, but no human being can opt out of this covenant arrangement either. Like natural law itself, the covenant with Noah is a great equalizer of the human race. All alike, as a great human family, stand blessed and accountable in this covenant. Second, with respect to the promise of preservation, classical natural law theory is about *nature*, that is, the natural order of this present world (and not about the future new creation that Christians ultimately expect). Classical natural law theory is also about *law*, not about the *gospel* (to use the terminology of the Reformation): natural law communicates moral obligation but does not deliver good news of divine salvation. Third, the substantive yet minimal requirements of the Noahic covenant pertain to the regulation of human conduct (traditionally the chief concern of natural *law*), but describe these regulations as intrinsic to, and constitutive of, the nature of human beings who act in the real world (the whole point of calling this law *natural*). Human beings have natural capacities for procreation and eating, they need to procreate and eat, and they generally desire to procreate and eat. Furthermore, the biblical text grounds the requirement of administering justice in the fact that humans bear God's image: "whoever sheds the blood of man, by man shall his blood be shed, *for God made man in his own image*" (9:6). Calling human beings the image of God is about as close as Scripture gets to defining human nature. Other animals have no wherewithal or authority to administer proportionate retributive justice for affronts to their dignity, but human beings do. We would be something less than human if we did not find ways to enforce at least the rudiments of justice in our communities.[24]

To summarize my basic conclusion about natural law and the Noahic covenant: Gen. 8:20–9:17 provides a theological explanation for the reality of a natural law. This text describes human life within the present world as orderly, meaningful, and purposeful because God has bound the whole creation to himself in a covenant that aims to guarantee this order, meaning, and purpose.[25]

---

[24] I believe the appeal to the image of God in Gen. 9:6 explains why God delegates the enforcement of justice to human beings, rather than explaining why murder is such a serious crime. For arguments in favor of this interpretation, see e.g. Steven D. Mason, "Another Flood? Genesis 9 and Isaiah's Broken Eternal Covenant," *Journal for the Study of the Old Testament* 32:2 (2007), 177–197: 192 f; and W. Randall Garr, *In His Own Image and Likeness: Humanity, Divinity, and Monotheism* (Leiden: Brill, 2003), 163.

[25] Judaism has long evaluated the moral obligation of Gentiles through the concept of the Noahide laws, and some Jewish thinkers have developed this tradition in a natural law direction. See especially the work of David Novak in *The Image of the Non-Jew in Judaism: An Historical and Constructive Study of the Noahide Laws* (New York: Edwin Mellen, 1983); and *Natural Law in Judaism* (Cambridge: Cambridge University Press, 1998).

Liberalism in Light of the Covenant with Noah

With this I return to the question of liberalism. I suggest that the Noahic covenant offers good reasons to support not only a conception of natural law but also liberalism of a certain kind. I offer several interrelated considerations in support of this claim, and thereby specify what kind of liberalism I have in mind.

First, the Noahic covenant suggests that seeking and maintaining a peaceful *pluralist* social order is a proper goal for human beings. By 'pluralist' I mean a social order consisting of all sorts of people, not one limited to those meeting certain ethnic, religious, or other special qualifications. In the Noahic covenant the only qualification for participating in human society seems to be refraining from violence against fellow human beings.[26] To put it in natural law terms, we all share a basic human dignity and equality, despite many real and important differences among us, and we are obligated to seek a harmonious and collaborative life together as far as possible. This is also a widely recognized goal of liberalism.

Second, the Noahic covenant, while offering a strong view of individual human worth, also recognizes the inherent and inevitable social dimension of individuals' lives. The inclusion of the entire human family in this covenant and its protection of all shed human blood testify to the dignity of each individual. Yet there is also no pretense here to an abstract individualism, for Gen. 9:1–7 presumes that these dignified individuals live in communities. It takes more than an individual to procreate (9:1, 7) and to rectify injustices (9:6), to state the obvious. Here again we find correspondence with liberalism, at least of certain sorts. Some liberal theories do tend toward an unqualified individualism or acknowledge equal dignity only for some individuals,[27] but more attractive renditions not only affirm the worth and privileges of each individual but also recognize that individuals can only achieve worthwhile goals and find genuine meaning to life in a range of communities. Thus a healthy liberalism

---

26   See Gen. 9:6. In this way of looking at things, a person does not have to love pluralism of every sort as an end in itself. One can view pluralism simply as a social fact that must be reckoned with: like it or not, individuals and groups are often very different from each other. Confronted with this fact, people might try to eliminate pluralism by expunging those who are different from the human community, or they can try to accommodate it by seeking peaceful means of co-existence (which does not rule out peaceful attempts at persuading others of one's own views). My account of natural law commends the latter.

27   E.g., Ackerman's theory in *Social Justice in the Liberal State* acknowledges rights only for those able to engage in political dialogue/conversation, hence excluding, for instance, "the idiot human," the unborn, and infants; see 79 f, 127 ff.

honors individual dignity by acknowledging important social roles for family and civil government and by allowing and encouraging people to form voluntary associations in order to achieve a host of objectives that human capabilities make possible but which are impossible to achieve in isolation.

A third consideration with respect to liberalism concerns the minimalist ethic presented in the Noahic covenant. According to my Noahic natural law proposal, there exists a minimal core of universal human obligation, aimed at the survival and extension of the human race in this world. This does not mean there are no other worthy human pursuits, or even that a more philosophically or theologically detailed natural law theory would fail to disclose them—far from it. But it does suggest that this minimal core of universal human obligation is genuinely *foundational*. There is much more to human life than this, but there cannot be less than this either, and the rest of the social edifice is built upon it. To the extent the foundation weakens, the whole structure becomes precarious. My natural law proposal encourages the active pursuit of a range of human goods and achievements, through the efforts of individuals and associations, but never in such a way that excludes other human beings from procreating, eating, and receiving justice when wronged. These matters too correspond to common liberal themes: the encouragement of human development and progress alongside refusal to exclude disfavored groups from participating in this project, whether through theocracy, nationalism, slavery, ethnic cleansing, or the like.

These considerations regarding the Noahic covenant and liberalism may raise specific questions about the nature of the state. Gen. 8:20–9:17 does not speak explicitly about the state or civil magistrates, but, when interpreted against the background of the larger canon of Scripture, it does suggest a view of the state harmonious with liberalism. Demonstrating this claim would require a much longer argument than is possible here, but a few reflections on Rom. 13:1–7 indicate the direction this argument would go. Rom. 13:1–7 has traditionally been the *locus classicus* for Christians seeking biblical guidance for political life. Among the teachings of this text that have deeply shaped Christian political thought are that every person should be subject to civil magistrates, that civil magistrates have authority as office-holders instituted by God, and that magistrates are God's servants who bear the sword to carry out his wrath against evildoers. One of this text's puzzles concerns how and when God instituted political office and endowed it with such authority. Clearly Paul is not saying that God was doing so through the very writing of Rom. 13:1–7, for Paul treats political authority as something already existing, as do many other texts throughout the biblical canon. I suggest that if there is any text in Scripture that describes God *instituting* political authority, Gen. 9:6 must be it. Rom.

13:1–7 says that civil magistrates have authority from God to do good for society through bearing the sword and carrying out God's wrath against evildoers; after Gen. 9:5 states how God himself will seek a reckoning from those who shed the blood of their fellow human beings, Gen. 9:6 explains that God delegates this work to the human community: "whoever sheds the blood of man, *by man shall his blood be shed."* This sounds precisely like the authoritative task of the magistrate described in Rom.13. While I do not claim that Paul is consciously alluding to Gen. 9:6, I would suggest that Gen. 9:6 provides the theological background and explanation for Paul's assertions. To put it more boldly: Gen. 9:6 provides a grid through which subsequent biblical teaching about the state ought to be interpreted.

If this is the case, the Noahic covenant offers a conception of the state harmonious with liberalism. This would seem to be true, if for no other reason, because the Noahic covenant as a whole presents a vision of human society consistent with several of the key tenets of liberalism, as argued above. In addition, however, the Noahic covenant seems compatible with the most common liberal conception of the state, the *protectionist* view: that is, the state's chief responsibility is to protect people's basic rights against violation, in distinction from a *perfectionist* conception in which the state seeks to promote individuals' and communities' virtue.[28] Gen. 9:6 speaks of the state's divinely instituted sword-bearing authority *only* in terms of punishing one who has wronged a fellow human being. Wolterstorff makes a good case, I believe, that Rom. 13:1–7 also presents a generally protectionist, rather than perfectionist, view of the state, which is not surprising in light of the organic connection between Gen. 9:6 and Rom. 13 suggested above.[29] In fact, while these two texts and many others present the state in (liberal-friendly) protectionist terms, no text of Scripture calls for the state, through its magistrates, to seek perfectionist goals.[30] I leave open the possibility that there exists a valid argument that the state ought to pursue some perfectionist task or another, since Gen. 9:6, Rom. 13:1–7, and other protectionist-sounding texts do not assert that the state may never undertake responsibilities other than those they explicitly mention. For

---

[28] Some liberals, however, do promote a version of perfectionism; see e.g. Joseph Raz, *The Morality of Freedom* (Oxford: Clarendon, 1986).

[29] Wolterstorff, *The Mighty and the Almighty*, ch. 8. I believe Wolterstorff's case could be strengthened by recognizing how Gen. 9:6 serves as part of the text's background.

[30] Of course I cannot prove here that there is no such text. I simply state here that I cannot think of one! I also note that I do not take texts speaking about civil authority under the Mosaic law as direct evidence of what "the state" should do, though such texts may provide indirect evidence.

purposes of this essay, however, the Noahic covenant at least provides a *prima facie* case for a liberal protectionist state.

To this point I have outlined an account of natural law from the Noahic covenant and argued that it is compatible with, and even favorable towards, important liberal themes. But readers will have noticed that both my natural law proposal and my conception of liberalism are modified versions of what one might consider ideologically pure forms of each. The natural law proposal, though organically related to Thomistic versions of natural law mentioned above, is significantly more modest, with a less ambitious account of the human good and the character of the good society, and with a more sober view of the prospects for human achievement in this present world.[31] With respect to liberalism, I prefer to think of my conception as a *penultimate* liberalism. I have not embraced liberalism as a worldview or a grand moral theory,[32] but focus upon some of its central themes—a pluralist social order, the dignity of all individuals, pursuit of cultural progress without excluding any peaceful person from the project, and the protectionist state—as consistent with my broader (and theologically-shaped) understanding of reality. Even if not ideologically pure, my proposal does suggest a way to bring the natural law and liberal traditions into a plausible harmony, and in a way that utilizes features of each that many people today still value: especially liberalism's defense of a peaceful pluralist social order and natural law theory's defense of the moral (and not simply pragmatic) reasons for the existence of necessary constraints and obligations in our dealings with one another.

A Noahic Natural Law Liberalism

In this final section I elaborate briefly on three important matters that may provoke questions or objections to my arguments above. I clarify the nature of the liberalism I defend, clarify the account of natural law I propose, and respond to common claims about liberalism's promotion of 'public reason' and 'secular' argumentation. In each case I believe grounding natural law and

---

31   For a detailed comparison of my theory with Thomistic theories, see VanDrunen, *Divine Covenants and Moral Order*, 22–36.

32   In other words, while I applaud liberalism's desire to unite people of various ultimate convictions in a single civil society, I do not thereby imply that there are no objective ultimate truths that all people can know and ought to acknowledge. My defense of natural law reflects my belief that there are indeed such objective ultimate truths. I address this issue again below.

liberalism in the Noahic covenant helps to stave off legitimate criticisms of both these traditions.

First, I return to my comment near the end of the previous section that I seek to defend a *penultimate* liberalism, not a comprehensive liberalism or liberalism as a worldview. I do indeed have, in Rawls's terms, a 'comprehensive view,' specifically a biblical and confessional Reformed theology (which includes convictions about the Noahic covenant described above). I find it attractive and even preferable to organize society as a liberal polity, understood in light of this theologically-shaped comprehensive view. The defense of liberalism offered above rests intimately upon a biblical Reformed theological foundation, and therefore my comprehensive view itself cannot be described as liberal.

Many prominent contemporary liberals may give the impression that they adopt a similar position with respect to the relation between liberal theory and comprehensive views. Rawls, for example, promotes a "political" liberalism that he explicitly differentiates from a "comprehensive" liberalism.[33] Political liberalism, for Rawls, represents an overlapping consensus among people of various comprehensive views, and it does not address controversial moral questions on which these comprehensive views divide. He envisions people defending political liberalism differently, from within their own incompatible comprehensive views. Nevertheless, Rawls believes that political liberalism's conception of justice, "justice as fairness," is itself independent of any of these comprehensive views, and hence "freestanding." And though Rawls thinks that a multitude of comprehensive views is the inevitable result of the use of human reason within free institutions, he deems only some of these to be "reasonable"—precisely those that embrace the liberal project.[34] Thus Rawls inevitably constructs a liberal theory that is decidedly not "impartial" among competing comprehensive views: no view of the perennially debated topic of justice could be freestanding and independent of a comprehensive view, and no judgment about the reasonability of a comprehensive view could plausibly proceed apart from the criteria some other comprehensive view provides.

When I claim to defend only a *penultimate* liberalism, therefore, I do so acknowledging that there is no single, thick Liberal Theory that all people can adopt. There are only multiple liberal theories, which depend upon the philosophical and theological commitments of particular comprehensive views. People who embrace a liberal theory may be able to offer other people attractive reasons to support liberal policies, but they will not be able to offer their

---

33   E.g., see Rawls, *Political Liberalism*, xxvii.
34   See Rawls, *Political Liberalism*, xix, xxvii f, 9 f, 39, 49 f, 60.

own particular liberal theory as one that should be equally acceptable to people of fundamentally different ultimate convictions.

Second, and along similar lines, I wish to clarify the understanding of natural law that I promote. Many people who hear an appeal to natural law assume that it refers to a universally common way of moral reasoning that can appeal and be compelling to all people of good will. That is an impossible ideal and not what I have in mind. As there can be no single liberal *theory* that all people of different comprehensive views could embrace, so there can be no natural law *theory* that could serve as a common ethic neutral among competing comprehensive views. Any thick theory of natural law must rest on certain convictions about human nature, the powers of human intellect and will, the order of the universe, and humanity's standing before God. There are natural law theories that correspond with various comprehensive views, but no single natural law theory that compels the allegiance of all.

Nevertheless, a theory of natural law can be extraordinarily useful for understanding and explaining life in this world. I mention two useful functions of the Noahic natural law proposal discussed above. For one thing, it has explanatory value: it provides theological rationale for why there often is considerable agreement about basic moral and social issues among people with different comprehensive views. Even where theoretical agreement is impossible, practical agreement is often possible. The reality of a natural moral order that presses itself upon the conscience and experience of all provides considerable help in explaining this remarkable phenomenon. Another useful function of my Noahic natural law proposal is as a corollary to a Noahic liberalism. Liberalisms that emphasize the quest to unite those divided by incompatible comprehensive views in a single political society often come to deny that there is any universal moral truth at all.[35] A Noahic liberalism, however, by virtue of its linkage to a Noahic account of natural law, with its conception of a minimalist ethic, is able to affirm that though there is no possibility of uniting political society around the highest goods, there are true (if limited) goods that all societies must and often do pursue. Liberalism does not have to mean forsaking the pursuit of moral good in political society altogether.

Third and finally, the Noahic natural law liberalism I propose here can provide clarity to the often frustrating discussions about notions of public or secular reason proposed by many liberal theorists. The basic problem these theorists try to address is an understandable one: if a liberal society is constituted by people of many different comprehensive views, how is mutually

---

[35] Well exemplified, e.g., in Richard Rorty, "Postmodernist Bourgeois Liberalism," *The Journal of Philosophy* 80 (October 1983), 583–589.

intelligible discourse to take place in political life? Rawls developed his theory of "public reason" to describe proper political advocacy concerning constitutional essentials and questions of basic justice in the public forum. While he envisioned citizens affirming the ideal of public reason "from within their own reasonable doctrines [i.e., comprehensive views]," public reason is to appeal "only to presently accepted general beliefs and forms of reasoning found in common sense, and the methods and conclusions of science when these are not controversial," such that discussions are "based on values that the others can reasonably be expected to endorse."[36] To mention one other example, Robert Audi has labored to elucidate the difference between "secular" and "religious" argumentation, the former of which should generally be the chief basis for political decision-making. Like many other liberal theorists, Audi believes protecting individuals' autonomy is paramount, and therefore he thinks coercing people is justified only when based on argumentation that the coerced people themselves would find persuasive, provided they had sufficient information and were thinking rationally—a requirement met by secular but not religious reasoning.[37] A problem arises similar to the ones addressed earlier in this section: so-called 'public' and 'secular' reason, no matter how assiduously it attempts to exclude assumptions dependent upon comprehensive views or religious doctrines, inevitably ends up importing such assumptions into its argumentation.[38] Many religious people, even those sympathetic to a liberal polity, are unable to meet Rawls's and Audi's requirements for political reason without giving up central convictions of their faith.[39]

The natural law liberalism defended here, in affirming that a liberal polity is authorized by God as part of his preservation of the natural order through the Noahic covenant, has to agree with Wolterstorff that the public reason idea is ultimately a failure.[40] But the question about how to make appropriate arguments in political debates within a liberal polity is still very important. Surely

---

36   Rawls, *Political Liberalism*, 213 ff, 218, 224, 226.
37   E.g., see Robert Audi, "The Place of Religious Argument in a Free and Democratic Society," *San Diego Law Review* 30 (1993), 677–702.
38   I cannot defend this claim in detail here, but for such a defense see Wolterstorff, *Understanding Liberal Democracy*, ch. 1. For other critical engagement of Rawls on public reason, see also Michael J. Perry, *Religion in Politics: Constitutional and Moral Perspectives* (New York: Oxford University Press, 1997), 54–59; and Kent Greenawalt, *Private Consciences and Public Reasons* (New York: Oxford University Press, 1995), ch. 10.
39   E.g., given Audi's "epistemic criterion" for what constitutes a "religious" argument in "The Place of Religious Argument," 680 f, I could never make a non-religious argument since I believe all knowledge is derived from revelation of some sort.
40   Wolterstorff, *Understanding Liberal Democracy*, 110.

Christian proponents of a Noahic natural law liberalism would not wish to engage in discourse in the liberal public forum in exactly the same way they engage in ecclesiastical debate. Rather than differentiating between secular and religious, or some other distinction bound to flounder, however, a Noahic natural law liberalism can distinguish between natural revelation and special revelation, to use classic Reformed categories. Christians ought to understand that all true knowledge, and hence any valid argument, must derive from natural and/or special revelation. And if God gives natural revelation to all people, as human beings created by him, while he has delivered special revelation, generally speaking, to Israel and the church, as people in redeemed covenant relationship with him,[41] then natural revelation would seem to be the more appropriate basis for political discourse in a liberal polity grounded in the universal Noahic covenant. As discussed above, arguments from natural law (as an aspect of natural revelation) are never secular, impartial, or neutral in the sense intended by many liberal theorists. But they are *appropriate* for political society, insofar as God does in fact hold all people accountable to himself through natural revelation, via the Noahic covenant.

Conclusion

The natural law and liberal traditions are central aspects of the heritage of Western civilization. Are these traditions also its future hope? For the Christian, there is no ultimate hope for anyone outside the coming kingdom of God, which natural law does not reveal and liberalism does not manifest. But I have argued, through consideration of the Noahic covenant, that Christian theology offers grounds for developing a natural law theory and promoting a liberal polity, in recognition of God's purposes in his ongoing preservation of this present age. Though Christians must dissociate natural law and liberalism from any utopian fantasies and futile aspirations for religious neutrality, they deserve an important place for Christians seeking a theologically sound perspective on the current predicaments of Western civilization.

---

[41] For a detailed Reformed exposition of the doctrines of natural and special revelation, see Herman Bavinck, *Reformed Dogmatics*, Vol. 1, *Prolegomena*, ed. John Bolt, trans. John Vriend (Grand Rapids: Baker Academic, 2003), 283 ff.

Bibliography

Ackerman, Bruce A., *Social Justice in the Liberal State* (New Haven: Yale University Press, 1980).

Audi, Robert, "The Place of Religious Argument in a Free and Democratic Society," *San Diego Law Review* 30 (1993), 677–702.

Baker, Robert C. & Roland Cap Ehlke (eds.), *Natural Law: A Lutheran Reappraisal* (St. Louis: Concordia, 2011).

Bavinck, Herman, *Reformed Dogmatics*, Vol. 1, *Prolegomena*, ed. John Bolt, trans. John Vriend (Grand Rapids: Baker Academic, 2003).

Bickel, Alexander M., *The Morality of Consent* (New Haven: Yale University Press, 1975).

Bratt, James, *Abraham Kuyper: Modern Calvinist, Christian Democrat* (Grand Rapids: Eerdmans, 2013).

Charles, J. Daryl, *Retrieving the Natural Law: A Return to Moral First Things* (Grand Rapids: Eerdmans, 2008).

Covington, Jesse; Bryan McGraw & Micah Watson (eds.), *Natural Law and Evangelical Political Thought* (Lanham: Lexington, 2012).

Cunningham, Lawrence S. (ed.), *Intractable Disputes About the Natural Law: Alasdair MacIntyre and Critics* (Notre Dame: University of Notre Dame Press, 2009).

Deneen, Patrick J., "Unsustainable Liberalism," *First Things* (August/September 2012), 25–31.

Garr, W. Randall, *In His Own Image and Likeness: Humanity, Divinity, and Monotheism* (Leiden: Brill, 2003).

George, Robert P., *Making Men Moral: Civil Liberties and Public Morality* (Oxford: Clarendon, 1993).

Grabill, Stephen J., *Rediscovering the Natural Law in Reformed Theological Ethics* (Grand Rapids: Eerdmans, 2006).

Greenawalt, Kent, *Private Consciences and Public Reasons* (New York: Oxford University Press, 1995).

Hayek, Friedrich A., *The Constitution of Liberty* (Chicago: University of Chicago Press, 1960).

———, *The Fortunes of Liberalism: Essays on Austrian Economics and the Ideal of Freedom*, ed. Peter G. Klein (Chicago: University of Chicago Press, 1992).

Johnson, Thomas K., *Natural Law Ethics: An Evangelical Proposal* (Bonn: Verlag für Kultur und Wissenschaft, 2005).

MacIntyre, Alasdair, *Whose Justice? Which Rationality?* (Notre Dame: University of Notre Dame Press, 1988), 210.

Mahoney, Daniel J. "The Art of Liberty," *First Things* (August/September 2012), 33–35.

Mason, Steven D., "Another Flood? Genesis 9 and Isaiah's Broken Eternal Covenant," *Journal for the Study of the Old Testament* 32:2 (2007), 177–197.

Mayes, A.D.H. & R.B. Salters (eds.), *Covenant as Context: Essays in Honour of E.W. Nicholson* (Oxford: Oxford University Press, 2003).

McConnell, Michael W., "Old Liberalism, New Liberalism, and People of Faith," in Michael W. McConnell, Robert F. Cochran, Jr. & Angela C. Carmella (eds.), *Christian Perspectives on Legal Thought* (New Haven: Yale University Press, 2001), 5–24.

Novak, David, *Natural Law in Judaism* (Cambridge: Cambridge University Press, 1998).

———, *The Image of the Non-Jew in Judaism: An Historical and Constructive Study of the Noahide Laws* (New York: Edwin Mellen, 1983).

Perry, Michael J., *Religion in Politics: Constitutional and Moral Perspectives* (New York: Oxford University Press, 1997).

Rawls, John, *Political Liberalism* (New York: Columbia University Press, 1993).

Raz, Joseph, *The Morality of Freedom* (Oxford: Clarendon, 1986).

Rorty, Richard, "Postmodernist Bourgeois Liberalism," *The Journal of Philosophy* 80 (October 1983), 583–589.

VanDrunen, David, *Divine Covenants and Moral Order: A Biblical Theology of Natural Law* (Grand Rapids: Eerdmans, 2014).

———, *Natural Law and the Two Kingdoms: A Study in the Development of Reformed Social Thought* (Grand Rapids: Eerdmans, 2010).

Vos, Geerhardus, "The Doctrine of the Covenant in Reformed Theology," in Richard B. Graffin Jr. (ed.), *Redemptive History and Biblical Interpretation: The Shorter Writings of Geerhardus Vos* (Phillipsburg: Presbyterian and Reformed, 1980), 234–267.

Wolfe, Christopher, *Natural Law Liberalism* (Cambridge: Cambridge University Press, 2006).

Wolterstorff, Nicholas, *Justice: Rights and Wrongs* (Princeton: Princeton University Press, 2008).

———, *The Mighty and the Almighty: An Essay in Political Theology* (Cambridge: Cambridge University Press, 2012).

———, *Understanding Liberal Democracy: Essays in Political Philosophy*, ed. Terrence Cuneo (Oxford: Oxford University Press, 2012).

The Empire and the Desert
Eastern Orthodox Theologians about Church and Civilization

Alfons Brüning

It does not take much effort to trace the contemporary application of the term 'civilization' in writings or statements of Eastern Orthodox churchmen and theologians. This is especially true for the Russian Orthodox Church. As the present patriarch of Moscow, Kirill frequently points out, Russia forms a particular civilization, distinct from others (and especially from 'the West'), based as it is on a specific set of social relations, political structures and moral customs with roots in Russian Orthodox tradition.[1] With his statements the patriarch gives voice not only to a widespread conviction but also to a related program of a sociopolitical character. Scientific institutions, faculties, and university departments are devoted to the discipline of 'culturology' (*kul'turologiia*), which are tasked with fostering the restoration of the traditional values of the Russian people, and therefore the re-birth of its indigenous culture. The focus of this—incidentally, rather new—academic discipline is not on the issue of culture or civilization in generalizing terms (although there are similarities in applied methods to Western 'cultural studies'), but first of all on the exploration of the 'Russian civilization' and its peculiarities, including their moral content, and methods of disseminating these values in today's Russia—and beyond.[2] Likewise, a foundation under the name 'The Russian World' (*Russkii mir*), founded in 2007 on the initiative of the Russian president Putin, is active in various cities in Russia's neighbor states (e.g., Ukraine, Moldova, Poland or the Baltic states), implementing projects cultivating and spreading Russian language, customs and culture.[3] To be sure, neither 'culturology' as an academic

---

1 See, as a most recent example, Kirill's opening speech, delivered on October 31, 2013, before the latest assembly of the All Russian National Council (*Vsemirnyi Russkii Narodnyi Sobor*—a platform established by the Moscow patriarchate and outwardly similar to, for example, the German *Kirchentag*, whereas the predominant political orientation of these assemblies is much more conservative and traditionalist), published on http://www.pravoslavie.ru/news/65312.htm.

2 Jutta Scherrer, *Kulturologie: Russland auf der Suche nach einer zivilisatorischen Identität*, Essener Kulturwissenschaftliche Vorträge, vol. 13 (Göttingen: Wallstein Verlag, 2003); Marlène Laruelle, "La discipline de la culturologie: un nouveau prêt-à-penser pour la Russie?" *Diogène* 204:4 (2003), 25–45.

3 http://www.russkiymir.ru/russkiymir/ru.

discipline nor the *Russkii mir* foundation are directly linked with the church or the Moscow patriarchate. But the ideological overlapping is difficult to ignore, when one hears the patriarch reflecting on ways how to strengthen and to develop 'The Russian World,'[4] or takes into account such facts as for example the recent establishment of a subject called 'Fundamentals of Orthodox Culture' (*osnovy pravoslavnoi kul'tury*) at public schools in Russia, as a result of long-standing lobbying by the Moscow patriarchate. In addition, the regions and cities where the *Russkii mir* foundation regularly pursues its activities are not only located on the territory of the former Soviet Union, but likewise in those countries which the Russian church continues to claim as part of its 'canonical territory.' In sum, the 'Russian civilization,' the 'Russian World' and Russian Orthodoxy's 'canonical territory' are concepts interconnected in terms of their content, meaning and territorial extension.[5]

Theological Difficulties of an 'Orthodox Civilization'

Concerning the perspective of the Orthodox church, the purely—at first sight—ecclesiological concept of a 'canonical territory' does have some merit, as critics have admitted, but at the same time it has been criticized as hardly applicable to a situation where religious pluralism exists, including 21st century Russia itself.[6] The claimed coincidence of the 'canonical territory' with that of a 'Russian civilization' seems even more problematic. Against the background just outlined, the use of terms like 'culture' or 'civilization'—with its apparent parallels to non-ecclesiological ways of thinking—opens the way to a perspective beyond proper theology. First, the context betrays rather geopolitical overtones next to the ecclesiological considerations that could be regarded as the actual domain of a Christian church. Secondly, the terms 'Russian civilization' or 'the Russian World' ideally operate if we understand 'civilization' in a plural sense: there are more than one 'civilization,' and the Orthodox therefore implicitly subscribe to a view which would divide the globe into several spheres of influence of a small number of civilizations, claiming one of

---

4 Kirill, Patriarch of Moscow, "Russkii Mir: puti ukrepleniia i razvitiia" (The Russian World: Ways how to Strengthen and to Develop it), *Tserkov i Vremia* (*Church and Time*) 49:4 (2009), https://mospat.ru/church-and-time/4.
5 For further evidence and a systematization see Katja Richters, *The Post-Soviet Russian Orthodox Church: Politics, Culture and Greater Russia* (London: Routledge, 2013).
6 Johannes Oeldemann, "The Concept of Canonical Territory in the Russian Orthodox Church," in Thomas Bremer (ed.), *Religion and the Conceptual Boundaries in Central and Eastern Europe: Encounters of Faith* (London: Palgrave MacMillan, 2008), 229–236.

them as their own. Again, the political implications are obvious. Already in theory, this kind of approach generates the need to clarify where exactly the borders between them run (a question that also occurs in connection with 'canonical territory'), and further, how these spheres of influence should relate to one another. Orthodox theorists applying the civilizational model have inherited these problems, with all their implications concerning jurisdiction and inter-confessional relations, from the model's inventors. They are borrowed from such global theorists of historiosophy as Oswald Spengler, or Arnold Toynbee, or from Toynbee's more recent revitalization in Samuel Huntington's *The Clash of Civilizations*.[7] The latter work in particular continues to enjoy some popularity in Orthodox circles, whereas its globalizing perspective and the concepts of 'civilization' applied therein have long become obsolete in the Western academic world. One reason for this might be that Huntington to a large extent grounds his concept of 'civilization' on religion as a constitutive factor, allowing the Orthodox to refer to Huntington's scheme as to that of a foreign and therefore allegedly 'objective' supporter of their own ideas. In fact the scheme seems to support ideas about a particular 'Orthodox civilization' distinct from others which have already been in existence for a long time, and are common amongst the Orthodox themselves.

There is an entire system of Orthodox anti-Western concepts, all of which more or less openly operate with some semantic relatives of 'civilization.' Suffice it here to mention briefly just the most important of these: the classical view (as one might call it) of a 'Holy Russia'[8] can be discerned through the lines of the above-mentioned geopolitical and civilizational descriptions, and stands in a row with similar ideas about distinctive Orthodox countries of the European East, almost each of them with strong emphasis not only on an Orthodox religious culture in general, but sometimes also on its national manifestations (like the 'Hellenism' of the Greek Christos Yannaras[9] or the Serbian concept of *svetosavlje*[10]). Even if the very terms 'culture' or 'civilization' are applied in quite a variety of ways and semantic content throughout all these

---

7   Samuel Huntington, *The Clash of Civilizations and the Remaking of World Order* (London: Simon & Schuster, 1996). For leanings from such works as applied in academic 'culturology' see Scherrer, *Kulturologie*, 34–38, 83, 107 ff; Laruelle, "Culturologie," 30–33.

8   Michael Cherniavsky, "'Holy Russia': A Study in the History of an Idea," *The American Historical Review* 63:3 (1958), 617–637.

9   Christos Yannaras, *Orthodoxy and the West: Hellenic Self-Identity in the Modern Age* (Brookline: H.C. Press, 2006).

10 Klaus Buchenau, "Svetosavlje und Pravoslavlje: Nationales und Universales in der serbischen Orthodoxie" (Sventosalje and Pravoslavlje: Nationals and Universals in the Serbian Orthodoxy), in Martin Schulze Wessel (ed.), *Nationalisierung der Religion und*

concepts, their inner structure and dynamics clearly follow the general patterns once described on the theoretical level for possible applications of the 'civilization' or 'culture' concepts.[11] There is not only a claim for a principal 'otherness' inherent in all these concepts, but also a more or less open feeling of superiority, always narrowly connected with the idea of a peculiar mission that would consist in the task to give back to the world (or to Europe or to 'the West') some of its lost values, moral consciousness or spiritual orientation. Conversely, 'the other' (civilization) is viewed as being either backwards or in decline. These missions might be expressed in various terms and formulas, and the alleged superiority leads to either more offensive or defensive conclusions, which consequently make 'the other' a threat or an inferior entity that is doomed to decay, or an object of missionary endeavors. The general theoretical pattern always active behind this variety is that 'civilization' in its singular meaning is quasi automatically superior to its opposite, to 'non-civilization.' The 'civilized' is automatically superior to any other 'less civilized' or 'not civilized.' 'Civilization' is opposed to 'nature' (with such negative connotations as 'barbarian,' 'uncivilized' and the like), while the process of 'civilization' is connected with advancement and progress. This means that the initial semantics of 'civilization' in the singular sense remain active behind the scenes, which the plural application constitutes. This cannot but have consequences for how one understands an encounter between 'civilizations' in the plural.[12]

Sakralisierung der Nation im östlichen Europa (Stuttgart: Franz Steiner Verlag, 2006), 203–232.

[11] For a thorough overview of such patterns and of their numerous historical applications see Jörg Fisch, s.v. "Zivilisation, Kultur," in Otto Brunner, Werner Conze & Reinhart Koselleck (eds.), *Geschichtliche Grundbegriffe*, Vol. 7 (Stuttgart: Klett-Cotta, 1997). Fisch on occasion also addresses the basic difference between the originally French *civilization* and its connotations of "civilized behavior and lifestyle" and the German *Kultur*, the latter being rather synonymous with 'education' and 'intellectual and moral advancement' (as first pointed out by Norbert Elias, *Über den Prozess der Zivilisation* (Basel: Verlag Haus zum Falken, 1939). This difference will further preoccupy us on due place below. For the moment it needs yet to be stated that this difference has generally become of less importance, against the background of a whole variety of applications of both terms, often with interchangeable significance.

[12] See Fisch, "Zivilisation, Kultur," 679–682. Huntington himself, when explaining the shift from the use of "civilization" in the older, singular sense towards a plurality of concepts, notes the same dichotomy when he writes: "Instead there were many civilizations, each of which was civilized in its own way. Civilization in the singular, in short, "lost some of its cachet," and a civilization in the plural sense could in fact be quite uncivilized in the singular sense" (Huntington, *Clash of Civilizations*, 41).

Widespread as such concepts and perspectives might be to this day among Orthodox believers and clerics,[13] they also often provoke negative reactions from other clerics and theologians, who vividly feel their inherent threat: does the adoption of the 'civilization' concept not come down to reducing the universalism of the Christian message, and the universal 'catholic and apostolic' character of the Christian church to a narrow-minded political or cultural ideology, in the end not defending the church, but a secondary and particular historical entity? Is the spiritual not in danger to be either captured or even replaced by ideology or even pure politics? In order to avoid this threat, some Orthodox theologians feel a need to think about an appropriate use of 'civilization' and its relatives, and therefore to clarify the actual relationship between Christianity and culture, and to express this relationship in less misleading terms.

Re-definitions in the Diaspora: Georges Florovsky

It probably does not come as a surprise that some of the first attempts toward a better assessment of this relationship were initiated in Western emigration centers of Orthodoxy around the middle of the 20th century. The situation of an Orthodox diaspora, placed within milieus of religious dissent, non-belief and cultural diversity created a spectrum of various reactions, ranging from a tendency to erect walls of defense around one's own sacred tradition on the one side to a new definition of the Orthodox mission within this new environment on the other. In the latter case, however, a new theoretical balance had to be found between the universal and the particular. To put it roughly, there hardly could be seen much sense in attempts to turn German, French or American people into Russians or Greeks, but what did it mean then to win them over for the Orthodox faith?[14]

A crucial personality among the theologians who would try and meet the challenge brought up by the new circumstances was the Russian born father Georges Florovsky (1893–1979), who left Revolutionary Russia for Western Eu-

---

13   Cf. the examples collected by Vasilios N. Makrides, "Orthodox Anti-Westernism Today: A Hindrance to European Integration?" *International Journal for the Study of the Christian Church* 9:3 (2009), 209–224, and the more systematical considerations in Vasilios N. Makrides & Dirk Uffelmann, "Studying Eastern Orthodox Anti-Westernism: The Need for a Comparative Research Agenda," in Jonathan Sutton & Wil van den Bercken (eds.), *Orthodox Christianity and Contemporary Europe* (Leuven: Peeters, 2003), 87–120.

14   Cf. the chapter entitled "The Twentieth Century: Diaspora and Mission," in Kallistos Ware, *The Orthodox Church*, 4th ed. (London: Penguin Books, 1997), 172–194.

rope in 1919. After sojourns in Bulgaria and Prague, he was among the founders of St. Serge Orthodox Theological Institute in Paris, where he taught patristics from 1925 until 1949, the year he left for the United States. Establishing himself in New York City, he took the position of Dean of St. Vladimir's Orthodox Theological Seminary, which he held until 1955. While there, he established contacts with the wider academic world, met with émigré scientists from other parts of Europe, and held lectures at Columbia University. Subsequently he became a professor of divinity at Harvard University, and ended his academic years as a professor at Princeton University.[15] Florovsky is probably not counted on the scale of the most illustrious theologians of the 20th century, but his influence in preparing new paths for Orthodox theology in his time was immense. First and foremost, his name is connected with the program of the so-called 'neo-patristic synthesis' (also called 'sacred Hellenism' by him), a significant part of which was the purification of the Orthodox tradition (and the Russian in particular) from distorting influences of Western theology throughout the preceding centuries. On the other hand, Florovsky played a major part in the early phase of the Ecumenical movement, and represented much of the Orthodox' voice in the process that would eventually lead to the foundation of the World Council of Churches after World War II. This rather cursory account of some pillars of his intellectual legacy may already betray the richness and the inner tensions of this work.

Over the years Florovsky dealt with the problem of 'church and culture' or 'church and civilization' on various occasions, to the extent that an entire volume of his collected works could eventually be devoted to this issue.[16] Among the articles gathered in this volume there is especially one that expressively (as the title indicates) addresses the theme of 'Christianity and Civilization,' written in the early 1950s, and published in the opening issue of St. Vladimir's periodical in 1952.[17] In this article, Florovsky, a specialist in patristic studies and in ancient history, starts his considerations with a most suggestive historical

---

15 Andrew Blane, "A Sketch of the Life of Georges Florovsky," in Andrew Blane (ed.), *Georges Florovsky: Russian Intellectual and Orthodox Churchman* (Crestwood: St Vladimir's Seminary Press, 1993), 11–217; Peter A. Chamberas, "Georges Vasilevich Florovsky (1893–1979)," *Modern Age* 45 (2003), 49–66. For an evaluation of father Florovsky's work and contribution to Orthodox theology see Paul L. Gavrilyuk, *Georges Florovsky and the Russian Religious Renaissance* (Oxford: Oxford University Press, 2014).

16 Georges Florovsky, *Church and Culture*, Collected Works, Vol. 2 (Belmont: Nordland Publishers, 1974).

17 Georges Florovsky, "Christianity and Civilization," *St Vladimir's Seminary Quarterly* 1:1 (1952), 13–20, republished in his *Collected Works*, to which I refer. Cf. Florovsky, *Church and Culture*, 121–130.

observation about early Byzantium. He points to the remarkable phenomenon that right at the moment when the ancient world became Christian through the baptism of Emperor Constantine, and the Roman and Greek civilization began to turn, step by step, into what could be called a 'Christian civilization,' as a parallel there commenced a massive monastic movement, with increasing numbers of people leaving the world for the desert, and a wave of new monasteries founded on places remote from the 'civilized' world. The birth of a new civilization was, therefore, immediately accompanied by an inner opposition.

> The whole of the inner life of the Hellenistic men had to undergo a drastic revaluation. The process … finally resolved in the birth of a new civilization, which we may describe as Byzantine. One has to realize that there was but one Christian civilization for centuries, the same for the East and the West, and this civilization was born and made in the East. A specifically Western civilization came much later.[18]

Then he continues: "And yet, it was precisely from this Christened Empire that the flight commences, the flight into the desert. It is true that individuals used to leave cities before … Yet, a movement begins only after Constantine."[19] Florovsky offers a peculiar interpretation of the phenomenon he describes, and of the motives that might have guided so many to flee the cities and the just emerging new Christian-Hellenic cultural symbiosis. In his view, these monks were much less inspired by the simple wish to 'leave the world' behind, and to separate from any human community in order to be free for an individual encounter with the Divine. "Monastic flight in the IV-th century was first of all *a withdrawal from the Empire*."[20] It was rather an attempt to preserve the actual substance of Christianity that was at stake. What those emigrants from the world actually did was to merely take their baptismal oaths seriously, and to take to heart that the true Christian always remains a homeless pilgrim, a stranger in this world. The threat that emerged from a Christian civilization, after the times of harsh persecutions, therefore went beyond the ambiguities of a kind of cultural triumphalism or the pure temptations of power. And the monks were looking for more than simply loneliness in the desert. Florovsky at this point refers to St. John Chrysostom, who had emphatically warned against the dangers of 'prosperity': security for this church father was the greatest of all persecutions, much worse than the bloodiest persecutions from outside.

---

18   Florovsky, "Christianity and Civilization," 122.
19   Florovsky, "Christianity and Civilization," 124.
20   Florovsky, "Christianity and Civilization," 125 (emphasis in the original).

The renouncement of any settling within a civilized context with all its implications like home and family life up to public functions, political power or economic welfare would already have constituted a critical element that was hard to ignore, even more so if it occurred with such quantitative strength. However, a movement of pure self-separation from a newly emerging cultural formation in the long run would rather have lost its critical potential, and ended up just in isolation from this culture. But the monks did more than just to disappear out of the context of civilization and Empire. They constituted a kind of 'anti-civilization' that would persistently strive to counterbalance a Christianity settling in worldly contexts. Florovsky at this point expressively emphasizes that monasticism has never been anti-social. But the communities they constituted in contrast to worldly cities were aimed at realizing the city of God, and the heavenly kingdom. "The fact that monasticism evades and denies the conception of the Christian Empire does not imply that it opposes culture ... first of all, monasticism succeeded, much more than the Empire ever did, to preserve the true ideal of culture in its purity and freedom."[21] Florovsky finds the roots for this true ideal in asceticism, which truly frees creativity. "Creativity is ultimately saved from all sorts of utilitarianism only through an ascetical re-interpretation."[22] It was out of this preserved ideal that monasteries would subsequently develop into centers of learning and original 'philosophy' throughout the Christian world. Likewise, it was not by accident that during the iconoclastic period in the 8th century monks were the first and most important defenders of art, "safeguarding the freedom of religious art from the oppression of the State, from 'enlightened' oppression and utilitarian simplification."[23]

Florovsky later elaborated his idea about "the Empire and the desert" in another study that takes a slightly more thorough look on the matter, whereas his basic approach remained the same.[24] Concerning the relationship between Christianity and 'civilization,' there remains a certain ambiguity in this approach, and probably in the whole work. Florovsky does not draw a clear fault line between, as it were, the spiritual and the cultural. Religion basically finds its expression through culture, but rather no worldly 'civilization' can claim for itself that it would have fully absorbed the richness of the spiritual element.

---

21 Florovsky, "Christianity and Civilization," 126.
22 Florovsky, "Christianity and Civilization," 127.
23 Florovsky, "Christianity and Civilization," 127.
24 Georges Florovsky, "Empire and Desert: Antinomies of Christian History," *The Greek Orthodox Theological Review* 3:2 (1957), 133–159. Reprinted in Florovsky, *Collected Works*, Vol. 2, 67–100.

But the ideal of perfection the monks take as their goal is also never to be achieved in this world, whereas the actual fruits of their efforts only in part are suitable for secular contexts. Their role therefore is rather that of a contrasting factor that counterbalances worldly manifestations of religion, in various fields including worship, ethics and even art, and in case of necessity calls for reconsideration and for new formulas and images. On the other hand, this scheme is not to be seen in terms of an antithesis between two entities, between 'civilization and anti-civilization.' Rather, both factors combine, and here the 'Christian civilization' has its ground. If these two factors are present, and complement one another, it is just this combination that in the long run might well deserve the name of a true Christian civilization, and Florovsky was obviously ready to ascribe this title to a long part of the historical path of Byzantium. Sure, the Christian civilization remained a model, an ideal, and as far as perfection is never to be achieved by man alone, it still waits for its complete realization on earth. Moreover, the monasteries had only started to turn the ideal of the 'City of God' into reality, and they remained a factor separate from the average world of human beings. The liturgy and the market belonged to different realms. Yet precisely from this outside position they nourished as well as challenged and corrected secular culture in Byzantium. Byzantium, or at least what Florovsky called the 'sacred Hellenism' within it, to some extent did achieve the realization of a Christian civilization through a creative combination of 'Empire and desert.' So while Florovsky proved reluctant to give the title of a Christian civilization exclusively to any political entity or cultural formation on earth, he nonetheless felt able to ultimately identify traces of this ideal in a particular part of history. Christian universalism and cultural or political particularity are specifically combined in his perspective, but the borderline between them is vague: the universal element in Christianity does not remain purely timeless, while particularity escapes the threat of being reduced to mere ideology.[25]

This ambiguity of Florovsky's 'sacred Hellenism' reflects the author's own inner history, an intellectual movement there and back again between Christian universalism and historical manifestations in time. When Florovsky had left his homeland in 1919, he left behind a newly established Soviet system in which he saw no perspective for either his belief or his philosophy; subsequently, he resided first in Sofia, and then in Prague in the early 1920s. Thanks to a supporting program of Czech president Tomas Masaryk, Prague by then had attracted quite a number of Russian emigrants and intellectuals, and in this environment the events of the time were vividly debated. One widespread

---

25 See also, for a more thorough description of the matter, Gavrilyuk, *Religious Renaissance*, 201–219.

theory that pretended to be able to explain the course of recent events, and to offer a perspective on Russia's role in history, was the 'Eurasian idea,' developed and propagated by such personalities as the linguist Nicholas Trubec'koy, or the historian George Vernadsky. In their theory, the 'Eurasians' tried to combine the Orthodox element in Russian culture with the influence from the Asian East, the Empire of Chingiz Khan and the Tatar political system with a likewise 'Christian' and anti-Western perspective, including the formulation of a missionary element for, as they perceived it, a Europe in decline. The response of these intellectuals to the challenges of World War I and the Russian Revolution was to interpret the historical situation as a crisis that paved the way for a new 'Eurasian' civilization to take over the position of a West in decay. The 'Eurasians' openly operated with pluralistic models of competing civilizations developed one generation before. Such global concepts about the course of history and the change of civilizations at use in those times were, first of all, that of the Russian Nikolai Danilevsky or the by then very popular, and very pessimistic work of the German Oswald Spengler.[26]

Florovsky was involved in these debates only for a short time. He eventually left the Eurasian circles and theory behind, with expressed dismay of the intolerant spirit and the political ambitions that he had found there: "... you want to be involved in political intrigue, and that is not for me."[27] Instead, Florovsky formulated a different program for himself. He argued that the historical problem raised and illustrated by the World War and the Russian Revolution could not be solved by the political and Slavophil concerns of the Eurasians.

> Seeing the impasse of all ideologies and philosophies of culture, Florovsky argued not for another alternative rational ideology, but for the revitalization of culture, for a spiritual reconstruction, without the deviations

---

26 Nikolai Danilevsky, in his work *Rossiia i Evropa: Vzgliad na kul'turnye I politicheskie otnosheniia slavianskogo mira k germano-romanskomu* (*Russia and Europe: A Perspective on the Political and Cultural Relations of the Slavic World to the German and Roman*), first published in 1869 (recently Moscow: Kniga, 2003) apparently was the first among modern theorists to apply a multiplied scheme of 'civilizations' which subsequently take over from one another their dominating role in history. His work was of considerable influence, among others, on Oswald Spengler, *Der Untergang des Abendlandes* (Vol. 1 Vienna: Braumüller, 1918, Vol. 2 Munich: C.H. Beck, 1922). Both schemes, next to some prophetic statements of Dostoevsky concerning Russia's future role in history, found their way into the ideas of the 'Eurasians.' Cf. Stefan Wiederkehr, *Die Eurasische Bewegung: Wissenschaft und Politik in der Russischen Emigration der Zwischenkriegszeit und im postsowjetischen Russland* (Cologne et.al.: Böhlau, 2007).

27 Blane, "Sketch," 39.

and perversions of previous generations. Florovsky recoiled from any political or even social program to fight revolution with its own violence or ideological utopianism.[28]

However, his further intellectual path also betrayed the considerable influence of his early engagement with the Eurasians and their views on civilization, as would become clear some years later on the pages of his first major work about *The Ways of Russian Orthodoxy*, published in Paris in 1937.[29] In this polarizing book, either celebrated or condemned by fellow theologians, Florovsky emphatically voted for a purification of Russian theological and spiritual tradition from foreign influences, as they had come over centuries from the West through either Catholic scholasticism or Protestant rationalism. Florovsky treats Kievan theology of the 17th, the Petrine reforms of the 18th, and academic theology in Russia of the 19th centuries with equal erudition, and argues that what all these influences (being in their origin and character strange to the Russian tradition) had produced was what he called a 'pseudomorphosis' of the Russian tradition. Yet this was still Spengler speaking behind the scenes, from whom Florovsky had taken both the term and the image: just like the former, Florovsky described the changes which had occurred through Western influences in Russia as an inappropriate transformation of an Orthodox substance into Western shapes, in a way comparable to how crystallographers would describe the emergence of otherwise unusual forms of a mineral due to huge external pressure.[30] His conclusion was simple: "Western influences on Russian theology must be overcome."[31] In place of these rather falsifying and distorting influences Florovsky recommended a return to the spiritual tradition of ancient Russia. This, again, in his view is a tradition much more of the monasteries than of the tsars, and secondly, it is a trace which ultimately led back to the writings of the Church fathers in Late Antiquity. Here Florovsky supposed the roots and the original substance of Christian tradition, before it got distorted in a variety of worldly cultural contexts, and before the painful division of Christianity into different branches in East and West had taken place. His program 'back to the fathers' therefore had as much of a certain

---

28 Chamberas, "Florovsky," 52.
29 Georgii Florovskii, *Puti russkago bogosloviia* (Paris: YMCA press, 1937); an English translation entitled *The Ways of Russian Theology* appeared as Vol. 5 (Belmont: Nordland Publ., 1979) and Vol. 6 (Vaduz: Büchervertriebsanstalt, 1987) of his *Collected Works*.
30 Florovskii, *Puti*, 49. Cf. Spengler, *Untergang des Abendlandes*, Vol. 2, 225 ff.
31 Taken from his programmatic summary: Georgii Florovskii, "Westliche Einflüsse in der russischen Theologie," *Kyrios* 2 (1937), 1–22: 14 (my translation, AB).

'fundamentalism,' a spirit of radical purification and a 'back to the true roots' impetus on the one hand, as of ecumenical encounter and reconciliation on the other. His argument went beyond historic-philosophical, and therefore secular theories about 'civilization,' but eventually did not evade the use of 'civilization' completely. The latter managed to enter his scheme again through the idea of a 'sacred Hellenism.' In this major work, therefore, the relationship between a timeless universalism and a secular plurality of 'civilizations' remained tense, and at the end unclear.

Florovsky's 'Hellenic' Followers

This also made Florovsky's legacy an ambiguous one. Among his many disciples who were inspired by his 'neo-patristic synthesis' there was to be found quite a variety of rather diverging conclusions and further elaborations of the program of 'back to the fathers' and of 'sacred Hellenism.'[32] The scale is marked by the same tension between religious universalism and 'civilizational' particularity. As for the latter, Greeks like John Romanides or Christos Yannaras strengthened the emphasis of the 'Hellenic' element in Florovsky's 'sacred Hellenism' and accordingly tried to keep the spiritual heritage of the Greek Church fathers and of Byzantium pure from illegitimate Western infiltrations. For them, the ultimate split between East and West had occurred in the late Middle Ages, when Byzantine hesychast theology appeared in opposition to Western scholasticism: hesychasm (derived from the Greek *hesycheia*, inner tranquility) was a label given to a set of models and practices of meditation and prayer, applied by monks in the East in order to come to a personal encounter with the Divine. A theological dispute ensued around these practices, as the question of whether to look for a direct relation to the Divine mystery is actually possible and would not end in obscure mysticism arose in the early 14th century. The Greek bishop Gregory of Palamas became the main theological defender of the hesychast tradition. After sharp controversies over several decades, the Eastern church at a council in 1356 decided the dispute in favor of this tradition, finally rejecting the objections raised from Italian monks (like Barlaam of Calabria), who were shaped by scholastic theology.

The debates surrounding hesychasm were of crucial significance already for Florovsky himself, who took much effort to defend the Orthodoxy of Palamas

---

32   Gavrilyuk, *Religious Renaissance*, 232–258.

and 'Palamism.'[33] Subsequently, taking the hesychast debates as a starting point, later theorists and followers of Florovsky like those mentioned above have developed the concept of what might be called—and often actually is called by themselves—an 'Orthodox civilization' distinct from others, and from the West in particular. As there are some basic differences about anthropology already inherent in the controversy, i.e., surrounding the spiritual nature of man and the role of mind and rationality, these theorists came to some specific conclusions concerning such modern phenomena as modernity, plurality, secularism or even human rights. Although still somewhat hidden at this point, theological anthropology subsequently began to gain a major significance in the debate. At the same time, these theorists developed concepts with at least indirect political implications (in the sense at least of a general political agenda), specifically regarding such issues as individual state or the secular state or the like. For this reason they have been labeled—appropriately or not—as 'political hesychasts' by adherents and critics alike. The political element, at any rate, is grounded on the presumption of a distinct 'Orthodox civilization,' that as a consequence cannot, or cannot directly adopt the named Western concepts of pluralism, secularism, human rights, and so forth.[34]

Yet, despite their anti-Western overtones and a certain striving for purity, these concepts cannot be simply categorized as 'fundamentalist.' It has to be stated that their conclusions usually result in a plausible critique of the West (that is often shared by inner Western critics as well), and in alternative visions of at least an aesthetic quality. Yannaras, for example, systematically tries to dissociate a spiritual and communitarian Orthodox tradition from that of the

---

[33] Georges Florovsky, "St Gregory Palamas and the Tradition of the Fathers," *Sobornost* 4:4 (1961), 165–176.

[34] Christos Yannaras, *Orthodoxy and the West*; cf. Gavrilyuk, *Religious Renaissance*, 247–251; Daniel P. Payne, *The Revival of Political Hesychasm in Contemporary Orthodox Thought: The Political Hesychasm of John S. Romanides and Christos Yannaras* (Lanham: Rowman and Littlefield, 2011). For a consideration of more direct political implications see Daniel P. Payne, "The Clash of Civilizations: The Church of Greece, the European Union and the Question of Human Rights," *Religion, State & Society* 31:3 (2003), 261–271. In Russia, some theorists have approved the widely discussed "Bases of a Social Concept," a comprehensive document adopted by the Russian Orthodox Church in 2000 (see https://mospat.ru/en/documents/social-concepts/), as a late manifestation of Byzantine heritage in Russia, and therefore as an expression of 'political hesychasm': Vladimir Petrunin, *Politicheskii isikhazm i ego traditsii v sotsial'noi kontseptsii Moskovskogo Patriarkha* (*Political Hesychasm and its Tradition in the Social Concept of the Moscow Patriarchate*) (St. Petersburg: Aleteiia, 2009). For a critical evaluation see the review article by Kristina Stoeckl, "The Revival of Political Hesychasm in Contemporary Orthodox Thought," *Journal of Contemporary Religion* 26:3 (2011), 499–502.

allegedly individualistic and rationalistic West, but in no way wants to be identified with anti-Western zealots and Orthodox fundamentalists. His thoughtful and nuanced work can rather be described, in more than one sense, as a Hellenic continuation of Florovsky's *Ways of Russian Theology*. Such authors adopt the 'civilization' paradigm in various ways, arguing in favor of an 'Orthodox civilization' that has to be reinstated in its dignity, and its distinctiveness from the Christian West, but does not necessarily have to be hostile to the latter. Yet, whereas this 'Orthodox civilization' might be universal in design and go beyond narrow ethno-national boundaries of both mind and territory, it is nonetheless 'Hellenic' in its roots and sources. So, in a way the above-mentioned ambiguity between universalism and civilizational particularity, already characteristic for Florovsky's considerations, continues to exist among his 'Hellenic' followers and apprentices.

A Step Further: The Universalism of Alexander Schmemann

Other followers of Florovsky have tried to take a path that would more decisively preserve the universal element and overcome the mentioned inner tension. In one of his later books, father Alexander Schmemann, by then dean of St. Vladimir's Orthodox Seminary and father Florovsky's successor on this post, noted in the late 1970s:

> Sooner or later it will become clear to all that it is not by concentrating on the preservation of 'Hellenism,' 'Russianism' or 'Serbianism' that we will preserve Orthodoxy; but, on the contrary, by preserving and fulfilling the demands of the Church we will salvage all that is essential in all incarnations of Christian faith and life. If Fr. Florovsky, a Russian theologian living and working 'in exile,' had the courage in his *Ways of Russian Theology* to denounce and to condemn the deviations of 'Russianism' from 'Christian Hellenism' and thus to liberate an entire generation of Russian theologians from the last hangups of any pseudo-messianism and religious nationalism, is it not time for a Greek to perform the same painful and yet necessary and liberating operations with the ambiguities of 'Hellenism'?[35]

---

35 Alexander Schmemann, *Church, World, Mission* (New York: St. Vladimir's Seminary Press, 1979), 115. Schmemann's book contains a row of critical remarks concerning the "tragedy of Fr. Florovsky."

Alexander Schmemann shared the fate of an Orthodox theologian working 'in exile' with father Florovsky, from whom he had learned much, but to whom in his later years he was in a relationship not without tensions. Schmemann was born in 1921 in Tallinn in Estonia as a son of Russian emigrants. When he was still a child, his parents moved to France, and Alexander received his education in Russian schools, and at a French Lyceum. Between 1940 and 1945 he studied at the University of Paris. After that, he finished his theological studies at St. Serge Orthodox Institute in Paris, where after 1946 he would teach church history for six years. Following a call by Florovsky, in 1951 he left for the United States and took a position as church historian at St. Vladimir's Orthodox Seminary in New York. After 1962 he was dean of St. Vladimir's, a post that he held until his death in 1983.[36]

Schmemann had completed his studies at the University of Paris with a thesis on the Byzantine Empire and theocracy which probably already denoted his first step towards an overcoming of what he saw as the myth of 'holy Byzantium': this Byzantine theocracy for him marked a historical deviation and an error. The veneration of God, and the consciousness of superiority thanks to God's guidance had, in Byzantium, turned into the idea and the messianism of a 'chosen people' and 'sacred state'—a development that had significantly contributed to its ultimate decline.[37] That the essential and the timeless of the Orthodox faith became hidden under particularisms of ethno-national or civilizational self-consciousness is, furthermore, not only the tragedy of Byzantium, but also a part of its legacy to Russia. Here, the new Russian messianism culminated in the theory of the 'Third Rome,' and fell victim to just the same confusion of church and civilization, and of grace and exclusivism. Schmemann later elaborated his visions on the history of the church in his widely read book *The Historical Road of Eastern Orthodoxy*, seen by many as a continuation of Florovsky's work just in the sense quoted from him above.[38] Its conclusions come down to the need for further purification. To put this

---

36   My article at this point owes much to the empathetic and well informed portrait of Alexander Schmemann drawn by Nikolay Gavriushin, "'Das Priestertum sollte kein Beruf sein,'—sagt Protopresbyter Alexander Schmemann: Nicht Religion und Ideologie, sondern Glaube an Christus," on http://de.bogoslov.ru/text/361386.html; see also Gavrilyuk, *Religious Renaissance*, 242–247.

37   A summary of his observations in Russian has been published as "Sud'ba vizantiiskoi teokratii" (The Fate of Byzantine Theocracy), *Pravoslavnaia mysl'* (*Orthodox Thought*) 5 (1947), 130–146.

38   Alexander Schmemann, *Istoricheskii put' pravoslaviia* (New York: Izdatel'stvo Imeni Chekhova, 1954); English translation: *The Historical Road of Eastern Orthodoxy* (London: Harvill Press, 1963).

program into action would mean to leave behind any further allusions to Orthodoxy as something constituting particular 'civilizations.' Father Alexander Schmemann, did not, however, fully avoid the problem of 'Christianity and civilization,' but rather addressed it in a different manner, one that put a much stronger accent on 'civilization' in the singular sense. The question to begin with, then, would be what he actually had in mind when he called to "preserve and fulfill all the demands of the Church" instead.

A possible answer can be found in an article Schmemann published in a Russian journal in Paris, in 1974, under the title "Can one be a believer, being civilized?"[39] Here he refrains from any reasoning about the general meaning of 'civilization,' but analyses what it would mean to be a believer under the circumstances of the present, 'civilized' world. 'Civilized' can mean two things, which both pertain to man's formation and behavior. In a way, therefore, Schmemann continues with the hidden focus on anthropology that is already present in the work of other followers of Florovsky. First, there is the current tension about the best path that would lead to the wealth and happiness of mankind on earth: is it offered by science (as the, for the time being, final achievement of human civilization), or rather by religion? As it turns out, the question at the given state of affairs is just left open on grounds of mutual agreement. Meanwhile adherents of both camps have become accustomed to approach each other in—the second meaning of the term—a 'civilized manner,' just living alongside each other in peace and without mutual disturbance. Yet, however preferable that might be to a situation elsewhere—as for example in the Communist states of his time, where the named antagonism was held in the more rigid form of a persecution of religion—this state of affairs still is disappointing. The superficial peace agreement includes a frozen silence with regard to any vision about the future of the world, and about the fate of man. And what appeared as a result—and as a price to be paid—was not a spirit of liberation, but an overwhelming feeling of grief and boredom. Christians on their part suffer from the same impoverishment. While a perspective on the eternal, a reminder of the transcendent would be precisely the possible contribution of the Christian faith towards bringing back the vision that man is destined to more than material welfare and a kind of bourgeois contentedness, the reality is as tempered and bored—or 'civilized'—as that of all others. "We, the Orthodox, love to say at ecumenical meetings: 'Orthodoxy, that is the

---

39 Alexander Schmemann, "Mozhno li verit', buduchi tsivilizovanym?" *Vestnik Russkogo studencheskogo khristianskogo dvizheniia* (*Messenger of the Russian Students Christian Movement*) 107 (1974), 145–152: also online on http://www.pravoslavie.by/page_book/mozhno-li-verit-buduchi-civilizovannym. I further refer to the online version.

transformation of world and life,' but in reality all is limited to tea in the parish."[40] What has to happen, instead, is to restore man's call to testify for a kingdom that does not come from himself, but was founded and revealed by God himself, through the mystery of incarnation, and of the Easter event. Schmemann cites the chants of the Orthodox Easter liturgy here: "'This is the calling of the human being in this world—communion with God [*bogoobshchenie*], joy, peace and rightfulness in the Holy Spirit.' This, and only this constitutes a sense and depth in human life."[41] Schmemann's thoughts rather come down to a critique of the 'civilized' world of his days, and at this point the words of the church father St. John Chrysostomos, that security entails the most dangerous of all temptations, might have appeared to him as suitable as they were for father Florovsky earlier. However, he speaks not within a framework of a historical analysis of earlier times, nor does he address the problem of civilization and civilizations in abstract terms. His eye and ear are directed towards the situation of man in his own present. Having left any theoretical problem of 'civilizations' in world history and their relation to faith behind, Schmemann, a French by education, operates with 'civilization' only in the singular meaning, and preferably in the French understanding, synonymous to 'cultivated behavior' and 'enlightened mind' alike.[42] Schmemann was sensible for a certain timeless, abstract component of 'civilization,' that in his eyes remains to be connected with sin: "The Fall of Adam and Eve happens, continues, always works, and the locus of this act is not any abstract 'nature,' which we allegedly have 'inherited' from Adam, but this locus is just civilization," he once noted in his diaries.[43] However, as this could be the diagnosis everywhere in history, his focus left historical-philosophical reasoning behind and concentrates on the image of man, the 'civilized' human being. And no philosophy is needed to find a cure: concerning the deficits and imperfections of the general, and the actual state of 'civilization' he looks to the Orthodox liturgy and to the sequences that call human beings to be 'salt to the world.' Apart from particular sets and historical contexts, it is this framework out of liturgy, revelation, the image of man with his call and with his sinfulness that stands in the center

---

40 Schmemann, "Mozhno li verit'..." (printed online version), 3.
41 Schmemann, "Mozhno li verit'...," 4.
42 Concerning the ambiguities of Enlightenment, Schmemann refers to Paul Hazard's famous work concerning *La crise de la conscience européenne* (Paris: Boivin et Cie, 1935), cf. Schmemann, "Mozhno li verit'...," 2. Cf. also footnote 11 above.
43 Protoierei Alexander Schmemann, *Dnevniki* (*Diaries*) 1973–1983 (Moscow: Russkii put', 2005), 383.

of what Fr. Schmemann identified as the timeless "essentials of the Church and the Christian faith."

Conclusions

The various uses, explicit or implicit, of the term 'civilization' and related concepts are, as this overview might have shown, still of significance within the Orthodox world. But if our analysis is right, there also continue attempts to overcome the inner tensions that certain applications of this paradigm have brought about in past and present. This, on the one hand, concerns a shift from any considerations about an 'Orthodox civilization' and its historical or future manifestations towards a focus on the image of man delivered by Orthodox Christian faith and theology, regarded as being of value beyond concrete historical constellations.[44] On the other hand, there are also continued efforts to either purify an understanding of the church from undue infiltrations of national ideologies and political theory[45] or to better define the relationship of the church towards modern society and politics, and to ascribe to it the role of a both independent and corrective force.[46]

This latter aspect might also evoke the question to what extent such attempts might find their parallels in theological thinking of other confessions, which equally felt challenged by the dramatic changes and turns of the 20th century. If, for example, the role of the church in relation to modern society is described with a special emphasis on eschatology, accompanied by concomitant efforts to distinguish between eschatology and mere utopianism, and between a simple NGO and a voice outside societal contexts, but to be listened to within these,[47] an external observer might feel inclined to note here certain parallels in 20th century Protestant theology. A particular example here is the 'protestant principle' as formulated by Paul Tillich, equally keen to keep a balance between the Christian church in its timeless dimension and particular cultural manifestations.[48] As a matter of fact, Tillich and Florovsky during their time in New York and as lecturers at Princeton University did meet from

---

44   Kallistos Ware, *Orthodox Theology in the 21st Century* (Geneva: WCC publications, 2012), esp. 19–33.
45   See the recent special issue devoted to "Ecclesiology and Nationalism" in *St. Vladimir's Theological Quarterly* 57:3–4 (2013).
46   Pantelis Kalaitzidis, *Orthodoxy and Political Theology* (Geneva: WCC publications, 2012).
47   Kalaitzidis, *Orthodox Political Theology*, 89–139.
48   Paul Tillich, "The Church and Contemporary Culture," *World Christian Education* 9 (1956), 41 ff (also online on http://www.religion-online.org/showarticle.asp?title=2521).

time to time, and they probably communicated. However, the impression one gets from the evidence of these encounters is still that of two different theological cultures, which only started to enter into dialogue.[49] How far these assumed parallels really go, and what a dialogue between confessions on this level would look like two generations later, is in need of further exploration.

Bibliography

Blane, Andrew, "A Sketch of the Life of Georges Florovsky," in Andrew Blane (ed.), *Georges Florovsky: Russian Intellectual and Orthodox Churchman* (Crestwood: St Vladimir's Seminary Press, 1993), 11–217.

Buchenau, Klaus, "Svetosavlje und Pravoslavlje: Nationales und Universales in der serbischen Orthodoxie" (Sventosalje and Pravoslavlje: Nationals and Universals in the Serbian Orthodoxy), in Martin Schulze Wessel (ed.), *Nationalisierung der Religion und Sakralisierung der Nation im östlichen Europa* (Stuttgart: Franz Steiner Verlag, 2006), 203–232.

Chamberas, Peter A., "Georges Vasilevich Florovsky (1893–1979)," *Modern Age* 45 (2003), 49–66.

Cherniavsky, Michael, "'Holy Russia': A Study in the History of an Idea," *The American Historical Review* 63:3 (1958), 617–637.

Danilevsky, Nikolai, *Rossiia i Evropa: Vzgliad na kul'turnye I politicheskie otnosheniia slavianskogo mira k germano-romanskomu* (*Russia and Europe: A Perspective on the Political and Cultural Relations of the Slavic World to the German and Roman*) (Moscow: Kniga, 2003 (1869)).

Elias, Norbert, *Über den Prozess der Zivilisation* (Basel: Verlag Haus zum Falken, 1939).

Fisch, Jörg, "Zivilisation, Kultur," in Otto Brunner, Werner Conze & Reinhart Koselleck (eds.), *Geschichtliche Grundbegriffe*, Vol. 7 (Stuttgart: Klett-Cotta, 1997).

Florovsky, Georges, "Christianity and Civilization," *St Vladimir's Seminary Quarterly* 1:1 (1952), 13–20.

———, *Collected Works*, Vol. 2 (Belmont: Nordland Publishers, 1974).

———, *Collected Works*, Vol. 5 (Belmont: Nordland Publishers, 1979).

———, *Collected Works*, Vol. 6 (Vaduz: Büchervertriebsanstalt, 1987).

———, "Empire and Desert: Antinomies of Christian History," *The Greek Orthodox Theological Review* 3:2 (1957), 133–159.

---

49 Cf. Florovsky's contribution "The Predicament of the Christian Historian," in Walter Leibrecht (ed.), *Religion and Culture: Essays in Honor of Paul Tillich* (New York: Harper, 1959), 140–166.

———, *Puti russkago bogosloviia* (*The Ways of Russian Theology*) (Paris: YMCA press, 1937).

———, "St Gregory Palamas and the Tradition of the Fathers," *Sobornost* 4:4 (1961), 165–176.

———, "The Predicament of the Christian Historian," in Walter Leibrecht (ed.), *Religion and Culture: Essays in Honor of Paul Tillich* (New York: Harper, 1959), 140–166.

———, "Westliche Einflüsse in der russischen Theologie," *Kyrios* 2 (1937), 1–22.

Gavrilyuk, Paul L., *Georges Florovsky and the Russian Religious Renaissance* (Oxford: Oxford University Press, 2014).

Gavriushin, Nikolay, "'Das Priestertum sollte kein Beruf sein,'—sagt Protopresbyter Alexander Schmemann: Nicht Religion und Ideologie, sondern Glaube an Christus," http://de.bogoslov.ru/text/361386.html.

Hazard, Paul, *La crise de la conscience européenne* (Paris: Boivin et Cie, 1935).

Huntington, Samuel, *The Clash of Civilizations and the Remaking of World Order* (London: Simon & Schuster, 1996).

Kalaitzidis, Pantelis, *Orthodoxy and Political Theology* (Geneva: WCC publications, 2012).

Kirill, Patriarch of Moscow, "Russkii Mir: puti ukrepleniia i razvitiia" (The Russian World: Ways how to Strengthen and to Develop it), *Tserkov i Vremia* (*Church and Time*) 49:4 (2009).

Laruelle, Marlène, "La discipline de la culturologie: un nouveau prêt-à-penser pour la Russie?" *Diogène* 204:4 (2003), 25–45.

Makrides, Vasilios N., "Orthodox Anti-Westernism Today: A Hindrance to European Integration?" *International Journal for the Study of the Christian Church* 9:3 (2009), 209–224.

Makrides, Vasilios N. & Dirk Uffelmann, "Studying Eastern Orthodox Anti-Westernism: The Need for a Comparative Research Agenda," in Jonathan Sutton & Wil van den Bercken (eds.), *Orthodox Christianity and Contemporary Europe* (Leuven: Peeters, 2003), 87–120.

Oeldemann, Johannes, "The Concept of Canonical Territory in the Russian Orthodox Church," in Thomas Bremer (ed.), *Religion and the Conceptual Boundaries in Central and Eastern Europe: Encounters of Faith* (London: Palgrave MacMillan, 2008), 229–236.

Payne, Daniel P., "The Clash of Civilizations: The Church of Greece, the European Union and the Question of Human Rights," *Religion, State & Society* 31:3 (2003), 261–271.

———, *The Revival of Political Hesychasm in Contemporary Orthodox Thought: The Political Hesychasm of John S. Romanides and Christos Yannaras* (Lanham: Rowman and Littlefield, 2011).

Petrunin, Vladimir, *Politicheskii isikhazm i ego traditsii v sotsial'noi kontseptsii Moskovskogo Patriarkha* (*Political Hesychasm and its Tradition in the Social Concept of the Moscow Patriarchate*) (St. Petersburg: Aleteiia, 2009).

Richters, Katja, *The Post-Soviet Russian Orthodox Church: Politics, Culture and Greater Russia* (London: Routledge, 2013).

Scherrer, Jutta, *Kulturologie: Russland auf der Suche nach einer zivilisatorischen Identität*, Essener Kulturwissenschaftliche Vorträge, Vol. 13 (Göttingen: Wallstein Verlag, 2003).

Schmemann, Alexander, *Church, World, Mission* (New York: St. Vladimir's Seminary Press, 1979).

———, *Dnevniki (Diaries)* 1973–1983 (Moscow: Russkii put', 2005).

———, *Istoricheskii put' pravoslaviia* (New York: Izdatel'stvo Imeni Chekhova, 1954).

———, "Mozhno li verit', buduchi tsivilizovanym?" *Vestnik Russkogo studencheskogo khristianskogo dvizheniia (Messenger of the Russian Students Christian Movement)* 107 (1974), 145–152 (also online on http://www.pravoslavie.by/page_book/mozhno-li-verit-buduchi-civilizovannym).

———, "Sud'ba vizantiiskoi teokratii" (The Fate of Byzantine Theocracy), *Pravoslavnaia mysl' (Orthodox Thought)* 5 (1947), 130–146.

———, *The Historical Road of Eastern Orthodoxy* (London: Harvill Press, 1963).

Spengler, Oswald, *Der Untergang des Abendlandes* (Vol. 1 Vienna: Braumüller, 1918, Vol. 2 Munich: C.H. Beck, 1922).

Stoeckl, Kristina, "The Revival of Political Hesychasm in Contemporary Orthodox Thought," *Journal of Contemporary Religion* 26:3 (2011), 499–502.

St. Vladimir's Theological Quarterly 57:3–4 (2013) (Special Issue on "Ecclesiology and Nationalism").

Tillich, Paul, "The Church and Contemporary Culture," *World Christian Education* 9 (1956), 41–43 (also online on http://www.religion-online.org/showarticle.asp?title=2521).

Ware, Kallistos, *Orthodox Theology in the 21st Century* (Geneva: WCC publications, 2012).

———, *The Orthodox Church*, 4th ed. (London: Penguin Books, 1997).

Wiederkehr, Stefan, *Die Eurasische Bewegung: Wissenschaft und Politik in der Russischen Emigration der Zwischenkriegszeit und im postsowjetischen Russland* (Cologne et.al.: Böhlau, 2007).

Yannaras, Christos, *Orthodoxy and the West: Hellenic Self-Identity in the Modern Age* (Brookline: H.C. Press, 2006).

Whose Civilization is Europe Today?
Encounters between Hungarian Reformed Faith and Secular Worldviews

Ábrahám Kovács

In the past century and a half, theologians and church leaders in Hungary have needed to apply God's law in very different forms of social order, such as constitutional monarchy (1867–1918), communist totalitarian dictatorship (1948–1989) and neoliberalism (1990–2014). In this essay, I attempt to describe and analyze the challenges faced by the Reformed Church of Hungary (hereafter RCH) during these three periods. By briefly sketching the various political, social and ecclesiastical contexts, we may get a picture of the kinds of challenges presented by contemporary secular worldviews. Each historical era posed questions for Reformed Hungarians who sought to find contemporary answers to the problem of living in accordance with God's will and commandments in their society. The first part of the essay presents a debate about true Calvinism and whether it should be seen as aristocratic or democratic. The second part scrutinizes the church's interpretations of the demands of God's law and will under communist dictatorship and explores the failures of Reformed leaders to respond to the message of the gospel. Finally, I intend to offer a reflection on some of the issues concerning the Reformed Church of Hungary today, its relationship with the state, and why a self-critical stance as well as a humble prophetic voice within society is essential for Christians.

God's Law in a Constitutional Monarchy: Is True Calvinism Aristocratic or Democratic?

The first era under discussion, the era of constitutional monarchy, was underpinned by idealized liberal nationalism. During the short-lived Austro-Hungarian Empire the political context of the Reformed Church of Hungary was particularly lively.[1] After the *Ausgleich* of 1867, a compromise was achieved between the Austrian and Hungarian aristocracy, the name of the Habsburg

---

1 Alan John P. Taylor, *The Habsburg Monarchy, 1809–1918: A History of the Austrian Empire and Austria-Hungary* (Harmondsworth: Penguin, 1981); John W. Mason, *The Dissolution of the Austro-Hungarian Empire, 1867–1918* (London: Longman, 1985).

Monarchy was changed and Hungary experienced rapid urbanization, industrial and economic development, as well as unprecedented political freedom.[2] These changes had a great impact on the various classes of society.[3] Hungarian society and economy during this era is best described as feudalist-capitalist. It was a time when an extraordinary shift took place from an agrarian to a more industrialized society. Large-scale socialism also appeared for the first time.[4] These rapid changes created many challenges for the Reformed Church of Hungary. Various theological trends surfaced on the platform of Hungarian Calvinism and many—evangelicals, pietists and liberals—expressed a great interest in social outreach.[5] This involvement also contributed to the development in which theologians tried to give answers to the question of how God's law should be best observed in the modern state, and what form civilization should take, whether aristocratic, feudalist, capitalist, socialist, or, indeed, a particular mixture of these elements. In this context, a heated debate emerged about how God's kingdom may relate to the kingdom of the world, in other words, to what social order Christians should subscribe.

Within the RCH a serious debate was sparked by a passing but pertinent remark made by Béla Kenessey (1858–1918), who was the Reformed bishop of the Transylvanian Reformed Diocese. In his annual report of 1911, he paid tribute to the recently deceased Count Dezső Bánffy (1843–1911), who was not only the lay president of the Transylvanian Synod of the Reformed Church but also a prime minister of the Hungarian Kingdom. Kenessey was formerly a professor of Biblical Studies[6] in Budapest before becoming the director of the Reformed Theological University in Kolozsvár, Transylvania. It was from this position that he moved further up in the ranks of the church. He was a bishop in the Transylvanian diocese from 1908 until his death in 1918. Kenessey's report introduced an astonishing concept that reflected how a member of the Reformed

---

2 *Magyarország története 1848–1890* (*History of Hungary 1848–1890*) (Főszerk.: Endre Kovács. Szerk.: Katus László.) 1–2. rész. (Budapest: Akadémiai Kiadó, 1979), 1760.

3 György Kövér, *Iparosodás agrárországban: Magyarország gazdaságtörténete 1848–1914* (*Industrialization in an Agrarian Country: A History of Economics of Hungary 1848–1914*) (Budapest: Gondolat Kiadó, 1982).

4 István Schlett, *A szociáldemokrácia és a magyar társadalom 1914-ig* (*Social Democracy and Hungarian Society until 1914*) (Budapest: Gondolat Kiadó, 1982).

5 Sándor Koncz, *Hit és vallás: A magyar vallástudományi teológia kibontakozása és hanyatlása* (*Faith and Religion: The Rise and Demise of Hungarian Liberal Theology*) (Debrecen: Csuka Nyomda, 1942).

6 Jenő Zoványi, *Magyar protestáns egyháztörténeti lexikon* (*Lexicon of Hungarian Protestant Church History*), 3. jav. bővített kiadás. szerk Ladányi Sándor (Budapest: MRE Zsinati Iroda, 1977), 306.

elite understood Calvinism. He held that Calvinism, in addition to being an expression of faith, existed as a worldview and that it justified the contemporary social order. As we will see, he provided little theological grounding for his aristocratic concept of Calvinism.

To be fair, Kenessey did not intend the report to be a theological treatise. For him it was an annual account of the year in the diocese. The bishops, deans and professors of Reformed Theology, as well as the lay leaders of the national church who were often nobleman belonging either to the gentry or to the aristocracy, were part of the old establishment of the feudalist-capitalist social order. For many of them the altar of the church and the throne of the Hungarian Kingdom were married. Christendom, as in Great Britain or the Netherlands, still had a strong hold on society. It is not surprising, therefore, that his theology corroborated and justified the divinely commanded and prevailing social order.[7] His view shows that Hungarian Reformed theology was not immune to the fashionable contemporary reasoning of the late nineteenth century which argued that Calvinism is aristocratic. In his words:

> The major question is whether there is a difference between the aristocracy of Calvinism and the principles of ordinary aristocracy. Calvinism is indeed an immeasurably special worldview. Besides being on the one hand, as it always had been, a source of power for liberalism, the ideas of equality and democracy, we deem that on the other hand it is as much conservative, aristocratic and stands in opposition to any kind of leveling principle of equality.[8]

Kenessey's report also articulated his thoughts on the ideal type of democracy:

> God executes all his things through the elected and there is no comparable aristocratic institution to his governance of the world on this earth. Thus, what is entirely ridiculous and stands in sharp contrast with our ancient Calvinist worldview is the 'catchword' democracy, which leads into a swamp and is too radical. This is loudly proclaimed by many Calvinist ministers in their quest for popularity. Count Bánffy was regarded as a great democratic and radical politician by many, although he was a member of a family stretching back nine hundred years, which had given

---

[7] One must also note that Kenessey was part of the Upper House of the Parliament by right of being a Reformed bishop.
[8] Jenő Sebestyén, *Kálvin és a demokrácia (Calvin and Democracy)* (Budapest: MRE, 1912), 39 (my translation, AK).

a Palatine, a Governor-General, many Ensign Lords to the king and nation. He could not help being a dominant personality, an autocrat and aristocrat in the noblest sense of the word. A Caesar-like individual, who would have been pre-eminent everywhere: in Rome as well as in the most remote village.[9]

The first quotation reveals Kenessey's view that Calvinism as a religion combined two opposing features. On the one hand, Calvinism was a source, the birthplace of liberal democratic values and ideas. On the other hand, it was a conservative worldview/religion that implicitly rejected the radical forms of democratic endeavor. As he began to develop his views, Kenessey was leaning more towards a conservative and aristocratic interpretation of Calvinism. Being part of the old establishment, he believed in a process of slow, gradual reform that maintained the privileges of the elite to some extent. Unfortunately, Kenessey did not precisely explicate his views on the theological understanding of aristocracy among Christians. It seems that what he meant by 'elected' was not the people chosen by God's salvific act—all who accepted Christ's atonement—but rather the elect who were the leaders of the church, oftentimes elite members of the prevailing social order. This is precisely the point seized upon by his critics in rejecting his support for the current social order of Hungarian society.

His statements were vehemently refuted by Zoltán Jánosi (1868–1942), a minister from Debrecen, who expressed his views in a periodical entitled *Association of Ministers* (*Lelkészegyesület*). Jánosi was astonished by the way Kenessey presented Calvinism and democracy as opposites. Refuting such a claim, Jánosi held that Calvinism should stand far from any aristocratic claims based on wealth or birthright.[10] The moral aristocracy of the Christian is the only acceptable realm. Indeed:

> In God's kingdom, only aspects of faith and morality determine who are aristocrats, but in worldly kingdoms it is the aspect of possessions and nativity. One is moral aristocracy and the other is aristocracy based on wealth and birth founded in civil law.[11]

---

9   Béla Kenessey, "Dr. Kenessey Béla éves püspöki jelentése" (Bishop Dr Béla Kenessey's Annual Report), *Református Szemle* (*Reformed Review*) 4 (1911), 805 (my translation, AK).
10 Zoltán Jánosi, "Kálvinizmus és demokráczia I." (Calvinism and Democracy I), *Lelkészegyesület* (*Pastor's Association*) 4 (1911), 2 f (my translation, AK).
11 Jánosi, "Kálvinizmus I.," 3.

Jánosi's article claims that God chooses the elect not from an earthly aristocracy but from among the people, the 'demos': shepherds,, fishermen and tax collectors. To bolster his argument he quotes 1 Cor. 1: 28 and draws attention to the fact that Jesus was not born in a palace to be king, a nobleman, but to be a simple carpenter in Nazareth. He rejects the charge of "populism" leveled by "certain ministers" who were championing radical democratic change, and believes that democracy is compatible "with our ancient Calvinist worldview."[12] Kenessey is accused of blurring the issue of democracy. For Jánosi, "It is not worldly democracy, established in state law, that has to be compared with moral aristocracy, but human aristocracy based on wealth and nativity."[13] Jánosi's penetrating eyes questioned the logic of Kenessey's argument. He dismantled the bishop's theological position, which initially wavered between two views of Calvinism, i.e. whether it was a democratic or aristocratic social order, before subscribing emphatically to the latter.

However, Kenessey did have a theological justification for his views, even if he did not skillfully present it in his report. From Jánosi's refutation one may infer that the bishop may have tried to allude to one of Calvin's arguments regarding social order. Jánosi's critique referred to Calvin's *Institutes* (Book IV, Chapter 20), which deals with the issue of proper state government. In particular, he cited the following excerpt:

> And certainly it was a very idle occupation for private men to discuss what would be the best form of polity in the place where they live, seeing these deliberations cannot have any influence in determining any public matter. Then, the thing itself could not be defined absolutely without rashness, since the nature of the discussion depends on circumstances. And if you compare the different states with each other, without regard to circumstances, it is not easy to determine which of these has the advantage in point of utility, so equal are the terms on which they meet. Monarchy is prone to tyranny. In an aristocracy, again, the tendency is not less to the faction of a few, while in popular ascendancy there is the strongest tendency to sedition. When these three forms of government, of which philosophers treat, are considered in themselves, I, for my part, am far from denying that the form which greatly surpasses the others is aristocracy, either pure or modified by popular government, not indeed in itself, but because it very rarely happens that kings so rule themselves as never to dissent from what is just and right, or are possessed of so much

---

12   Jánosi, "Kálvinizmus I.," 3.
13   Jánosi, "Kálvinizmus I.," 3.

> acuteness and prudence as always to see correctly. Owing, therefore, to the vices or defects of men, it is safer and more tolerable when several bear rule, that they may thus mutually assist, instruct, and admonish each other, and should any one be disposed to go too far, the others are censors and masters to curb his excess.[14]

Jánosi reasoned that Calvin chose the best civil order available under the circumstances—a democracy constituted by a mixture of noblemen as well as the new order, the bourgeoisie.[15] He did not cease to emphasize that the "aristocratic civil government, or one which consists of aristocracy as well as bourgeoisie, which Calvin reckoned as an optimum, was not an autarchy but a republic."[16] Jánosi perceived the civil order in Geneva to be aristocratic in Calvin's time, when inhabitants of the city shared similar rights and the final power rested with the nobility and the wealthy tradesman and merchants. He pointed out that Calvin preferred the rule of the bourgeoisie, but "its prime place is argued only over against monarchy."[17] Jánosi highlighted that Calvin, like other contemporary political writers, accepted the "relative rights" of all forms of civil government. In his interpretation, Calvin presented a clear political principle: "there is no kind of government happier than where liberty is framed with becoming moderation."[18]

But Jánosi's most decisive premise rested not on theories of state law and order as expounded by Calvin. He reasoned that the true "Calvinist worldview" is informed by two of Calvinism's much more characteristic principles, those of faith and church governance. These ideas swing the pendulum towards a democratic civil governance instead of an "aristocratic and bourgeois" civil order of a state. In support of his opinion, Jánosi refers to the egalitarian principle of the procedural election of the 'servants' (*ministri*) governing the church. All members of the congregations are eligible to elect their leaders. This was the most appropriate and proper worldview of Calvinism on which the most preferable form of democratic government should rest.[19] Overall, the debate between Jánosi and Kenessey reveals several notable political alignments within early twentieth century Calvinism. Kenessey represented a conservative

---

14 John Calvin, *Institutes of the Christian Religion*, trans. Henry Beveridge (London: James Clarke, 1949), IV.20.8.
15 Jánosi, "Kálvinizmus I.," 1.
16 Jánosi, "Kálvinizmus I.," 1.
17 Jánosi, "Kálvinizmus I.," 1.
18 Calvin, *Institutes*, I.20.8.
19 Jánosi, "Kálvinizmus I.," 1.

position which sided with the current state order and supported aristocratic Calvinism when it was convenient. This conservative view was content with the marriage of state and church. In opposition to this, Jánosi's views represent a much more progressive interpretation of Calvinism and democracy. In the first case, God's kingdom and his law were seen as compatible with the settlement of state order of the Austro-Hungarian Monarchy. It was a constitutional monarchy with a feudalist-capitalist character that gave little freedom to average citizens, such as the right to vote, education and a more equal distribution of wealth. In contrast, the liberal vision of society emphasized progress towards full equality of all people in Hungarian society, as in Western Europe. Of course, many issues were still waiting to be changed and reformed. Jánosi was a socialist and he believed that Calvinism offered a theology from which one was able to forge a worldview for a proper democracy which warranted equal rights to all citizens, not just the privileged few. Using a form of historical theology, Jánosi held that Calvin's views were progressive in the sixteenth century and this led him to argue for the twentieth-century institution of the truly democratic values inherent in Calvinism.

Kenessey's conservatism and Jánosi's social liberalism represent two major political viewpoints held by members of the RCH between the two world wars. Full democracy was realized more than three decades later by the leadership of another Reformed minister, Rev. Zoltán Tildy, who was party leader of the Smallholders' Party and won the first entirely free general elections in 1945.[20] Between 1946 and 1948 Tildy served as president of the Hungarian Republic and later was imprisoned by the communists.[21] The communist dictatorship slowly began to undermine these recent advances and Reformed people were again exposed to new challenges and persecutions.

God's Law and the Law of Atheism during Communism

During communism religion was regarded as a danger to the development of a new civilization that was to achieve its highest and finest form in the egalitar-

---

[20] His theological views in relation to his political ones have not yet been researched, although he held a very high position in an extremely difficult time.

[21] György Gyarmati & Tibor Valuch (eds.), *Hungary under Soviet Domination 1944–1989* (New York: Columbia University Press, 2009). See also Paul Lendvai, *Hungary between Democracy and Authoritarianism*, trans. Keith Chester (London: Hurst & Co, 2012).

ian and classless society envisioned by Hungarian advocates of Marxism.[22] The materialistic and atheist ideology of communist regimes was totalitarian.[23] Christians who wished to live their lives in accordance with God's will, his law, and observe morals set by the teaching of the church, were portrayed as an evil threat. Communists also believed that religion only stupefied and cheated people. It lured them into a non-rationalistic, alien and detested spirituality. Marx expressed this notion when he wrote:

> Religion is the sigh of the oppressed creature, the heart of a heartless world ... It is the opium of the people ... The abolition of religion as the illusory happiness of the people is required for their real happiness ... Thus the criticism of heaven turns into the criticism of the earth ... the criticism of theology into the criticism of politics.[24]

Religion in its Christian forms, including the Reformed Church of Hungary, represented a danger to the communists, because they promoted a different kind of secularization of former Latin Christendom in Central Europe than what was happening in the West.

From the 1940s onward, the RCH experienced a totalitarian form of secularization with its scorning dismissal of Christian religion. People wishing to continue their religious activities were imprisoned, tortured and killed by fanatical communists.[25] The ideological tenet of dialectical materialism functioned like a fundamentalist quasi-religion and led to persecution of the Christian church.[26] Christians trying to obey the word of God and follow the teachings of Jesus were forced to turn their back on their faith. In this regard the situation was comparable to the suffering of Christians under Diocletian and other Roman rulers, as Füsti-Molnár has pointed out.[27] Many people gave up religion

---

22 Karl Marx, "Critique of the Gotha Program," in Robert C. Tucker (ed.), *The Marx-Engels Reader* (New York: W.W. Norton 1978), 525–541.
23 Arthur Koestler, *Darkness at Noon* (London: Cape, 1940).
24 Karl Marx, "Critique of Hegel's Philosophy of Right," in *Karl Marx and Friedrich Engels on Religion* (New York: Schocken Books, 1964), 42. The essay was originally published in the *Deutsch-Französische Jahrbücher* (1844).
25 Seth Ronald, *For My Name's Sake: A Brief Account of the Struggle of the Roman Catholic Church against the Nazis in Western Europe and against Communist Persecution in Eastern Europe* (London: Bles, 1958).
26 John E. Smith, *Quasi-Religions: Humanism, Marxism and Nationalism* (Basingstoke: Macmillan, 1994).
27 Szilveszter Füsti-Molnár, *Ecclesia sine Macula et Ruga: Donatist Factors among the Ecclesiological Challenges for the Reformed Church of Hungary Especially after 1989/90* (Sárospatak: Sárospataki Református Teológiai Akadémia, 2008).

with its public practices for fear of losing their jobs or their lives. Others resisted, arguing that they only obeyed God's law, that is, to be a witness to the world, preach the good news of Jesus Christ, man's corruption in sin and his need for salvation. To them, true discipleship and authentic Christian life was dear. They argued: how could one collaborate with an openly atheist ideology which hated religion, in particular Christianity? To be an authentic Christian, a key element was not to give up faith in the salvific message of the gospel. These voices were gradually suppressed by state power. The worst crime in communist eyes was if someone took God's law, his commandment of Matthew 28:19, so seriously that they dared preach the gospel, did mission work and reached out to the poor in a state which endeavored to root out Christianity.[28]

Those resisting the secularization of communism acted in good conscience despite the threatening actions of the dictatorship. However, some of the leaders of the Reformed Churches collaborated with the atheist state and helped to produce a distorted and false theology, the 'theology of the serving church', which attempted to harmonize God's law with the official ideology and requirements of the state. To marry the two opposing worldviews was a highly controversial move. The gospel envisions a society where the elect are called to be the salt and light of the world, and where the Kingdom of God and the world of human beings are in no way identical. However, for many centuries, particularly in Europe, Christianity with its development into Christendom drifted far from the biblical vision. During communism the temptation arrived from a different angle. The communist state sought to subjugate, even to eradicate Christianity.[29] This meant that Calvinists had to consider whether God's law and his will for human beings, relating to the shape and form of society and civilization, was compatible with the materialist ideology of the communist regime. A peculiar theology, mentioned above, was created in Hungary after the Communist Party began its rule with the effective and brutal assistance of the occupying Soviet Army. This theology effectively reinterpreted various aspects of Calvinism in a way that was sympathetic to communism. There were three phases of this reinterpretation.

The contributors to the formulation of a 'theology of the serving church' arrived at the concept from various theological viewpoints. Nonetheless, it is claimed that a key and common feature of that theology was developed by

---

28 Herbert Schlossberg, *A Fragrance of Oppression: The Church and its Persecutors* (Wheaton: Crossway, 1991).

29 Attila Molnár, "A vallásos világnézet elleni harcról. Az MSZMP Politikai Bizottsága 1958. július s 22-i határozata" (About the Battle against the Religious Worldview: The Decree of the Political Committee of Hungarian Socialist Work Party), *Protestáns Szemle* (*Protestant Review*) 1 (1994), 44–66.

bishops and the ruling elite of the church who sought to satisfy an overtly atheist state. It was Bishop Albert Bereczky who began to use the term 'theology of the narrow way' in the 1950s.[30] As the presiding bishop of the Synod of the Reformed Church of Hungary he was responsible for the Agreement between the Reformed Church of Hungary and the totalitarian state.[31] The first phase of reinterpretation, named 'the period of trying to *find orientation*' started in 1948 and lasted until 1958.[32] Shortly after the initial collaboration with communism, Reformed participants began to formulate a 'theology of service' and the term 'theology of the serving church' was coined.

At first these key 'ideological phrases' made their way into church talks. Then they became theological concepts. The emergence and presence of these terms was thought to assure its wide acceptance by the church and please the atheist state. Many theologians, ministers and lay people did not subscribe to this theology and they were often in consequence marginalized, removed and disadvantaged. However, it was to be the official theology of the church, in the search for compatibility with the atheist communist regime's ideology. As Tibor Fabiny has pointed out, this happened in other Hungarian Protestant churches as well. His work on the Lutheran Church of Hungary shows that church leaders developed a 'theology of *diakonia*' that followed much the same pattern.[33]

In the second phase of reinterpretation, new terms were offered for basically the same theology of appeasement. When Bishop Tibor Bartha of the Transtibiscan Reformed Diocese succeeded Bereckzy as presiding bishop of the RCH after the Hungarian revolution of 1956, he introduced a new term, 'Evangelical Calvinism,' to denote the same theological system. The term 'the theology of the serving church' was chosen to describe how God's law had to be made compatible with atheist state law. The second period was called '*learning* how to walk on the road of a serving church' (1958–1968). This 'learning' cynically indicated the stance of collaborating church officials. Except for a short period in 1956, from the mid-1950s onwards no open debate was possible

---

30   Albert Bereczky, *A keskeny út* (*The Narrow Way*) (Budapest: 1953).
31   However, some new sources, not yet analyzed, suggest that others such as József Éliás may have had a decisive role.
32   Tibor Bartha, "Zsinat elnöki székfoglaló. 1970. jan. 21" (Inauguration Speech as President of the Synod), *Református Egyház* (*Reformed Church*) 22:4 (1970), 74–76. See also: Károly Tóth, "A Zsinati Tanács nyilatkozata az Egyezmény 30. évfordulójára. 1978. dec. 1" (A Declaration of the Council of the Synod on the Occasion of the Agreement's Thirtieth Anniversary), *Református Egyház* (*Reformed Church*) 12 (1978), 268.
33   Tibor Fabiny, "Theologies of Church Government in the Hungarian Lutheran Church during Communism (1945–1990)," *Religion in Eastern Europe* 24:4 (2004), 11–29.

within the RCH about the ideological relationship between Calvinism and communism.[34] After the revolution was brutally suppressed, ministers and theologians who dared to challenge and criticize the basic elements of this theology were accused of a "revolt against the Word of God"[35] and were stigmatized as "agents of the imperialists." István Bogárdi Szabó has described it as a "dishonest debate" in which the 'official' theologians often alluded to pieces of criticism which were not accessible to the church public, simply because it was forbidden to publish them.[36]

The third phase of reinterpretation also fell under the presidency of Bishop Bartha and might be labeled as 'the era of developing the theology of the serving church' (1968–1978). In fact this was a time of soft persecution of ministers and lay people. All were expected to collaborate with the 'humble servants of the serving theology,' enabling them to fulfill the expectations of the atheist state.[37]

To understand the main constituent parts of the 'theology of the serving church', we must turn our attention to the historical context. After World War II, the Hungarian people experienced a severe trauma in the reaffirmation of the Trianon Treaty Dictatum. The original treaty had been made at the end of World War I. It reduced Hungary to a country that was around one third of the size it had been before the war. This belligerent and, in many ways, unjust decision of the Western powers effectively punished Hungary for being on the losing side. The social and cultural impact of the treaty was immense, since it left every third Hungarian person living outside their former home country in newly formed states which had often never existed before.[38] Many Hungarian Reformed lay people, theologians and church leaders lived in these areas, and they tried to find biblical answers, particularly from the prophetic language of the Old Testament, to explain this trauma. Like the Jews, they asked: Why has God punished us so severely? What did we do wrong?

Various theological trends gave different answers. What interests us here is how the proponents of the theology of the serving church made an attempt to

---

34   István Bogárdi Szabó, *Egyházvezetés és teológia Magyarországi Református Egyházban 1948–1989* (*Church Leadership and Theology in the Reformed Church of Hungary 1948–1989*) (Debrecen: DRTA, 1995), 66 f.
35   István Török, *Kereszténységünk a szocializmus történelmi korszakában* (*Our Christian Life during the Historical Time of Socialism*), Unpublished manuscript, 3. Quoted by Bogárdi Szabó, *Egyházvezetés*, 120.
36   Bogárdi Szabó, *Egyházvezetés*, 66 f.
37   Bogárdi Szabó, *Egyházvezetés*, 25. He speaks of a "double system of guarantees."
38   Ignác Romsic, *The Dismantling of Historic Hungary: The Peace Treaty of Trianon, 1920*, trans. Mario D. Fenyo (Boulder: Wayne, 2002).

understand contemporary events. The hermeneutical key to this was a well-known parallelism found in the language of the prophets scourging the elected nation.[39] The historical parallels using the Old Testament schemes of 'judgment-mercy' and 'past-present' were taken up again by theologians. This phenomenon was already present in the Hungarian Reformed tradition, as János Győri and others have pointed out.[40]

During the Reformation in Hungary, the same pattern was used by Gáspár Károli and others.[41] They drew parallels between the fate of the biblical Israel and the Hungarian nation.[42] The arguments contained elements such as: the Hungarian nation sinned against God through religious inobservance and social injustice, so God sent the 'pagans,' i.e. Muslim Turks, to Hungary as a punishment.[43] Therefore, the nation should repent and hope that God will remove the punishment. Similarly, the proponents of the newly emerging theology claimed that Hungarians[44] acted against God, therefore the Trianon Treaty was reaffirmed; we lost the war because we did not heed 'God's will.'

László Gonda is right to point out that many leaders of the first period came from a revivalist background, like Bereczky.[45] I may add that their leftist political orientation also contributed to their eagerness to work closely with the new

---

[39] On this point I would not label it pietist as Gonda does. "When speaking about judgment and mercy, it is exceedingly apparent that a Pietistic terminology is implemented here" (László Gonda, *The Service of Evangelism, the Evangelism of Service* (Utrecht: University Press, 2008), 58).

[40] Graeme Murdock, *Calvinism on the Frontier 1600–1660: International Calvinism and the Reformed Church in Hungary and Transylvania* (Oxford: Clarendon, 2000).

[41] Győri L. János, *A magyar reformáció irodalmi hagyományai (The Literary Traditions of the Hungarian Reformation)* (Budapest: MRE, 1997), 38. See also: Czeglédy Sándor, *A választott nép (The Chosen People)* (Budapest: MRE, 1940), 12.

[42] Bogárdi Szabó, *Egyházvezetés*, 87.

[43] Pál Fodor, "A törökök magyar szemmel" (The Turks through the Eyes of Hungarians), *Magyar Tudomány*, 4 (2011); *A magyar irodalom története, 1600-tól 1772-ig. A szigeti veszedelem (A History of Hungarian Literature from 1600 to 1772: The Fall of Szigetvár)*, szerk. Klaniczay Tibor, 6 Vols. (Budapest: Akadémiai kiadó, 1964), Vol. 2., 168; see also: István Magyari, *Az országokban való sok romlásoknak okairól (About the Many Reasons of Destruction)* (Budapest: Európa kiadó, 1979); András Szkhárosi Horváth, *A török Isten csapása: A református és a zsidó magyar párhuzam (The Turks are God's Punishment: The Reformed and Jewish Hungarian Parallel)* (Budapest: Magyar Helikon).

[44] This generalizing term is often unjust and improper, since the authors in question do not always make it clear whether they speak of the entire Hungarian nation regarded as Christians, or the Reformed Christians only.

[45] Gonda, *The Service of Evangelism*, 68 f.

regime.[46] No wonder that some of the former revivalists (evangelicals and pietists) shifted their allegiance, either knowingly or subconsciously, much more readily than others. Their rhetoric was in tone deceptively similar to the Reformers. However, they only applied the judgment-mercy dialectical parallelism, the opposing terms, to excite the interest of the believer and offer a seemingly biblical explanation. This action provided them with the opportunity to coin the term 'theology of the serving church.' After doing so, they began to create a framework of reference by elevating the categories often used for individual piety to a national level. Thus, following an old method, they transferred ideas originally applied to the individual to general, corporate concepts such as church (the Reformed people) and nation.

After describing the political-social impact on people's emotions and the immense impact on their spirituality, we should understand there was a receptive soil for the development of such a theology. It did not take too long for many to discern where the development began to drift away, even at its outset, from the biblical Reformed faith. The credit goes to Bogárdi Szabó for identifying the sources for the development of 'serving theology' and its characteristics. He drew attention to the fact that the theological notion of "grace working from the outside"[47] was introduced by János Victor.[48] The person who does not recognize, with a grateful and humble heart, that God works in the lives of humans outside His Word as well, and that numberless morally good acts can proceed from that, such a person has not understood the majestic testimony of the Word about God's 'universal grace.' Among the factors that God's 'universal grace' uses to transform the moral lives of men, we find the political, legal, so-

---

[46] To see how influential or at times how misleading political views may be for a Christian stance is well seen in the case of Karl Barth, who as a socialist was lenient towards the extremism of the left, e.g. communism, but highly critical about the extremism of the right-wing political scale. In my opinion, evil has no color or sides. István Pásztori-Kupán, "Hallgatni: arany-e vagy cinkosság? Karl Barthnak az 1956-os magyar szabadságharc kapcsán tanúsított „hallgatása" Reinhold Niebuhr értelmezésében" (To Be Silent Is To Be Wise or To Become a Pander? Karl Barth's Attitude of Silence in Relation to the Hungarian Revolution in the Interpretation of Reinhold Niebuhr), *Református Szemle (Reformed Review)* 1 (2009), 103–125.

[47] János Victor, "Kívülről befelé is munkálkodó kegyelem" (The Grace which Works from the Inside towards the Outside), *Református Egyház (Reformed Church)* 4 (1952), 3.

[48] He was a professor of Systematic Theology at the Reformed Theological Academy in Budapest and minister of the Budapest-Szabadság téri Reformed Church, an outstanding theologian with close links to the Awakening movement. For a detailed analysis of Victor's oeuvre, cf. Sándor Gaál, *Kezdeményező egyház (The Initiative Church)* (Debrecen: DRTA, 2006).

cial, and economic orders that humans live in. And this order does not only form one's outward deeds, but one's thinking, emotions and spirituality as well. There is something indeed that forms humans from outside.[49] This concept later played a key role in the structure of the theology of the serving church.[50] Victor reasoned that in the context of general revelation God uses instruments in human history to instruct and correct the church. He regarded socialism as such an instrument which is in accordance with the will of God. Albert Berecky held the same opinion. He "saw God's judgment in the catastrophes of the war (judgment on the old feudal system and Nazism), and he saw God's act of mercy in the liberation by socialism."[51] In order to equate God's kingdom with communism, the biblical message was distorted. Three major features of the 'theology of the serving church' were developed by various collaborators: a selective Christology, a corrupted ecclesiology and a distorted eschatology.

Benő Békefi,[52] another proponent of the theology of the serving church, states in an article on "Our Diakonia as a Part of the Diakonia of Jesus Christ"[53] the following:

> If the church understands that she is in the world to carry out Christ's diaconia, she will die of that, because she will not be needed anymore. For the church does not exist to assure her own existence to eternity, but that by sacrificing herself, by sharing in Christ's suffering, a new creation will come, in which there will be no temple, but where God dwells in the universality of the people: in the city without temple. ... let us learn that such a world is made by his salvation where finally the Son himself will be submitted to the One who had cast all things under his feet and where God will be all in all.[54]

As a former revivalist, Békefi tended to connect the idea of biblical new creation with the ushering in of a new civilization initiated by communism. One is left pondering how ill-informed these church leaders were, and how oblivious to the materialist and atheist form of Marxism as realized in Hungarian communism. It is conspicuous that this 'self-dissolving' program of the diaconal

---

49 Bogárdi Szabó, *Egyházvezetés*, 76.
50 Bogárdi Szabó, *Egházvezetés*, 70–85.
51 Füsti-Molnár, *Ecclesia*, 55.
52 Benő Békefi was senior of the classis Nyírségi, theological professor in Debrecen, later bishop of the Dunántúli (Transdanubian) church district.
53 Benő Békefi, "Diakóniánk, mint Jézus Krisztus diakóniájának része," *Református Egyház (Reformed Church)* 3 (1951), 4 ff.
54 Békefi, "Diakóniánk," 6. I owe the translation to Szilveszter Füsti-Molnár.

church coincides with the Marxist utopia of the spontaneous disappearance of religion in developed communism. One cannot help thinking that Békefi was either a dilettante theologian or a soulless former Christian who consciously sought to undermine the church and satisfied the oppressors by any means. It is more than perplexing to realize that they willingly cooperated with an atheist ideology "whose final purpose was to liquidate Christian thought and life."[55] Füsti was quick to highlight a disturbing point: "the church with its obedient suffering takes part in the liquidation of the church."[56]

Bogárdi Szabó convincingly demonstrates that a selective Christology is used in Békefi's argumentation (and in several other places). The kenotic element of Christ's earthly ministry is highlighted (suffering, passion and death), but His resurrection, ascension and glorification are ignored. As a result, in the words of one author, the ministry of the church becomes "a one-way kenotic movement towards the world."[57] One must also point to the lack of preaching about the corruption of man due to original sin which calls every human being to turn to God, confess sin and accept his salvific grace offered through the death of Christ. Bogárdi Szabó is right in saying together with Stephen Sykes "this constant 'evacuation' of Christ's power leads to an ecclesial practice of letting the 'world set the agenda'."[58] The second problematic point here is the notion of the participation of the church in Christ's *diakonia*. In this case the unique character of the vicarious suffering, death (and then the resurrection!) of Christ—as classically taught in Reformed theology—is lost. The third characteristic element of the theology of the serving church was its ecclesiological exclusiveness, which was articulated very clearly over against the associations and societies of home and foreign mission in Hungary.[59] Here, we propose that one of the greatest dangers for communists were not the sleepy nominal Christians and masses of traditionalist Christianity, though nationalism and traditional forms of Christianity formed a very significant aspect of Christian faith in the Reformed Church, but the well-organized evangelicals, pietists and other devout Christians who held key positions in several church organizations. They were the people who had to be suppressed and posed a threat to the communists. No wonder the leaders of the totalitarian state sought and

---

55 Füsti-Molnár, *Ecclesia*, 156.
56 Füsti-Molnár, *Ecclesia*, 158.
57 Bogárdi Szabó, *Egyházvezetés*, 100.
58 Bogárdi Szabó, *Egyházvezetés*, 104.
59 I believe the irony of history is that the evangelical-pietist movement initiated most of the societies and it was mainly people from the same circle who vastly contributed to its eradication. However, this area requires more research.

unfortunately found some leaders who compromised the gospel, and more importantly placed them in key positions. These leaders could be easily yoked. Fellow revivalists as well as traditionalists who resisted experienced harsh persecution. Later, Tibor Bartha expressed his conviction that "Christians do not participate directly in the salvific work of Christ [sic!], but indirectly, in the fellowship of the church ... The Revelation informs us that the church is the mandate of the Christian service."[60] Bogárdi Szabó points out that a hierarchy of communication and of participation is applied here (Christ—church—individual) which is contradictory to the classical Reformed doctrine of the church.[61]

It is truly revealing to study the statements made by the chief promoters of the 'theology of the serving church.' I believe it was a distorted interpretation of Deuteronomist historiography found in the Old Testament. Bogárdi-Szabó clearly articulates the line of argumentation of those who developed the 'theology of serving church' doctrine. In their self-assigned prophetic role, many of the proponents went astray and created a theological heresy: the affirmation of God's special revelation of himself in the events of world history was taken together and combined with God's revelation of himself in Jesus Christ. Many church leaders believed that God's kingdom could be realized in its entirety on earth and that therefore a paradise-like state could be achieved. This is what Cromwell and other militant Puritans believed, but this eschatological view is not biblical. A true follower of Christ cannot confuse the Kingdom of God with a Christian political state nor with a communist one, which superficially proclaimed similar goals such as equality and social justice, but denied the salvific deed of Jesus Christ. Instead it placed itself in the role of the Savior. This is apparent from the zeal with which revivalist evangelical-pietists flagellated the church.

The first statement was that the RCH was not faithful to the Lord in the decades before World War II.[62] This was a grossly generalizing and superficial theological assertion. Theologians often fall into the mistake of projecting

---

60   Tibor Bartha, "A keresztyén szolgálatunk ekkléziológiai összefüggései" (The Ecclesiological Relationship of our Christian Service), *Theológiai Szemle (Theological Review)* 1 (1973), 9. Although this publication comes from after 1968, there are good reasons to suppose that these insights were characteristic of the whole period discussed.

61   Bogárdi-Szabó, *Egyházvezetés*, 127.

62   Tibor Bartha, "Megtérés Krisztushoz és a felebaráthoz" (Conversion to Christ and to the Neighbor), in Tibor Bartha, *Ige, egyház, nép (Word, Church, People)* (Budapest: MRE Zsinati Iroda, 1972), 95 ff. I owe the English translation to László Gonda (*The Service of Evangelism*, 58).

their own interpretation of the Bible on historical, political, social or economic events. What does it mean to be 'not faithful to the Lord'? Has there ever really been a true and faithful church on earth? Is it not rather that we live with the tension of knowing that neither a believer nor a church can live up to God's requirements (commands, law, and teachings of the gospel), but that human beings can and should always endeavor to do so? This tension, if it is understood properly and lived out humbly and honestly, may be responsible for a healthy attitude to do everything 'before God.' This creative tension lends an eschatological flavor and may result in a devout Christian life. Christians have to have a critical, alert, loving and uncompromising stance regardless of whatever ideology controls the state and shapes human civilization. If the church's worldview is made compatible with that of the State, a compromise is struck and a crisis of faith emerges which may lead to the denial of God's glory and his salvation.

Secondly, the theology of the servant church asserted about the RCH:

> ... she was too much incorporated into the civic structures of the Hungarian establishment, she did not side with the poor, the underprivileged and the oppressed, she did not protest strongly enough against the persecution of Jews,[63] she failed to proclaim the Gospel clearly and failed to call the nation to repentance and thus she failed altogether to fulfill her prophetic task.[64]

The charges were only partly true for the Reformed Church. As one of the national churches of Hungary it was, beyond recovery, part of Christendom taking shape in Europe, in our case the Reformed Church of Hungary. This self-flagellating criticism distorts the fact that a lot of organizations, mission societies and the like were set up by church members to respond to the needs of society from 1870s onward, due to the impact of Scottish-English evangelicals and German pietists.[65] While certain historians are quick to paint a dismissive picture of the RCH, it has to be stated that Bishop László Ravasz was

---

63 This is a strongly distorted picture as there were several initiatives within the Reformed Church of Hungary to save the Jews and a good number of ministers individually defied the Nazis. On the history of Good Shepherd Mission (*Jó Pásztor misszió*) see Ábrahám Kovács, *A Jó Pásztor bizottság története* (*Good Shepherd Committee*) (Debrecen: DRTA, 1997; dissertation).

64 Bartha, "Megtérés," 95 ff.

65 Ábrahám Kovács, *The History of the Free Church of Scotland's Mission to the Jews in Budapest and its Impact on the Reformed Church of Hungary 1841–1914* (Wien: Peter Lang, 2006).

supportive of mission[66] and during the war allowed room for the Good Shepherd Mission and the Scottish Mission, which was legally incorporated into the Reformed Church to save the Jews, where Jane Haining worked.[67] Many other Reformed ministers and laypeople took a strong biblical stance to protect the suffering Jewish people.

The third statement of collaborating Reformed theologians is highly questionable as it stands: "God, the Lord of history, uses communism as a means of discipline in order to call the church to repentance of her former sins and failures. Through the social program of Marxism-Leninism, the churches are taught to work for social justice."[68] It is a remarkable phenomenon to observe here how the desire of fervent revivalism to realize God's Kingdom on earth overlaps with a very similar endeavor of staunch believers in communism. Both adhered to the notion of social and economic equality among all people and sought to realize a classless egalitarian society, but their worldviews rested on different tenets and their unveiled doctrines had a different flavor, one theist, the other atheist. The former could see the positive aspects of communism and sought to work closely with it, but the latter rejected any fair cooperation. The way of Marxist ideology as understood and realized by Hungarian communists was brutally oppressive and incited hatred against Christians.

Finally, it is perplexing to see what Bishop Bartha claimed:

> ... the church must humble herself under the discipline of God and accept communism as His instrument. She must give up any aspiration to power and influence in society and should be a follower of the *diakonos Christos*, the servant Christ. She should also make a clear decision to support the cause of social justice and world peace (which is in harmony with God's will). Thus the churches (and the RCH) should convert to Christ and to the neighbor.[69]

This theology superficially appears agreeable since it refers to the second clause of the Great Commandment "love your neighbor as yourself." This always implies or should imply a strongly social element to care for and reach out to the people next door. However, it is debatable in what sense communism can be seen as a tool in God's hand. What is often neglected is that this

---

66 Anne-Marie Kool, *God moves in Mysterious Ways: The Hungarian Protestant Foreign Mission Movement 1756–1951* (Zoetermeer: Boekencentrum, 1993).
67 Kovács, *A Jó Pásztor bizottság története*, 35.
68 Bartha, "Megtérés," 95 ff.
69 Bartha, "Megtérés," 95 ff.

second statement of God's law has a spiritual aspect as well. This is responsible for the missionary fervor of Christians, who are 'constrained by the love of God' to preach that 'all have sinned against God' and every human being needs to turn to Jesus. Christians have a very different understanding of salvation from communists. God's law asks that one first of all obeys with joy to express one's love for God, an anathema to atheist communism, the chief ideology of the Hungarian ruling Socialist Party.

Calvinism did provide Hungarian ministers with a theology from which they could form a Christian worldview of egalitarian democracy which Jánosi promoted and Tildy managed to realize, though only for a short while. The theology of the servant church caused deep wounds within the very bosom of the RCH. After the collapse of communism the church has not yet recovered from its past hurt. In the third part of this article, I try to delineate some of the crucial challenges which the Reformed Church faces in a new secular state exposed to globalization, secularization and modern humanism.

A Self-critical Church in a Neoliberal Age

Entering the new world of freedom, which Hungarians gladly embraced, was an unknown experience for Reformed Christians after the collapse of communism. People in the West welcomed the change and thought everything had *completely* changed. However, there is a frightening reality that is often ignored. Former atheism, which had placed a severe limitation on freedom of speech and religion and vehemently denied any form of pluralism, still keeps a grip on Hungarian society, but under a different guise. Our first observation is that communism as a form of civilization may officially have disappeared, but the very people who participated in directing, governing and controlling society did not just vanish from the scene. In the public sphere, politics and in ecclesiastical structures many of the former key figures remained in power, unlike in (East) Germany. And it is still like that today. Vogelaar expertly grasped the essence of the situation: "In Hungary Communism was not beaten, it simply collapsed in mid-1989."[70] There was no revolution. Consequently, no people were summoned to courts for their past deeds and not one single political leader was taken into custody and held accountable for what he had done. Former political and social powers were quietly and cunningly converted into economic advantage. The most ironic examples of this 'development'

---

70   Huub Vogelaar, "Ecumenical Relations in Hungary since 1990," *Exchange* 35 (2006), 398–422: 401.

are current socialist or liberal politicians who are businessmen with economic empires. In addition they, or their relatives and circles of friends, again managed to translate and transform power into political capital. Only a handful of key figures from the former regime admitted the evil deeds of communism.[71] The majority later presented themselves as liberals, or progressive socialists, a disguise that managed to mislead the West and also the people of Hungary. Not until 2014 was a national committee set up to deal with the past.[72] Not much has happened in Hungary in the past 23 years which can be compared with the reconciliatory and healing process in Germany or South Africa.

A similar process can be discerned in the church. It was not until nineteen years after the official collapse of communism that a committee consisting of historians was officially set up by the Reformed Church. Its lateness speaks for itself. Their task is "to collect and evaluate the historical evidence."[73] Their aim is to investigate and disclose who collaborated with the atheist state, why and to what extent they did so. Apart from this initiative, other independent researchers and historians have endeavored to uncover who gave up their faith and compromised with communism.[74] Both initiatives attempt to collect data, but the most imperative task is to describe how the system between the church and state worked.[75] To sum up, the lack of a proper process for dealing with the past on a national scale both within the church and civil society, which would create room for repentance and forgiveness, impedes spiritual renewal within the church and makes healing impossible in society. It must be underlined that there were some sporadic, sincere and moving confessions of collaborators within the church. It is also true that some of the collaborators were victims themselves. The situation was and is highly complex. Yet it is precisely this observation which calls for sober and well-analyzed research from church historians, whose intention should only be to promote reconciliation. Church leaders too should promote intra-church talks and facilitate a process of

---

[71] E.g. Imre Pozsgay, who was responsible for the transition from communism to democracy.

[72] http://www.magyarhirlap.hu/elnokot-kapott-a-multat-feltaro-bizottsag.

[73] http://www.reformatus.hu/egyhazunk/mutat/6512/. It describes very briefly the task of Tényfeltáró Történész Bizottság (A Committee of Historians to Unveil the Facts).

[74] László Kósa, "Az állambiztonsági szervezet hálózata a református egyházban a diktatúra idején" (The Network of the State Security Association in the Reformed Church during the Dictatorship), *Théma* 12:1–2 (2010).

[75] The only truly excellent and sober analysis is that of István Bogárdi Szabó, who critically analyzed texts and offered reflections (see second subsection). Such works are really needed for progress on the road of reconciliation.

reconciliation similar to that in South Africa, which had to learn to how to handle the misdeeds of apartheid. Germany dealt with its communist past in the same kind of way.

Reformed Christians need to be vigilant and have a prophetic voice. This involves the twofold task of applying God's law expressed in the Great Commandment and the Lord's Prayer. First, they must exercise self-criticism with a repentant and humble heart and second, they should not be afraid to offer a healthy critique of all aspects of public life.

Before turning our attention to the first issue, we must point to a popular notion which seems to survive like a myth. Politicians, public figures and chief exponents of the intelligentsia on both sides of the political scale wrongly assume that the church still has enormous power. I believe that those days have gone. The Hungarian population is highly secular. According to the census of 2011, slightly more than fifty percent of the total population indicated some form of religious affiliation (mostly Christian, but including other world religions). Even this group of people is slow to practice religion on a regular basis and does not even go to church on Sunday. Hungary is a secular country, and therefore genuine Reformed Christian witness and mission is an imperative for all believers in Christ. God's law and teaching should be lived out in all sectors of public life.

Before spelling out how the church should carry out its public role, one must state that the church has a place, rights and responsibilities in the public sphere. It should not be marginalized in the public arena. To remind the secular state of the historical and cultural impact of Christianity is necessary and healthy for society.[76] Duncan Forrester has stated that public theology

> ... seeks the welfare of the city before protecting the interests of the Church, or its proper liberty to preach the Gospel and celebrate the sacraments ... It strives to offer something that is distinctive, and that is gospel, rather than simply adding the voice of theology to what everyone is saying already.[77]

Regarding the church's self-criticism, first, reconciliation must be at the top of the church's agenda, as all aspects of public life are closely interwoven with

---

76 András Reuss, "Vitázva a társadalommal és egymással. A keresztyének és a politika" (Debating with Society and Each Other), *Credo* 7 (2002), 93–105.

77 Duncan B. Forrester, "The Scope of Public Theology," *Studies in Christian Ethics* 17:2 (2004), 5–19: 6.

stances marked by unhealed wounds in different circles of society. Reformed Christians need to confess, repent and forgive one another and initiate a spiritual renewal amongst themselves to set an example for society.

The second feature of having a healthy 'self-criticism' is that Reformed Christians must be aware that they live in a secular and pluralistic society in which Christendom has run its course. Tolerance is vital in all aspects of life, but it does not mean that a believer gives up his or her opinion. Rather it insists on the message of God's law of love, which is communicated and unveiled to the church through the work of the Holy Spirit and at the same time respects the identity of the other person. The deep and dearly held Christian belief about every human being, that all of us, regardless of race, color and ethnicity, are created in the image of God, calls us to value all human beings and reminds us to respect human dignity. Christians should not give up their deepest conviction that God's word, his law, teaches about his salvific love and that the morals taught in the gospel are valid claims on the individual as well as on society.

Thirdly, the church must resist the temptation to seal any form of marriage between throne and altar. Neither the rhetoric and speeches of political leaders evoking ideas of Christendom nor the financial subsidies given to the church by civil governments, regardless of whether the political right or left is in power, should be allowed to exert influence on the understanding of God's word. The leaders and theologians of the Reformed Church must remind themselves of the misdeeds of Christendom's past and warn and instruct their members that the marriage of throne and altar is not what the gospel teaches. Neither the feudalist-capitalist form of old establishment with its culture of dominant Christendom nor the forced marriage of communism and religion is desirable. We have seen that theology may misuse the gospel and that the word of God has often been abused. This has been and continues to be a shame to Christianity.

A truly evangelical Christianity of Reformed faith with its rich heritage of resistance against evil powers and tradition of holding firm for justice should provide a ground for today's Hungarian Calvinists. The Heidelberg Catechism teaches that all deeds of Reformed people flow from the immense gratitude of the converted Christian's heart to God for his salvation through Jesus Christ. Consequently, Christian morals, if a believer exhibits an authentic and committed Christian life, may offer a healthy critique of a society. In all spheres of public life Christians must follow God's basic law, the Great Commandment: "You shall love the Lord your God with all your heart and with all your soul and with all your mind. This is the great and first commandment. And a second is like it: You shall love your neighbor as yourself" (Matt. 22: 37–39). But the question arises as to how we apply this teaching. The declaration of the Evangelical Churches of Germany (EKD)[78] offers a valuable guide to be followed sincerely by Christians in Hungary too. The declaration spells out how Christians could relate to various issues emerging in society.[79] By following the guidelines and adding some other themes which concern them, Hungarian Christians are called to offer a healthy and responsible critique of society. When a believer faces a decision to choose a political party, he or she needs to pay attention to the legislative attitude of all parties concerning churches. Apart from observing how they deal with material and financial issues, it is vital to examine to what extent they really deal with moral and spiritual issues. Reformed Christians should investigate the public statements of parties. They should scrutinize what their stances are on protecting the natural world, strengthening families, raising children, the rights of single parents, minorities and marginalized groups.[80] When making a decision, it is also crucial to consider how they deal with unemployment, what their concept on equitable taxation is and how they envision the relationship between people speaking different languages and adhering to various religions and worldviews.

Concluding Thoughts

In an age of secularism underpinned by various Western European ideologies and worldviews, such as neoliberalism with its modern humanism, Reformed Christians believe that the church proclaims the word of God about the cross, which is the good news to all human beings. This realization of the message of the gospel obliges all Christians to appreciate the other's otherness, yet at the same time calls for a biblically based criticism of views, morals and acts that are contrary to God's commandment and his vision for a civilization where human beings live in peace. The church must articulate her thoughts clearly without any ambiguity on issues concerning society and has to learn how to

---

78   *Evangelische Kirche in Deutschland* (EKD). This body is the main representative of German Protestantism joining Lutheran, Reformed and United churches under one council. The statement was issued in October 1997.

79   "Gerechtigkeit erhöht ein Volk": Erklärung des Rates der Evangelischen Kirche in Deutschland (EKD) zur Parteispendenaffäre, Chorin (Brandenburg), 28. Januar 2000, cited by Reuss, "Vitázva," 103.

80   Péter Balla, "Reformed Identity in Eastern Europe with a Particular Focus on Hungary," *Presbyterion* 36 (2010), 65–70: 69 f. I entirely agree with the author that Christian families with strong Reformed identity may healthily contribute to the building up of congregation and society.

relate to pluralism. She should never attempt to impose her understanding on society, but present a life that will convince others to consider God's message.

It is a privilege to live in a modern democracy.[81] Christians must repent with sincere hearts that the gospel was interpreted incorrectly through the centuries with the false belief that God's kingdom and any form of human civilization may have common boundaries on earth before Christ's return. They have to learn to live with the eschatological tension of the 'already but not yet' realization of God's kingdom. Christians are called to be light and salt in the world, but not to be the sole constituents of the world. They may endeavor to express how much human beings may learn from God's law and the gospel about Jesus Christ, which may well be a cohesive force for society and state. It is right for Christians to hope that a democratic state with respect for the law will realize the positive message of Christianity.[82] Finally, Christians live in an increasingly pluralistic and advanced modern society. In that context, while witnessing their faith, they encounter science as well as various worldviews and religions. Reformed Christians of Hungary need to learn how to deal with these challenges. It is possible to draw on our rich tradition of denominational tolerance, which was one of the earliest European examples of accepting the others' otherness, witness the edict of Torda.[83] In that spirit a healthy society may be built. Interreligious dialogue and a constant conversation with science and different worldviews is an essential step for a democratic society but also for an open-minded Christian life. One can only agree with Rüdiger Noll that it is not the task of the government to dialogue with religions but of given communities within society.[84] This is true for science and worldviews too. One of the preconditions for engaging in such an enterprise is to proclaim freedom of conscience and religion. Living with the healthy tension of endeavoring to fulfill God's law and being aware of our sinful nature and iniquity which impede us from living up to the very high moral criteria Jesus set for Christians should remind all Christians that every human being needs to be saved. With such a view Christian testimony—our mission in the world and to the members of

---

81 András Bozóki, András Körösényi & George Schöpflin (eds.), *Transition: Emerging Pluralism in Hungary* (New York: St. Martin's Press, 1992).
82 Reuss, "Vitázva," 104.
83 István Pásztori-Kupán, "The Spirit of Religious Tolerance: A Transylvanian 'extra calvinisticum?'" in Ábrahám Kovács & Béla Baráth (eds.), *Calvinism on the Peripheries: Religion and Civil Society in Europe* (Budapest: L'Harmattan, 2009), 155–179.
84 http://www.meot.hu/index.php?option=com_content&view=category&layout=blog&id =77&Itemid=74 (downloaded 11 January 2014).

our societies—is maintained and a constant self-critical attitude is developed to foster humility.

Bibliography

A magyar irodalom története, 1600-tól 1772-ig. A szigeti veszedelem (A History of Hungarian Literature from 1600 to 1772: The Fall of Szigetvár), szerk. Klaniczay Tibor, 6 Vols. (Budapest: Akadémiai kiadó, 1964).

Balla, Péter, "Reformed Identity in Eastern Europe with a Particular Focus on Hungary," *Presbyterion* 36 (2010), 65–70.

Bartha, Tibor, "A keresztyén szolgálatunk ekkléziológiai összefüggései" (The Ecclesiological Relationship of our Christian Service), *Theológiai Szemle (Theological Review)* 16:1–2 (1973), 7–12.

———, "Megtérés Krisztushoz és a felebaráthoz" (Conversion to Christ and to the Neighbor), in Tibor Bartha, *Ige, egyház, nép (Word, Church, People)* (Budapest: MRE Zsinati Iroda, 1972), 95–97.

———, "Zsinat elnöki székfoglaló. 1970. jan. 21" (Inauguration Speech as President of the Synod), *Református Egyház (Reformed Church)* 22:4 (1970), 74–76.

Békefi, Benő, "Diakóniánk, mint Jézus Krisztus diakóniájának része," *Református Egyház (Reformed Church)* 3:18 (1951), 4–6.

Bereczky, Albert, *A keskeny út (The Narrow Way)* (Budapest: 1953).

Bogárdi, István Szabó, *Egyházvezetés és teológia Magyarországi Református Egyházban 1948–1989 (Church Leadership and Theology in the Reformed Church of Hungary 1948–1989)* (Debrecen: DRTA, 1995).

Bozóki, András; András Körösényi & George Schöpflin (eds.), *Transition: Emerging Pluralism in Hungary* (New York: St. Martin's Press, 1992).

Calvin, John, *Institutes of the Christian Religion*, trans. Henry Beveridge (London: James Clarke, 1949).

Fabiny, Tibor, "Theologies of Church Government in the Hungarian Lutheran Church during Communism (1945–1990)," *Religion in Eastern Europe* 24:4 (2004), 11–29.

Fodor, Pál, "A törökök magyar szemmel" (The Turks through the Eyes of Hungarians), *Magyar Tudomány*, 4 (2011).

Forrester, Duncan B., "The Scope of Public Theology," *Studies in Christian Ethics* 17:2 (2004), 5–19.

Füsti-Molnár, Szilveszter, *Ecclesia sine Macula et Ruga: Donatist Factors among the Ecclesiological Challenges for the Reformed Church of Hungary Especially after 1989/90* (Sárospatak: Sárospataki Református Teológiai Akadémia, 2008).

Gaál, Sándor, *Kezdeményező egyház (The Initiative Church)* (Debrecen: DRTA, 2006).

Gonda, László, *The Service of Evangelism, the Evangelism of Service* (Utrecht: University Press, 2008).

Gyarmati, György & Tibor Valuch (eds.), *Hungary under Soviet Domination 1944–1989* (New York: Columbia University Press, 2009).

János, Győri L., *A magyar reformáció irodalmi hagyományai (The Literary Traditions of the Hungarian Reformation)* (Budapest: MRE, 1997).

Jánosi, Zoltán, "Kálvinizmus és demokráczia I." (Calvinism and Democracy I), *Lelkészegyesület (Pastor's Association)*, 4:52–53 (1911), 2–3, 21–23.

Kenessey, Béla, "Dr. Kenessey Béla éves püspöki jelentése" (Bishop Dr Béla Kenessey's Annual Report), *Református Szemle (Reformed Review)*, 4:22 (1911), 339–342.

Koestler, Arthur, *Darkness at Noon* (London: Cape, 1940).

Koncz, Sándor, *Hit és vallás: A magyar vallástudományi teológia kibontakozása és hanyatlása (Faith and Religion: The Rise and Demise of Hungarian Liberal Theology)* (Debrecen: Csuka Nyomda, 1942).

Kool, Anne-Marie, *God moves in Mysterious Ways: The Hungarian Protestant Foreign Mission Movement 1756–1951* (Zoetermeer: Boekencentrum, 1993).

Kósa, László, "Az állambiztonsági szervezet hálózata a református egyházban a diktatúra idején" (The Network of the State Security Association in the Reformed Church during the Dictatorship), *Théma* 12:1–2 (2010), 1–45.

Kovács, Ábrahám, *A Jó Pásztor bizottság története (Good Shepherd Committee)* (Debrecen: DRTA, 1997).

———, *The History of the Free Church of Scotland's Mission to the Jews in Budapest and its Impact on the Reformed Church of Hungary 1841–1914* (Wien: Peter Lang, 2006).

Kövér, György, *Iparosodás agrárországban: Magyarország gazdaságtörténete 1848–1914 (Industrialization in an Agrarian Country: A History of Economics of Hungary 1848–1914)* (Budapest: Gondolat Kiadó, 1982).

Lendvai, Paul, *Hungary between Democracy and Authoritarianism*, trans. Keith Chester (London: Hurst & Co, 2012).

Magyari, István, *Az országokban való sok romlásoknak okairól (About the Many Reasons of Destruction)* (Budapest: Európa kiadó, 1979).

Magyarország története 1848–1890 (History of Hungary 1848–1890) (Főszerk.: Endre Kovács. Szerk.: Katus László.) 1–2. rész. (Budapest: Akadémiai Kiadó, 1979), 1760.

Marx, Karl, "Critique of Hegel's Philosophy of Right," in *Karl Marx and Friedrich Engels on Religion* (New York: Schocken Books, 1964), 41–58.

———, "Critique of the Gotha Program," in Robert C. Tucker (ed.), *The Marx-Engels Reader* (New York: W.W. Norton 1978), 525–541.

Mason, John W., *The Dissolution of the Austro-Hungarian Empire, 1867–1918* (London: Longman, 1985).

Molnár, Attila, "A vallásos világnézet elleni harcról. Az MSZMP Politikai Bizottsága 1958. július s 22-i határozata" (About the Battle against the Religious Worldview: The Decree of the Political Committee of Hungarian Socialist Work Party), *Protestáns Szemle (Protestant Review)* 1 (1994), 44–66.

Murdock, Graeme, *Calvinism on the Frontier 1600–1660: International Calvinism and the Reformed Church in Hungary and Transylvania* (Oxford: Clarendon, 2000).

Pásztori-Kupán, István, "Hallgatni: arany-e vagy cinkosság? Karl Barthnak az 1956-os magyar szabadságharc kapcsán tanúsított „hallgatása" Reinhold Niebuhr értelmezésében" (To Be Silent Is To Be Wise or To Become a Pander? Karl Barth's Attitude of Silence in Relation to the Hungarian Revolution in the Interpretation of Reinhold Niebuhr), *Református Szemle (Reformed Review)* 1 (2009), 103–125.

———, "The Spirit of Religious Tolerance: A Transylvanian 'extra calvinisticum?'" in Ábrahám Kovács & Béla Baráth (eds.), *Calvinism on the Peripheries: Religion and Civil Society in Europe* (Budapest: L'Harmattan, 2009), 155–179.

Reuss, András, "Vitázva a társadalommal és egymással. A keresztyének és a politika" (Debating with Society and Each Other), *Credo* 7 (2002), 93–105.

Romsic, Ignác, *The Dismantling of Historic Hungary: The Peace Treaty of Trianon, 1920*, trans. Mario D. Fenyo (Boulder: Wayne, 2002).

Sándor, Czeglédy, *A választott nép (The Chosen People)* (Budapest: MRE, 1940).

Schlett, István, *A szociáldemokrácia és a magyar társadalom 1914-ig (Social Democracy and Hungarian Society until 1914)* (Budapest: Gondolat Kiadó, 1982).

Schlossberg, Herbert, *A Fragrance of Oppression: The Church and its Persecutors* (Wheaton: Crossway, 1991).

Sebestyén, Jenő, *Kálvin és a demokrácia (Calvin and Democracy)* (Budapest: MRE, 1912).

Seth, Ronald, *For My Name's Sake: A Brief Account of the Struggle of the Roman Catholic Church against the Nazis in Western Europe and against Communist Persecution in Eastern Europe* (London: Bles, 1958).

Smith, John E., *Quasi-Religions: Humanism, Marxism and Nationalism* (Basingstoke: Macmillan, 1994).

Szkhárosi Horváth, András, *A török Isten csapása: A református és a zsidó magyar párhuzam (The Turks are God's Punishment: The Reformed and Jewish Hungarian Parallel)* (Budapest: Magyar Helikon).

Taylor, Alan John P., *The Habsburg Monarchy, 1809–1918: A History of the Austrian Empire and Austria-Hungary* (Harmondsworth: Penguin, 1981).

Török, István, *Keresztyénségünk a szocializmus történelmi korszakában (Our Christian Life during the Historical Time of Socialism)*, unpublished manuscript.

Tóth, Károly, "A Zsinati Tanács nyilatkozata az Egyezmény 30. évfordulójára. 1978. dec. 1" (A Declaration of the Council of the Synod on the Occasion of the Agreement's Thirtieth Anniversary), *Református Egyház (Reformed Church)*, 30:12 (1978), 268–269.

Victor, János, "Kívülről befelé is munkálkodó kegyelem" (The Grace which Works from the Inside towards the Outside), *Református Egyház (Reformed Church)*, 4:4 (1952), 1–3.

Vogelaar, Huub, "Ecumenical Relations in Hungary since 1990," *Exchange* 35 (2006), 398–422.

Zoványi, Jenő, *Magyar protestáns egyháztörténeti lexikon (Lexicon of Hungarian Protestant Church History)*, 3. jav. bővített kiadás. szerk Ladányi Sándor (Budapest: MRE Zsinati Iroda, 1977).

PART 2

Monotheism

∴

The Aniconic God in Isaiah 43:10 and the Contemporary Discourse on Monotheism[1]

Emanuel Gerrit Singgih

On Friday, September 18, 2011, after Friday prayers, hordes of people stormed out of the mosques to destroy four statues placed in a public space in the town of Purwakarta, West Java. They are statues of Semar, Bima, Gatutkaca and Yudisthira, well-known figures from the *wayang* stories, which are part of the popular culture of both the Javanese and the Sundanese people. The group named itself 'Masyarakat Peduli Purwakarta' (the Concerned Community of Purwakarta), and gave six reasons why they destroyed the statues: (1) the statues are of no utilitarian value; (2) they are an economic waste; (3) they are not relevant to the history of Purwakarta, as the figures are not heroes of the region; (4) they are detrimental to the values of Islam and *mushriq* (creatures are equated with the creator); (5) they are proof of political moves to lead people back to superstition, and (6) they are figures of illusion.[2]

I disagree with all six reasons and condemn the destruction of the statues of these popular folk figures. In the post-reformation era of Indonesia, similar incidents frequently occur. These phenomena seem to repeat what happened in Afghanistan during the reign of the Taliban, namely the destruction of ancient Buddhist statues from the Gandharan period. They also show some changes in the cultural and religious views of present-day Indonesians. Although the majority of the Indonesian people are Muslims and Christians, followers of monotheistic religions, until now they were tolerant of iconic expressions of faith within the respective communities. But recently there are militant groups that harbor aniconic attitudes and that do not tolerate statues, especially statues that are placed in public spaces. As can be seen from the six reasons above, they make a distinction between statues of the heroes of Indonesia, which can be found in every major city, and the statues of the *wayang* stories, which are inherited from Hindu religious mythology. This contemporary *beeldenstorm* (iconoclasm or image-breaking) is therefore an expression of violence against the symbolic existence of other religions that is contained

---

[1] I am grateful to my colleagues Robert Setio and Chang Yau Hoon, and my friends Ekaputra Tupamahu and Daniel Sihombing for reading an earlier draft.
[2] Dedy Riyadi, "Kisruh Patung Wayang di Purwakarta" (The storming of wayang-statues in Purwakarta), in http://regional.kompasiana.com/2011/09/19/kisruh-patung-wayang-di-purwakarta-396722.html.

in the people's cultural heritage. Many people regard the statues as cultural objects. They are not worshipped or even venerated. At most, the figures are regarded as exemplary figures, and many have patterned their lives according to the character of one of the figures. But that is not the view of these militant groups, which I think are convinced that a monotheistic religion such as Islam should not tolerate past heritages that contain elements of polytheistic religions.

This brings me to the theme of our subject, which relates to 'the law of God,' 'civilization' and 'monotheism.' I will look at it in the context of the Christians in Indonesia, especially those who come from the Calvinist tradition, which in the past was also known for its iconoclasm (hence the Dutch expression above). What makes people destroy statues? Do we agree with the ideology/theology of these Taliban-like radical groups? What are we to make of biblical references to statues as idols and the ban on graven images? What is the difference between *elohim* (God) and *elohim* (the gods)? How do we look at monotheism? Can we as Calvinists in Indonesia live our monotheistic faith without becoming iconoclasts? In this paper I will first look at a biblical passage, Is. 43:10. Then I will use the findings to evaluate the theological discourse concerning monotheism, which recently has been revived by the books of Jan Assmann, the German Egyptologist,[3] and which includes discussions on whether the concepts of deity are translatable or not.[4] Finally I shall present my conclusions and return to the context of Indonesia.

"Before me no God was formed": Is. 43:10 in the Context of Is. 40–55

As is well known, Is. 40–55 forms a separate part in the book of Isaiah in the Old Testament, and its historical background is that of the Babylonian Exile (586–538 BCE). Its core goes to a poet-prophet, who produces verses of encouragement for the people of Israel exiled in Babylon, in the wake of the victories of Cyrus, the Persian conqueror. He had defeated many rulers, the latest of whom was the Lydian king, Croesos, and finally stood threateningly on the horizon of Babylon. The victories of Cyrus were interpreted as part of God's plan to liberate His people, and Cyrus was seen as God's Messiah (Is. 45:1). The

---

3 Jan Assmann, *Moses the Egyptian: The Memory of Egypt in Western Monotheism* (Cambridge/London: Harvard University Press, 1998, digitally reprinted); Jan Assmann, *The Price of Monotheism* (Stanford: Stanford University Press, 2010).
4 Mark S. Smith, *God in Translation: Deities in Cross-Cultural Discourse in the Biblical World* (Grand Rapids: Eerdmans, 2010).

poet-prophet (who is named 'Deutero-Isaiah' by the commentators) exhorts the Israelites to welcome this new event and prepare themselves for the homeward journey. The verses are full of references to creation theology, but also of references to God's incomparability and singleness. On the other hand, the gods are portrayed as being powerless and even non-existent. In the other parts of the Old Testament, the existence of other deities is not disputed; what matters is that an Israelite cannot worship any other than Yahweh, the God of Israel. But in Is. 40–55, there is only Yahweh as *the* God, all the others are nothing, they are images or idols, statues made of metal or wood. According to Wildberger, it is only in Isaiah 40–55 that we can refer with certainty to the idea of monotheism as the belief in one god and the denial of the existence of other gods.[5]

In Is. 40:19–20; 41:6–7; 42:17; 44:9–20; 45:16 and 46:1–2, 6–7, the gods are described as lifeless idols, and all of them, the idols and their makers and worshippers, are ridiculed. In the long passage of idol mockery in Is. 44:9–20 the idol worshippers are seen as stupid (Is. 44:18), because they use the same material (wood) for heating and cooking and for making their idols, whom later on they ask for help. Because the passage was (formerly) in prose (whereas almost all the verses in Is. 40–55 are poems), many commentators think that these idol passages are insertions from a later period.[6] But I doubt this. The existence of prose in poetic passages does not necessarily indicate different dates. In Is. 52:1–6 there is again prose in the middle of a poetic passage (vv. 3–6). The arguments of Yahweh's incomparability and singleness and the emphasis that only the God of Israel exists and there is no other[7] are well suited to the passages of idol mockery. Both can come from the same period.[8]

The context of Is. 43:10 is Is. 43:1–9 and Is. 43:11–28. In Is. 43:1–9, Yahweh is the Creator and the Redeemer of Israel. He guarantees that Israel shall survive the journey back home, as fire and water (common hazards faced by travelers) cannot prevail against them. Yahweh has redeemed Israel in exchange for three

---

5 Hans Wildberger, "Der Monotheismus Deuterojesajas," in Herbert Donner et al., *Beiträge zur Alttestamentlichen Theologie, Festschrift Walther Zimmerli* (Gottingen: Vandenhoeck & Ruprecht, 1977) 506–530. This Deutero-Isaianic monotheism concurs with similar understandings of monotheism in our contemporary world.
6 For instance, Claus Westermann, *Isaiah 40–66* (London: SCM Press, 1978) 146–152; Marie-Claire Barth, *Kitab Yesaya 40–55 (The book of Isaiah 40–55)* (Jakarta: BPK Gunung Mulia, 2003) 176 f.
7 See the Hebrew text of Is. 45:6, אֲנִי יְהוָה וְאֵין עוֹד, "I am Yahweh and there is no other!"
8 J. Muilenburg, "Isaiah 40–66," in *The Interpreter's Bible*, Vol. 5 (Nashville: Abingdon Press, 1978) 381–773; R.J. Clifford, who confirms Muilenburg, "The Function of Idol Passages in Deutero Isaiah," *The Catholic Bible Quarterly* 42 (1980) 450–464.

African countries (Egypt, Ethiopia and Seba). They may return to Jerusalem from the four corners of the world, as may their descendants, and it is precisely the descendants who are projected as a future creation, with many verbs of creation used (Is. 43:7, ברא, יצר, and עשה). Is. 43:8–13 is reminiscent of a judicial court-scene (Hebr: ריב), but with emphasis on the witnesses. On the one hand, the nations are implored to bring their witnesses, and on the other hand, the people of Israel are called to serve as witnesses of Yahweh. Is. 43:14–28 contains separate items: in Is. 43:14 there is an announcement that Yahweh the Single One is sending a Liberator to defeat the Babylonians and set the exiled Israelites free.

I adhere to the Hebrew text of Is. 43:14, although members of United Bible Society choose to follow the Vulgate rendering, which tries to relate Is. 43:14 to Is. 42:7. If we follow the Vulgate, then the Liberator is the Servant of Yahweh, but if we follow the Hebrew text, then the Liberator is Cyrus the Persian, who indeed conquered Babylon in 539 BCE. The victory of Cyrus is paralleled with the Exodus, where Yahweh makes a way through the sea, so that the people of Israel under Moses can escape Pharaoh and his army, who later are crushed under the waters. Surprisingly, the people are exhorted not to remember the past Exodus, because Yahweh is going to make something new and much better, namely roads in the wilderness and rivers in the desert, for the sake of Israel His people. Wild animals will praise Yahweh, and He will provide drinking-water for the journey. The text of Is. 43:10 emphasizes the people of Israel as Yahweh's witnesses, *who shall know and believe* in the constancy of Yahweh, that before this event of Israel's liberation, Yahweh is the Single One and after this, Yahweh is still the Single One. There is only one Savior (Hebr: מוֹשִׁיעַ) and the Savior is not a strange or alien (Hebr: זָר) god. It is a matter of knowing and believing in a future event, or especially a future understanding of God.

From the examination of both the passage and the text we can conclude that the context of Is. 43:10 is about the single existence of Yahweh as God and the non-existence of formed gods. The English translation I use at the head of this section is taken from NRSV (the complete text: "Before me no god was formed, nor shall there be any after me"). The Hebrew text is as follows, לְפָנַי לֹא־נוֹצַר אֵל וְאַחֲרַי לֹא יִהְיֶה. The Indonesian Bible (TB-LAI), "Sebelum Aku tidak ada Allah dibentuk, dan sesudah Aku tidak akan ada lagi" (Before Me no God was formed, and after Me there shall be none). Other renderings could be consulted, but what is the Hebrew text implying? There are two possibilities: first, Yahweh the God of Israel is unformed and second, before Yahweh, there are no formed gods, and after Him there shall be no other formed gods. Formed gods are not gods! That, I think, is the general meaning of the text.

Jan Assmann and the "Mosaic Distinction"

Jan Assmann has recently attempted an explanation of the development of monotheism in religion. His book *Moses the Egyptian* starts with an elaboration of the concept of "Mosaic distinction," which is about the distinction between true and false in religion.[9] Although tradition ascribes it to Moses, we cannot be sure that Moses ever lived because there are no traces of his existence outside tradition. But we can be sure that Moses was not the first to draw the distinction. In the fourteenth century BCE, king Akhenaten (Amenophis IV) of Egypt introduced a monotheistic religion. However, Akhenaten did not live on in the traditions of Egypt, as all that he introduced was wiped from Egypt's memory. Even his name does not appear in the Egyptian king list. It was only after archaeological excavations in the nineteenth century revealed his existence that people came to know about Akhenaten.[10] Assmann provides an interesting comparison of Moses and Akhenaten. While Moses is a figure of memory but not of history, Akhenaten is a figure of history but not of memory. Since memory is all that counts in the sphere of cultural distinctions and constructions, we are justified in speaking not of 'Akhenaten's distinction' but of the 'Mosaic distinction.'[11] It is therefore not just history as such which is important, even more important is how a certain community remembers its past. Assmann refers to this as 'mnemohistory.'[12]

What is the cause of Akhenaten's disappearance from Egypt's history? According to Assmann, the sudden and drastic introduction of Akhenaten's monotheism has the character of a revolution, and this revolution caused many traumatic experiences. Before the reign of Akhenaten, Egypt belonged to the world of polytheism, where the gods fulfill a cosmic function. Although the names may differ per religion, their function is the same: the sun god of one religion can be easily equated with the sun god of another religion. Because they have identical functions, the name of the gods can be translated. "The cultures, languages and customs may have been different as ever: the religions always had a common ground. Thus they functioned as a means of intercultural translatability."[13] For this reason, even when people worship their own gods, the reality of foreign gods and the legitimacy of foreign forms of worship are not rejected. Polytheism is a great achievement, as it allows for the articula-

---

9   Assmann, *Moses*, 2.
10 Assmann, *Moses*, 23.
11 Assmann, *Moses*, 2.
12 Assmann, *Moses*, 8–15.
13 Assmann, *Moses*, 3.

tion of a common semantic universe. It is this semantic dimension that makes the names translatable.[14] However, Akhenaten's religion is a new type of religion, which rejects and repudiates everything that went before as "paganism." It is a "counter-religion" and functions as a means of intercultural estrangement rather than as a means of intercultural translation. It blocks intercultural translatability. Pagan or false gods cannot be translated.[15] As we have seen in Deutero-Isaiah, to proclaim the singleness of a deity is to deny the plurality of the gods.

Akhenaten's monotheistic revolution came as a shock to the people of Egypt. Temples were closed, images of the gods were destroyed, their names were erased and their cults were discontinued. If no ritual is performed and festival celebrated, then for the people, there is no guarantee that the cosmic and social order will be maintained. For them, the new religion is catastrophic and criminal. To this experience is added another tribulation in the form of a plague from Asia that swept over the entire Near East and probably Egypt as well and raged for twenty years. It was these two phenomena, the experience of facing a violent counter-religion and the experience of a plague, that formed a collective traumatic memory. An example of this can be seen in a later memorial such as Tutankhamun's "Restoration Stela."[16] These traumatic experiences caused people to restore the old religion when Akhenaten died after a seventeen-year reign, and to erase anything related to Akhenaten.

Traumatic experiences are suppressed, but surface again in different, *inverted* forms. Assmann examines Greek and Latin literature concerning Egypt and is successful in detecting possible traces of "Amarna experience" left within the Egyptian tradition. This includes Manetho's *Aigyptiaka* from the first half of the third century BCE, Hecataeus of Abdera, who came to Egypt in about 320 BCE, Lysimachos from the second century BCE, Chaeremon from the first half of the first century BCE, Pompeius Trogus' *Historicae Phillipicae*, Artapanos, Tacitus, Apion and Strabo.[17] Space does not permit me to describe each instance here. I will therefore summarize Assmann's description of Manetho's *Aigyptiaka* as an example of 'mnemohistory.' The latter was an Egyptian priest who wrote his history of Egypt under Ptolemy II. We know about Manetho's history because it is referred to by Flavius Josephus in *Contra Apionem*. Josephus provides two excerpts from Manetho. The first he regards as proof of the antiquity of the Jewish people and therefore as true, and the second he regards

---

14   Assmann, *Moses*, 45.
15   Assmann, *Moses*, 3.
16   Assmann, *Moses*, 27.
17   Assmann, *Moses*, 29–39.

as an example of anti-Jewish calumny and therefore as false. The first is about the Hyksos people, who conquered Egypt for more than five hundred years, until they were driven out of their capital Avaris and settled down in what is now called Judaea.

Josephus's second excerpt from Manetho is about the lepers. The king of Egypt has banished all the lepers to the eastern desert. The lepers are allowed to settle down in Avaris, the former capital of the Hyksos people. They choose a priest, Osarsiph, as their leader. He makes a law for his people the lepers, following the principle of normative inversion, *prescribing all that is forbidden in Egypt and forbidding all that is prescribed there*. It has the characteristics of a counter-religion. The first and foremost commandment is not to worship the gods, not to spare any of their sacred animals, not to abstain from other forbidden food.[18] These references could be to the Jews, who came to Egypt as refugees in the sixth century and as Jewish mercenaries that settled in colonies like the one at Elephantine. But according to Assmann, we cannot rule out the possibility that they stem from an older experience—the "Amarna experience"— which gives way to the "Amarna complex."[19]

After establishing his counter-religion, Osarsiph invited the Hyksos to join them in their revolution against Egypt, and so the Hyksos people returned to Egypt. King Amenophis escaped to Ethiopia. The Hyksos and the lepers ruled Egypt for thirteen years. Osarsiph took the name 'Moses.' In the end, king Amenophis and his grandson Ramses returned and drove out the lepers and the Hyksos people. This is the story in which Akhenaten in the guise of 'Osarsiph' or 'Moses' re-enters the literary tradition of Egypt. The only reference with historical foundation is the reference to the Hyksos people, who came to Egypt from Asia in the seventeenth century BCE and ruled Egypt for a hundred years (and not for five hundred years as in Manetho's history). In Egypt, the experience of the Hyksos invasion and expulsion is reported in the official king list tradition. Assmann's thesis is that after the traumatic Amarna experience the Hyksos tradition received a semantic coloring, in which Hyksos people play the role of the "religious enemy," a role subsequently filled by the Assyrians, the Persians, the Greeks and finally the Jews.[20]

References to lepers involved considerations about purity and defilement. We are used to seeing these considerations from the point of view of those who loathe idolatry, the "iconoclasts." But Manetho's story reflects the loathing from

---

18 Assmann, *Moses*, 31.
19 Assmann, *Monotheism*, 66.
20 Assmann, *Moses*, 41. Through the Greeks (Hellenistic Egypt) this stereotypical hatred of the Jews spread to Europe and became known as anti-Semitism (Assmann, *Moses*, 43 f).

the other side, the side of the "idolaters," the "iconists" (or better, "iconodulists," EGS). For them, destroying the images caused deadly pollution or defilement, and can be compared to leprosy or the plague.[21] Assmann's merit is to remind experts from the Jewish and Christian traditions to try—once in a while—a change in their perspective, to move from the side of the Israelites to the side of the Egyptians. Although his first book is about Moses (alias Akhenaten) the Egyptian, his "thesis problem" is: "how the Jew came to attract this undying hatred."[22]

In the other chapters Assmann embarks on a brilliant journey across the centuries to see the development of 'mnemohistory' in the form of "encrypted" traumatic experience. He discusses John Spencer the Egyptologist, the Moses discourse in the eighteenth century and Sigmund Freud, the author of *Moses and Monotheism*. In themselves, these chapters are fascinating to read. But the first and the second chapters of Assmann's first book best serve our purpose. There Assmann tries to construct a theory of the rise of monotheism as a counter-religion in the Ancient Near East. As a counter-religion it breaks radically with all that went before. Because of his profession as an Egyptologist, it is not surprising that his frame of reference is Akhenaten. But influenced by his reading of the texts mentioned above, especially by Freud, Assmann identifies Akhenaten with Moses, and "Akhenaten's distinction" becomes the "Mosaic distinction." Then of course he has to prove that there is such an understanding in the Hebrew Bible. In his first book he assumes rather than argues the existence of the "Mosaic distinction" in the Hebrew Bible and Ancient Israel. It is on account of this view (and its corollary that monotheism is a violent belief) that Assmann is attacked by many critics, including two German Old Testament scholars (Rolf Rendtorff and Klaus Koch). It is time to evaluate Assmann's findings.

Divine Translatability and Untranslatability

We have seen that Assmann describes the gods of the polytheistic world as having the same function and their names as being translatable. But the rise of monotheism makes it impossible to continue the practice of translation. The world, especially the world of the gods, is no longer an oecumene. Mark Smith has devoted a whole book to this problem.[23] Smith does not state that his book

---

21 Assmann, *Moses*, 42 f.
22 Assmann, *Moses*, 5.
23 Smith, *God*.

is a reply to Assmann, but he discusses Assmann right at the beginning (where he examines both *Moses the Egyptian* and *The Price of Monotheism*), sets aside a special section for Assmann in chapter V, and appraises Assmann again in the epilogue, where Smith explains that each chapter of his book alludes to certain aspects in Assmann's book.

Smith's goal is to counter Assmann's "Mosaic distinction" by showing that both the notion of translatability and the notion of untranslatability exist in Ancient Israel. The term is therefore not rejected outright, but modified. Smith marshals many passages with admirably detailed arguments to prove that there is translatability in Ancient Israel: the Balaam poem in Num. 23–24, which portrays El, Elyon and Shadday as independent beings (following Levine); Gen. 31:43–53, especially Gen. 31:53, "May the god of Abraham and the god of Nahor adjudicate between us" (Smith's translation); Judg. 3:20, where Ehud informs the obese king Eglon that he has a divine message for him. The phrase דְּבַר־אֱלֹהִים לִי אֵלֶיךָ literally means "I have a divine word (or matter)/word of God for you." The use of *elohim* suggests that the term of divinity is shared by Israel and Moab and was operative in the worldview of the author(s) during the monarchy.[24] Indeed, in Smith's book, the evidence for translatability is located in monarchic Israel.

The same evidence can be seen in Judg. 7:12–15, where Gideon overheard someone in the enemy camp telling another about the dream that he had, a dream favorable to Gideon. This passage represents an Israelite view that a non-Israelite could have an authentic dream involving the Israelite deity, and that a second non-Israelite could properly interpret the dream as such. Also, the term *elohim* is used by the foreigner in verse 14 and the fact that it is understood by Gideon shows that they have a shared discourse about divinity. In Judg. 11:23–24 both Yahweh and Chemosh are mentioned in the context of international relations. Smith quotes Burney: "The speaker assumes just as real an *existence* for Chemosh as for Yahweh."[25] In 1 Kgs. 20, an Israelite author could represent Arameans as recognizing the Israelite god in his capacity as a divine warrior, and in 2 Kgs. 1, the Israelites are represented as discussing the relative ability of the Philistine and Israelite gods to provide a divine word. Here translatability is an implicit assumption made by both parties in their dispute. Finally, 2 Kgs. 3 refers to implicit recognition of the Moabite national god by Israel.[26]

---

24 Smith, *God*, 96–108.
25 C.F. Burney, *The Book of Judges: With Introduction and Notes* (London: Rivingtons, 1918), 314 f.
26 Smith, *God*, 109–118.

On the other hand, Smith also offers evidence for the rejection of translatability in Ancient Israel. He presents a very detailed exegesis of Ps. 82, where all the *elohim* are indicted by *Elohim*, the God of Israel. In Deut. 32, Yahweh is identified with Elyon, and in Deut.6:4, the application of אֶחָד (one) to Yahweh implies that Yahweh is for Israel the one god deserving and requiring Israel's covenantal obedience and allegiance. These passages acknowledge but at the same time reject the older worldview in which each nation is headed by its own god. Here Smith agrees with Assmann. Still, Smith holds that the rejection of translatability is not a fundamental, original feature of Israel.[27] In both Israel and Mesopotamia, reference to one god does not necessarily imply monotheism. Smith, following Machinist and Greenstein, proposes the term "one god" theism, which is similar to the term "henotheism" (Max Müller) or "summodeism" (Eric Voegelin). Even Deutero-Isaiah, which is markedly polemical against the Mesopotamian gods, does not place much importance on the name of Yahweh itself, but still refers to El (El is not Mesopotamian but Canaanite, EGS). It is only later, in the post-exilic period and beyond, that the very name of Yahweh comes to assume a particular religious importance as the one and the only name. Thus divinity ends generally in non-translatability in Ancient Israel.[28]

Assmann's Reply to his Critics in his Second Book

I dwell on Smith at some length, as he offers convincing evidence that Assmann's claim of the existence of a "Mosaic distinction" in Ancient Israel is hasty and overstated. But before I come to my conclusions, to be fair to Assmann, we have to look at his reply to his critics in his second book, *The Price of Monotheism*, which is ignored in Smith's *God in Translation*.[29] In *The Price of Monotheism,* Assmann acknowledges that his (former) reading of Freud is wrong. Far from being a regression from intellectuality, monotheism is a progression towards intellectuality.[30] Although Assmann acknowledges in his second book that he had misread Freud in his first book, Smith still accuses him of

---

27 Smith, *God*, 131–147.
28 Smith, *God*, 157–178.
29 Smith, *God*, 23–29. On the other hand, in *The Price of Monotheism*, Assmann never refers to Smith's book, which is strange, since *God in Translation* was first published in 2008 by Mohr & Siebeck in Tübingen.
30 Assmann, *Monotheism*, 85 f.

misusing Freud.[31] Assmann also replies to criticisms that he construed violence as being inherent in monotheism. The idea that monotheism is inherently violent does not of course originate with Assmann. Among others, two feminists, Regina Schwartz and Kune Biezeveld, share the same idea.[32] Smith reports that this view of Assmann evoked a vigorous response from Cardinal Joseph Ratzinger (now the retired Pope), who states that polytheistic religions are no less violent. "The gods were by no means always peaceful and interchangeable. They were just often, indeed more often, the reason for people using violence against each other."[33] For Smith, both Assmann and Ratzinger are wrong, because in the history of the Ancient Near East, violence is not inherent in either monotheism or polytheism. "It is not a function of the form of theism, whether polytheism or monotheism; it is a function of power and the capacity to wield it."[34] This sounds like an attempt to cut the Gordian knot.

Assmann, however, has a more nuanced view than his critics suggest. He is not stating that polytheism is less violent than monotheism. The "Mosaic distinction" is not a permanent process in the history of Ancient Israel from the beginning to the end, but happens momentarily. Or, to use his poetic formulation, "The Mosaic distinction is the melody sung by a particular voice, not the refrain of a permanently established religion."[35] It is not a historical shift, but an event or a moment. The Bible reports several "monotheistic moments," which subsequently relapsed into polytheistic or syncretistic practice.[36] Here the "Mosaic distinction" shared the fate of Akhenaten's distinction, which rose like a meteor, only to disappear in the black of the night. The difference is that the first has its moments of resurgence. As a counter-religion, monotheism in Israel is therefore unable to erase polytheism, which Assmann regards positively as "cosmotheism." In the Hebrew Bible they exist side by side, in opposition to one another. Cosmotheism can be seen in the Priestly tradition, and monotheism can be seen in the Deuteronomic tradition.[37]

---

31   Smith, *God*, 25, especially fn 28.
32   Regina M. Schwartz, *The Curse of Cain: The Violent Legacy of Monotheism* (Chicago and London: The University of Chicago Press, 1997); Kune Biezeveld, "The One and Only God: Revaluating the Process of Violence and Exclusion," in Dirk van Keulen and Martien Brinkman (eds.), *Christian Faith and Violence*, Vol. 1 (Zoetermeer: Meinema, 2005), 47–68.
33   Smith, *God*, 26; Joseph Ratzinger, *Truth and Tolerance: Christian Belief and World Religions* (San Francisco: Ignatius, 2004), 219.
34   Smith, *God*, 28.
35   Assmann, *Monotheism*, 34.
36   Assmann, *Monotheism*, 32 f.
37   Assmann, *Monotheism*, 8 f. The recent trend in Old Testament studies on sources is to refer only to "P-Komposition" (KP) and "D-Komposition" (KD), instead of to J, E, P and D

According to Assmann, 'violence' in the context of monotheism is more a matter of the weight of incompatibility than of violence in a concrete sense. To explain this, Assmann looks for a parallel in the history of science, in Parmenides' distinction between "wild thought" and "logical thought." From its beginning, science has been based on the distinction between true and false cognition. Scientific knowledge is "counter-knowledge" because it knows what is incompatible with its propositions. The Parmenidean distinction between true and false has the potential for negation, and that is why, according to Assmann, scientific knowledge is "intolerant."[38] But we need this intolerance, if science is to progress. The same applies *mutatis mutandis* to monotheism in religion. Assmann believes to have discovered in Egypt the repressed and forgotten side of monotheism, *the dark side of monotheism*, which has remained present in the cultural memory of the West.[39] He urges his readers to be aware of this dark side. He is not rejecting monotheism because it is violent, or advocating a return to polytheism because it is non-violent.

But what about the *beeldenstorm* in the town of Purwakarta? Of course in this case it is the statues that are attacked and not the worshippers. Still, it gives us images of a truly violent counter-religion, and sometimes the worshippers are also attacked if they try to protect the statues. According to Assmann, this is the result of conflicting worldviews. For this explanation we have to look to Assmann's concept of cosmotheism. In Ancient Egypt, the gods are not set in opposition to the world made up of the cosmos, humankind and society, but endow them with meaning as a structuring and ordering principle. The gods encompass both cosmos and society. That is why every city and settlement has its own gods. Polytheism is actually cosmotheism.[40] The divine cannot be separated from the world. Monotheism is a violent effort to separate the world from the gods. Assmann borrows Max Weber's definition of secularization to describe monotheism as a similar project of "disenchantment of the world."[41] The ban on graven images is to be seen in the light of this project. Graven images are intended to establish contact between humankind and the gods, or they are symbols of the gods. Even more, depicting the gods is considered an act of worship. "One should avoid depicting things of this world lest one fell into the trap of worshipping them. That is why humankind ought to rule the

---

from the old Documentary hypothesis, see Erhard Blum, *Studien zur Komposition des Pentateuch*, BZAW 189 (Berlin: de Gruyter, 1990).

38   Assmann, *Monotheism*, 12 f.
39   Assmann, *Monotheism*, 119 f.
40   Assmann, *Monotheism*, 40 f.
41   Assmann, *Monotheism*, 102. Or is it "disenchantment of nature"? (EGS)

world: not in order that it may be exploited, but to resist turning it into an object of veneration."[42] This view reminds me of Gerhard von Rad, who, despite his agreement that no theological or pedagogic reasons can be found behind the ban on graven images, insists that its background is one of conflicting worldviews.[43] The rejection of graven images is therefore also an act to prevent humankind from worshipping the world.

In trying to understand this Weberian argument, one cannot escape the feeling that it involves a change of perspective, which could confuse the reader. Is Assmann here still looking at the problem from the perspective of the Egyptians, or has he shifted to the side of the Israelites? I suspect that the corrected view about Freud, in which monotheism is an achievement and not a failure, persuades Assmann to modify his stance in his second book. Although he explains the reason for the ban on graven images as the result of conflicting worldviews, it is still not clear in what ways they conflict. If it is because of creation theology, then precisely creation theology can be said to be operative in cosmotheism. Robert Carroll has examined several reasons for the ban on images, and deems them unsatisfactory.[44] Assmann might arrive at a better explanation if he takes into consideration the findings of researchers into Asian iconic *living* religions like Wilfred Cantwell Smith, who states that while these religions highly regard their icons, they are aware that the icons are not the gods. Even in a polytheistic milieu, one finds tributes to God such as "Thou art formless. Thy only form is our knowledge of thee."[45]

Conclusions

First, both Assmann's first and second book are helpful in enlightening the reader on the subject of 'mnemohistory' or psychohistory. Here I agree with my fellow Indonesian, Ekaputra Tupamahu, who observed that Assmann approaches history as a way of digging into the collective memory of the people

---

42 Assmann, *Monotheism*, 69.
43 Gerhard von Rad, *Old Testament Theology*, Vol. 1 (London: SCM Press, 1977), 217 f. I might be wrong, since in the impressive list of literature on biblical ban on images in Assmann's second book (*Monotheism*, 131), von Rad's name does not appear.
44 Robert Carroll, "The Aniconic God and the Cult of Images," *Studia Theologica* 31 (1977) 51–64. The reasons are a belief in Yahweh's invisibility, the prohibition against the vain use of Yahweh's name, the nature of God who appeared to Moses in the burning bush as a presence, and the belief that insofar as there is an image of God in the world, it is man.
45 Wilfred Cantwell Smith, "Idolatry in Comparative Perspective," in John Hick and Paul Knitter (eds.), *The Myth of Christian Uniqueness* (London: SCM Press, 1988), 53–68.

in order to explain their current condition. Through this approach, Assmann contributes significantly to the study of monotheism.[46]

Second, Assmann's effort to prove the prevalence of the "Mosaic distinction" in Ancient Israel appears to be unsatisfactory, and so he modifies his view in his second book, claiming that the "Mosaic distinction" is a momentary movement, appearing from time to time on Israel's horizon. More important is his finding that this "Mosaic distinction" is not wholly identical with monotheism, as polytheism or cosmotheism is still operative in Israel. It is not that there is one god and no other, but "that alongside the True One God, there are only false gods, whom it is strictly forbidden to worship."[47] According to Assmann, it is different from and less radical than the case of Akhenaten, as it recognizes the existence of other gods. "Otherwise the requirement of loyalty would be meaningless. These other gods are not denied, they are expressly *forbidden*."[48]

Third, for Smith the existence of other gods in Israel is recognized until the end of the exilic era. Even statements on the incomparability and singleness of God and the nothingness of other gods in Deutero-Isaiah do not negate the existence of other gods. It is only during the post-exilic era that Israel comes to hold on to Yahweh's untranslatability. However, in my exegesis of Is. 43:10 within the context of Deutero-Isaiah, the existence of other gods is denied. Other parts of the Hebrew Bible may refer to henotheism or monolatry, but Deutero-Isaiah refers to monotheism pure and proper. Here I differ from both Assmann and Smith. Even when the gods are vehemently mocked as in Is. 44:9–20, their powers are still a subject of concern, as we can see in Is. 48:5.

Fourth, when we come to questions concerning the relationship between monotheism and polytheism, the existence of God and the gods, between the invisible gods and the visible gods (statues), we are facing a false problem. The same situation can be seen in philosophy, when people discuss "the One" and "the Many," or monism and pluralism.[49] Our job is to remove this false problem and squarely face the overlapping of the concepts in concrete everyday life avoiding any attempt to make a general theory out of this apparent "mess" (Robert Setio). It does not mean that we shun the problem. It is good that Assmann and Smith have renewed the discourse on monotheism, and of course we have to continue discussing it. But we always have to bear in mind the

---

46   Ekaputra Tupamahu, "Review of Jan Assmann, *The Price of Monotheism*," *Indonesian Journal of Theology* 1:2 (December 2013), see http://indonesiantheology.org.
47   Assmann, *Monotheism*, 34.
48   Assmann, *Monotheism*, 38.
49   Alfred C. Ewing, *The Fundamental Questions in Philosophy* (New York: Collier Books, 1962), 225 f.

warning of Robert Carroll (Robert Setio's teacher) that we are entering the realm of speculative thinking or speculative theology.[50]

Fifth, when we come to the context of Asia, where the iconic religions (Hinduism, Buddhism, the Chinese and primal/natural religions) are *living realities*, and especially in the context of Indonesia, Christians, in this case Calvinists, can continue to live their belief in a monotheistic God, but with modesty and moderation, and mindful of what Assmann says about the dark side of monotheism, which may unleash violent reactions to different views. They should dissociate themselves from the Taliban-like, radically aniconic Muslims with their *beeldenstorm* spirit, and side with both the moderate Muslims who form the majority in Indonesia and their fellow Christians, the Catholics, who are iconic and who, like Mark Smith at the end of his book, hold on to the idea of translatability.[51] Indonesian theological students who are studying the Bible should always be aware that biblical references concerning idols, idolatry, graven images and statues are not only about the ancient past, but also about their present neighbors, who try to practice their religion in public by appreciating their cultural iconic heritage. Theological teachers have to show respect for other people's faith and their cultural iconic heritage (which is also *ours!*) when they are explaining biblical texts that refer to idolatry. Only then can we contribute to a better future for religious communities in Indonesia.

Bibliography

Assmann, Jan, *Moses the Egyptian: The Memory of Egypt in Western Monotheism* (Cambridge/London: Harvard University Press, 1998, digitally reprinted).

———, *The Price of Monotheism* (Stanford: Stanford University Press, 2010).

Barth, Marie-Claire, *Kitab Yesaya 40–55 (The book of Isaiah 40–55)* (Jakarta: BPK Gunung Mulia, 2003).

Biezeveld, Kune, "The One and Only God: Revaluating the Process of Violence and Exclusion," in Dirk van Keulen and Martien Brinkman (eds.), *Christian Faith and Violence*, Vol. 1 (Zoetermeer: Meinema, 2005), 47–68.

Blum, Erhard, *Studien zur Komposition des Pentateuch*, BZAW 189 (Berlin: de Gruyter, 1990).

Burney, C.F., *The Book of Judges: With Introduction and Notes* (London: Rivingtons, 1918).

Carroll, Robert, "The Aniconic God and the Cult of Images," *Studia Theologica* 31 (1977) 51–64.

---

[50] See Robert Carroll, "The Aniconic God and the Cult of Images," 64.
[51] Smith, *God*, 340.

Clifford, R.J., "The Function of Idol Passages in Deutero Isaiah," *The Catholic Bible Quarterly* 42 (1980) 450–464.

Ewing, Alfred C., *The Fundamental Questions in Philosophy* (New York: Collier Books, 1962).

Muilenburg, J., "Isaiah 40–66," in *The Interpreter's Bible*, Vol. 5 (Nashville: Abingdon Press, 1978) 381–773.

Rad, Gerhard von, *Old Testament Theology*, Vol. 1 (London: SCM Press, 1977).

Ratzinger, Joseph, *Truth and Tolerance: Christian Belief and World Religions* (San Francisco: Ignatius, 2004)

Riyadi, Dedy, "Kisruh Patung Wayang di Purwakarta" (The storming of wayang-statues in Purwakarta), in http://regional.kompasiana.com/2011/09/19/kisruh-patung-wayang-di-purwakarta-396722.html.

Schwartz, Regina M., *The Curse of Cain: The Violent Legacy of Monotheism* (Chicago and London: The University of Chicago Press, 1997).

Smith, Wilfred Cantwell, "Idolatry in Comparative Perspective," in John Hick and Paul Knitter (eds.), *The Myth of Christian Uniqueness* (London: SCM Press, 1988), 53–68.

Smith, Mark S., *God in Translation: Deities in Cross-Cultural Discourse in the Biblical World* (Grand Rapids: Eerdmans, 2010).

Tupamahu, Ekaputra, "Review of Jan Assmann, *The Price of Monotheism*," *Indonesian Journal of Theology* 1:2 (December 2013), see http://indonesiantheology.org.

Westermann, Claus, *Isaiah 40–66* (London: SCM Press, 1978).

Wildberger, Hans, "Der Monotheismus Deuterojesajas," in Herbert Donner et al., *Beiträge zur Alttestamentlichen Theologie, Festschrift Walther Zimmerli* (Gottingen: Vandenhoeck & Ruprecht, 1977) 506–530.

Is Christ Among Us?
Mystical Christology from the Perspective of Pseudo-Dionysius and Taoism

Jaeseung Cha

Regina M. Schwartz argues in her book, *The Curse of Cain: The Violent Legacy of Monotheism*, that monotheism stands for a collective identity and that biblical narratives have become the foundation of a prevailing understanding of collective identity over against *others*.[1] Although Christianity is closer to a Trinitarian monotheism or multiform monotheism and Schwartz's definition of violence is broad,[2] the critical view that a Christian understanding of the monotheistic God could be the very source of human violence is painfully realistic. In this article I will articulate an essential aspect of Christianity by discussing Christology on the basis of two presupposed and paradoxical claims: (1) Christ's incarnation is the heart of Christian mystery that gives space for *others*; and (2) Christ's incarnation is the concrete reality of the God-man, in his humanity as well as in his divinity, who remains in, shares, and bears human suffering from violence.

Critical concerns that the monotheistic God is violent and even a threat to human civilization need to be nuanced by mystic and apophatic traditions that have been at least part, if not the majority, of the Christian understanding of God. God is hidden, not fully revealed, and humans are therefore limited in comprehending the relation of God with God's own creatures, as the author of Isaiah states: "For my thoughts are not your thoughts, nor are your ways my ways, says the LORD. For as the heavens are higher than the earth, so are my ways higher than your ways and my thoughts than your thoughts."[3] This mystic aspect of God gives others space beyond the exclusive paradigm of monotheism.[4]

---

1 Regina M. Schwartz, *The Curse of Cain: The Violent Legacy of Monotheism* (Chicago: The University of Chicago, 1997), x.
2 "This book argues that acts of identity formation are themselves acts of violence" (Schwartz, *Curse*, 5).
3 Is. 55:8–9 (NSRV).
4 On the other hand, mysticism can be a challenge to human civilization in different ways. If the divine is ontologically too distant for humans to approach (absolute mysticism), the divine may be free from human violence, but a deistic remoteness or a Kabalistic contraction would provoke questions of how the divine being actively engages in this violent world. If humans

Furthermore, Christian mysticism is centered in the mystery of Christ, who lived in a historical setting and is at the same time ontologically and epistemologically beyond any human criterion. That the Christian God in Christ is both transcendent and immanent suggests a third way between a violently monotheistic god and a mystically apophatic god. God is revealed in Christ, who demonstrates a unique way of dealing with human violence and suffering. In order to understand this unique nature of Christianity, this article will deal with mystical Christology from the perspective of Pseudo-Dionysius and Taoism. Comparing Dionysius' view of Christ's incarnation with Taoist in-naturation (the Tao's presence in nature) is intriguing in that we can find surprising similarities between them in the mysticism of the impersonal essence of God (Tao), incarnation (in-naturation), and procession and return (Tao's in-naturation and return to itself). They share problems too: an advanced theology of how Christ's incarnation (Tao's in-naturation) works for human existential realities is all but absent in both.

However, the view that even different mysticisms share commonalities confronts us with a critical question: "Is there a common core mystical experience or not?"[5] Christian scholars with an awareness of the plurality of religions are beginning to see that different religions share some commonalities in mysticism.[6] Perennialists have attempted to identify common mystical experience

---

    can be fully united with the divine (complete mysticism), a cosmic and ontological gap between the human and the divine disappears and only a few mystics can be free from human violence; this view can be found in Taoism. Or, if mysticism suggests that humans are absolutely unable to comprehend the divine (apophatic mysticism), there is no way for humans to follow the divine. Mysticism in its varieties may save God from violence but may not save this violent world and humans with whom God is engaged. Bernard McGinn summarizes Almond's five views of mysticism and its interpretation: (1) all mystical experience is the same; (2) mystical experience is always the same but the interpretations of it vary according to the religious and philosophical frameworks employed; (3) a certain type of mysticism transcends religious barriers; (4) in mysticism there are paradigmatic expressions which refer to the central focus, aim, or nature of the experience, and (5) mystical experiences are as diverse as incorporated interpretations of it (*The Foundations of Mysticism* (New York: Crossroad, 1991), 321). The focus of this typology is on the relationship between mysticism and its interpretation. The distinctions between different types of mysticism this article mentions are based more on the ontological and epistemological relations of humans to the divine.

5 Ekman P.C. Tam, "Another Look at the Theory of a Common Core Mysticism," *Dialogue and Alliance* 11:2 (1997), 31.
6 Tam, "Another Look," 32.

across cultures and traditions.[7] It is paradoxical that mysticisms share commonalities in their core values. On the one hand, it may give an ecumenical zeal for dialogues with people of other religious traditions. Similarities between Dionysius' Christology and Taoism surpass the simple expectation that mystical *experiences* can be common in their attributes: their essential core values and perspectives can be shared.[8] On the other hand, it is contradictory to the nature of mysticism that they share similarities even in their core values; those shared values are no longer mystical. The suspicion is that human imagination and projection, not the divine and mystical beings, are the origin of mysticism. God in Christ, however, is uniquely mystical not only in the sense that Christ's incarnation is beyond—and thus never consumed—by human mind but also in the sense that the incarnated Christ mystically remains among us, shares human suffering, and bears human violence in his life, death and resurrection.

In what follows, I will explore Dionysian mysticism focusing on Christ's person and work. Four points will be discussed, namely, Dionysius' philosophized view of the mystical God, his accent on Christ's divine nature, his use of the word "theandric," and his theology of Christ's crucifixion. Then, I will move on to discussing Taoism as having much to commend itself to Christological reflection with reference to the Tao's in-naturation and the divinization of humans in their return to the Tao. In conclusion, I will discuss the values of incarnational mysticism in Christ's sharing and bearing.[9] The contrast between them will enlighten for us the deeper mystery of Christ, who constantly challenges the human ideology and philosophy of a violently monotheistic god as well as a mystically apophatic god.

Dionysian Mysticism and Christ's Incarnation

In the writings of Pseudo-Dionysius, God is transcendent, mystical, and apophatic. The nature of God is beyond all intellect and all being and all

---

7 Jerome Gellman, "Mysticism," in Edward N. Zalta (ed.), *The Stanford Encyclopedia of Philosophy*, http://plato.stanford.edu/archives/sum2011/entries/mysticism (summer 2011).
8 "In other words, the mystics' experiences before any form of expressions are universal; only the overt written expressions of the mystics' experiences appear to be theologically or doctrinally different from one to the other" (Tam, "Another Look," 32).
9 Paul Rorem enumerates three different types of negative theology—progress, complete, and incarnational—and classifies Dionysius' theology as complete and Luther's theology as incarnational (Paul Rorem, "Negative Theology and the Cross," *Lutheran Quarterly* 23 (2009), 314–331).

knowledge,[10] and thus there are no words or concepts to express this hidden, transcendent God.[11] God is the nameless One, the wonderful name, which is above every name and is therefore without a name.[12] God is also one, one source or cause, not so much in the sense of a single being as in the sense of supernatural simplicity and indivisible unity.[13] More philosophically speaking, God is not a being but the essence of beings:

> God is not some kind of being. No. But in a way that is simple and indefinable he gathers into himself and anticipates every existence. So he is called, "King of the ages," for in him and around him all being is and subsists. He was not. He will not be. He did not come to be. He is not in the midst of becoming. He will not come to be. No. He is not. Rather, he is the essence of being for the things which have being.[14]

The author of *The Divine Names* unfolds his purpose for writing this part not as revealing the transcendent being but as singing a hymn of praise for the being-making procession of the absolute divine Source.[15] Thus, we should not press this philosophized part too far for a generalized Dionysian view of God. Still, it cannot be denied that God in Dionysius has a philosophized impersonal nature, which can be easily related to the Taoistic divinity.[16]

The genuine mystery of God in Dionysius is that the transcendent God is immanent in and underlying all things,[17] pouring out overwhelming light on what is most manifest.[18] God is in our minds, in our soul, in our bodies, and in and around and above the world, while remaining ever within Godself.[19] Thus,

---

10   *The Divine Names* (hereafter *DN*) 2.7–8, *Pseudo-Dionysius: The Complete Works* (hereafter *CW*), trans. Colm Luibheid (New York: Paulist, 1987), 63 f.
11   *DN* 1.1–2, *CW* 50.
12   *DN* 1.6, *CW* 54.
13   *DN* 1.4, *CW* 51.
14   *DN* 5.4, *CW* 98.
15   *DN* 5.1, *CW* 96.
16   Because of this nature of God, negation or even negation of negation (*negatio negationis*) is more suitable to the realm of the divine being, since positive affirmations are unfitting to the hiddenness of the inexpressible (*The Mystical Theology* 3, hereafter *MT*, *CW* 139–140). By negation, however, Dionysius does not mean "to negate the divine God." Rather, negation in him is close to "removing" obstacles to the pure view of the hidden image that sculptors have in mind as they carve images. So, negation is negation of things in the world and of our limited ideas.
17   *DN* 5.4, *CW* 98.
18   *MT* 1.1, *CW* 135.
19   *DN* 1.6, *CW* 55 f.

God in Dionysius is hardly to be compared with a deistic god. However, we need to note the way Dionysius' transcendent God is immanent: (1) the Godhead proceeds to all and returns to Godself in the sense of movement and (2) God is always one within Godself in the sense of the intrinsic identity, dwelling indivisibly in every individual.[20] Dionysius states:

> For the blessed divinity, which transcends all being, while proceeding gradually outward because of goodness to commune with those who partake of him, never actually departs from his essential stability and immobility... And it is the same with the divine hierarchy. He generously hands down to his inferiors that unique hierarchic understanding which is especially his own. He resorts to a multitude of sacred enigmas. Then, freely and untrammeled by anything beneath him, he returns to his own starting point without having any loss.[21]

Undeniably, Neo-Platonic influence can be seen here in the procession of and return to the divinity itself.[22] In this movement, God remains one amid plurality, unified throughout, and God is one and dispenses his oneness to every part of the universe as well as to its totality, to the single as well as to the multiple.[23] God penetrates all things and yet remains unapparent to all.[24]

The philosophized image of God in Dionysius is balanced with Christ's incarnation. Christ, who is timeless and totally transcends the natural order of the world, took on the duration of the temporal and entered our human nature.[25] It is Jesus himself who sustains the whole process of procession of light from the Father and lifts us up back to the oneness. Interestingly, both *The Celestial Hierarchy* and *The Ecclesiastical Hierarchy* begin by describing Jesus as the one who became one of us and lifts us up back to God, which implies that Jesus himself unites all the hierarchical steps in both directions.[26] Golitzin

---

20   *DN* 2.11, *CW* 66 f.
21   *The Ecclesiastical Hierarchy* (hereafter *EH*) 3.3.3, *CW* 212 f.
22   *CW* 145, note 4.
23   *DN* 2.11, *CW* 66 f.
24   *The Celestial Hierarchy* (hereafter *CH*) 13.3, *CW* 177.
25   *DN* 1.4, *CW* 52.
26   "Let us, then, call upon Jesus, the Light of the Father, the 'true light enlightening every man coming into the world,' 'through whom we have obtained access' to the Father, the light which is the source of all light" (*CH* 1.2, *CW* 145). "Indeed the Word of God teaches those of us who are its disciples that in this fashion—though more clearly and more intellectually—Jesus enlightens our blessed superiors ..." (*EH* 1.1, *CW* 195).

even argues that Moses' ascents in *Mystical Theology* should be interpreted in a Christological context, even though there is no mention of Christ.[27]

A critical question can be raised: what is the nature of Christ's incarnation in Dionysius? Is it simply an abstract movement of procession and return to his own identity, without experiencing any change in his nature, or is it a substantial union with humanity as Christ shares and bears human sufferings, not only in his divinity but also in his *humanity*? In his *Letter 4*, Dionysius seems to understand Christ's incarnation in a more substantial way than as a transitional procession and return; Jesus, even though he is not called a man in the context of being the cause of man, is as himself truly a man according to the whole essence (ὡς αὐτὸς κατ᾽ οὐσίαν ὅλη ἀληθῶς ἄνθρωπος).[28] The philanthropic Jesus puts aside his own hiddenness and reveals himself to us by becoming a human being.[29] Dionysius writes in his *The Divine Names*:

> An instance of differentiation is that benevolent act of God (θεουργίας) in our favor by which *the transcendent Word wholly and completely* (ὁλικῶς καὶ ἀληθῶς) *took on our human substance and acted in such a way as to do and to suffer all that was particularly appropriate and exalted within his divinely human activity* (τῆς ἀνθρωπικῆς αὐτοῦ θεουργίας). This was something in which the Father and the Spirit had no share, unless, of course, one is talking of the benevolent and loving divine will and of the entire supreme and ineffable act of God performed in the human realm by him who as God and as Word of God is immutable (emphasis mine, JC).[30]

Here, the idea of the completeness of Christ's incarnation is stressed to the extent that Christ had something not to be shared with the Father and the Spirit and he suffers all. Hence, one can argue that Dionysius follows the ortho-

---

27 Alexander Golitzin, "Dionysius Areopagita: A Christian Mysticism?" *Pro Ecclesia* 12:2 (2002), 198.
28 *Letter 4*, *Patrologia Cursus Completus Series Graeca*, ed. Jacques Paul Migne (Paris: Apud J.-P.), 3.1072A (hereafter *MPG*). English translation in CW 264 is "as being himself quite truly a man in all essential respects."
29 *Letter 3*, CW 264.
30 2.6, CW 63. MPG 3.644C. A literal translation of τῆς ἀνθρωπικῆς αὐτοῦ θεουργίας is rather closer to "His humanly God-work" than to "his divinely human activity" in this text and to "action of His Divine Humanity" in *Dionysius the Areopagite on the Divine Names* and *The Mystical Theology*, trans. C.E. Rolt (New York: The Macmillan, 1920), 73. The difference between them is not trivial, because the original text focuses on the divine work while the two translations focus on humanity.

dox view of Christ's incarnation and develops the idea of the unique aspect of Christ's work.

It is, however, not clear whether Dionysius develops a full scale Christology or that his focus is placed only on the fact of the incarnation. Presumably, it may be difficult to enhance a sophisticated view of Christ's person and works when one is overwhelmed with the idea of the profound mystery of the transcendent God. Still, several points are worth noting. First of all, Christ's divine nature is strongly emphasized. Of course, Dionysius never denies the reality of Christ's humanity: not once did Jesus abandon the human form.[31] In many places, however, the accent seems to be placed on Christ's unchangeable *divine nature*. Christ's nature remains *forever unchanged* and *unmixed*: (1) Jesus remains *forever unchanged* even when fully and truly made one of us[32] and (2) Christ emerged from the hiddenness of his divinity to be utterly incarnate among us while remaining *unmixed*.[33] No significant line of thought can be found on Jesus' humanity other than simply mentioning the fact itself that Christ was incarnate as a man. Instead, the divine aspect of Jesus is underscored: "The divinity of Jesus is the fulfilling cause of all, and the parts of that divinity so related to the whole that it is neither whole nor part while being at the same time both whole and part."[34]

What is the genuine meaning of mystery if Christ's divine nature remains unchanged and unmixed even in his incarnation? Is not incarnation a radical change of Christ's nature? If not, then Christ's incarnation seems to be similar to a docetic pretense. Agreeing that Dionysian mysticism is undergirded by an emphasis on Jesus' unchangeable and unmixed divine nature, we should further discuss Dionysius' expressions of Christ's person and nature that can be found in the following four paragraphs: (1) Jesus is neither human nor nonhuman, neither being God for the divine things, nor being a man for human things, but rather by being God-made-man (ἀνδρωθέντος Θεοῦ) he accomplished something new (καινήν τινα) in our midst, the activity of the God-man (τὴν θεανδρικὴν ἐνέργειαν, literally the "theandric activity");[35] (2) an instance of differentiation is that benevolent act of God (θεουργίας) in our favor by which the transcendent Word wholly and completely took on our human substance and acted in such a way as to do and to suffer all that was particularly appropri-

---

31   *CH* 4.4, *CW* 158.
32   *EH* 4.3.10, *CW* 231.
33   *EH* 3.3.13, *CW* 222.
34   *DN* 2.10, *CW* 65.
35   *Letter* 4, *CW* 265, *MPG* 3.1072C.

ate and exalted within his humanly God-work (τῆς ἀνθρωπικῆς αὐτοῦ θεουργίας);[36] (3) for because of his goodness and his love for humanity the simple, hidden oneness of Jesus, the most divine Word, has taken the route of incarnation for us and, without undergoing any change, has become a reality that is composite and visible (συνθετόν τε καὶ ὁρατὸν);[37] and (4) in a fashion beyond words, the simplicity of Jesus became something complex (ὁ ἁπλοῦς Ἰησοῦς συνετέθη), the timeless took on the duration of the temporal, and, with neither change nor confusion of what constitutes him, he came into our human nature, he who totally transcends the natural order of the world.[38]

Based on the texts cited above, many have debated whether Dionysius' view of Christ's nature is close to monophysitism and monenergism, or to that of Chalcedonean Christology.[39] However, the expressions 'composite' and 'complex' in (3) and (4) above do not necessarily imply 'one united nature and work.' On the contrary, their contexts tell us that one Christ proceeds to a multiplicity, symbolized by the bread of the Lord's Supper: "The bread ... is now uncovered and divided into many parts."[40] As for *Letter* 4 described above in point (1), the word 'theandric' for the nature and operation of Christ may suggest monophysitism and monenergism: the theandric Christ accomplished something new, neither human nor nonhuman. Yet, the context of *Letter* 4 is perhaps inconclusive, because the first part of the letter is closer to the idea of Christ as *both* human *and* superhuman than to the idea of Christ as neither human nor nonhuman.[41] In addition, the idea of 'not by being God for doing divine things, not by being a man for doing human things' can be interpreted as similar to the notion of *communicatio idiomatum*. Note that in *Letter* 4, which includes the expression *theandric*, Dionysius repeatedly uses the word Jesus instead of Christ. This may suggest that Dionysius' idea of the theandric includes the notion of the 'divine humanity' of Christ. In fact, David Coffey

---

36   DN 2.6, CW 63, MPG 3. 644C. CW interprets τῆς ἀνθρωπικῆς αὐτοῦ θεουργίας into "his divinely human activity" but I correct it as "his humanly God-work," in order to stick to the technical meaning of θεουργίας as the God-work.

37   EH 3.3.12, CW 222, MPG 3.444A.

38   DN 1.4, CW 52, MPG 3.592A.

39   E.g., David Coffey quotes John of Damascus and Thomas Aquinas for the interpretation of Dionysius as two operations ("The Theandric Nature of Christ," *Theological Studies* 60 (1999), 407 f), while Pelikan seems to understand Dionysius' view as a monenergism ("The Odyssey of Dionysian Spirituality" in CW 21).

40   EH 3.3.12, CW 222.

41   "Out of his very great love for humanity, he became quite truly a human, both superhuman and among humans; and, through himself beyond being, he took upon himself the being of humans" (*The Letter* 4, CW 264).

follows this line of thought when he argues, "This tells us that his human nature is unique, theandric."[42] If this interpretation is accepted, *Letter* 4 may disclose both the idea of Jesus' unique theandric humanity and that of his identity as *truly* identical with our humanity, according to the whole essence (κατ' οὐσίαν ὅλη ἀληθῶς ἄνθρωπος).[43] But we must remember that the word 'Jesus' in Dionysius is often employed to imply the divine nature of Christ; "The divinity of Jesus (τοῦ Ἰησοῦ θεότης) is the fulfilling cause of all ...,"[44] and "For this mystery of Jesus remains hidden and can be drawn out by no word or mind."[45] Thus, it is unlikely that Dionysius specifies Christ's humanity with the word theandric. More importantly, the content of *Letter* 4 does not seem to show evidence that the word theandric concretely points to Christ's humanity, considering that it also views Jesus as the overflowing transcendence. We cannot find any particular connotation of Christ's humanity in the expression of the humanly God-work in point (2) above either. All four references, therefore, do not tell us in what ways and how crucially Jesus' nature and person, especially his human nature, are manifest in his incarnation, and, more critically, how his nature cannot experience any change even in this radical change of incarnation.

Finally, how existentially Dionysius sees Christ's incarnation needs to be viewed in relation to his theology of the cross. Dionysius writes:

> For it is on Jesus himself, our most divine altar, that there is achieved the divine consecration (ἀφιέρωσις) of intelligent beings. In him, as scripture says, "we have access" to consecration (ἀφιερούμενοι) and are mystically offered as a holocaust ... For it is the most holy Jesus who consecrates (ἁγιάζει) himself for us ... God, first of all, having become man, was consecrated (ἁγιάζεσθαι) for us and, secondly, this divine act is the source of all perfection and of all consecration (ἁγιάζειν).[46]

A sacrificial motif is manifested in this passage; Jesus is our altar and consecrates himself for us, and we are offered as holocaust. Jesus who consecrates the consecrated willingly died on the cross for the sake of our divine birth.[47]

---

42 "The Theandric," 425.
43 *Letter* 4, CW 264, MPG 3.1072A.
44 DN 2.10, CW 65, MPG 3.648C.
45 *Letter* 3, CW 264. The Latin text includes *mysterium* where the Greek text omits it. But the context regards the hiddenness of Christ even after his incarnation, which may imply that the word 'Jesus' here does not denote the humanity of Christ (MPG 3.1069B, 1070B).
46 EH 4.3.12, CW 232, MPG 3.484D-485A.
47 EH 4.3.10, CW 231.

Yet even in this text, human sacrifice as holocaust seems to be more focused than Christ's sacrifice.[48] In *Letter* 8, Christ's death is briefly related to salvation from sin: Jesus endured suffering on the cross to keep us from sin.[49] Apart from the few references noted above, hardly any substantial theology of Christ's crucifixion can be found in Dionysius. Instead, Dionysius describes Christ's death as a moral example. The sign of the cross indicates the renunciation of all the desires of the flesh and points to a life given over to the imitation of God.[50]

Who is Christ and how are Christ's works actualized as he proceeds and returns to himself? It is apparent in Dionysius that God is the source of all divinization.[51] We enter into God through God and God for Dionysius in *The Mystical Theology* means Jesus Christ,[52] who "generously hands down to his inferiors that unique hierarchic understanding" and returns to his own starting point without any loss, drawing all varied symbols together into one.[53] But, how can this happen? Can it be possible because Jesus has one, divine, unchangeable, and unmixed nature? Does Jesus unite all with himself simply because his divine nature is the fulfilling source of all as both *part* and *all*?[54] Or, if Jesus makes this possible in his incarnational works, how does his *extus-reditus* (procession and return) actually work out for *our divinization*? Is Jesus an instructor who teaches us to unite ourselves with him by showing his example,[55] and are we sculptors who carve a statue and remove every obstacle to the pure view of the hidden?[56] Can any instructor unite us with himself by teaching? Defining Dionysius' theology as Christ-less mysticism may not be a balanced evaluation, because Christ's incarnation is one of the central points of mysticism in

---

48   Alexander Golitzen includes this text in his Christological interpretation of Dionysius and relates the sacrifice of the consecrated as holocaust to the reminiscence of the second-century description of the Christian martyr as sacrificial offering ("Dionysius Areopagita," 188). Yet the notable feature here is how concretely Dionysius describes the reality and meaning of Christ's crucifixion. He simply mentions the sacrificial motif of the cross without any further explanation while emphasizing that it works for the consecration of Christ's followers.

49   *Letter* 8.6, CW 280.

50   EH 5.3.4, CW 240. "The sign of the cross proclaims ... the death of all fleshly desire" (EH 6.3.3, CW 247).

51   EH 1.4, CW 198.

52   Golitzin, "Dionysius Areopagita," 189.

53   EH 3.3.3, CW 213.

54   DN 2.10, CW 65.

55   CH 7.3, CW 164.

56   MT 2, CW 138.

his writings.[57] But it is fair to say that a developed view of Christ's human nature and his crucifixion is all but lacking in Dionysius' writings.[58]

The mystical reality of God who is hidden in Christ's incarnation and crucifixion gives us space by liberating us from the idea that God is exclusively tied up with violence. God tests the view of the ontological bond of God with human suffering, when God challenges Job with questions, "Do you know?" (Job 37:14–39:30). But the agnostic distance of God from human reality should not be the predominant answer to the question of God's relation to human violence. God in Christ is God incarnated and crucified. Hence, the question must include how this God in Christ relates to human violence and suffering. A Christology for human violence must reflect the biblical reality that Christ is among us in his humanity as well as in his divinity, and shares and bears human suffering and violence on the cross. It is critical that Dionysius' mysticism lacks a developed view of Christ's humanity and crucifixion because neither the apophatic Christ nor Christ as a teacher can share and take up human violence and suffering in existential and extensive ways.

The challenge over Dionysius' Christology is intensified when compared with Taoistic mysticism in which the Tao is both transcendent and immanent and teaches us how to be harmonized with the Tao. Furthermore, the Tao's in-naturation seems to be more inclusive than Christ's incarnation, as the Taoistic in-naturation surpasses the boundaries between being and non-being and between humans, nature, and cosmos. Shared core values may challenge the nature of mysticism and the uniqueness of Christ's incarnation. This leads us to the next section, in which we will discuss Taoistic in-naturation and its return to itself.

---

57 Golitzin, "Dionysius Areopagita," 198.
58 The sacrificial view of the atonement, for instance, logically precedes the moral exemplary theology. If Christ shows nothing but a moral value on the cross, his death cannot be a moral example at all; for death as such is not a moral value but a reality of human beings. Only after his death embraces a sacrificial reality can such specific death as sacrifice have a moral value (Jaeseung Cha, *The Mystery and Paradox of the Cross: Jesus' Proclamation of the Crucifixion in his Five Statements* (Seoul: Saemulkyulplus, 2013), 243–248.

The Tao's In-naturation and its Relevance to Christology[59]

The Tao (道) literally means "the way," which can be related to Christ's declaration in John 14:6, "I am the Way."[60] But the Tao in Taoism is far more than a path. The Tao is *both* beyond a being *and* a being, *both* a cosmological principle *and* a personal being, and *both* present in cosmos *and* in humans. This extremely inclusive attribute of the Tao grounds its cosmological harmony with humans. On the other hand, it may prevent us from drawing any concrete and analytical conclusions for Christology: all including all excludes particular details, just as a simple declaration of the divine incarnation itself cannot demonstrate how the incarnated one relates to the world and humans. Thus, further discussion is required on three points: (1) the mystical nature of the Tao, (2) the

---

59   Taoism is a Chinese religion and philosophy that is believed to have begun between the 6th and 5th centuries B.C. It was embodied in three major scriptures: *Tao Te Ching, Chuang Tzu,* and *I Ching*. This article will use two texts, *Tao Te Ching* and *Chuang Tzu. Tao Te Ching* (道德經, 6th-4th cent. B.C) literally means "scripture of way and virtue." Opinions about the authorship have varied: some maintain Lao Tzu as the sole author, while others attribute it to his followers. Yet the consensus is that Lao Tzu (老子 6th cent. B.C.) himself was critically involved in constructing the essential contents. *Tao Te Ching* consists of two parts: *Tao* (道, cosmic, ontological, or true reality, and nature, 37 chapters) and *Te* (德, virtues humans may acquire by harmonizing with *Tao*, 44 chapters). While Confucianism mostly deals with human affairs in society, *Tao Te Ching* presents cosmology, metaphysics of beings and truth, and anthropology. *Chuang Tzu* (莊子, 4th-2nd cent. B.C.) is named eponymously after *Chuang Tzu* (4th-3rd cent. B.C.), whose life is little known. Probably written by *Chuang Tzu* himself and later his followers, the book has had great influence on the development of Taoism and Zen Buddhism. Extant in various editions, it comprises 5 parts and 33 chapters. It treats of the great freedom of the human mind, which can reach far beyond ordinary matters and nature (*ziran*, 自然 literally means "self that is what it should be," and signifies both nature and essence, just like "φύσις" in Greek and "nature" in English). It also deals with continuous flux and yin-yang, as well as with union between heaven and the human (天人合一) (William. L. Reese, *Dictionary of Philosophy and Religion: Eastern and Western Thought* (New Jersey: Humanities Press, 1980) is partly referred to for this introduction. See also Jung Young Lee, *The Trinity in Asian Perspective* (Nashville: Abingdon Press, 1996), 39–44). Some parts of this section are modified from my writing, "Taoistic Implications for Christology: Grand Unity, *datong* (大同) and Valley-god, *gushen* (谷神)," in Eddy Van der Borght & Paul van Geest (eds.), *Strangers and Pilgrims on Earth: Essays in Honour of Abraham van de Beek* (Leiden: Brill, 2012), 189–208.

60   Michael Amaladoss begins the chapter "Jesus, the Way" with John 14:6 and proceeds to explain the Tao in *Tao Te Ching* and Confucianism (*The Asian Jesus* (Maryknoll: Orbis, 2006), 51–55).

mystical nature of the Tao's in-naturation, and (3) the union (divinization) with the Tao as a return to the Tao.

First of all, both *Tao Te Ching* and *Chuang Tzu* disclose mystical aspects of the Tao. The Tao is dark and obscure,[61] and indescribably deep and unrecognizably indistinct.[62] Whoever thinks he or she knows the Tao in fact does not know what the Tao is because the Tao cannot be heard, seen, and spoken of, and if we understand that the formless Tao gives forms to all things, we must not name it.[63] More critically, the Tao is related to nothingness, *wu* (無), of name and form. The unknown feature of the Tao leads us to question the ontological status of the Tao: is it because the Tao does not exist that the Tao cannot be seen, heard, and spoken of? If the formless Tao negates its existence as it returns to nothingness, all theological concerns would seem to be of irrelevance to Taoism. Nonetheless, philosophical and cultural expressions of Taoism may not be fully apprehended by a strict dualism in which distinctions between being and non-being, ontology and epistemology, and humanity and the cosmos are not easily reconciled. The Tao as non-being reaches negation of nothingness, exists before the creator,[64] and produces all beings.[65] Book 22 (知北遊) of *Chuang Tzu* uses two intriguing expressions in relation to the concept of nothingness (無): *youwu* (有無, there is nothingness) and *wuwu* (無無, there is no nothingness).[66] It is the very nature of the Tao that it freely crosses

---

61 沌沌 *Tao Te Ching* 20. The original text of *Tao Te Ching* is from Sang Dae Kim, *Dodukkyung Kangui* (*Lectures of Tao Te Ching*) (Kukhakjaroywon, 1996) and Chinese Text Project (http://ctext.org/dao-de-jing). The English translation is my own with reference to R.L. Wing, *The Tao of Power* included in Sang Dae Kim & Stephen Mitchel, *Tao Te Ching* (New York: HarperCollins, 1988), and Victor H. Mair, *Tao Te Ching: The Classic Book of Integrity and the Way* (New York: Bantam Books, 1990).

62 "窅然難言 冥冥" *Chuang Tzu* 22 (知北遊). *Chuang Tzu*, ed. and trans. Dong Lim An (Hyunamsa, 1993), 541. The original text of *Chuang Tzu* is from Dong Lim An, *Chuang Tzu* and the Chinese Text Project (http://ctext.org/zhuangzi), and the English translation is my own with reference to Dong Lim An's and Hak Chu Kim's complete Korean translation (Yunamseoka, 2010).

63 "孰知不知之知 无始曰 道不可聞 聞而非也 道不可見 見而非也 道不可言 言而非也 知形形之不形乎 道不當名" *Chuang Tzu* 22 (知北遊), Dong Lim An, 552. The literal translation is, "Who knows that not knowing is knowing? Wushi (without beginning) says, 'The Tao cannot be heard, if it is heard, it is not. The Tao is not seen, if it is seen, it is not. The Tao is not spoken of, if it is spoken of, it is not. If we know that the one who gives forms to forms is formless, it is unnatural to name the Tao.'"

64 "象帝之先" *Tao Te Ching* 4.

65 "有生於無" *Tao Te Ching* 40.

66 *Chuang Tzu* 22 (知北遊), Dong Lim An, 553.

the boundaries between non-being and being.[67] In the metaphor of a human body, non-being is the head and becomes one with being.[68] This cosmically inclusive Tao is also described as the One, which is the divine nature in *Tao Te Ching*.[69]

Secondly, the Tao is both transcendent and immanent. The first chapter of *Tao-Te Ching* states:

> The Tao that can be expressed is not the absolute (eternal) Tao. The name that can be named is not the absolute name. The nameless originated Heaven and Earth (eternal things) while the named is the mother of all things (manifested things). Free from desire one sees the mystery and caught with desire one sees only the manifestation. Yet, mystery and manifestation arise from the same source with different names, both of which are called, *xuan* (玄, profundity), *xuan* upon *xuan* (玄之又玄, profundity upon profundity), the gate to collective subtlety.[70]

Like God, who is the unsearchable, inscrutable, and nameless one in Dionysius, the Tao cannot be named.[71] But the Tao without name is the originator of heaven and earth and the Tao with names is the mother of all things. The real profundity is that these two are not separable but are united arising from the same source: mystery and its manifestation are one. This paradoxical yet natural attribute of the Tao's in-naturation is abundant in the texts. The cosmic oneness of the Tao is related to the omnipresent nature of the Tao: the Tao is

---

67 Sung Hae Kim, "What is Taoistic Culture? From a Christian Perspective," in *Taoism and Christianity* (Seoul: Pauline, 2003), 26, Gu Ying Chen (陳鼓應), *A New Perspective of Lao-Chuang* (老莊新論), trans. Jin Sik Choi (Seoul: Sonamu, 1997), 23 f.

68 "以无有爲首⋯孰知有无死生之一守者" *Chuang Tzu* 23 (庚桑楚).13, Dong Lim An, 580. A similar idea is seen in 6 (大宗師).22, Dong Lim An, 197.

69 "The things which from old had the One (or the Tao) are; by having the One heaven becomes clear; by having the One the earth becomes firm" (昔之得一者 天得一以清 地得一以寧, *Tao Te Ching* 39). "The Tao produced the One, the One produced the Two, the Two produced the Three, the Three produced all things" (道生一 一生二 二生三 三生萬物, *Tao Te Ching* 42).

70 "道可道非常道 名可名非常名 無名天地之始 有名萬物之母 故常無欲以觀其妙 常有欲以觀其徼 此兩者同出而異名 同謂之玄 眾妙之門" *Tao Te Ching* 1.

71 "The Tao is always nameless" (道常無名, *Tao Te Ching* 32). "Many scripture writers will tell you that the divinity is not only invisible and incomprehensible, but also 'unsearchable and inscrutable,'..." (*DN* 1.2, *CW* 50). "Realizing all this, the theologians praise it by every name—and as the Nameless one" (*DN* 1.6, *CW* 54).

one because the Tao includes all[72] and is present in all, namely, in ants, grass, earthenware tile, and even in excrement.[73] An interesting distinction between Dionysius and Taoism is that while pure simplicity is the foundation of the divine One in Dionysius, all-embracing multiplicity is the very root of the Tao's oneness.[74]

The way the Tao relates to the world is mysteriously humble, as we can read:

> The great Tao is overflowing everywhere, on the left and the right. All things depend on it for their production; it does not deny them. When it achieves its purpose, it does not claim the name of having done it. It clothes and cultivates all but never has a desire to act as their master. It can be named Small, (because of this), all things return to (the Tao) and do not know that the Tao is their master …[75]

The Tao is humbly present in nature to the extent that it is united with dust, the smallest thing.[76] The biblical proclamation of Jesus' humble incarnation in his becoming flesh and of the world not knowing him as the Son of God can be viewed as parallel with the humble Tao that, although the originator of all, does not act as a master and, because of this, one cannot recognize the Tao as the master of all.

Mysticism of the Tao in its humble presence in nature can be centered in the expressions, *xuan* (玄, mysterious, obscure, dark), *xuantong* (玄同, mysterious identification), and *xuante* (玄德, mysterious virtue). The first chapter of *Tao Te Ching* repeats *xuan* three times to express the mysterious in-naturation of the Tao. *Xuan* is also employed when the Valley-god that never dies is called

---

72 "All things are reduced to One through the Tao" (道通為一, *Chuang Tzu* 2 [齊物論]12, *Dong Lim An* 62).

73 *Chuang Tzu* 22 (知北遊), Dong Lim An, 546. According to *Tao Te Ching*, the Tao can be found in an empty container (4), in a valley and in a female (6, 28), in water (8), in infants (10, 28), in a bamboo tree (15, 32, 37), in heaven (16), in the heart of the Sage (22), in a king (25), and in heaven, earth, the divine being, and the valley (39).

74 Dong-guo Zi asked Chuang Tzu, saying, "Where can you find the Tao?" Chuang Tzu replied, "Everywhere." There is not a single thing without (the Tao). There are the three terms, "Complete," "All-embracing," "the Whole." These names are different, but the reality is the same; referring to the One thing (*Chuang Tzu* 22 [知北遊], Dong Lim An, 546).

75 "大道汎兮其可左右 萬物恃之而生而不辭 功成不名有 衣養萬物而不為主 常無欲 可名於小 萬物歸焉 而不為主" *Tao Te Ching* 34.

76 "同其塵" *Tao Te Ching* 4, 56.

"mysterious female and the root of all things."[77] This *xuan*, mystery, has two further concrete realties, *xuantong* and *xuante*. These two concepts overlap, because the Tao's in-naturation and its actualization by humans are interchangeable, so that the distinction between them may be obscure. For example, the concept of "identification with dust" expresses the Tao in the chapter four of *Tao Te Ching* whereas the same expression is employed in the chapter 56 for the one who knows the Tao. What is of significance is that both articulate the mystical presence of the Tao in nature and humans. It is called *xuantong*, mysterious identification, that the Tao is united with the smallest, dust.[78] When one denies one's own virtue, *te* (德), the virtue of heaven and earth begins being united profoundly (*xuantong*).[79] Thus, the Tao's mysterious identification is the source of the sage's mysterious virtue and, in turn, the mysterious virtue is the very reflection of the profound identification of the Tao: "(The Tao) produces (all things) and nourishes (them); it produces (them) but does not possess (them). It does all, and yet does not boast of it; it presides over all, and yet does not control them. This is what is called *xuante*, (玄德, mysterious virtue)."[80] The sacrificial nature of the Tao, producing all but not possessing them, is surprisingly similar to the sacrificial God in Christ. However, the pivotal questions of how the Tao works for the world and humans is not yet concretely answered. Indeed, Taoism may not have any interest in explaining it, given the Tao's own nature of hidden humbleness. Regardless of whether the Tao is personal or impersonal, the best way to explain how the Tao works for us seems to be through metaphors. The valley itself may not be the Tao, but it may be the presence of the Tao, metaphorically speaking (*pi*, 譬), like (*you*, 猶) the valley stream joining the rivers and seas.[81] Chapter 15 of *Tao Te Ching* is all about this metaphorical description of the one who knows the Tao: the wise are so mysterious (*xuan*) that they cannot be recognized; they are extremely cautious, like (*rou*, 若) those who wade through a stream in the winter; grave like a guest; evanescent like ice that is melting away; unpretentious like wood that has not been fashioned into anything; vacant like a valley, and dull like

---

77 "谷神不死 是謂玄牝 玄牝之門 是謂天地根" *Tao Te Ching* 6. Bang Xiong Wang interprets *xzuan* as twofold reality of the Tao, namely, being and non-being and further relates it to the Tao's procession and return (Bang Xiong Wang 王邦雄, *Lao-Tzu: Philosophy of Life* (老子的哲學, Taoistic Philosophy), trans. Byung Don Chun (Seoul: Kleine Iyaghi, 2007), 114–118).
78 "同其塵 是謂玄同" *Tao Te Ching* 56.
79 *Chuang Tzu* 10 (胠篋), Dong Lim An, 275.
80 "生之畜之 生而不有 為而不恃 長而不宰 是謂玄德" *Tao Te Ching* 10.
81 "譬道之在天下 猶川谷之與江海" *Tao Te Ching* 32. *Peyou* (譬猶) means metaphor.

muddy water.[82] In this sense, what the Tao does in its in-naturation seems to give way to what humans do, which leads us to the last point, the divinization of the sage.

Thirdly, the mystical identification of the Tao can be accomplished by the sage who knows, finds, and follows the Tao. "Return" is the very nature of the Tao, as we can read in the expression, *fan* (反, return, paradoxical):

> There was something undefined and complete, before Heaven and Earth were born; silent, vast, independent, and unchanging. ... It is the mother of heaven and earth. I do not know the name, and the word I say is Tao. Forced to give it name, I say Great. Great means continuing; continuing means going far; going far means return, *fan*.[83]

The unnamable Tao is the great being of all things as mother and at the same time can be described in two movements: great is it going far and great is it returning back. *Fan,* return, is the movement of the Tao (反者道之動).[84] This nature of the Tao is also called *fu* (復, return, repetition) of the Tao. We do not know the Tao as such but the clue to the Tao is its return, *fu*, to its own nature of nothingness (復歸於無物): this is called the form of the formless, and the visible image of the invisible; we meet it and do not see its front; we follow it, and do not see its back.[85] Union with the Tao is one of the major themes of *Chuang Tzu*. Heaven and earth (all things) and the sage were produced together, and thus all things and the sage become one.[86] The boldest thought of the grand unity between the Tao and humans can be found in *Chuang Tzu* 23 (庚桑楚): above, the sage plays with the Creator; below, he has a friend who considers life and death as having neither beginning nor end.[87] In this stage, being,

---

82. "古之善為士者 微妙玄通 深不可識 ... 豫兮若冬涉川 猶兮若畏四鄰 儼兮其若容 渙兮若冰之將釋 敦兮其若樸 曠兮其若谷 混兮其若濁" *Tao Te Ching* 15.
83. "有物混成 先天地生 寂兮寥兮 獨立不改 周行而不殆 可以為天下母 吾不知其名 字之曰道 強為之名曰大 大曰逝 逝曰遠 遠曰反 故道大" *Tao Te Ching* 25.
84. *Tao Te Ching* 40. Se Hyung Lee argues that the Tao has two movements: ontological-cosmological and cosmological-ontological, creating and receiving, going far and returning back (Se Hyung Lee, *Theology of the Tao: A Taoistic Reinterpretation of Christian God and Evil* (Seoul: Handul, 2002), 58). Bang Xiong Wang defines *fan* as the return of the Tao to itself, not surpassing itself (Bang Xiong Wang, *Lao-Tzu: Philosophy of Life*, 140).
85. "是謂無狀之狀 無物之象 是謂惚恍 迎之不見其首 隨之不見其後" *Tao Te Ching* 14.
86. "天地與我並生 而萬物與我為一" *Chuang Tzu* 2 (齊物論), Dong Lim An, 70.
87. "上與造物者遊 而下與外死生" Dong Lim An, 796.

non-being, life, and death all become part of the sage's body,[88] which can be called "Great Return" to the Tao[89] and "Great Identification with the Tao."[90]

How then do we find and follow the Tao when the Tao returns to itself? Mysticism here is a serious challenge. What Taoism suggests is that since the Tao is the origin of all things and we as children of the Tao return to the mother Tao,[91] we have to *perceive* the principle of return in each thing in nature: we see all things (in the vegetable world) return to its root, having displayed their luxuriant growth; roots return to stillness, stillness returns to destiny; and destiny returns to unchanging eternity, and so on.[92] Thus, the Tao's return to itself becomes the sage's return to the Tao: they are united with the Tao by returning to infants, the valley, the bamboo tree, and the empty container, which remain in their primitive status.[93] The sage embraces the One (the Tao) but does not display himself, and the humility of the sage following the Tao can become an example to the world.[94] Again, what the Tao does in the world and humans is unclear, apart from the fact that the Tao *teaches* us to find itself and that it is *we* who must find the mysterious Tao in nature and in humans.

Conclusion

In what ways does the Christian understanding of God give space for *others*? Hosea 11:8 declares, "I am God and no mortal, the Holy One in your midst, and I will not come in wrath." That God is ontologically different from us, but is among us, grounds Christian mysticism, in which we can find space liberated from an exclusive bond between human violence and divine intervention. A transcendent and immanent god is definitely a more sophisticated god than a violent or an apophatic god. Yet, Christian mysticism in Christ goes deeper than this paradoxical reality of God. What matters in giving space for others in a Christian way is not so much that God is both transcendent and immanent; for this can be found in Taoism as well. The actual content of how Christ relates to human beings must be considered. In this sense, examining Dionysian and

---

88 "生俄而死 以無有為首 以生為體" *Chuang Tzu* 23 (庚桑楚), Dong Lim An, 580.
89 "乃大歸乎" *Chuang Tzu* 22 (知北遊), Dong Lim An, 545.
90 "同於大通" *Chuang Tzu* 6 (大宗師), Dong Lim An, 215.
91 "天下有始 以為天下母 既得其母 以知其子 既知其子 復守其母" *Tao Te Ching* 52.
92 "吾以觀復 夫物芸芸 各復歸其根 歸根曰靜 是謂復命 復命曰常" *Tao Te Ching* 16.
93 *Tao Te Ching* 28.
94 "是以聖人抱一為天下式 不自見故明" *Tao Te Ching* 22.

Taoistic mysticism is a significant resource in appreciating the profundity of Christ's incarnation, which uniquely gives us space for others.

We have discussed four pivotal points in Dionysius: (1) Mysticism in Dionysius includes a philosophical perspective that God is not a being but an essence of being; (2) Christ's mystical incarnation is based on his divinity; (3) Dionysius' concept of *theandric* is less a developed idea of Christ's person with a twofold nature than something closer to a simple description of the God-man's incarnation; and (4) a developed theology of the cross is all but absent in Dionysius. Christ, according to Dionysius, is the subject who, ultimate in divine power, assimilates us to his own light,[95] and Christ's divine life makes the human race participate in his perfection.[96] This divine aspect of Christ could be interpreted as a divine aspect of Christ's humanity if we extended his word *theandric* to apply to Christ's humanity. Yet, Dionysius seldom pays attention to *Christ's humanity* as distinct from Christ's divinity. The divine presence in nature and human beings is a common concept in human religiosity. It is what we aspire to and thus can be easily imagined by us. Mystical presence of Christ in his humanity as well as his divinity is far beyond this common expectation since his body is shared on the cross and at the Lord's Supper. As for Christ's crucifixion, Dionysius mentions the victory over death[97] and suffering for human sin.[98] A greater emphasis, however, falls on the union with Christ by *imitating* him. Dionysius does not further develop the theandric Christ for his theology of Christ's crucifixion. Can this God as depicted by Dionysius give us space for others?

What puzzles me in Dionysius is how he misses the theology of the cross while he explicates the mystical reality of the Christian God. Is not God in Christ truly mystical, not only in the sense that God visits us and takes us along with Godself, but in the sense that God remains *in nobis*, suffers human brokenness, and unites all others in his death? Is not God's space in Christ a space for others, not only in that we are free from exclusive ties with God and thus are solitary in ourselves but also in that Christ penetrates into human space of suffering, draws all into his space, i.e., his body and blood, of reconciliation?[99]

---

[95] *EH* 1.1, *CW* 196.

[96] *EH* 3.3.13, *CW* 222 f.

[97] *EH* 2.3.6, *CW* 207.

[98] "Here I am, ready once again to suffer for the salvation of man and I would very gladly endure it if in this way I could keep men from sin" (*The Letter* 8.6, *CW* 280).

[99] "And I, when I am lifted up from the earth, will draw all people to myself" (John 12:32). "But now in Christ Jesus you who once were far off have been brought near by the blood of Christ. For he is our peace; in his flesh he has made both groups into one and has broken down the dividing wall, that is, the hostility between us" (Eph. 2:13–14).

Considering this problem in Dionysius, the Neo-Platonic influence seems to be critical. The idealism of the two directions of the movement, Christ's procession toward humanity and returning to his own unchangeable nature with humanity, is the major framework of what constitutes Dionysius' Christology, while the biblical reality of Christ who *remains* with us in our sorrow, pain, sins, and death, and even remains in the grave, is absent in Dionysius. In this sense, the divine humanity or theandric nature of Christ in Dionysius is neither *fully* human in his incarnation nor *uniquely* divine in his crucifixion.

Interestingly, my criticism of Dionysius can be more fully comprehended if we see it through the lens of Taoism. The nameless, mystical, and apophatic Tao is the creator of all and yet present in nature, humans, and even in dust. The Tao's profundity is disclosed in its movements to proceed to the world and return to itself. We find even sacrificial and humble attributes of the Tao as the Tao produces all but does not possess. More surprisingly, the mystical union between the Tao and the sage is an essential part of Taoistic ideals. It is of great importance to understand the historical and social settings in which Taoism was formulated in China: people greatly suffered from all sorts of political and social instabilities in the days of Lao Tzu and Chuang Tzu. The Tao was not the reality that ordinary people enjoyed but an idealistic vision that they had in order to *escape* their hardships in life.[100] It is not clear in what way the Tao sacrifices itself for the ordinary people in violence and suffering. What is at stake here is that it would be contradictory to the nature of "sacrifice" if the Tao simply demonstrates and teaches us "sacrificial nature."

Jesus is incarnate not in an ideal society or nature, but in a chaotic, violent, and sorrowful world where people experience all sorts of poverty, suffering, and brokenness. Jesus is the Lord of the oppressed and broken human beings, not only as one who demonstrates and teaches the sacrificial nature of the divinity, but as one who remains in our misery and sacrifices himself on the cross. Jesus shares his body and blood,[101] is abandoned into humanity,[102] gives his life as ransom for many,[103] completes his works,[104] and draws and reconciles all into himself.[105] Although it is far beyond our ability to comprehend this mystical reality of Christ's incarnation and crucifixion, Jesus' own proclamation is the ceaselessly overflowing *Ursprung* of Christian mysticism. Only

---

100 Chen, *New Perspective of Lao-Chuang*, 73 f.
101 Mk. 14:22–24.
102 Mk. 15:34.
103 Mk. 10:45.
104 Jh. 19:30.
105 Jh. 12:32; Col. 1:20.

when we encounter this Jesus sharing and bearing human violence and sufferings, can this crucified Jesus be the *way* for us to take little steps toward overcoming human violence and suffering that plague human civilization. Space for others in Christ is not a space outside of Jesus. He himself is the mystical space where he takes up human suffering and violence.

Bibliography

Amaladoss, Michael, *The Asian Jesus* (Maryknoll: Orbis, 2006).

Cha, Jaeseung, "Taoistic Implications for Christology: Grand Unity, *datong* (大同) and Valley-god, *gushen* (谷神)," in Eddy Van der Borght & Paul van Geest (eds.), *Strangers and Pilgrims on Earth: Essays in Honour of Abraham van de Beek* (Leiden: Brill, 2012), 189–208.

———, *The Mystery and Paradox of the Cross: Jesus' Proclamation of the Crucifixion in his Five Statements* (Seoul: Saemulkyulplus, 2013).

Chen, Gu Ying (陳鼓應), *A New Perspective of Lao-Chuang* (老莊新論), trans. Jin Sik Choi (Seoul: Sonamu, 1997).

Chuang Tzu, ed. and trans. Dong Lim An (Hyunamsa, 1993).

Coffey, David, "The Theandric Nature of Christ," *Theological Studies* 60 (1999).

Dionysius the Areopagite on the Divine Names and *The Mystical Theology*, trans. C.E. Rolt (New York: The Macmillan, 1920).

Gellman, Jerome, "Mysticism," in Edward N. Zalta (ed.), *The Stanford Encyclopedia of Philosophy*, http://plato.stanford.edu/archives/sum2011/entries/mysticism.

Golitzin, Alexander, "Dionysius Areopagita: A Christian Mysticism?" *Pro Ecclesia* 12:2 (2002), 161–212

Kim, Sang Dae, *Dodukkyung Kangui* (*Lectures of Tao Te Ching*) (Kukhakjaroywon, 1996).

Kim, Sung Hae, "What is Taoistic Culture? From a Christian Perspective," in *Taoism and Christianity* (Seoul: Pauline, 2003).

Lee, Jung Young, *The Trinity in Asian Perspective* (Nashville: Abingdon Press, 1996).

Lee, Se Hyung, *Theology of the Tao: A Taoistic Reinterpretation of Christian God and Evil* (Seoul: Handul, 2002).

Mair, Victor H., *Tao Te Ching: The Classic Book of Integrity and the Way* (New York: Bantam Books, 1990).

McGinn, Bernard, *The Foundations of Mysticism* (New York: Crossroad, 1991).

Patrologia Cursus Completus Series Graeca, ed. Jacques Paul Migne (Paris: Apud J.-P.).

Pseudo-Dionysius, *The Complete Works*, trans. Colm Luibheid (New York: Paulist, 1987).

Reese, William. L., *Dictionary of Philosophy and Religion: Eastern and Western Thought* (New Jersey: Humanities Press, 1980).

Rorem, Paul, "Negative Theology and the Cross," *Lutheran Quarterly* 23 (2009), 314–331.
Schwartz, Regina M., *The Curse of Cain: The Violent Legacy of Monotheism* (Chicago: The University of Chicago, 1997).
Tam, Ekman P.C., "Another Look at the Theory of a Common Core Mysticism," *Dialogue and Alliance* 11:2 (1997), 31–42
Wang, Bang Xiong (王邦雄), *Lao-Tzu: Philosophy of Life* (老子的哲學, Taoistic Philosophy), trans. Byung Don Chun (Seoul: Kleine Iyaghi, 2007).
Wing, R.L., *The Tao of Power*, in Sang Dae Kim & Stephen Mitchel, *Tao Te Ching* (New York: HarperCollins, 1988).

A Violent God?
Philosophical Reflections on Monotheism and Genesis 22

Renée van Riessen

> Part of what has happened in our time is that God has shifted over from the side of civilization to the side of barbarism
> TERRY EAGLETON[1]

∴

Religion in today's society is sometimes seen as a positive force, but the negative aspects are underlined too, because, as philosopher and declared atheist A.C. Grayling argues, religious faith is neither kind nor attractive:

> Religions have often been cruel in their effects, and remain so today: homosexuals are hanged in Iran, adulterous women are beheaded in Afghanistan and stoned to death in Saudi Arabia, 'witches' are murdered in Africa, women and children are subordinated in fundamentalist households in the Bible Belt of the United States and in many parts of the Islamic world.[2]

Among the types of religion that are criticized for their detrimental effects on civilization, monotheism has a special place. Traditionally it was seen as the most rationally defendable and civilized form of religion by Jewish, Christian and Muslim theologians and philosophers alike. However, as Terry Eagleton points out: in present times, God has shifted over from the side of civilization to the side of barbarism. By 'civilization' Eagleton means the ability to reason, participation in universality and autonomy, the faculty of rational speculation and, even more important, a capacity for irony. Opposed to civilization is the notion of 'culture,' alongside 'barbarism'; culture thus understood refers to "the

---

[1] Terry Eagleton, *Reason, Faith and Revolution, Reflections on the God Debate* (New Haven & London: Yale University Press, 2009), 154.
[2] A.C. Grayling, *The God Argument: The Case* against *Religion and* for *Humanism* (London/New York: Bloomsbury, 2013).

customary, collective, passionate, spontaneous, unreflective, un-ironic and a-rational."[3]

Shifting from civilization to culture and barbarism, theism (or monotheism) indeed has a double face in our time. On the one hand, it can still be seen as a type of religion that admits of rational justification, and thus understood monotheism is defended by philosophers of religion like Richard Swinburne and Alvin Plantinga.[4] On the other hand, monotheism is criticized for its irrational and even violent character, which paves the way for religious intolerance. This line of criticism started with David Hume's verdict on the "intolerance of almost all religions which have maintained the unity of God," which he observes to be just as remarkable as the contrary principle of polytheists.[5] Following David Hume, (mono)theism must be criticized for the intolerance inherent in its very character, as well as for the subsequent tendency to become violent towards others who uphold a different set of beliefs. The biblical God is not only imagined and portrayed as 'One,' but also as jealous of his oneness. As He asks to be worshipped as a unique God, He also inspires a typical zeal that is often difficult to temper.[6] In addition, the biblical God is repeatedly presented as acting in passion. His behavior and attitude towards mankind is not rational, but full of *pathos*; and his reaction to idolatry can be compared with that of a passionate lover, so that idolatry (not surprisingly) is often seen as a form of adultery.[7] Therefore, the biblical God is not a God of reason, but rather a God of *pathos*.

The changing political situation after the 9/11 attacks has put monotheism under even more pressure. The resulting 'clash of civilizations' (Huntington) has given rise to new forms of religion critique that are not only philosophi-

---

3 Eagleton, *Reason, Faith and Revolution*, 155.
4 Swinburne defended theism as being a simpler hypothesis than polytheism, since simpler hypotheses turn out more often to be true. Moreover, the universe exhibits a unity, in its universal natural laws for example. This unity argues for one deity as its originator (Richard Swinburne, *The Existence of God* (Oxford: Oxford University Press, 1991), 141 f). This thesis is complicated by the outcome of Assmann's research into the development of biblical monotheism, see below.
5 David Hume, *The Natural History of Religion* (Stanford: Stanford University Press, 1957), 48–51.
6 Peter Sloterdijk, *God's Zeal: The Battle of the Three Monotheisms* (Cambridge: Polity Press, 2009), 3, 160. (first published in German as: *Gottes Eifer: Vom Kampf der drei Monotheismen* (Frankfurt a. M.: Suhrkamp, 2007)).
7 As Moshe Halbertal and Avishai Margalit point out in their study of idolatry: the prohibition of idolatry can be seen as the fundamental difference between pagan and non-pagan (i.e. monotheist) religions (Moshe Halbertal & Avishai Margalit, *Idolatry* (Cambridge/ London: Harvard University Press, 1992), 10–14, 25–30).

cally inspired, but also motivated by concern about detrimental effects of theism/monotheism on contemporary society. Parallels are drawn between the monotheism of the three Abrahamic religions, with a keen eye for especially those religious expressions and actions that threaten or cause damage in society. Worshipping one God is not only an intellectual or rational act that can be defended in a civilized way; it is also, and perhaps in the first place, an expression of belonging to a certain culture that asks to be defended against others. A particular monotheist religion inevitably makes distinctions between those who partake in the right religion and those who do not: between friends and foes. Recent examples of the consequences following from such religiously inspired distinctions are the atrocities of the Boko Haram movement in Nigeria and the violence of anti-abortion activists in the US. The present article contains an analysis and comparison of the arguments put forward by two prominent contemporary critics of monotheism: Paul Cliteur and Peter Sloterdijk. Both question the influence of religious attitudes in modern society, although for different reasons, and in doing so, both concentrate on the relation between violence and monotheism. Further reflection on the question of what characterizes monotheistic violence will lead us to the work of Egyptologist Jan Assmann, who bases his perspective on historical research into the origins of monotheism. Finally, the discussion about monotheism and violence will be related to the controversial story of Abraham's trial in Genesis 22, which in many interpretations (in our time, but also in the past) was a reason for rejecting not only the 'violent' God of Abraham, but also Abraham's way of being faithful.

Monotheism

One of the stumbling blocks for Christian theology as well as Christian philosophy seems to be their commitment to monotheism as an essential feature of Christian faith. Of course, essential features do not exist. They are constantly under construction, in revision, and receive criticism from different perspectives. One could question whether Christian faith is essentially monotheist, or one could try to overcome certain problems of monotheism by a weaker form of theism (Vattimo). From a different perspective, Slavoj Žižek has repeatedly claimed that Christianity is a consistent form of atheism. Some theologians opt for a mild form of polytheism, to evade the problematic consequences of monotheism.[8] However, for this occasion I propose to leave aside these

---

8 See several articles in Anne-Marie Korte & Maaike de Haardt (eds.), *The Boundaries of Monotheism: Interdisciplinary Explorations into the Foundations of Western Monotheism* (Leiden/Boston: Brill, 2009).

nuanced discussions about monotheism among theologians and academics, to concentrate on another, related question that is important when reflecting on the recent struggle between God and civilization: What representations of Christian faith do we meet in the public debate and in the public domain? When we look at Christian faith from this perspective, the conclusion is evident: Christianity is seen as one of the three great monotheist traditions; which means that Christians are seen as humans who believe that reality's ultimate principle is God, understood as a Being that is omnipotent, omniscient and good; and that as such He is the creative ground of everything other than Himself. Monotheism is the view that there is only one such God.[9]

This perspective on Christianity can be found in the writings of 'outsiders' like Paul Cliteur and Peter Sloterdijk. In their recent publications on religion Christianity is taken with Judaism and Islam as a theist (or monotheist) religion. Furthermore, both Cliteur and Sloterdijk see a connection between monotheism and violence. It is this aspect of their representation of monotheism in the public domain that I would like to concentrate on in what follows.

One preliminary remark: the motivation and outcome of both Cliteur's and Sloterdijk's reflection on Christian faith as monotheism is above all critical. Sometimes they seem to be driven not by the desire to understand, but by a desire not to understand. The result is that Christians (and others, also religious Jews and Muslims) will react by saying that they are not 'properly understood.' In my view, this can be the basis for a fruitful discussion. It is the hermeneutics of such a discussion that needs to be thought through for any religious or theological debate that sets itself the task of reflecting on the relation between 'God' and 'civilization.'

Cliteur's Critique of Monotheism

For Paul Cliteur it is clear that Christian religion should be seen as a monotheist religion. In his perspective, there is no real difference between monotheism and theism. Theists, he argues, are adherents of one of the three theist religions, Judaism, Christianity and Islam. Theists believe in one God (strictly speaking, monotheism is therefore a pleonasm).[10] Theists have specific ideas

---

9   *Stanford Encyclopedia of Philosophy*, lemma "Monotheism": http://plato.stanford.edu/entries/monotheism/.
10 Paul Cliteur, *The Secular Outlook: In Defense of Moral and Political Secularism* (Oxford: Wiley/Blackwell, 2010), 17. See also Paul Cliteur, *Het monotheïstisch dilemma* of *De theolo-*

about their God. 'He' is good, even perfectly good, eternal, the creator of the universe, omniscient, almighty, transcendent, holy and He is seen as a person.

Of course, Cliteur is also aware that not all Christians would agree with this summary of what they believe in. He mentions other perspectives on God, such as Tillich's translation of God in terms of an 'ultimate concern,' and Robinson's death-of-God or atheist theology. But ultimately Cliteur evaluates these options as not being very influential on the main course of his argument. For him, such 'liberal' points of view are only deviant perspectives that, in the end, will make people who agree with the 'liberal outlook' on Christian faith more open to the strictly secular perspective that Cliteur argues for. For liberal believers, religious faith has become optional, and ultimately not of any importance for culture and society. In Cliteur's eyes, liberal theologians and liberal believers in fact already share his perspective on society, which ideally would have to be secular.

It is clear that Cliteur rejects both the option of a multicultural society and the option of a dialogue between different religious groups. In his perspective the nature or character of monotheism itself prevents it from fully participating in a multireligious, multicultural discussion.[11] This can be deduced from what he calls the 'logic' of monotheism. Monotheism, in the end, cannot avoid confronting its adherents with the dilemma of whom they should follow and obey, the commandments of their God that apply in their religious community, or the laws of the country they live in.

What vice can be discovered in the nature of monotheism (or theism) that justifies Cliteur's quite vigorous critique? The root of all problems of course has to be sought in what is seen as the nature or character of monotheism itself: religion that proclaims the existence of one God as the 'One and Only.' This monotheist 'root decree' already contains a first explanation of its inherent violence. The declaration that there is and only can be 'One God' provokes antagonism towards beliefs of a different type. In the line of David Hume's critique of monotheist religions, Cliteur also concludes that polytheism must be a more peaceful conception of religion. Nevertheless, he has to admit that certain questions can be raised about the strictness of monotheist belief from the outset. How monotheistic were the Israelites if one can conclude from biblical sources that they still had the tendency to worship other gods? Apparently, these gods 'existed' in their religious imagination, besides the God that should be worshipped as the 'One and Only.' Cliteur solves this problem by regarding

---

    gie van het terrorisme (*The Monotheist Dilemma* or *The Theology of Terrorism*) (Amsterdam/Antwerpen: De Arbeiderspers, 2010).

11   Cliteur, *Secular Outlook*, 5 f; and Cliteur, *Monotheïstisch dilemma*, 17.

the religion of Israel as 'incipiently,' in principle, monotheist, but sometimes polytheist in practice.[12]

Another line of thought is the relation of monotheism to ethics. This seems to be Cliteur's most urgent problem with monotheism, as it is related to its concrete ethical and political effect. Here, his argument is as follows: if God is really the One and Only, then his commandments are absolute and have to be obeyed. Cliteur holds that the effect of this monotheist point of view can most clearly be seen in the story about the sacrifice of Abraham (or *Aqedah*, Gen. 22), and accordingly he reads this story as an illustration of the attitude that theist believers would regard as 'morally right': it is right to perform an action commanded by God.[13] This is a problematic inference that fails to do justice to the many different ways the story has been read in Jewish, Christian and Islamic tradition;[14] but that is not Cliteur's point here. We will leave this interesting discussion, because the point that Cliteur wants to make is clear for our purposes: he makes use of the story of Abraham's sacrifice—and to a lesser extent of Old Testament stories like that of Jephtah (Judg. 11) and Phineas (Num. 25)—as an abhorrent example of the violence that is hidden in theist (monotheist) religion. From an ethical perspective he concludes that theism provides ethics with the most secure basis one can imagine: absolute divine certainty. Even among unbelievers and relativists, the Divine Command Theory has the reputation of being objective, universal and a stable basis for morality.

One of Cliteur's reasons for rejecting the Divine Command Theory is that it provides a perfect basis for religious terrorism. In this way the connection with the violent character of monotheism is easily made. Cliteur underlines it by quoting the Dutch jihadist Jason W.: "I do not do this because I like fighting, but because the Almighty has commanded this: Fighting is obligatory for you, much as you dislike it. But you may hate a thing although it is good for you and love a thing although it is bad for you. God knows, but you know not."[15] He then draws a comparison with the dilemma Abraham was facing: should I substitute

---

12   Cliteur sees a development from this incipient form of monotheism towards the unequivocally monotheist religion of the prophets in Babylonian captivity (SO 188). See Isaiah 45:5: "I am the Lord, and there is no other; besides Me there is no God." He declares that this 'mature' conception of monotheism is the focus of his book (*Secular Outlook*, 188).

13   Cliteur, *Secular Outlook*, 189.

14   For a selection of different interpretations of Gen. 22 see: Ed Noort & Eibert Tigchelaar (eds.), *The Sacrifice of Isaac: The Aqedah (Genesis 22) and Its Interpretations* (Leiden/Boston: Brill, 2002).

15   Cliteur, *Secular Outlook*, 216. The quotation is from the farewell letter of Jason W. that was found after he had been arrested in The Hague on November 10, 2004. The arrest took

my own human judgment for that of God? From the perspective of ethics according to the Divine Command Theory as understood by Cliteur, the answer is clearly: no.

The hopeful part of this story is that, according to Cliteur, liberal democracies will be able to deal with the problems of religious violence and religious terrorism. The problematic part is that this may require complete re-evaluation of their religious traditions, in particular certain violent elements that are inherent in the theist conception of God.[16]

Does Monotheism Imply a Divine Command Theory?

Cliteur's critique of monotheism raises several questions. First there is the problem of whom he in fact addresses, for, as we have seen, several forms of monotheism are seen as harmless in *The Secular Outlook*. Liberal monotheists, whether Jew, Muslim or Christian, will not cause great difficulties in the society of which they form part. The critique is in fact limited to the orthodox and more extremist types of monotheism. Cliteur solves this puzzle by narrowing down the definition of monotheism in such a way that liberal believers are not included. This makes it easy to 'prove' the inherent violence of monotheism: groups that do not show violent behavior in words or deeds are not 'real monotheists.' This is not only evident case of begging the question, but also a line of arguing that negates the right of liberal believers to participate in discussions concerning religion on their own terms.

Another, related problem is Cliteur's quite narrow perspective on monotheism itself, which neglects its complicated history, and hence creates uncertainty as to the type of violence that originates in monotheism. As we have seen, Cliteur sees a strong connection between the monotheist type of violence and the Divine Command Theory. His critique of this theory is based on his reading of Gen. 22 and Kierkegaard's reception of the story in *Fear and Trembling*. But there are good grounds for arguing that neither Gen. 22 nor its interpretation in *Fear and Trembling* is about Divine Command Theory at all.[17] Here too, as in

---

place after a prolonged siege, during which Jason W. threw a hand grenade at police officers. In March 2006 he was convicted and sentenced to 15 years' imprisonment.

16   Cliteur, *Secular Outlook*, 218.

17   John Lippitt, *Kierkegaard and Fear and Trembling* (New York: Routledge, 2003) concedes that this is the most natural 'superficial' way to read the text, but also gives arguments why this simple reading is unsatisfactory as an interpretation of Kierkegaard's text as a whole (145 ff). See also Ed Noort, "Genesis 22: Human Sacrifice and Theology in the Hebrew Bible," in Noort & Tigchelaar, *Sacrifice of Isaac*, 1–20. Noort concludes that Gen.

the definition of monotheism, Cliteur's perspective is highly problematic, as he chooses the simplest interpretation of both theism and the form of ethics that seems to follow from it. When we look closely, there is no clear link between the nature of monotheism and the corresponding theory of Divine Command Ethics.[18]

Peter Sloterdijk: A Hygienic Perspective on Monotheism

Peter Sloterdijk, who in *God's Zeal* recounts the story of monotheist religions, reveals other aspects of the inherent violence of monotheism. The title of the book, *God's Zeal* (in German *Gottes Eifer, Vom Kampf der drei Monotheismen*), is telling: monotheist religions fire up their adherents, they become inspired by a holy zeal for God. A constant theme in Sloterdijk's book is the necessity of civilization. Its spiritual mission is the attempt to convert the treasures of transcultural knowledge into a living form of capital that can be invested in all existing cultures. Eventually, Sloterdijk returns to this theme when, in the conclusion of *God's Zeal*, he says that "the path of civilisation is the only one that is still open."[19]

Sloterdijk mentions several problems and tensions between monotheism and civilization. Referring to Derrida's *Spectres of Marx* (1994), he considers monotheist religions as conflict parties, whose belief structure contains radioactive material ("a manic-activist or messianic mass"[20]). It is this mass that requires analysis in order to open it up to the path of civilization Sloterdijk has in mind. What all monotheisms share is the transcendent character of their 'object,' and therefore Sloterdijk opens his deliberations (which he compares with performing open heart surgery) with a survey of the premises of monotheism,

---

22 is "a tale about a deadly threat and the rescue from it" (19). For an analysis based on biblical evidence, see Ed Noort, "Over het gebruik van Bijbelse teksten: Paul Cliteur en zijn monotheïstisch dilemma" (On the Use of Biblical Texts: Paul Cliteur and his Monotheist Dilemma), in Theo Boer, Heleen Maat et al. (eds.), *Van God gesproken: Over religieuze taal en relationele theologie* (*Speaking about God: On Religious Language and Relational Theology*), Valedictory volume Prof. Luco J. van den Brom (Zoetermeer: Boekencentrum, 2011), 188–202. See also the next chapter in the present volume, "The Irreducibility of Religious Faith" by Pieter Vos.

18   In addition, one wonders why a philosopher of law like Cliteur pays no attention at all to the doctrine of the two kingdoms (Augustine, Luther) and the way it was received in Calvinism.

19   Sloterdijk, *God's Zeal*, 160.

20   Sloterdijk, *God's Zeal*, 3.

meaning the structure of transcendence implied in it. Several aspects of transcendence are mentioned and four of them are singled out as forms of misunderstood transcendence (for instance: transcendence seen as an effect of the inaccessibility of the other).[21] But three other aspects are features of genuine transcendence, because they are irreducible—which means that the desire for transcendence cannot be fulfilled by other means (naturalist or functionalist). One such irreducible aspect of transcendence is that it offers the possibility to imagine another intelligence superior to human intelligence. Here Sloterdijk sees intelligence grow, choosing its own form of transcendence. This 'gesture' lives on in the world of books—the civilized world—as the piety of eager readers.[22]

Death is also connected with transcendence in a genuine way. As human beings need to imagine the place the dead have 'gone to,' the place of the dead remains transcendent, their 'abode' is represented as an elsewhere that eludes the alternatives of somewhere and nowhere. Tradition offers for this the words: 'with God,' 'Nirvana,' 'in the memory of those who love.'

The last and most precious aspect of genuine transcendence (as a gift to humanity and civilization) is the concept of revelation as the possibility to receive a message from beyond. A strong sender (and a metaphysics of the strong sender) is necessary for such a revelation, and transcendence in this context indicates the possibility of receiving a message that has life-altering significance.[23]

Sloterdijk hastens to add that the concept of revelation has become complex nowadays because of the modern turn to the subject. Since the Enlightenment, it has been replaced by the activist culture of rationality.[24] The positive outcome of this development is that theology is under constant pressure to consult not only divine words (in the form of revelation), but also to learn from others, and to interact with other ways of knowing, like arts and sciences. This is in line with an overall shift from a passive to an active attitude, also when faith is involved, for—as Sloterdijk brings forward—in the post-secular world, being a believer is an active decision which depends on the will to believe and less on the gift of faith.[25] Cultural science should be the true moderator of

---

21 Sloterdijk, *God's Zeal*, 9.
22 Sloterdijk, *God's Zeal*, 14.
23 Sloterdijk, *God's Zeal*, 15.
24 Sloterdijk, *God's Zeal*, 16.
25 Thus Sloterdijk in *God's Zeal*, 16; Sloterdijk's approach to secularity/post-secularity in this respect shows similarity to Charles Taylor's perspective in *A Secular Age* (Cambridge & London: Harvard University Press, 2007), 1–22.

global ecumenism. It has the responsibility to show why the path of civilization is the only one still open.

Sloterdijk also pays ample attention to the formation of monotheist religions. How did they develop: in sequence from one another or from older sources?[26] Referring to Thomas Mann's novel *Joseph and his Brothers*, he portrays Abraham as the protagonist in the drama of monotheism. With Abraham, the question whom humanity should serve came into being. The answer was: "the highest alone." In Thomas Mann's narration, Abraham imagined different possibilities (humanity could also worship mother earth or the sky as highest authority). But looking closer, the father of the faithful reached the conclusion that neither the earth nor the sky can be given the highest place: "No, they are not worthy to be my gods." Abraham thus arrives at the concept of an absolutely supreme, powerful and otherworldly God.[27] This impulse has been called the 'summotheistic affect,' a feeling that is paradigmatic for monotheist belief.

This affect calls for a relationship that Sloterdijk refers to as a "summotheistic alliance." The monotheist chain of reaction is typified from its very beginning by this contract between a great, serious psyche and a great, serious God.[28] It gives the believers stableness and satisfaction because, by submitting to the Highest, they share in His sovereignty. One consequence of monotheism is monolatry. It is the price that has to be paid for the singular alliance by the ruling out of lesser alliances.[29] Hence, there can never be monotheism without a form of ranking-based jealousy. Here, Sloterdijk finds the origin of the zeal and subsequent violence that monotheism produces.[30]

---

26   Sloterdijk announces that he will restrict himself to typological descriptions here, and will not focus on the history of the holy texts. His aim is to present the 'conflict parties' in the field (*God's Zeal*, 19).

27   Sloterdijk, *God's Zeal*, 20 f.

28   Sloterdijk, *God's Zeal*, 22.

29   Sloterdijk, *God's Zeal*, 24, with reference to the great scholar of language and religion Friedrich Max Müller (1823–1900), who coined the term *henotheism* for the evolutionary phase that precedes monotheism.

30   One of the most characteristic features of monotheism is the imagination of God as a person. Sloterdijk's interpretation of this invention is remarkable. He has a keen eye for the theoretical difficulty of this perspective, but also points to the practical advantage: God's actions towards the world become more comprehensible and communicable when seen as the actions of a person who can create, destroy, forbid, reward and punish like any other person.

God's Zeal and the Zeal of his Followers

A personal, jealous God that is presented as the One and Only can create dangerous forms of affectivity in the faithful who follow Him. In the Jewish Bible the examples are never far. Take Moses' commandment in Ex. 32:27: "let every man kill his brother, his friend and his neighbor." For Sloterdijk, the implication is that at Mount Sinai a "new moral quality for killing" was found: "it no longer served the survival of a tribe, but rather the triumph of a principle. This is the outcome of the evolution towards monotheism, in which God 'becomes an idea.'"[31] Consequently, God becomes a principle that asks for obeisance.

One effect of monotheism is that it changed the position of human beings in relation to God. The so-called 'summotheist alliance' also changed the idea that humankind forms of its own position. Sloterdijk pays attention to this aspect when he discusses the different forms of 'summotheism' that can be found in Western thought: varying from religious (belief in a personal God, Highest Being) to philosophical (the highest is the impersonal universe, as in Spinoza). The latter variant is inspired by a passion for depersonalization characteristic of Indian metaphysics. Sloterdijk calls this "impersonal supremacism."[32] The most subtle variant, which can be recognized in its latest form in the philosophy of Eckhart and Hegel, is noetic supremacism, in which the human mind is an important factor in the development and realization of the highest, which is now mainly seen as 'intelligence' (nous).

Sloterdijk describes personal supremacism as the most explosive and dangerous variant. The consequence of this form of summotheism is that man, in relation to the Most High, can only play the role of vassal or employee. "Whether they like it or not, the supremacization of the personal God inevitably assigns humans for an inferior status."[33] Therefore, human beings that participate in personal supremacism will develop an extreme will to obey the most rigid laws and commandments. The examples mentioned are not encouraging: they vary from the servant syndrome, which underlies suicide attacks, to the moderate version encountered in the Roman Catholic organization Opus Dei. Part of the structure is an irrational tendency to sacrifice, including (if necessary) the tendency to sacrifice reason itself. A striking example here is Abraham's sacrifice of Isaac, i.e., Abraham's willingness to obey God's commanding

---

31   Sloterdijk, *God's Zeal*, 26; this could be a reference to a later work of Levinas (*De Dieu qui vient à l'idée*, usually translated as *Of God who Comes to Mind*, but sometimes (wrongly) understood as *Of God who becomes an idea*).
32   Sloterdijk, *God's Zeal*, 85.
33   Sloterdijk, *God's Zeal*, 85.

voice. Abraham seems to be willing to obey even (or especially) when the command seems unfathomable.[34]

Reflecting on Sloterdijk and Cliteur: Monotheism and Its Discontents

Our theme was the image of God in the public domain. For Sloterdijk and Cliteur, this image is determined and problematized by the monotheist idea of God and religion in the three Abrahamic religions. Both point to monotheism to explain religiously inspired violence, although for different reasons. Cliteur focuses on the alleged relation between monotheism and the Divine Command Theory. Sloterdijk's arguments against monotheism emphasize the psychological aspect: for him the main problem is formed by the possibilities of monotheist religion to kindle religious zeal in its supporters. To put it differently: whereas Cliteur is an apostle of Enlightenment, as he repeats the Enlightened objections to monotheism, Sloterdijk's perspective on the problems of religion in general and monotheism in particular is inspired by the works of Friedrich Nietzsche and Sigmund Freud.

There is a close connection between the problem of the view of monotheism in the public domain and the position of human beings towards God, as represented in monotheist religions. The critics of monotheism bring forward that this position seems to be incompatible with (and does not stimulate) human autonomy and the possibility of free and critical thought. Both Sloterdijk and Cliteur refer to the stories about Abraham here, and their critique is ultimately the same: from the moment that one God is seen as the highest and most worthy to be revered, the position of human beings in relation to God can be no other than that of a servant or vassal who is obedient to the words of the Most High.

For this reason, Abraham's position is ambiguous. In the memory and tradition of monotheism his importance is undisputed (see Sloterdijk's positive evaluation of the 'invention' of transcendence by Abraham). But both authors express strong doubts as to whether this tradition is still worth following. Wasn't Abraham the one who listened when God asked him to sacrifice his only son? Should he have listened to God at that moment? Wouldn't it have been more advisable to consult his own conscience and enter into a discussion with God? (The questions asked here are the same that philosophers like Kant

---

34 Here too, as in Cliteur, especially Kierkegaard's account of Abraham's sacrifice influences the interpretation of what monotheism (understood as personal supremacism) is.

and Levinas raise in connection with Gen. 22—Levinas does so in relation to Kierkegaard's *Fear and Trembling*. I will return to this later.)

A last word on the differences in approach between Sloterdijk and Cliteur. Whereas Sloterdijk starts with a respectful overview of perspectives on transcendence, and praises some of them as being both characteristic of monotheist belief and uniquely significant for human civilization, Cliteur's account of monotheist belief is—as we have seen—strikingly shallow. He acts like an anthropologist who visits a strange clan with beliefs and superstitions, and sees no other way than to address them with a 'hermeneutics of condescension'— the expression is gratefully borrowed from the author Marilynne Robinson, who used it to characterize the modern 'enlightened' attitude towards religion.[35]

Sloterdijk does not share Cliteur's 'missionary of enlightenment' attitude; and his ironic account of the zealous effects of religion seems to be more open to a discussion that makes the crossing of boundaries possible. But ultimately he too adopts an attitude of condescension towards religious belief. In *God's Zeal* the leading perspective is Nietzsche's critique of culture with emphasis on the psycho-hygienic part of this project. In this approach, religious acts like worshipping (the name of) God appear as the expression of a desire for destruction that is present in every religious soul.[36] Monotheist religion is at best a form of illness that has to be cured. It is true that Sloterdijk distinguishes between mild and acute forms of the disease, but this difference is only gradual. In sum, both for Sloterdijk and Cliteur, monotheist religions are not judged in their own right, but merely evaluated according to their ability to restrain the existential rage of their more extremist followers.

Assmann: Monotheism as Counter-Religion

After we have reflected on the differences and similarities in the attitudes of Cliteur and Sloterdijk on monotheism, there are two aspects of the field of discussion they open that I would like to look further into. First, Assmann's study on the origins of monotheism, is mentioned by both, but—in my view—not

---

35 Marilynne Robinson, *Absence of Mind: The Dispelling of Inwardness from the Modern Myth of the Self* (New Haven & London: Yale University Press, 2010), 14: "[Religion is] treated as a proof of persisting primitivity among human beings, ... [it] legitimizes ... the assumption that humankind is itself fearful, irrational, deluded, and self-deceived, excepting, of course, these missionaries of enlightenment."

36 Sloterdijk, *God's Zeal*, 156 f.

properly valued as regards its consequence for the meaning of monotheism. Second, and finally, the interpretation of Gen. 22, being a familiar topic in the discussion about the inherent violent character of monotheism, deserves some attention.

Both Sloterdijk and Cliteur refer to the work of the German Egyptologist Jan Assmann, but surprisingly enough without mentioning those aspects of Assmann's research which could help to understand the relation between monotheism and violence.[37] This subject was brought into discussion by the release of *Moses the Egyptian* (1998);[38] the most important reactions to this book were reprinted in *Die Mosaische Unterscheidung* (2003), where Assmann attempts to answer his critics. We will here follow Assmann's argumentation regarding the violence of monotheism as it is given in *Of God and gods*.[39]

In Assmann's perspective, biblical monotheism is not the outcome of an evolution from polytheism to the conviction that there is 'only one God.' He shows that various tendencies towards a hierarchy are present in polytheism itself, as one can take the many gods to be represented in one higher God. In fact, there is no polytheist confession that 'God is manifold' or 'many Gods exist.'

Therefore, monotheism must not be seen as the outcome of an evolution from many representations of the divine to one representation. Especially biblical monotheism can best be understood as an ongoing attempt to make a distinction between true and false religion.[40] What makes biblical monotheism different and new is its concept of reality and of the relation between the divine and the human sphere. The cosmos ceases to appear as a manifestation of divine presence, and is seen as a 'creation' of God. Another difference is the

---

37   Sloterdijk, *God's Zeal*, 151–154; Cliteur, *Monotheïstisch dilemma*, 191–194.

38   Jan Assmann, *Moses the Egyptian* (Cambridge: Harvard University Press, 1997); *Die Mosaische Unterscheidung, oder der Preis des Monotheismus* (*The Mosaic Distinction: or the Price of Monotheism*) (Munich: Carl Hanser, 2003), translated as *The Price of Monotheism* (Stanford: Stanford University Press, 2003)—this edition omits the critical articles mentioned before. Cliteur refers to this discussion in *Monotheïstisch dilemma*, 191–194.

39   Jan Assmann, *Of God and gods: Egypt, Israel and the Rise of Monotheism* (London/Wisconsin: University of Wisconsin Press 2008).

40   In Assmann's view, it was not Moses, but the Egyptian pharaoh Akhenaten (Echnaton) who 'invented' this distinction. Akhenaten was especially noted for abandoning traditional Egyptian polytheism and introducing a form of religion which is sometimes described as monotheistic or henotheistic. But Moses made a deeper and more lasting inscription in our collective cultural memory; and it is for this reason that the distinction so characteristic of biblical monotheism is called a Mosaic distinction in Assmann's research (*Of God and gods*, 107 f).

place of stories about the divine: the narrations are no longer seen as stories told about the gods, but as a *historia sacra* (sacred history), while their written codification no longer has the function of presenting the divine in a magical way.[41] As a result, biblical monotheism has the effect of creating a sphere with a normativity of its own, which is separated (therefore 'distinct') from other spheres, like the cultural and/or political realm.[42] Its effect is an emancipation from the political and cosmic power structure of the ancient world. This separation between religion and other cultural factors implies a distinction between true and false expressions of religion. As Assmann formulates it:

> ... this distinction, rather than the widespread idea of the unity of the divine, was the great innovation that transformed the ancient world in the form of an axial breakthrough. The distinction between true and false was alien to 'primary religion' which was based on distinctions as pure and impure, sacred and profane. Its introduction signalled a revolutionary step in creating a new type of religion. For the first time—and quite unlike primary religion—this new type sets itself apart not only from other religions, including its own religious tradition, but also from such other spheres of culture as politics, law, and economics.[43]

One of the questions Assmann keeps returning to is about the consequences of this discovery for the relation between religion and violence. Is violence the natural implication of this 'Mosaic distinction?' He argues that, in order to approach this question in the right framework, it is necessary to distinguish different types of violence. Violence, also religious violence, can be intra-systemic and extra-systemic. Sacrifice, for instance, and particularly the sacrifice of humans, is a form of intra-systemic violence that plays a central role where monotheism sets itself against paganism. One of the examples is Gen. 22, where one of the sub-themes of the story is the possible critical view of human sacrifice (although, as Assmann rightly observes, this is not the only and certainly not the most interesting interpretation of the *Aqedah*).[44]

In this respect, biblical monotheism brought a movement towards humanism; which would make it absurd to assume that it was monotheism that introduced violence into the world. The only new form of violence that comes into being with the invention of monotheism is extra-systemic violence: violence

---

41 Assmann, *Of God and gods*, 26 f.
42 Assmann, *Of God and gods*, 84.
43 Assmann, *Of God and gods*, 84.
44 Assmann, *Of God and gods*, 31.

against idolaters and heresy. This, however, is more a question of theory than practice.[45] In sum, Assmann's perspective leads towards an interpretation of biblical monotheism as a counter-religion. Its critique of others who worship other gods is typical of the kind of revolution it brought about. Its fundamental form is not: 'There is only one god,' but rather: 'no other Gods,' or 'no god but God.'

Assmann's ideas about the cultural and religious roots of monotheism give insight into the kind of violence it produces, and relativize the assumption that violence is inherent in monotheism by distinguishing intra- and extra-systemic violence. Nevertheless, it is clear that monotheism is not completely without violence, because new boundaries are drawn, between God and other gods, truth and untruth, us and them, present and past, the new and the old.

One strong characteristic of this monotheism is its rhetoric of conversion. Here we see that its violence lies not in the idea of truth itself, but rather in the conviction that untruth must be persecuted. However, as Assmann brings forward: there is no logical necessity for the distinction between true and untrue to turn into violence. This only turns real if the distinction truth-untruth is interpreted in terms of friend and foe, but again, this step is not necessary.[46]

Monotheism, Violence and Genesis 22

Finally, I would like to return to the story of Abraham's trial in Gen. 22, which is referred to by both Cliteur and Sloterdijk as a dangerous story about a violent God who provokes acts of violence in His people. Abraham, who is seen by all faithful monotheists as their forefather and example, was in fact prepared to sacrifice (murder) his beloved son Isaac, solely because God asked him to do so. The critique is that Abraham failed to see that he should have thought for himself. He missed the autonomous aspect of human subjectivity and wrongly focused only on a Voice that told him to act against ethics. This critique of Abraham's attitude is not new; in fact, Kant already expressed it.[47] It was Kierkegaard who, in search of a genuine 'Christian thought,' found the way back to Abraham and started to write on faith as a passion for paradox and for the absurd, starting from the story about Abraham's trial in Gen. 22.

---

45 Assmann, *Of God and gods*, 31
46 Assmann rightly underlines in this connection that the Jewish version of biblical monotheism has never led to a violent outcome (*Of God and gods*, 111).
47 Immanuel Kant, *Der Streit der Fakultäten*, in Immanuel Kant, *Werke* (ed. Wilhelm Weischedel), Vol. 9 (Darmstadt: Wissenschaftliche Buchgesellschaft, 1983), A 103.

For this moment, I will not enter into the details of the complex interpretation history of Gen. 22, but will confine myself to a few remarks about the story of Abraham's trial as a contribution to reflection on the theme of God's violence in relation to the image of God in the public sphere.

First, even a short look at this story and the very diverse ways it has been interpreted shows that it is not about Divine Commandment. What's more, every attempt to listen to and react to this story is itself embedded in a history of interpretations. In Jewish perspective, it is called the *Aqedah*, with Isaac as the center of attention: he is bound to the altar place, and it is his faithful surrender to what has to happen to him that, surprisingly enough, has been a source of inspiration for the Jewish people through the ages.[48]

How about the violence of the story? Asking for the sacrifice of a son is one thing, but in the end, the performance of the offering is prevented. For this reason, the practice of child sacrifice is possibly a subtext of Genesis but, as Noort argues, it can never be its main theme.[49] In that case, the story would have been less influential and would have lost its relevance for later times, where human sacrifices are a matter of the past.

It is Kierkegaard's merit both to have insisted on the abiding relevance of the account of Abraham's trial and to give insight into the deeper meaning of Abraham's attitude towards God against the critique of both Kant and Hegel.[50] Kierkegaard does not take the story for granted, but starts with the great difficulties it presents to readers and interpreters. "How to preach about Abraham?" is the constantly repeated question throughout *Fear and Trembling*. How to enter this story without pretending to know what the ending will be? Is it possible to understand Abraham in the situation where he answered to both commandments: the voice of God who asked him to sacrifice Isaac and the

---

48 Eli Wiesel, *Messengers of God* (New York: Random House, 1976). For more aspects of the Jewish interpretation of Gen. 22, see W.J. van Bekkum, "The Aqedah and Its Interpretations in Midrash and Piyyut," in Noort & Tigchelaar, *Sacrifice of Isaac*, 86.

49 Noort, "Human Sacrifice," 19 f.

50 On *Fear and Trembling* and Hegel, see Lippitt, *Kierkegaard and Fear and Trembling*, 85–91. The sections in *Fear and Trembling* on the relation of faith and reason, on the meaning of the ethical and on the problem of communicating religious belief should be interpreted as an answer to Hegel's position towards religion. For Hegel, Abraham represents an 'unhappy consciousness,' i.e. an inability to account for the unity of all things. This is not only the case in *Phenomenologie des Geistes*, but also in Hegel's earlier text *Der Geist des Christentums*. Here, Abraham's form of monotheism and his willingness to sacrifice Isaac are seen as signs of an attitude of deep estrangement that is rooted in his relation to a strange God (Georg W.F. Hegel, *Der Geist des Christentums*, in Georg W.F. Hegel, *Werke I (Frühe Schriften)* (Frankfurt a/M: Suhrkamp, 1972), 278 f).

voice of God who told him to do no harm to the boy on the altar? Here, the drama of the faithful begins, and it seems no easy task to make it communicable. Therefore, if we want to think about Gen. 22, we should take it up, as Kierkegaard does in *Fear and Trembling*, as a story that confronts us with the problem of communication of faith, the more so because Kierkegaard gives a reading of this story against the grain of his rational and idealistic predecessors, who are troubled by the dark side of the covenant between God and human beings.[51]

The Pathos of Monotheism? Concluding Remarks

We started this article by asking what perspective on the potential violence of monotheism was developed by contemporary critical voices like those of Paul Cliteur, Peter Sloterdijk and Jan Assmann. Paul Cliteur is apparently the most critical towards the violence implicit in the Divine Command Theory that (he assumes) can be derived from the story of Abraham's sacrifice in Gen. 22 and its influential interpretation by Kierkegaard in *Fear and Trembling*. But we also discovered that neither Gen. 22 nor its interpretation in *Fear and Trembling* gives rise to a genuine Divine Command Theory. Besides, Cliteur's approach clearly begs the question because he refuses liberal believers the right to call themselves 'monotheist' or 'theist' on the basis of his own (narrow) definition of monotheism. Cliteur's critique falls short in both respects because he misinterprets the material.

Peter Sloterdijk puts forward another interpretation of the potential violence of monotheism. He gives strong emphasis to the zealous effects of monotheist religions. According to Sloterdijk, monotheist religion is at best a form of illness that needs proper treatment. Here too, as in the approach of Paul Cliteur, we perceived a difficulty because faith is not considered a phenomenon that deserves respect in its own right; rather the attitude is one of condescendence. Finally, both Sloterdijk and Cliteur mainly evaluate monotheist religions according to their 'hygienic' capacities, i.e. their ability to restrain the existential rage of their followers.

Assmann, on the contrary, presents a more congenial attitude towards monotheism, without sharing its presuppositions. Reflecting on historical research into the origins of monotheism in what he calls the 'Mosaic distinction' (the distinction between true and untrue forms of worship that is triggered by the conception that no other god should be worshipped but 'God'), he

---

51   On the dark side of God in Gen. 22, see also Noort, "Human Sacrifice," 20.

differentiates between various types of religious violence. Consequently, with reference to the story of Gen. 22, he argues that it would be absurd to assume that it was monotheism that brought violence into the world. On the other hand, monotheism too is not without violence. This leads to the insight that the only new form of violence created by the invention of monotheism is 'extra-systemic violence,' i.e. violence against idolaters and heresy.

Turning, for the last time, to the story of Abraham's sacrifice and its interpretation by Kierkegaard, we discovered through the reading of *Fear and Trembling* that Gen. 22 should not be considered a story about the violence of the divine commandment, but rather a story that confronts the reader with the difficult question of how to communicate faith. Especially Kierkegaard's reading of the story in *Fear and Trembling* conveys in a persuasive and palpable way that faith cannot be seen as the reflection of objectified truth. Therefore, the communication of faith is not the communication of certain truths 'about God,' but rather means an initiation into the relationship that Abraham J. Heschel named *'pathos'*, with reference to the state of mind of the Old Testament prophets. Claiming that *pathos* is not without an element of reason, Heschel emphasized that *pathos* is a characteristic element in the relation between God and human beings, as both are engaged in relating to each other, which provokes a movement without certainty that asks for mutual trust.[52] Perhaps reflection on this 'pathological' aspect of faith could help us to discover what monotheist religion really is about, and why it possesses certain features that are strange and indeed uncommon in modern society.

Bibliography

Assmann, Jan, *Die Mosaische Unterscheidung, oder der Preis des Monotheismus (The Mosaic Distinction, or the Price of Monotheism)* (Munich: Carl Hanser, 2003).
———, *Moses the Egyptian* (Cambridge: Harvard University Press, 1997).
———, *Of God and gods: Egypt, Israel and the Rise of Monotheism* (London/Wisconsin: University of Wisconsin Press, 2008).
———, *The Price of Monotheism* (Stanford: Stanford University Press, 2003).
Bekkum, W.J. van, "The Aqedah and Its Interpretations in Midrash and Piyyut," in Ed Noort & Eibert Tigchelaar (eds.), *The Sacrifice of Isaac: The Aqedah (Genesis 22) and Its Interpretations* (Leiden/Boston: Brill, 2002).

---

52   Abraham J. Heschel, *The Prophets* (New York: Harper&Row, 1962), 221–231.

Cliteur, Paul, *Het monotheïstisch dilemma* of *De theologie van het terrorisme* (*The Monotheist Dilemma* or *The Theology of Terrorism*) (Amsterdam/Antwerpen: De Arbeiderspers, 2010).

———, *The Secular Outlook: In Defense of Moral and Political Secularism* (Oxford: Wiley/Blackwell, 2010).

Eagleton, Terry, *Reason, Faith and Revolution, Reflections on the God Debate* (New Haven & London: Yale University Press, 2009).

Grayling, A.C., *The God Argument: The Case* against *Religion and* for *Humanism* (London/New York: Bloomsbury, 2013).

Halbertal, Moshe & Avishai Margalit, *Idolatry* (Cambridge/ London: Harvard University Press, 1992).

Hegel, Georg W.F., *Der Geist des Christentums*, in Georg W.F. Hegel, *Werke I* (*Frühe Schriften*) (Frankfurt a/M: Suhrkamp, 1972).

Heschel, Abraham J., *The Prophets* (New York: Harper&Row, 1962).

Hume, David, *The Natural History of Religion* (Stanford: Stanford University Press, 1957).

Kant, Immanuel, *Der Streit der Fakultäten*, in Immanuel Kant, *Werke* (ed. Wilhelm Weischedel), Vol. 9 (Darmstadt: Wissenschaftliche Buchgesellschaft, 1983), 371–393.

Kierkegaard, Søren A., *Fear and Trembling & Repetition, Kierkegaard's Writings*, Vol. VI, ed. and trans. Howard V. Hong & Edna H. Hong (Princeton: Princeton University Press, 1983).

Korte, Anne-Marie & Maaike de Haardt (eds.), *The Boundaries of Monotheism: Interdisciplinary Explorations into the Foundations of Western Monotheism* (Leiden/Boston: Brill, 2009).

Lippitt, John, *Kierkegaard and Fear and Trembling* (New York: Routledge, 2003).

"Monotheism," in *Stanford Encyclopedia of Philosophy*, http://plato.stanford.edu/entries/monotheism/.

Noort, Ed, "Genesis 22: Human Sacrifice and Theology in the Hebrew Bible," in Ed Noort & Eibert Tigchelaar (eds.), *The Sacrifice of Isaac: The Aqedah* (*Genesis 22*) *and Its Interpretations* (Leiden/Boston: Brill, 2002), 1–20.

———, "Over het gebruik van Bijbelse teksten: Paul Cliteur en zijn monotheïstisch dilemma" (On the Use of Biblical Texts: Paul Cliteur and his Monotheist Dilemma), in Theo Boer, Heleen Maat et al. (eds.), *Van God gesproken: Over religieuze taal en relationele theologie* (*Speaking about God: On Religious Language and Relational Theology*), Valedictory volume Prof. Luco J. van den Brom (Zoetermeer: Boekencentrum, 2011), 188–202.

Noort, Ed & Eibert Tigchelaar (eds.), *The Sacrifice of Isaac: The Aqedah* (*Genesis 22*) *and Its Interpretations* (Leiden/Boston: Brill, 2002).

Robinson, Marilynne, *Absence of Mind: The Dispelling of Inwardness from the Modern Myth of the Self* (New Haven & London: Yale University Press, 2010).

Sloterdijk, Peter, *God's Zeal: The Battle of the Three Monotheisms* (Cambridge: Polity Press, 2009).

———, *Gottes Eifer: Vom Kampf der drei Monotheismen* (Frankfurt a. M.: Suhrkamp, 2007).

Swinburne, Richard, *The Existence of God* (Oxford: Oxford University Press, 1991).

Taylor, Charles, *A Secular Age* (Cambridge & London: Harvard University Press, 2007).

Wiesel, Eli, *Messengers of God* (New York: Random House, 1976).

The Irreducibility of Religious Faith
Kierkegaard on Civilization and the Aqedah

Pieter Vos

Since many theorists in the fields of religious studies and sociology have pointed out the end of the secularization thesis, religion returned in debates on civilization, civil society, the public domain, education, and *Bildung*. In these debates several (contradictory) positions can be distinguished. Some advocate a greater influence of religion in these domains on religious grounds. Others support this view on non-religious grounds, pleading for a rehabilitation of religion as cultural inheritance ('the Jewish-Christian tradition') and emphasizing its civilizing potential for society. To give an example, in the domain of education civilization has been connected to the concept of *Bildung*,[1] originally understood in religious terms as it was related to the German word *bilden* meaning 'to shape' or 'to form' (cf. Latin *formatio*) and referring to the Genesis narrative in which man was formed in the image of God (*imago Dei*). Since the Enlightenment the concept generally secularized,[2] but nowadays several philosophical educationalists plead for reconnecting the concept of *Bildung* with 'the Other' or with God, in order to come up with inadequacies of the secularist outlook of modern education and formation theories.[3]

Others, however, precisely make a new strong case for secularism, being aware of the threats of religious violence, in particular terrorism. The Dutch philosopher of law Paul Cliteur defends a 'secular outlook' on life as the only

---

1 Especially in Germany but also in other countries where the word is adopted as an untranslatable but still valuable concept. Initially, the German *Bildung* had a meaning parallel to the French and English *civilisation*. Since the beginning of the nineteenth century in Germany the concept of *Kultur* including *Bildung* was contrasted against the English and French *civilisation (Zivilization)*. See Pim den Boer, "Vergelijkende begripsgeschiedenis," in Pim den Boer (ed.), *Beschaving: Een geschiedenis van de begrippen hoofsheid, heusheid, beschaving en cultuur (Civilization: A History of the Concepts Courtliness, Courtesy, Civilization, and Culture)* (Amsterdam: Amsterdam University Press, 2001), 15–78: 37.
2 Hans-Jürgen Fraas, *Bildung und Menschenbild in theologischer Perspektive* (Göttingen: Vandenhoeck & Ruprecht, 2000), 42–105.
3 Michael Wimmer, "The Gift of *Bildung*: Reflections on the Relationship between Singularity and Justice in the Concept of *Bildung*," in Gert J.J. Biesta & Denise Egéa-Kuehne (eds.), *Derrida & Education* (London & New York: Routledge, 2001), 150–175; Herner Sæverot, "Bildung, God, and the Ethical School," Conference paper Philosophy of Education Society of Australasia 2010, retrieved from http://www.pesa.org.au, on 17 February 2012.

condition for making peaceful living of believers and non-believers possible. In this view it is a matter of civilization to teach the basic principles of moral secularism and moral autonomy over against religious heteronomy as the only guarantee for the continuation of Western civilization.[4]

One of the key issues in secularism is the promotion of an autonomous morality against religious (mono)theism (Judaism, Christianity, and Islam) and its presumed ethics. As Renée van Riessen has pointed out in the previous chapter, according to Cliteur (mono)theism's ethics (or meta-ethics) is what is known as the Divine Command Theory assuming that what is morally right is synonymous with what has been commanded, prescribed, or ordered by God.[5] The classic example of this ethics is found with the father of the Abrahamic religions: Abraham, who proved to be the father of faith by his willingness to obey the divine command to kill his only son Isaac (or in the Islamic version: Isma'il), as described in Gen. 22 and in the Qu'ran, 37:91–110. In the Divine Command Theory, God's command to Abraham is seen as the proof of the supremacy of faith over reason in a religious ethics.

One of the most evocative interpretations of the *Aqedah*, the Binding of Isaac, is found in Søren Kierkegaard's *Fear and Trembling*,[6] for the divine command to offer one's son is presented here as a real dilemma, a *horror religiosus*, between we could say the law of God and 'civilized' morality.[7] Kierkegaard's pseudonymous author Johannes *de silentio* sets the dilemma: either ethics legislates religion or religion legislates ethics. Or, to frame it in Plato's famous Euthyphro-dilemma: is something good because God wills it, or does God will the good because it is good?

According to Cliteur, however, Kierkegaard's alter ego chooses the wrong side. In advocating 'a teleological suspension of the ethical' the author

---

4 Paul Cliteur, *The Secular Outlook: In Defense of Moral and Political Secularism* (Oxford: Wiley-Blackwell, 2010).
5 Cliteur, *Secular Outlook*, 189–194.
6 Søren A. Kierkegaard, *Fear and Trembling & Repetition, Kierkegaard's Writings*, Vol. VI, ed. and trans. Howard V. Hong & Edna H. Hong (Princeton: Princeton University Press, 1983), 1–123. In this article I will quote from this edition. References to the new standard Danish edition will be added between brackets: *Søren Kierkegaard Skrifter* (København: Gads Forlag 1997–2013), abbreviated as SKS, of which volume 4 contains *Frygt og Bæven*.
7 The title of the book illustrates this *horror religiosus* referring to the Pauline word in Phil. 2: 12–13. Kierkegaard himself was well aware of the importance of his book, as he wrote in one of his *Papirer* (Journals and Notebooks): "Once I am dead, *Fear and Trembling* alone will be enough for an imperishable name as an author. Then it will be read, translated into foreign languages as well" (SKS 22, 235; NB12: 147).

"legitimizes religiously motivated terrorism and fundamentalism."[8] Therefore, *Fear and Trembling* must be disqualified as one of the most dangerous books in the history of philosophy. We had better follow Immanuel Kant, who, every time God commands something that violates the moral law, simply said: 'this cannot be the voice of God.'[9] A rejection of the Divine Command Theory implicit in the story of Abraham and in Kierkegaard's book is all the more pertinent once we realize that this attitude is not something that is to be found only in old religious books, but in real life as well. Abraham's attitude can result in a total rejection of legal authority and in a direct claim to operate as the executor of God's own will, a view that religious extremists actually subscribe to and which brings them into conflict with the great values of Western democracy and civilization.

In this contribution, I will demonstrate that Cliteur is not right in interpreting the juxtaposition of moral reason and Abraham's faith in *Fear and Trembling* as a choice in favor of a divine command ethics. An in-depth reading of Kierkegaard's book will reveal that with Kierkegaard the relation between ethics and religion is more complicated than Cliteur presents it. It is not simply a matter of deciding what is highest: the religious or the ethical. To understand this, specific characteristics of Kierkegaard's book have to be taken into account. It is not without meaning that *Fear and Trembling* is published under a pseudonym. Johannes *de silentio* writes from a specific perspective, i.e. of a person who neither has faith nor understands it. From an outsider's perspective the author nevertheless has an illuminating understanding of what faith is *not*. Furthermore, as a 'dialectical lyric' (subtitle) the book cannot be reduced to a systematic treatise on ethics and religion. In the text multiple levels of meaning are present, each level having its own narrative and significance.

The aim of this article is to reinvestigate the relationship between religion and ethics, divine command and human morality in Kierkegaard's *Fear and Trembling*, in dialogue with modern thinkers such as Kant and Hegel, with a focus on issues of civilization and *Bildung*. Numerous interpretations of Kierkegaard's book have been offered, but less attention has been paid to the implications for these themes. In Kierkegaard's use of the Danish word *Dannelse* both the concepts of civilization and *Bildung* come together. By analyzing the book as a discourse on five distinct levels,[10] I will argue that Kierkegaard helps us to understand that religion is irreducible to what it contributes to morality

---

8   Paul Cliteur in *Filosofie magazine* (*Philosophy Magazine*) 13:10 (2004), 29.
9   Cliteur, *Secular Outlook*, 217.
10 I derive the first four levels from Ronald M. Green, "'Developing' *Fear and Trembling*," in Alastair Hannay & Gordon D. Marino (eds.), *The Cambridge Companion to Kierkegaard*

and civilization and that it is precisely this that makes it possible to connect religion and ethics, God and civilization in a more appropriate and promising way.

First Level: A Critique of Christian Civilization

On the first level of meaning *Fear and Trembling* is a vehement critique of both the popular and cultured Christianity of Kierkegaard's day and a reminder of the original meaning of Christian faith. Abraham and the Genesis 22 narrative are chosen as paradigms of faith. According to Kierkegaard, the cultural triumph of Christian civilization had effaced the primitive meaning of Christianity. In his works, he criticizes that religious identity whose acquisition once entailed great individual risk, suffering, abandonment, and even martyrdom, had now become a matter of merely being born to Christian parents in a Christian nation. As an antidote, the pseudonymous author Johannes *de silentio* offers "a theological shock treatment"[11] portraying Abraham in the full terror of his encounter with the divine command against the clichés in which the story is usually told by the preachers.

To illustrate the profound tragic-comic misunderstanding of the age, Johannes *de silentio* introduces an imaginary churchgoer who is moved by the story and wants to imitate Abraham. Suppose this man literally intends to act like Abraham, then the preacher would shout: "You despicable man, you scum of society, what devil has so possessed you that you want to murder your son." The parishioner would reply: "But, after all, that was what you yourself preached about on Sunday,"[12] ironically portraying the spirit of the age, in which faith is no longer a task for a lifetime full of risks. In the world of ideas our age stages a real sale, having everything at a bargain price, Johannes *de silentio* remarks[13] referring to the Hegelians who want to 'go further,' transcending faith as a rudimentary phase of intellectual development. Johannes portrays the *Aqedah* full of anxiety, distress and paradox, to raise the price of faith as a counterweight to cultural Christianity including the established church[14] and Hegelian philosophy. He emphasizes faith as an act of will rather than of reason, illustrating it

---

(Cambridge: Cambridge University Press, 1998), 157–281, but I give my own interpretation of these levels and add a fifth level.
11 Green, "'Developing' *Fear and Trembling*," 258.
12 Kierkegaard, *Fear and Trembling*, 28 (SKS 4, 124 f).
13 Kierkegaard, *Fear and Trembling*, 5 (SKS 4, 101).
14 Kierkegaard, *Fear and Trembling*, 74 (SKS 4, 166).

by the irrationality of Abraham's faith, his belief that he will get Isaac back "by virtue of the absurd," thus offering the story as a *reductio ad absurdum* of what it means to believe.

When we connect this first level of meaning to the theme of God and civilization, the conclusion is that *Fear and Trembling* is written in the context of modernity in which *Christendom* is coming to an end. In this lone of thought, the solution is not to reestablish the religious underpinnings of Western civilization, like those who defend the civilizing meaning of religion. Kierkegaard's shock therapy reveals the irreducibility of faith to its cultural manifestation. God cannot be reduced to a function of society.

So far so good, but religious faith may not legitimize murder. What is the nature of this faith and how does it relate to the finite life and to moral responsibility?

Second Level: The Paradoxical Movements of Faith

On a second level of meaning, *Fear and Trembling* involves an exploration of what Green calls "the psychology of faith."[15] On this level the text is less polemical and subtler in meaning, focusing on various exemplars of faith, including ordinary people who do not look like 'knights of faith.' These faithful ordinary people remind us not to be distracted by the terrifying event on the mountain of Moriah and to pay attention to the inwardness of faith. Faith is depicted as a "double movement," open to everyone who understands that 'outward' codes of morality and faith are always at risk.[16]

Faith is contrasted with "infinite resignation," consisting only in one movement, the first movement of faith. This is the movement in which one resigns the finite infinitely, e.g., in the case of a young man who accepts the fact that the great love of his life lies forever beyond his reach and by infinite resignation discovers his "eternal consciousness." If Abraham would have resigned, he would have said: "Now all is lost, God demands Isaac, I sacrifice him and along with him all my joy."[17]

The double movement of faith adds a second movement to resignation, and thereby makes it completely different from the movement of infinite resignation: the beloved is relinquished by "virtue of the absurd, by virtue of the fact

---

15   Green, "'Developing' *Fear and Trembling*," 260 ff.
16   Kierkegaard, *Fear and Trembling*, 36 (SKS 4, 131).
17   Kierkegaard, *Fear and Trembling*, 35 (SKS 4, 130).

that for God all things are possible,"[18] i.e. that what is given up is regained at the same time. The crux is that Abraham believed that in some way or another he would keep Isaac, although he was going to sacrifice him: "He climbed the mountain, and even in the moment when the knife gleamed he had faith— that God would not require Isaac. No doubt he was surprised at the outcome, but through a double-movement he had attained his first condition, and therefore he received Isaac more joyfully than the first time."[19]

Although Abraham's faith is "by virtue of the absurd," the capacity for such knighthood is not confined to Abraham but remains available to every human being.[20] This becomes clear where Johannes *de silentio* imagines a knight of faith residing in the Copenhagen of his day. Outwardly this person's spiritual depth is not revealed, on the contrary, he looks like a bourgeois philistine, even a tax collector, enjoying all good finite things of life, "and yet every moment of his life he buys the opportune time at the highest price, ... at every moment making the movement of infinity,"[21] renouncing everything and at the same time grasping finitude back.

The double movement means that one renounces all *claims* to the finite, while at the same time keeping all *care* for it.[22] This has important implications for the interpretation of the dilemma between moral responsibility for the son and the divine command to sacrifice him. On this level of meaning *Fear and Trembling* is not quite the terrifying defense of a religiously commanded murder, but a more traditional defense of self-renunciation and selfless love as central features of religious life.[23] Abraham hands over his son, but without giving him up, "for the movement of faith must continually be made ..., but yet in such a way, please note, that one does not lose the finite but gains it whole and intact."[24] In this hermeneutical interpretation of the biblical narrative in its meaning for religious life, it is obvious that we should not imitate Abraham in his willingness to kill his son, but in his faith.

---

18   Kierkegaard, *Fear and Trembling*, 46 (SKS 4, 141).
19   Kierkegaard, *Fear and Trembling*, 36 (SKS 4, 131).
20   Kierkegaard, *Fear and Trembling*, 67 (SKS 4,159): "Faith is a marvel, and yet no human being is excluded from it."
21   Kierkegaard, *Fear and Trembling*, 40 (SKS 4, 135).
22   Edward F. Mooney, "Understanding Abraham: Care, Faith, and the Absurd," in Robert L. Perkins (ed.), *Kierkegaard's* Fear and Trembling: *Critical Appraisals* (Alabama: University of Alabama Press, 1981), 108.
23   Green, "'Developing' *Fear and Trembling*," 262.
24   Kierkegaard, *Fear and Trembling*, 37 (SKS 4, 132).

Third Level: The Relation between Ethics and Religion

On a third level, *Fear and Trembling* contains something of a study in the relationship between ethics and religion, especially in the three *problemata* of the second part of the book. Johannes' position on the "teleological suspension of the ethical," his concept of the "absolute duty to God" and his discussion of the question whether it was "ethically defensible for Abraham to conceal his undertaking" is more complex and confusing than his explorations on the second level. For, the author insists that we cannot understand Abraham's behavior in ethical terms, and that is why *Fear and Trembling* seems to hold up as exemplary a kind of conduct that we cannot understand in terms of general moral values.

On this core issue in *Fear and Trembling* many conflicting interpretations have been offered. I agree with those scholars who interpret the book as a critique of both Kantian and Hegelian ethics, a critique that would also apply to modern ethical theories, in which universalizability is required (e.g. R.M. Hare). However, I disagree with those who detect an *alternative religious ethics* in the book, like the Reformed theologian Seung-Goo Lee, who interprets the problemata as a defense of a religious understanding of ethics against the rationalistic conception of Kantian and Hegelian ethics,[25] and the Reformed philosopher C. Stephen Evans, who tries to make Abraham's act of obedience to the divine command morally intelligible as it was rooted in the trust that it was indeed God's (good) command and therefore Abraham's duty to obey, coming close to a divine command ethics.[26] Although Abraham's conduct evidently originates from a divine command, the book is completely lacking in the development of a divine command *ethics*. It is not about absolute obedience to a divine command (intelligible or not) or trust in the goodness of God's command as such, but about the inwardness of faith. From an ethical perspective the command is still *un*intelligible. Furthermore, God is not pictured as a tyrant forcing people through a test of absolute obedience.[27] This becomes clear in the four sketches of the 'Exordium' at the beginning of the book, where blind obedience to the divine command in each case really has bad outcomes

---

25 Seung-Goo Lee, "The Antithesis between the Religious View of Ethics and the Rationalistic View of Ethics in *Fear and Trembling*," in Robert L. Perkins (ed.), *International Kierkegaard Commentary*, Vol. 6, 101–126.

26 C.Stephen Evans, "Is the Concept of an Absolute Duty toward God Morally Unintelligible?" in Robert L. Perkins (ed.), *Kierkegaard's* Fear and Trembling, 141–151.

27 Edward F. Mooney, *Selves in Discord and Resolve: Kierkegaard's Moral-Religious Psychology from* Either/Or *to* The Sickness unto Death (New York/ London: Routledge, 1996), 50.

(losing one's faith, losing the faith that God is good, forsaking the duty to care for one's son)—yet each of these stories are mocked as false and unfaithful.[28]

In my interpretation, *Fear and Trembling* does not provide us with an alternative religious ethics, but limits itself to a critique of the pretensions of a rationalistic ethics, while at the same time affirming that the ethical as the ethical is not unjustified at all. "In ethical terms, Abraham's relation to Isaac is quite simply this: the father shall love the son more than himself."[29] This moral imperative may not be set aside. Abraham's responsibility for his son Isaac is nowhere annulled. The religious perspective does not overrule this responsibility, but puts it in a different perspective. The tension between the ethical and the religious is not one-sidedly solved in the direction of a legitimization of a religious murder. Moral responsibility, in this case of a father for his son, is maintained till the end.

The focus in *Fear and Trembling* is not on a religious *ethics*, but on the nature of *faith*, i.e. that the religious cannot be fully comprehended in ethical terms: from an ethical perspective it is even 'absurd.' Johannes' main thesis is that faith is irreducible to a life of moral striving. This becomes clear in three oppositions represented in the three problemata. In each of these problemata a characteristic of the ethical is provided: the ethical is a) the universal, b) immanent (external) and c) disclosed or manifest. Abraham's faith respectively contradicts each of these characteristics, for it is a) individual, b) transcendent (inward) and c) concealed. I give a brief description of these three characteristics of both the general understanding of the ethical and the transcendent conception of religion.

First, Johannes *de silentio* determines that "the ethical as such is the universal" and as the universal the ethical "applies to everyone, which from another angle means that it applies all times."[30] Here the author seems to point to Kant's categorical imperative, i.e. a moral maxim that is obligatory on all persons in all circumstances, and to Hegel's idea of the ethical life as the identity of the universal good with the subjective will. In Hegel's *Grundlinien der Philosophie des Rechts* the focus is on public morality and social roles embodied in his idea of *Sittlichkeit* (morality), consisting in a system of duties that parents, children, civilians, etc. have toward each other. That the ethical is the universal implies a condemnation of the suspension of universal moral law in favor of a single individual's interest. Hegel considers the individual determination of

---

28 Kierkegaard, *Fear and Trembling*, 9–14 (SKS 4, 105–111).
29 Kierkegaard, *Fear and Trembling*, 57 (SKS 4, 151), cf. 20 (SKS 4, 116 f).
30 Kierkegaard, *Fear and Trembling*, 54 (SKS 4, 148).

ethics as 'moral evil.'[31] The universal in ethics must take form in the public life of a people, institutionalized in family, civil society, and the state.[32]

Abraham violates the universal characteristic of the ethical: "By his act he transgressed the ethical altogether and had a higher τέλος outside it, in relation to which he suspended it."[33] The question whether there is a teleological suspension of the ethical is thus answered in the affirmative. However, this does not mean that what Abraham intended to do can be justified from a religious-*ethical* perspective. Johannes *de silentio* means that the ethical *as a whole* is suspended for the interests of a higher *telos outside* the ethical sphere. He understands that faith cannot be reduced to the ethical realm, as is the case in Hegel's attempt to mediate Abraham's faith, with the ethical as the universal. Abraham's faith is a paradox, it means that the single individual is higher than the universal, i.e. "that the single individual ... determines his relation to the universal by his relation to the absolute, not his relation to the absolute by his relation to the universal."[34] Abraham acts as a single individual by virtue of his relationship with God and this is beyond what his social roles and duties—as a husband, father and ancestor—require of him. Religion demands a disconnection from these roles and duties in order to reconnect to them in a proper way, as the 'double movement of faith' shows.

Second, problema II in *Fear and Trembling* criticizes the *immanent* conception of the divine within the ethical by advocating a *transcendent* perspective. Ethics rests immanent in itself, "has nothing outside itself that is the τέλος but is itself the τέλος for everything outside itself, and when the ethical has absorbed this into itself, it goes not further."[35] From this perspective the divine is not essentially distinguished from the ethical. Moral duty can be religiously motivated, in the sense that every universally required duty is identical with what God requires. The ethical itself is the absolute and we do not have a special duty to God. From the perspective of the ethical view, even God must be subjected to the ethical, i.e. the universal. In his *Philosophy of History* Hegel writes: "Morality and Justice in the State are also divine and commanded by God, and that in point of substance there is nothing higher or more sacred."[36]

---

31 Kierkegaard, *Fear and Trembling*, 54 (SKS 4, 149). Cf. Georg W.F. Hegel, *Elements of the Philosophy of Right*, ed. and trans. Allen Wood (Cambridge: Cambridge University Press, 1991), § 140.

32 Cf. Hegel, *Philosophy of Right*, § 260–262, 270 ff, cf. Green, "'Developing' *Fear and Trembling*," 265.

33 Kierkegaard, *Fear and Trembling*, 59 (SKS 4, 152). Cf. 60 ff (SKS 4, 153 ff).

34 Kierkegaard, *Fear and Trembling*, 70 (SKS 4, 162).

35 Kierkegaard, *Fear and Trembling*, 54 (SKS 4, 148).

36 Georg W.F. Hegel, *Philosophy of History*, trans. John Sibree (New York: Dover, 1956), 422.

This is in line with his overall speculative idea that his philosophy contains the same content as the Christian religion, but in the superior form of the philosophical concept (*Begriff*) rather than the religious form which he labels *Vorstellung*.[37] Elsewhere Hegel states: "The true reconciliation, whereby the divine realizes itself in the domain of actuality, consists in the ethical and juridical life of the state."[38] The state itself is an "earthly divinity" that commands our highest loyalties.[39] *De silentio* summarizes: the ethical is the divine.[40]

Kant does not accept an absolute duty to God which contradicts rational morality either: "even though something is represented as commanded by God, through a direct manifestation of Him, yet, if it flatly contradicts morality, it cannot, despite all appearances, be of God (for example, where a father ordered to kill his son who is, so far as he knows, perfectly innocent)."[41] Therefore, Kant condemns Abraham's willingness to sacrifice his son and adds that a god who demands sacrificing a human being can never be the true God, for God is good and what is good is determined by moral reason. Abraham ought to have replied to the so-called divine voice: "That I ought not to kill my good son is quite certain. But that you, this apparition, are God—of that I am not certain, and never can be, not even if this voice rings down to me from (visible) heaven."[42]

Johannes' critique is not that a divine command can morally be justified, but that both with Hegel and with Kant the specifically religious sphere disappears: God comes to be "an invisible vanishing point, an impotent thought; his power is only in the ethical."[43] Religious experience is only valuable insofar as

---

37   Merold Westphal, "Abraham and Hegel," in Robert L. Perkins (ed.), *Kierkegaard's* Fear and Trembling, 62–80: 63.
38   Georg W.F. Hegel, *Lectures on the Philosophy of Religion*, ed. and trans. Peter C. Hodgson (Berkeley: University of California Press, 1988), 484.
39   Hegel, *Philosophy of Right*, § 272, 307.
40   Kierkegaard, *Fear and Trembling*, 60 (SKS 4, 153). Note that these characteristics are quite similar to Judge William's understanding of ethics, Kierkegaard's pseudonymous author of part two of *Either/Or*. Also for the Judge, God is not separated from the universal and ethics and religion are never in conflict. Thus, the discussion on the distinction between ethics and religion is also a discussion between two positions within Kierkegaard's authorship.
41   Immanuel Kant, *Religion within the Limits of Reason Alone*, ed. and trans. Theodore M. Green & Hoyt H. Hudson (New York: Harper & Row, 1960), 81 f (*Die Religion innerhalb der Grenzen der bloßen Vernunft*, A 111 f).
42   Immanuel Kant, *The Conflict of the Faculties*, trans. Mary J. Gregor (New York: Abaris Books, 1979, 115n, cf. 119 (*Streit der Fakultäten*, A 103–104). Cf. Kant, *Religion Reason Alone*, 175.
43   Kierkegaard, *Fear and Trembling*, 68 (SKS 4, 160).

it motivates people to do what is morally good. *De silentio*'s critique does not imply a heteronomous view on the Euthyphro-dilemma advocating a divine command ethics. It rather seems that both sides of the dilemma are paradoxically maintained: God's command to sacrifice the son is 'good' simply because God has commanded it, but at the same time the good command to love the son is God's command as well, because it is good. Not the ethical, but its absolute presumptions are criticized. Although the ethical is reduced to the relative, "it does not follow that the ethical should be invalidated; rather, the ethical receives a completely different expression, a paradoxical expression, such as, for example, that love to God may bring the knight of faith to give his love to the neighbor—an expression opposite to that which, ethically speaking, is duty."[44]

Third, the ethical is the *disclosed* or manifest, i.e. the ethical task is "to become disclosed to the universal"[45] and a moral actor has to explain his motives for his moral conduct, in order that others can judge whether he has done the right thing. Ethical language is public language. Abraham, however, concealed his undertaking from the relevant "ethical authorities"[46]—his wife Sarah, his servant Eliezer, and his son Isaac—and the question is whether this is ethically defensible (problema III). Kantian and Hegelian ethics would answer in the negative, for the ethical is the universal and it does not accept any concealment, it demands disclosure. Contrary to the esthete, who thinks he can protect the other by not telling the truth, ethics is right.[47] Abraham, however, did not speak, because no one would have understood him. Just one word from him has been preserved, in answer to Isaac's question where the lamb is: "God himself will provide the lamb for the burnt offering, my son."[48] This word does not explain anything, but is an expression of Abraham's faith that he in one way or another would receive Isaac back.

In sum, on this third level the book takes the story of the *Aqedah* as a starting point to criticize a rationalistic, self-sufficient ethics insofar it absorbs the religious as the individual relationship with God. However, this does not mean that ethics is completely suspended by religion, as Ronald Green assumes in his interpretation of this level of meaning.[49] The ethical life must be purged of its absoluteness and then reappears as an essential component of the reli-

---

44 Kierkegaard, *Fear and Trembling*, 68 (SKS 4, 160).
45 Kierkegaard, *Fear and Trembling*, 82 (SKS 4, 172).
46 Kierkegaard, *Fear and Trembling*, 112 (SKS 4, 200).
47 Note that in *Either/Or* the ethicist also criticizes the esthete's concealment.
48 Gen. 22: 8; Kierkegaard, *Fear and Trembling*, 115 f (SKS 4, 203).
49 Green, "'Developing' *Fear and Trembling*," 268.

gious life. The tension between the religious and the ethical results from claims and pretensions made on behalf of the ethical, claims that are not essential to the ethical life as such. The ethical returns in the religious, like the pseudonym Johannes Climacus says in his explanation of *Fear and Trembling*: "an ordeal is a passing through; the person tested comes back again to exist in the ethical, even though he retains an everlasting impression of the terror."[50] *Fear and Trembling* thus opens the *possibility* of a religious ethics, without *exploring* this ethics—that is done in Kierkegaard's later work *Works of Love*. Yet, it is evident that religious ethics is not autonomous but originates from one's relation to God. Religion may require that one go beyond the confines of civilized moral order to establish one's own relation to the absolute.

Fourth Level: Sin and Grace, or Bridging the Moral Gap

While on the third level the religious may not be reduced to the ethical, on the forth level it turns out that the religious is actually 'higher' than the ethical, for it makes it possible to deal with something that ethics cannot deal with sufficiently: moral guilt. From an ethical perspective the highest one can do is willing and doing the good. It is assumed that 'ought' implies 'can' and since I ought to become a good person, I must believe that I am able to do so. The religious life begins where one discovers that this assumption is contradicted by experience, the discovery that actual existence is incommensurable with the demands of ethics.[51]

Kant also struggled with the problem of what John Hare calls "the moral gap," a gap between the unconditional demand of the moral law and our human incapacities to live according to this law. John Hare points out that there is a three-partite structure in Kant's ethical theory consisting in (1) the moral demand on us, (2) our natural (in)capacities, and (3) the source of the demand. This structure presents a potential moral gap between the unconditional demand of the moral law and our human incapacities to then live according to this law. Kant's problem with this gap is acute, because he believes that 'ought'

---

50   Søren A. Kierkegaard *Concluding Unscientific Postscript to* Philosophical Fragments, *Kierkegaard's Writings*, Vol. XII.1, ed. and trans. Howard V. Hong & Edna H. Hong (Princeton: Princeton University Press, 1992), 266 (SKS 7, 243).

51   C.Stephen Evans, "Faith as the *Telos* of Morality: A Reading of *Fear and Trembling*," in Robert L. Perkins (ed.), *International Kierkegaard Commentary*, Vol. 6: Fear and Trembling *and* Repetition (Macon: Mercer University Press, 1993), 9–27: 19.

implies 'can.'[52] In *Religion Within the Limits of Reason Alone* it is clear that the propensity to evil is radical, and inextirpable by human powers, "since extirpation could occur only through good maxims, and cannot take place when the ultimate subjective ground of all maxims is postulated as corrupt."[53] In order to persevere in the moral life we must have 'moral faith.' This requires belief in God's work on our behalf. Kant appeals to the possibility of assistance by God. God is the authority we need in order to actually do the good and to bridge the moral gap. The divine assistance consists in His teaching us to live according to the archetype of His will. Thus, Kant uses the third part of the structure of morality (the source of the demand) to bridge the gap between the first (the moral demand) and the second (our incapacity to meet this demand).

In Kant's solution God's assistance is essentially ethical in nature. God commands us again to do the good and supports us with *moral* faith. Ultimately, it is man himself as a moral actor—albeit with divine assistance—who must bridge the gap. This is nothing else than a reestablishment of the belief in the boundless possibilities of the ethical and hence the belief in God becomes obsolete.[54] After all, by doing good again I do not release myself of previously incurred guilt. This guilt cannot be absolved within a purely ethical perspective. The moral law is in the end an accuser that repeatedly indicts me.

Fear and Trembling hints to an alternative to bridging the moral gap. Not before the end of the book does this become clear, i.e. where the religious concepts of sin and repentance are introduced in a footnote where Johannes *de silentio* says: "Up until now I have assiduously avoided any reference to the question of sin and its reality. ... As soon as sin emerges, ethics founders precisely on repentance; for repentance is the highest ethical expression, but precisely as such it is the deepest ethical self-contradiction."[55] Moral obligation in the end leads one to an unsolvable guilt. An immanent ethical perspective, such as Kant's, cannot sufficiently deal with this guilt and the anxiety resulting from it, for in ethics the moral capability of man is presupposed. The religious God-relationship, on the contrary, makes one aware of an infinite responsibility that one cannot live up to, because of human finiteness and one's position as a sinner, and at the same time offers a way out: repentance, which is not in

---

52 John E. Hare, *The Moral Gap: Kantian Ethics, Human Limits, and God's Assistance* (Oxford: Clarendon Press, 1996), 38.
53 Kant, *Religion Reason Alone*, 32.
54 Cf. Gerrit Manenschijn, *De mythe van de autonomie (The Myth of Autonomy)* (Kampen: Kok, 1999), 67–73.
55 Kierkegaard, *Fear and Trembling*, 98 (SKS 4, 188).

itself closed, but appeals to Someone *beyond the ethical*: God who overcomes sin by divine grace and forgiveness.

Fear and Trembling only briefly deals with the concepts of sin and forgiveness, for these are Christian categories that are not at stake in Gen. 22. A Christological reading is needed, a tradition which started in Gal. 3: 13–14 and Heb. 11: 17–19, with which Kierkegaard was not unfamiliar,[56] and in which Abraham is interpreted as a type of God symbolizing His involvement in crucifixion and resurrection. Johannes *de silentio* alludes to this Christological reading, suggesting that moral responsibility can be reestablished in an ethics that is founded in the God relationship, in which sin is acknowledged: "An ethics that ignores sin is a completely futile discipline, but if it affirms sin, then it has *eo ipso* exceeded itself."[57] *The Concept of Anxiety* explores this kind of ethics as a 'second ethics': "This ethics does not ignore sin, and it does not have its ideality in making ideal demands; rather, it has its ideality in the penetrating consciousness of actuality, of the actuality of sin ... It is easy to see the difference in the movements, to see that the ethics of which we are now speaking belongs to a different order of things. The first ethics was shipwrecked on the sinfulness of the single individual ... instead of being able to explain this sinfulness."[58]

On this forth level of meaning, *Fear and Trembling* offers a more or less hidden discourse on sin and forgiveness, making apparent again the limits of the ethical; the meaning of religion does not consist in overruling ethics but in the redemption from inevitable guilt resulting from its imperatives.

Fifth Level: *Bildung* and Becoming a Self

On a fifth and final level, *Fear and Trembling* is a book about *Bildung* and becoming a self. The text indicates that one may be called to individual existence beyond what others demand from you, beyond any social integration or cultivation of the self, in a life received as a gift from God. The book wants to make the reader aware of himself 'before God,' presenting Abraham as a hero of

---

56   SKS 18, 62; EE 184: "And He who spared Abraham's firstborn, and only tested the patriarch's faith, He did not spare his only begotten Son." (dated 11 Sept. 1839) Cf. Green, "'Developing' *Fear and Trembling*," 270.

57   Kierkegaard, *Fear and Trembling*, 98 f (SKS 4, 188).

58   Søren A. Kierkegaard, *The Concept of Anxiety: A Simple Psychologically Orienting Deliberation on the Dogmatic Issue of Hereditary Sin, Kierkegaard's Writings*, Vol. VIII, ed. and trans. Reidar Thomte & Albert B. Anderson (Princeton: Princeton University Press, 1980), 20 (SKS 4, 328).

faith, inviting to articulate one's own conviction, inwardness, and identity through attention to Someone both outer and other than oneself.[59]

This process of becoming a self is not a matter of objectivity. It requires passion and is also a task for a lifetime, as *De silentio* claims in the 'Preface.'[60] Passion is neither reducible to, nor deducible from any form of learning, the theoretical learning of the learned or the practical learning of the socialized. Passions like love, faith, or longing, which are constitutive of the process of becoming a self, cannot be acquired by mere education or cultivation, i.e. by what is handed over from previous generations.[61] "Whatever one generation learns from another, no generation learns the essentially human from a previous one. ... The essentially human is passion ... [N]o generation is able to begin at any other point than at the beginning, no later generation has a more abridged task than the previous one."[62] The book presents faith as the highest passion and attacks the Hegelian idea that one could 'go further.' The same holds for all passions: "There perhaps are many in every generation who do not come to faith, but no one goes further. ... life has tasks enough also for the person who does not come to faith."[63]

In the 'Preliminary Expectoration' the same idea is discussed in relation to *Bildung*: "What, then, is education [Danish: *Dannelse*, equivalent for *Bildung*]? I believed it is the course the individual goes through in order to catch up with himself, and the person who will not go through this course is not much helped by being born in the most enlightened age."[64] This comment appears where *De silentio* discusses the importance of spirit and spiritual development of the self in making the movements of infinite resignation and faith. He refers to the way Hegel connects *Bildung* and God, making God part of world history.

Hegel states that what has to be cultivated in *Bildung* by the subject is something objective: "What is there in human inwardness, i.e. in one's rational spirit, is therefore brought to consciousness for the individual as something objective ... This is the concern of education [*Bildung*]."[65] The aim of Hegel's notion of *Bildung* turns on conceptualizing God: our initial notions of God (*Vorstellung*) have to be transformed into those of *Begriff*. God or 'Spirit' must be conceptualized as one does in philosophy. In *The Philosophy of History*

---

59 Mooney, *Selves in Discord and Resolve*, 43.
60 Kierkegaard, *Fear and Trembling*, 7 f (SKS 4, 102 f).
61 Merold Westphal, "Abraham and Hegel," 64.
62 Kierkegaard, *Fear and Trembling*, 121 (SKS 4, 208).
63 Kierkegaard, *Fear and Trembling*, 122 (SKS 4, 209).
64 Kierkegaard, *Fear and Trembling*, 46 (SKS 4, 140).
65 Hegel, *Philosophy of Religion*, 478.

Hegel explains how the Spirit develops himself in the development of history and civilization, in which the process of *Bildung* is involved, making progressions during this development.[66] This objective development is parallel to a subjective, psychological process of *Bildung*, its highest aim consisting in understanding World History as a whole, so that the Spirit of history is conceptually understood.

Kierkegaard disassembles Hegel's determination of *Bildung* as cultivation of World History. The reason for his critique is that on Hegel's position each individual must step aside in order to accept the cultural and historic tradition. In *Fear and Trembling* a religious-existential concept of *Bildung* is emphasized where God has a distinguished role and not only a supporting role, as with Hegel. By adhering to history and culture each individual becomes part of the collective. To adhere to God, on the contrary, means that each individual becomes a singular and unique person. The story of Abraham makes clear that one has to learn to exist as the single individual, which is both the most terrible and the greatest of all. In that sense existing before God cannot be achieved by incorporating cultural values and norms, or 'the universal' in the Hegelian way.[67] Rather, it is the other way around: only by becoming a single individual before God can one enter into the universal.[68] This makes *Bildung* primarily not a matter of entering the universal in which the collective (We) decides for the individual (I), but of a difficult process of becoming a self by catching up with oneself, i.e. by repeating oneself. Then, instead of being cultured one has found the way back to oneself in God.

This does not mean that Kierkegaard promotes a romantic idea of personal authentic development rooted in subjective feelings and passions. On this point Kierkegaard follows Hegel's critique of romanticism's aesthetic immediacy: "The first immediacy is the aesthetic, and here the Hegelian philosophy certainly may very well be right."[69] However, this does not apply to faith. Faith is not the aesthetic, it is a second immediacy in which one catches up with oneself. Kierkegaard's concept of passion is ethically and religiously determined.

By reintroducing God as the transcendent and critical moment in *Bildung* before or beyond what culture and civilization offer one to cultivate, Kierkegaard opens up the possibility to discover the 'gift character' of *Bildung*, which

---

66 Hegel, *Philosophy of History*, 54–79.
67 Sæverot, "Bildung, God, and the Ethical School," 5; Westphal, "Abraham and Hegel," 66 f.
68 Kierkegaard, *Fear and Trembling* 75 (SKS 4, 166).
69 Kierkegaard, *Fear and Trembling* 82 (SKS 4, 87).

is open to everyone and as such is universal, as he emphasizes elsewhere.[70] The inward passion of faith is related to outward cultivation and *Bildung*[71] in such a manner that the religious thwarts *Bildung* and at the same time makes it possible to receive *Bildung* as a gift 'from above.' Then, *Bildung* becomes something 'passive' which cannot be a matter of mere self-realization, of an activity, an active pursuit to become a self-realized human being.

Note that this passive aspect of *Bildung* was also present in the original idea of the concept in the Christian mystic tradition according to which man carries in his soul an *imago dei*, an image of God, which man must cultivate in himself. The process of *Bildung* depended upon cultivating this image. In one of his upbuilding discourses Kierkegaard interprets the image of God as invisible, making formation to that image essentially into something spiritual, i.e. worship of God: "worship is what makes the human being resemble God, and to be able truly to worship is the excellence of the invisible glory above all creation."[72] The greatness of the human being is not his reason or cultivation. Man's formation in the image of God means that he becomes a worshiping human being, a 'praying animal' instead of a 'rational animal,' saying grace to the Giver of "every good and every perfect gift which is from above."[73] Following this line of thought, my conclusion is that this receptivity may count as the pre-eminent religious moment in *Bildung*, criticizing both an elitist conception of *Bildung* and an in itself closed Hegelian conception.

Conclusion

Kierkegaard's *Fear and Trembling* can be read as an illuminating discourse on religious *Bildung*, reintroducing God as the transcendent and critical moment in *Bildung* beyond what culture and civilization offer the individual to cultivate. This reading is opposed to interpretations, such as Paul Cliteur's, in which the book is contested because of its supposed legitimization of a religiously motivated murder. In the end, devotion to God proves to be a matter of worship and not of obedience to an unethical command.

---

70 Søren A. Kierkegaard, *Upbuilding Discourses, Kierkegaard's Writings*, Vol. V, ed. and trans. Howard V. Hong & Edna H. Hong (Princeton: Princeton University Press, 1990), 12 f (SKS 5, 22).

71 Cf. SKS 18, 242, JJ:323.

72 Søren A. Kierkegaard, *Upbuilding Discourses in Various Spirits, Kierkegaard's Writings*, Vol. XV, ed. and trans. Howard V. Hong & Edna H. Hong (Princeton: Princeton University Press, 1993), 193 (SKS 8, 290).

73 James 1: 17–22, one of Kierkegaard's favorite texts in his upbuilding discourses.

In order to read the text in this manner, I offered an interpretation of Kierkegaard's book as a discourse on multiple levels. First, the book can be read as a vehement critique of Christian civilization as it was present in Kierkegaard's age: the narrative of the *Aqedah* is maieutically pictured as a *horror religiosus* against the mass produced bargain-priced faith of established Christianity. Beyond this critical stance, the book contains on a second level a much more subtle language, spelling out 'the movements of faith' consisting in both giving up what one loves the most in life and at the same time believing that one will receive it back. When it comes to ethics, *Fear and Trembling* limits itself to a critique of the pretensions of a rationalistic ethics, while at the same time affirming the ethical as such. The book does not provide us with a divine command ethics, nor is it a serious ethical discourse on a threatening moral dilemma in real life. The real contribution of the book consists in offering a religious perspective emphasizing the incommensurability and irreducibility of religious faith, in opposition to Kant and Hegel, who make the divine part of ethical life. As such, the religious signifies a movement of disconnection, of letting go of all godly qualifications of what is immanent, in order to reconnect to immanence in a more appropriate way, i.e. as not possessing but receiving all one is given in social, moral and cultural life. The meaning of this radical plea for the religious 'without ulterior motive' becomes clear on the fourth level of meaning dealing with guilt and repentance as religious 'solutions' to the ethical problem of the 'moral gap.' Finally, the book is about the religious moment of *Bildung* interpreted as formation of the self 'before God.' By stressing this moment as distinguished from what culture and civilization offer to cultivate, Kierkegaard's book opens up the possibility of criticizing what is recognized as moral or civilized, without, however, violently making one's own point of view absolute. For, the openness is directed toward God as the Absolute, the Other, preventing us from making any absolute claim for a relative reality including one's own (individual or collective) moral, cultural or religious stance or conviction.

Thinking through this Kierkegaardian line of thought, I would argue that *Bildung* is something more than the individual's realization within the sphere of a common universal morality as part of civilization. *Bildung* interpreted from the traditional notion of *imago Dei*, in the sense of man's God-relatedness, is a possibility for everyone and *as such* it includes a universal meaning. The crux is not a general socialization into a given civilized culture but that everyone resembles God, which makes distinctions between man and female, slave and free man, civilized and barbarian, etc., relative[74] and thereby criticizes

---

74 Cf. Gal. 3: 28.

any kind of superiority. Furthermore, in my view the *Aqedah* is the story of a process of both letting go and receiving back of what one 'possesses' as the most beloved. Aligning this narrative with the notions of *Bildung* and *imago Dei* the conclusion can be drawn that nobody is anyone's possession, not even one's beloved son of whom one takes care. From this perspective, I think it is possible to interpret *Bildung* in the sense of formation in the image of God as essentially *ethical Bildung*. The meaning of the story of the *Aqedah* is not to justify incredible divine commands. As a narrative of faith, it points at the ethical perspective *as such*. In my interpretation, the narrative opens up the possibility of an ethics in which the dignity of each human being is valued 'before God.' The story tells that *Bildung* is something else than mere self-realization. In the end, it is formation of the self 'before God' and in 'fear and trembling.' One receives oneself as a gift 'from above' and also discovers that every other human being is such a gift and may never be reduced to mere possession.

In sum, Kierkegaard's interpretation of the *Aqedah* makes us aware of both the irreducibility of religion and religion's specific contribution to civilization. In the openness to God as the critical, religious moment in *Bildung* and as non-identical with projects of self-development, moral cultivation and disciplining into a civilization, lies the real civilizing meaning of religious faith.

Bibliography

Boer, Pim den, "Vergelijkende begripsgeschiedenis," in Pim den Boer (ed.), *Beschaving: Een geschiedenis van de begrippen hoofsheid, heusheid, beschaving en cultuur* (*Civilization: A History of the Concepts Courtliness, Courtesy, Civilization, and Culture*) (Amsterdam: Amsterdam University Press, 2001), 9–28.

Cliteur, Paul, *The Secular Outlook: In Defense of Moral and Political Secularism* (Oxford: Wiley-Blackwell, 2010).

Evans, C.Stephen, "Faith as the *Telos* of Morality: A Reading of *Fear and Trembling*," in Robert L. Perkins (ed.), *International Kierkegaard Commentary*, Vol. 6: Fear and Trembling *and* Repetition (Macon: Mercer University Press, 1993), 9–27.

———, "Is the Concept of an Absolute Duty toward God Morally Unintelligible?" in Robert L. Perkins (ed.), *Kierkegaard's* Fear and Trembling: *Critical Appraisals* (Tuscalosa: University of Alabama Press, 1981), 141–151.

Filosofie magazine (*Philosophy Magazine*) 13:10 (2004).

Fraas, Hans-Jürgen, *Bildung und Menschenbild in theologischer Perspektive* (Göttingen: Vandenhoeck & Ruprecht, 2000).

Green, Ronald M., "'Developing' *Fear and Trembling*," in Alastair Hannay & Gordon D. Marino (eds.), *The Cambridge Companion to Kierkegaard* (Cambridge: Cambridge University Press, 1998), 157–281.
Hare, John E., *The Moral Gap: Kantian Ethics, Human Limits, and God's Assistance* (Oxford: Clarendon Press, 1996).
Hegel, Georg W.F., *Elements of the Philosophy of Right*, ed. and trans. Allen Wood (Cambridge: Cambridge University Press, 1991).
———, *Lectures on the Philosophy of Religion*, ed. and trans. Peter C. Hodgson (Berkeley: University of California Press, 1988).
———, *Philosophy of History*, trans. John Sibree (New York: Dover, 1956).
Kant, Immanuel, *Religion within the Limits of Reason Alone*, ed. and trans. Theodore M. Green & Hoyt H. Hudson (New York: Harper & Row, 1960).
———, *The Conflict of the Faculties*, trans. Mary J. Gregor (New York: Abaris Books, 1979).
Kierkegaard, Søren A., *Concluding Unscientific Postscript to* Philosophical Fragments, *Kierkegaard's Writings*, Vol. XII.1, ed. and trans. Howard V. Hong & Edna H. Hong (Princeton: Princeton University Press, 1992), 266.
———, *Fear and Trembling & Repetition*, *Kierkegaard's Writings*, Vol. VI, ed. and trans. Howard V. Hong & Edna H. Hong (Princeton: Princeton University Press, 1983).
———, *The Concept of Anxiety: A Simple Psychologically Orienting Deliberation on the Dogmatic Issue of Hereditary Sin*, *Kierkegaard's Writings*, Vol. VIII, ed. and trans. Reidar Thomte & Albert B. Anderson (Princeton: Princeton University Press, 1980).
———, *Upbuilding Discourses*, *Kierkegaard's Writings*, Vol. V, ed. and trans. Howard V. Hong & Edna H. Hong (Princeton: Princeton University Press, 1990).
———, *Upbuilding Discourses in Various Spirits*, *Kierkegaard's Writings*, Vol. XV, ed. and trans. Howard V. Hong & Edna H. Hong (Princeton: Princeton University Press, 1993).
Lee, Seung-Goo, "The Antithesis between the Religious View of Ethics and the Rationalistic View of Ethics in *Fear and Trembling*," in Robert L. Perkins (ed.), *International Kierkegaard Commentary*, Vol. 6, 101–126.
Manenschijn, Gerrit, *De mythe van de autonomie (The Myth of Autonomy)* (Kampen: Kok, 1999).
Mooney, Edward F., *Selves in Discord and Resolve: Kierkegaard's Moral-Religious Psychology from* Either/Or *to* The Sickness unto Death (New York/ London: Routledge, 1996).
———, "Understanding Abraham: Care, Faith, and the Absurd," in Robert L. Perkins (ed.), *Kierkegaard's* Fear and Trembling: *Critical Appraisals* (Tuscalosa: University of Alabama Press, 1981), 100–114.
Sæverot, Herner, "Bildung, God, and the Ethical School," Conference paper Philosophy of Education Society of Australasia 2010, retrieved from http://www.pesa.org.au, on 17 February 2012.
Søren Kierkegaard Skrifter (København: Gads Forlag 1997–2013).

Westphal, Merold, "Abraham and Hegel," Robert L. Perkins (ed.), *Kierkegaard's* Fear and Trembling: *Critical Appraisals* (Tuscalosa: University of Alabama Press, 1981), 62–80.

Wimmer, Michael, "The Gift of *Bildung*: Reflections on the Relationship between Singularity and Justice in the Concept of *Bildung*," in Gert J.J. Biesta & Denise Egéa-Kuehne (eds.), *Derrida & Education* (London & New York: Routledge, 2001), 150–175.

PART 3
Transformation

Civic Integration
A Mission to Civilize Religious Believers?

Mechteld Jansen

A comparison of Integration Programs in the EU[1] shows that obligatory participation in such programs is a regular requirement for becoming a legalized citizen and having access to a secure legal status. Along with Austria, Belgium (Flanders), Denmark, and Germany, the Netherlands currently requires mandatory integration courses. These courses must be successfully completed before the immigrant has the right to stay and have access to social and welfare benefits. Integration is increasingly viewed as a one-way process of adapting to the receiving country, with responsibilities and duties placed exclusively on the side of the immigrants. Integration has become a border between those who are in and those who are out. Behind this view of integration lies the idea of an already integrated, receiving society that the newcomer must strive to become part of. Yet it is difficult for the receiving society to say what this already united identity consists of. Many attempts to describe the 'national identity' of any one country stick to traditional stereotypes and are used to 'normalize,' 'modernize,' 'civilize,' and 'assimilate' the newcomers.[2] From a missiological viewpoint, this leads to the question: how do integration courses exemplify the attempt to normalize newcomers into *secularized* civilians. As Berger, Davies, and Fokas put it: " ... in Europe to be modern, to be with the times as against being backward, has come to mean being secular."[3] I will focus here on the Netherlands, presupposing that some of my findings will apply to other West European countries as well. First, I will discuss the whole project of this book, aligning my contribution with the debate on God and civilization.

---

[1] Sergio Carrera, "A Comparison of Integration Programmes in the EU: Trends and Weaknesses," CEPS CHALLENGE Papers No. 1 (2006); this comparison included Austria, Belgium, Denmark, France, Germany, Poland, Spain, and the Netherlands (available from the website of the Centre for European Policy Studies, http://www.ceps.be/book/comparison-integration-programmes-eu-trends-and-weaknesses).

[2] Sergio Carrera, *In Search of the Perfect Citizen? The Intersection between Integration, Immigration and nationality in the EU* (Leiden: Brill, 2009), 89; Sergio Carrera, "Integration as a Process of Inclusion for Migrants? The Case of Long-term Residents in the EU," in H. Schneider (ed.), *Migration, Integration and Citizenship: A Challenge for Europe's Future* (Maastricht: Maastricht University, 2005), 109–138.

[3] Peter Berger, Grace Davie & Effie Fokas, *Religious America, Secular Europe: A Theme and Variations* (Farnham: Ashgate, 2008), 19.

Second, I will sketch some of the background of Dutch immigration and integration history. Third, from a missiological perspective, I will reflect on key issues of *mission civilisatrice* as these issues appear in both 19th-century Christian missions and 21st-century attempts to modernize religious newcomers.

Alignment with the Project

In this book project, we are searching for both critical and renewing potential of the Law of God in relation to civilization. The history of the concept of civilization in different European contexts, the parallel and sometimes paralyzing use of civilizations (plural) as a synonym of cultures, does not make ours an easy job. For now, I will assume that civilizations (plural) differ from cultures in size, organization, and complexity. Civilizations have emerged with the accumulation of wealth, the development of scientific research, art, architecture, and customs defined by a certain elite.[4] We propose to think about God in terms of giving *room* to both *connect* and *disconnect* with the civilization as well as the religion in which we participate. The combination of *God and civilization* then means that we do not have a total commitment to our own civilization but always remain open to what is different, strange, i.e. to the 'other'. From a Protestant point of view, *God* prevents us from making any absolute claim for a relative reality, including religion (cf. Tillich's formula of the Protestant Principle).

I will refer to Western civilization as the temporary result of the process of civilization in North Atlantic cultures. Western civilization includes the social ideal and hope of fraternity/sorority, equality, liberty, justice, and peace. Christianity cannot but connect and sympathize with that hope because it taught this hope itself. In this contribution I will confine myself to one aspect of civilization, namely, the corollary division of people into binary categories like legal/illegal, citizen/alien, the included/the excluded. Modern Western thought on civilization is built in large measure on this division, which was erected on the basis of the distinction between a 'state of nature' where pre-civil savages live and a civil state where civilized live, the latter in close connection with urban culture.[5] Christianity and civilization have always lived in an uneasy al-

---

[4] J. Andrew Kirk, *Civilizations in Conflict? Islam, the West and Christian Faith* (Oxford: Regnum, 2011), 17.

[5] Fred Dallmayer, *Dialogue Among Civilizations: Some Exemplary Voices* (New York: Palgrave Macmillan, 2002), 19 f; Charles Taylor, *A Secular Age* (Cambridge: Harvard University Press, 2007), 455.

liance, with the accent sometimes on the uneasiness and at other times on the alliance. With its "radically secularizing and often anti-religious bent,"[6] however, Western post-Enlightenment civilization makes it hard for believers (of any religion and especially newcomers to Western countries) to partake in the alliance. Although religion has not disappeared from the lives of many West European citizens,[7] it seems that it has vanished from the screens of those who are responsible for Dutch immigration and integration laws and processes. In these policy-making circles "the intensity with which critique attaches itself to secularism, articulates itself as a secularizing project, and identifies itself with the dethroning of God" is sharply felt.[8] It seems that, to enter our civilization, one needs to accept the discipline of secularism.[9]

The Background of Dutch Immigration and Integration History

Neither the immigration of Jews and French Huguenots (16th and 17th century) nor the influx of people from former Dutch colonies after World War II caused heated political debates on integration and adaptation. Dutch society was de facto multicultural, allowing people of all cultural or ethnic backgrounds to cherish their own heritage, provided they obeyed the law. Slowly but surely, the fact of a multicultural society became loaded with the moral and political overtones of multiculturalism understood as the "recognition of group difference in the public sphere of laws, policies, democratic discourse and the terms of shared citizenship and national identity."[10] The turn of the

---

6   Dallmayer, *Dialogue*, 25.
7   Several—sometimes paradoxical—developments are taking place simultaneously: ongoing secularization regarding church attendance, endorsement of religious doctrine, and affiliation to institutions on the one hand and a resurgence or metamorphosis of religion in non traditional, non institutionalized forms on the other, thus raising the question of a 'post-secular society.' See Erik Borgman & Anton van Harskamp, "Tussen seculansering en hernieuwde sacralisering" (Between Secularization and Renewed Sacralization), in Meerten ter Borg et al., *Handboek Religie in Nederland* (Zoetermeer: Meinema, 2008), 14–25; Erik Borgman, *Metamorfosen: Over religie en moderne cultuur (Metamorphoses: On Religion and Modern Culture)* (Kampen: Klement, 2006); Jürgen Habermas, "Notes on Post-Secular Society," *New Perspectives Quarterly* 25 (2008), 17–29.
8   Wendy Brown, "Introduction," in Talal Asad, Wendy Brown, Judith Butler & Saba Mahmood (eds.), *Is Critique Secular? Blasphemy, Injury, and Free Speech* (Berkeley: University of California, 2009), 11.
9   For 'secularism' as a political doctrine and 'the secular' as an epistemic category, see Gé Speelman's chapter on Talal Assad, in this volume.
10 Tariq Modood, *Multiculturalism* (London: Polity Press, 2007), 2.

century brought a political change, yielding to the disqualification of multiculturalism as a viable political approach. In the eyes of its attackers, multiculturalism has produced nothing more than the stagnant integration of newcomers, increased segregation, and feelings of estrangement and deprivation on the part of many Dutch citizens.[11] A new, more coercive policy should discourage immigration and help immigrants *adapt* to Dutch culture.

Church and State

Ever since 1798, the Netherlands has followed the principle of separation of church and state in the sense that local and national governments are to treat all religions and worldviews equally and to refrain from any interference in the internal theological affairs of those religions. This principle was never understood to mean that the government could not protect the rights of religious minorities or support religious groups consisting of people with a weak social and economic position. In fact, the religious institutions of Moluccans, Surinamese, Turkish, and Moroccan immigrants were supported when this was deemed necessary for their well-being in the Netherlands with respect to building churches and mosques, for example.[12] Opposition to this settlement started with criticism of the 'imported' imams and fear of the radicalization of Muslims after 9/11. In 2006, the boundary of the principle of separation of church and state were certainly crossed when a governmental Action Plan against polarization and radicalization was accepted that aimed to stimulate a multiform offer of non-extremist interpretations of Islam. This plan was corrected in 2009 when it was recognized that it is not up to the government to decide which interpretations of Islam are the right ones.[13] Nonetheless, some sociologists continue to argue for normative governmental action against orthodox religious values, Christian or Muslim. Their mission is to herald a new

---

[11] The term "multicultural tragedy" was introduced by Paul Scheffer in NRC Handelsblad (January 2000). With Pieter Dronkers, however, we can ask if multiculturalism has not been put aside too quickly as a political ideal; see "Loyal to the Tricolour: Changing Regimes of Belonging in the Netherlands," http://www.raison-publique.fr/IMG/pdf/Dronkers_-_Loyal_to_the_tricolouri.pdf.

[12] Ben Koolen, "Godsdienst en levensovertuiging in het integratiebeleid etnische minderheden," (Religion and Philosophy of Life in Integration Policy for Ethnic Minorities), *Tijdschrift voor Religie, Recht en Beleid* 1:1 (2010), 5–27.

[13] Koolen, "Godsdienst," 25.

civilizing liberal relativism, not necessarily a secular one, but one that tames the dangers of orthodoxy.[14]

The European Context

An analysis of the current situation by the Spanish sociologist of religion José Casanova is helpful for seeing the Dutch debates in a wider European context.[15] Many Europeans share a complex and rarely verbalized mode of intertwining secular and Christian cultural identities. Secularism is seen as a "quasi-normative consequence of being a 'modern' and 'enlightened' European,"[16] and religions should not disrupt the program of a modern secular and progressive Europe.

West European countries use various ways to accommodate and regulate immigrant religions. The Netherlands tried to extend the model of pillarization: via means tolerated by the state, the Muslims were to organize themselves, to establish schools, mosque associations, and services for work and housing. Since 2002, however, this model of extended pillarization has been questioned by those who want to set clearer limits to the tolerance of what are perceived to be un-modern and un-European habits or behavior. In the perception of many Europeans, 'the' immigrant is Muslim, and, increasingly, his or her otherness does not consist in being non-Christian or having a different religion but in *religiousness per se,* which makes the European mind "shaped by the hegemonic knowledge regime of secularism" anxious.[17] Migrants, be they Muslim or Christian, experience an anti-religious aversion.[18] In general, liberal

---

14 Dick Pels, *Opium van het volk: Over religie en politiek in seculier Nederland* (*Opium of the People: On Religion and Politics in Secular Netherlands*) (Amsterdam: De Bezige Bij, 2008), 138 ff, and 157. Pels calls for a new "beschavingsoffensief," i.e., a new civilizing offensive.

15 José Casanova, "Religion, European Secular Identities and European Integration," in Timothy A. Byrnes & Peter J. Katzenstein (eds.), *Religion in an Expanding Europe* (Cambridge: Cambridge University Press, 2006), 65–92.

16 Casanova, "Religion," 66. As Casanova also indicates, however, the revitalization of Catholicism in Poland as well as the debates on the incorporation of Turkey into Europe, and on the European Constitution have indicated that there is a certain mixture of Christian and secularist views that still prevail—or at least prevent Muslims from becoming part of Europe.

17 Casanova, "Religion," 76.

18 Cf. Oscar Verkaaik, *Ritueel Burgerschap: Een essay over nationalisme en secularisme in Nederland* (*Ritual Citizenship: An Essay on Nationalism and Secularism in the Netherlands*) (Amsterdam: Amsterdam University Press, 2009), 34 f. Verkaaik interprets the new Dutch

secularist European politicians and intellectuals do not want to be accused of religious intolerance. They will not utter xenophobic or anti-religious speech publicly but use politically correct statements about welcoming all immigrants as long as they respect and accept modern liberal, secular European norms. Casanova views more restrictive legislative measures against Muslims in the Netherlands as part of constructing a new boundary against those who do not accept these modern liberal, secular norms. New immigrants have to adapt to the principles of secularism. If they fail to do so, they are marked as reactionary, fundamentalist, and anti-modern.[19] In what follows, I will focus on the hegemonic secularist worldview and ask if it is indeed this secular repression of religious heritages that animates the Dutch civic integration of immigrants. Although I endorse Casanova's comments on the Dutch situation, many Dutch people will say that extreme secularism is not part of mainstream Dutch society.

Integration Trajectory

All individuals who wish to stay longer than three months in the Netherlands must apply for a temporary residence permit and pass a *Basic Integration Exam*. This exam—the first of its kind in the world—must be taken before the applicant arrives in the Netherlands at the Dutch embassy in the country where he or she resides. The exam consists of two parts: a) knowledge of the Dutch language and b) knowledge of Dutch society. The test is available in 138 Dutch embassies around the world and it costs € 360 to take it.[20] On April 1, 2011, the level of this examination was raised by an added test in reading and understanding Dutch and requiring a higher minimum passing score for the existing oral language test. Once this exam has been passed and the newcomer has arrived in the Netherlands, residence permits are tied to the passing of further civic integration requirements. With these pre-entry requirements and

---

anti-religious nationalism as fear of Dutch modernists facing parts of their own religious past they tried to do away with.

19 Casanova, "Religion," 80.

20 To prepare for the Basic Integration Exam, an examination package can be ordered that contains no teaching material for the Dutch language, only a 105-minute film "Going to the Netherlands," an Instruction manual, and a photo book with pictures from the film and 100 questions about these pictures. 30 of these 100 questions are asked during the computerized exam taken at the Dutch embassy. The film is available in Dutch, French, English, Spanish, Kurmanci, Portugese, Turkish, Standard Arabic, Moroccan Arabic, Rif Berber, Chinese, Russian, Indonesian, and Thai.

the penalties for not engaging in further civic integration—no residence permit, no working permit—the Dutch integration program is currently the strictest in Europe.[21]

The *Civic Integration Exam*[22] requires that the applicant display a certain level of oral and written Dutch language and pass a digital test of knowledge of Dutch society.[23] This exam has to be taken by all foreigners between sixteen and sixty-five years old, with the exception of EU citizens and people earning more than € 40.000 a year. Here the link between integration and poverty becomes apparent. Poor people face more obstacles than the rich do. For expatriates earning enough to be exempted from participation in integration courses, it appears to be obvious that they speak the right language, are used to secularism, and will not discriminate against women or gay people. In general, West European governments apply a 'red carpet policy' to highly skilled people and well-educated professionals. This is understandable as far as non-dependency on welfare is concerned, but it becomes far less understandable insofar as being based on the assumed worldview of rich immigrants.

In addition to these exams, there are special requirements for preachers and religious teachers of all religions. As of September 2010, a compulsory trajectory for preachers and religious teachers was set up that takes about eighteen months and is divided into three parts: a) an intensive language course of ten days (custom-made and offered at different locations in the Netherlands); b) nine sessions with other preachers and teachers with assignments such as interviewing key figures within and visits to educational, medical, judicial and municipal institutions; c) coaching and supervision of practice assignments in the participant's own working environment. They also need to produce an ex-

---

21　Christian Joppke, "Beyond National Models: Civic Integration Policies for Immigrants in Western Europe," *West-European Politics* 30:1 (2007), 1–22.

22　Civic Integration Courses leading to this examination are called *Inburgeringscursussen* in Dutch, a word containing the word *burger* (which means 'citizen'). The denotation of the term *inburgeringcursus* is not that of becoming a national citizen in the sense of naturalization, but in the sense of economic integration: becoming a part of the workforce, Cf. María Bruquetas-Callejo, Blanca Garcés-Mascareñas, Rinus Penninx & Peter Scholten, "Policymaking Related to Immigration and Integration: The Dutch Case," *IMISCOE Working Paper 15,* Country Report Amsterdam (2007), 18, note 10. Since January 2013 foreigners have to prepare for their integration exam on their own, i.e., the government no longer offers free courses; foreigners can, however, follow these courses at private companies for a fee.

23　The passing rate of the examination is 75%, i.e., 17,582 persons, according to Minister van der Laan, February 2010.

tra six proofs of being able to render appropriate social assistance to others.[24] It is up to the religious communities to report preachers and teachers who have newly arrived and to enroll them in the course.

Looking at Civic Integration from a Missiological Perspective

There are several reasons to take a look at civic integration programs, courses, and exams from a missiological perspective. First of all, Christian mission history shows many examples of Christianity mixing with Western civilization.[25] Viewed as part of colonialism, the mission movement can be characterized by David Bosch's famous three C's: Christianity, Commerce, and Civilization.[26] To become Christian was to become civilized and modern, to leave behind all uncivilized, pagan, non-Western ideas and practices. This is not to deny the fact that there have always been missionary forces that worked against colonialism,[27] but these forces never proved strong enough to totally eradicate the contamination of mission by Western feelings of superiority, political expansion, and economic aggression. Mission was *mission civilisatrice*, civilizing mission, binding God and Western civilization dangerously close together. Some Christian missionaries become tired of the accusations and guilt laid on them, even by those who never have studied any page of mission history or made any attempt to share their life and goods with others. They will reply that if the mission part of civilizing mission is left out, only the civilizing part remains—which is worse. Missiologists, however, should not be content themselves with such a defense. They must show how God's mission—and mission in the footsteps of Christ—can be both a critique and renewal of civilization.

Second, there is a certain missionary zeal among those who want to integrate newcomers into Western society. A new preponderance of secularism challenges the long-standing notion of secularity as a means for balancing religious and ideological diversity. In the new assertive secularity, only the

---

24 The preparation for the civic integration exam for this group is entrusted to the Wico Bunskoek Academy, a Center for Religion and Society in Kontakt der Kontinenten, that has been working on integration courses since 2002. Until 2013 participation in the course was free, but since then participants have to pay for the course.

25 See Dana L. Robert (ed.), *Converting Colonialism: Visions and Realities in Mission History 1706–1914* (Grand Rapids: Eerdmans, 2008), 1–21.

26 David Bosch, *Transforming Mission: Paradigm Shifts in Theology of Mission* (Maryknoll: Orbis, 1991), 302 ff.

27 Paul Hiebert, *Anthropological Reflections on Missiological Issues* (Grand Rapids: Baker, 1994), 81 f.

secular ontology is 'real.' Religions represent historical vestiges of the past, and their protection should be subordinated to universalistic notions of civic liberties. This new assertive secularity is shaped to reflect national integration.[28]

Third, among the newcomers subjected to the civic integration programs, courses, and exams, we find many Christians and Muslims who consider their migration to the Netherlands a missionary activity. They have come because God has sent them. And, as soon as they arrive, it becomes clear in their eyes why they were sent: to rescue fellow migrants and wider European society from modernism, individualism, secularism, and all their alleged troubles.[29] Missiology contends that the shift of Christianity's center of gravity to the global south has huge implications for the intercultural communication between Christians worldwide.[30] Studies of Christian immigrants in the Netherlands show that this communication implies a struggle over the values of modernity. The core of this struggle is found in liberal individualism, with Western Christians adhering to the idea that the individual is a rational being, free to determine his or her own life. Non-Western Christian immigrants, on the other hand, emphasize that to be human is to live in community and to obey God's will.

Bildung and 'Normalizing'

As we saw in the previous chapter, *Bildung*, at least according to Kierkegaard, has a gift-like character, with God as its transcendent and critical moment. It does not content itself with what culture or civilization has to offer. This opens up the possibility of criticizing existing integration programs and integration demands whenever they are aimed at normalizing immigrants to what is recognized as moral or civilized at the time. *Bildung* is never finished. This

---

28 See Cora Schuh, Marian Burchardt & Monika Wohlrab-Sahr, "Contested Secularities: Religious Minorities and Secular Progressivism in the Netherlands," *Journal of Religion in Europe* 5:3 (2012), 349–383.

29 Jehu Hanciles, for example, is convinced that international migration and missionary expansion are inextricably connected; see Jehu J. Hanciles, "Migration and Mission: The Religious Significance of the North-South Divide," in Andrew Walls & Cathy Ross (eds.), *Mission in the 21st Century: Exploring the Five Marks of Global Mission* (Maryknoll: Orbis, 2008), 118–129.

30 Frans Wijsen, "Global Christianity: A European Perspective," *Exchange* 38 (2009), 147–160; Mechteld Jansen, *Inter Related Stories: Intercultural Pastoral Theology* (Zürich/Berlin: LiT Verlag, 2011), 81.

understanding of *Bildung* and its critical potential comes close to Paul Tillich's formulation of a core Protestant principle.

> The Protestant principle ... contains the divine and human protest against any absolute claim made for a relative reality, even if this claim is made by a Protestant church. The Protestant principle is the judge of every religious and cultural reality, including the religion and culture which calls itself 'Protestant.'[31]

This living, moving, restless principle exists beyond all its realizations; it cannot be captured in any civilization or ecclesial structure.

The Dutch Civic Integration Courses, especially the pre-entry courses and courses taken without any personal guidance from or debate with teachers and learners, have been criticized for drawing a stereotypical image of the Netherlands as well as targeting Muslim immigrants.[32] Moreover, citizenship education, as offered to immigrants during the integration trajectory, is a disciplinary program. It works with an often tacitly acknowledged teleological view of education: the goals are achieved and the diplomas can be offered when the trained people have come to accept liberal democracy and the freedom of the expressive individual. This includes the fact that many participants will pass the test, but there will also be many who will fail and 'remain behind.' They cannot enter the Promised Land. Consider the following example:

Question in the final integration exam:
1. Ali's neighbors have placed a statue of the Holy Virgin Mary in their garden. How can Ali best respond to this:
    a. Remove the statue at night
    b. Do nothing; the neighbors may do whatever they like with their garden

---

31   Paul Tillich, *The Protestant Era* (Chicago: University of Chicago Press, 1948), 163; Paul Tillich, *Systematic Theology* (Chicago: University of Chicago Press, 1967, 3 Vols. in 1), Vol. 3, 177 and passim.

32   Cf. Amitai Etzioni, "Citizenship Tests: A Comparative, Communitarian Perspective," *Political Quarterly* 78:3 (2007), 353–363, who mentions (360) the "'Coming to the Netherlands' video, with its sexually explicit scenes as well as depictions of crime-ridden immigrant ghettos in the Netherlands. It focuses largely on acceptance of key values, but mostly those that are related to rights (e.g., tolerance, the rights of women and freedom of expression) and not to shared responsibilities."

c. Ask the neighbors to remove the statue.[33]

In this example, only option b is correct, according to the civilizing goals of this program. Ali, supposedly a male Muslim, needs to understand that only answer b takes the tolerant position: tolerance takes the place of truth, and absolute tolerance takes the place of absolute truth. One has to obey the demand to drop all convictions that would openly contradict other convictions. *We have a culture of tolerance, and those who cannot live with that represent a backward culture.*[34] One wonders if a more critical *Bildung* perspective would not lead to a preference for option c and—provided these neighbors stay on speaking terms—to more *Bildung* on both sides.

Civic Integration Courses presuppose the model of 'the good citizen' who is responsible, capable of self-criticism, clean, and patient. The good citizen does not seek to satisfy all personal needs immediately. Implicitly, the participants learn what it means to be a good Dutch citizen and to adapt to Dutch civilization as in the following examples:

> Many Dutch people are set on their privacy; some are quite easily bothered ... In case of disputes between neighbors, you first try to discuss the problems. If that does not help, you can call the police. Parents in the Netherlands talk a lot with their children. They try to explain as much as possible, e.g., why something is forbidden or how something works. In the Netherlands, a child is not considered impudent when asking for an explanation or expressing an opinion (although in the eyes of the Dutch as well, children can go too far) ...
>
> When people meet each other for the first time in an informal setting, they do not ask questions like: How old are you? Are you married? How much do you earn? Are you religious? Such questions are considered improper ... Furthermore, people often look directly into each other's eyes during a conversation but do not touch each other, keeping a small distance from each other ...
>
> In conversations people often talk in a direct way; they do not keep their opinions to themselves ... It is not wrong to say 'no' if you do not

---

33 http://www.inburgeren.nl/inburgeraar/examen/centrale_examens/kennis_samenleving.asp.

34 Wendy Brown, "Why We Are Civilized and They Are the Barbarians," in Wendy Brown, *Regulating Aversion: Tolerance in an Age of Identity and Empire* (Princeton: Princeton University Press, 2006), 149 ff.

know the answer to a question. It is no problem if you contradict one another. But the way you say something is important.[35]

My point here is not that these broad descriptions of cultural patterns in the Netherlands are wrong, but that the newcomer must subscribe to them in order to obtain the rights of real citizens. After all, the final integration exams do not ask the participants to say what the Dutch normally think or do but to say what is best to do. If the participant does not subscribe to Dutch views and behavior, he or she will continue to remain a person without status, somewhere in the wasteland between exile and belonging.

A more subtle example can be found in the training material for the new integration exam:

> Question from the training material:
> Maliki's school celebrates Christmas and Easter. Maliki's mother does not consider this necessary. Religion is something that belongs in the home. She is looking for another school for Malika. Which school is the best for her?
> a. a Catholic school
> b. a public school
> c. a school for special education.[36]

Here, of course, only option b is right, since the 'normal' way of thinking has already been put into the mother's mind: it mirrors the views of those who want to keep religion out of the public domain. While this was never intended in Dutch tradition by those who defended state neutrality in religious affairs, it seems to be promoted now as the norm of the majority.

As a missiologist, I want to raise two questions that stem from Christian mission history with respect to present civic integration courses and exams. The first deals with the difference between civilizing as the core business of civic integration on the one hand and discipling on the other hand. Could the biblical idea and Christian practice of discipling be a counterforce to integration as the assimilation of believers to secular civilization? The second question is

---

35   Inge van Baalen & Wim Coumou, *Denkend aan Holland: Een programma Maatschappij-oriëntatie voor nieuwkomers* (*Thinking of Holland: Orientation on Dutch Society Textbook for Newcomers*) (Utrecht: NCB, 2004), 70, 129, 151.

36   DUO Inburgeren voorbeeldexamen Kennis Nederlandse Samenleving, example from Exam Knowledge of Dutch Society, question 17. http: www. inburgeren.nl (accessed on 31 July 2013).

about the similarity between *Bildung* and mission. Could both be forces of transformative thought, also when the integration of newcomers into Dutch society is at issue?

Discipling, Bildung, and Civilizing

As we have seen, both Christian mission and integration courses easily fall back into molding other people into one's own cultural (or even denominational!) and civil shape. This molding takes place when people who want to become Christian or to peacefully participate in Western civilization refrain from thinking differently and acting in a different way than the missionary teaches or the textbook says. Some might state that this molding is just a normal means of socialization, education, and disciplining. From a missiological view, however, we need to differentiate between disciplining and discipling as well as between civilizing and *Bildung*.

Discipling is about being transformed and letting one's life be gradually filled with God's Spirit. But can one really disciple other persons? Throughout history, great teachers and leaders may have had circles of disciples, but it was surely never intended in Christian tradition that Christian leaders or teachers form circles of disciples around themselves. Discipling, it seems to me, aims at growth and development from glory to glory in the image of Christ, as stated in 2 Cor. 3:18: "And all of us, with unveiled faces, seeing the glory of the Lord as though reflected in a mirror, are being transformed into the same image from one degree of glory to another; for this comes from the Lord, the Spirit."[37] As we saw in the previous chapter, discipling means spiritual formation, essentially through worship; becoming a true disciple takes a lifetime of learning and asking for feedback on what one practices (Luke 10:17–20). Discipling has been hijacked by many recipe books describing how some already 'arrived' church or community leaders can disciple new converts in nicely defined steps.

Despite this, it is important to note that discipling does indeed entail a reorientation of life, a resituating of ourselves, supported by the teachings of tradition, fellowship, the breaking of the bread, and prayer.[38] Thus, discipling

---

[37] New Standard Revised Version; this theme of discipling and discipleship is elaborated in Wonsuk Ma & Kenneth Ross (eds.), *Mission Spirituality and Authentic Discipleship* (Oxford: Regnum Books, 2013).

[38] Walter Brueggemann, "Evangelism and Discipleship: The God who Calls, the God who Sends," *Word and World* 24:2 (2004), 121–135: 131 f.

comes with discipline, which means control over oneself, following a path in obedience, having oneself under control, and following a rhythm in life. The risk, however, of conflating disciplining with discipline are rather high: command and control by the church leadership and punishment in the case of disobedience.

In the next step we turn to the concept of *Bildung*. At first sight, it might seem rather odd to combine the words mission and *Bildung*. In the eyes of many West Europeans, *Bildung* is far more subject-oriented and open-ended than mission. But both *Bildung* and mission are not about imposing a completed product on an individual or a group but about a process of appropriation. Nonetheless, precisely because both church and state know all too well the pitfalls of fostering discipline, it is worthwhile looking into missiological endeavors that fuel the profile of *Bildung*. Conversely, the idea of *Bildung* as a critical-constructive counterbalance to the discipline of civilizing might fuel practices and an understanding of Christian mission in a post-Christian era.[39] Both mission and *Bildung* are concerned with existential orientation, the ability to make political and ethical judgments, and the motivation to assume responsibility. *Bildung* fuels mission with questions like: how does this person (this group) discover the talents (s)he has? How do we deal with crises in life and faith? Does Christian mission increase proper assertiveness or does it promote submission to authorities?

We can compare the Dutch Civic Integration Courses with simple, sometimes oversimplified, courses in Christianity for dummies and the ABC's of the Christian faith. Although these courses certainly have their value, they cannot be taken as formative education (*Bildung*) and they should be constantly reevaluated, screening any attempt to mold believers and non-believers and to reduce them to either one type of secular citizen or one type of Christian dummy forever. Taken together, the concepts of disciplining and *Bildung* can serve as a warning against the civilizing discipline in church and society. Yet, as we can see in Christian mission history as well as in modern secularist mission, both disciplining and *Bildung* are jeopardized when certain frames of the 'target group' are in use. We will highlight these frames in the next sections.

---

39 Cf. Michael Herbst, "Bildsame Mission—Missionarische Bildung?" in Michael Herbst, Roland Rosenstock & Frank Bothe (eds.), *Zeitumstände: Bildung und Mission* (Frankfurt am Main: Peter Lang, 2009), 153–178; Johannes Zimmermann (ed.), *Darf Bildung missionarisch sein? Beiträge zum Verhältnis von Bildung und Mission* (Neukirchen-Vluyn: Neukirchener Verlag, 2010).

Framing the Believer as Backward

Many definitions of 'progress' are loaded with the idea that not all people can keep up with this progress—some will be left behind. This applies in particular to those forms of 'progress' philosophies that promise final redemption. This has certainly been the case in Christianity where it modeled the Christian life as a progressive way to heaven. In that model, non-believers are left behind. In modern West European discourse, however, the idea of progress excludes religious people. Those who cannot cope with the rapid change, i.e. the believers, will be left behind. Jews and Christians can perhaps partake in the final redemption if and when they accept the only true modernism, i.e. secularism.[40]

A fierce critique of this idea of progress comes from the American philosopher Judith Butler,[41] who attacks the division of people and cultures into modern progressive freedom-minded groups on the one side and non-modern, regressive religious minorities on the other. According to Butler, the progressive secular language of freedom can be deployed as an instrument of bigotry and coercion. In fact, it has been deployed that way in the war on terror with its embarrassing low points in the Abu Ghraib prison and Guantánamo. Those who remain behind, the Muslims, are labeled pre-modern. By forcing their prisoners to watch pornography, American soldiers try to discipline them and teach them what liberated modern, secular society means. In the same vein, Butler also points to the Dutch pre-entry integration course. She states that in this course "… modernity is being defined as sexual freedom, and the particular sexual freedom of gay people is understood to exemplify a culturally advanced position as opposed to one that would be deemed pre-modern."[42] This is clearly shown when

> new applicants for immigration are asked to look at photos of two men kissing, and asked to report whether those photos are offensive, whether they are understood to express personal liberties, and whether the view-

---

[40] For an example of this, I refer to the question asked by an MP in Dutch Parliament of the Minister of Internal Affairs on February 11, 2011: "Do you share the estimation that, owing to progressive secularization, Dutch Muslims will pass through a similar development like Christians have? If not, why?" see http://www.rijksoverheid.nl/documenten-en-publicaties/kamerstukken/2011/03/04/vragen-bericht-islamisering-europa.html (accessed November 2012).

[41] Judith Butler, "Sexual Politics, Torture, and Secular Time," *British Journal of Sociology* 59:1 (2008), 1–23.

[42] Butler, "Sexual Politics," 3.

ers are willing to live in a democracy that values the rights of gay people to open and free expression.[43]

In the pre-entry exam's film, the camera focuses on a topless woman emerging from the sea and walking onto a crowded beach. For people considering immigration into the Netherlands, it seems that acceptance of openly expressed homosexuality and female nudity is a litmus test for embracing modernity. Those who have objections would be deemed pre-modern because the state discourse, through these texts and photos, is a discourse of progress leading to freedom. The point is that it is taken for granted that only a secularist discourse can liberate people from homophobia and discrimination against women. Reasoning along the lines of this secularist discourse, one risks fighting serious forms of exclusion with another form of exclusion—the exclusion of religious people.

In the same vein, Tariq Modood sees today's world dominated by a definite predilection for secularism and panic about religious diktats.[44] To counterbalance this predilection for secularism, Modood points out that national law is never value-free and remains connected to the worldviews of people who make that law. Secularism is only one of them and cannot claim to have a privileged position. The secular liberal interpretation of reality assumes that secularism is more 'mature' than religious interpretations. Moreover, Christianity sometimes claims secularity as its own offspring, leaving Islam behind as the truly immature view. At other times, major Western thinkers and politicians are sending the message that *all* religions are problematic.[45]

Before I leave this section about 'framing' I need to point to a mirroring phenomenon to give a balanced account. Countless examples of mission history give evidence of the fact that non-Christians have been framed as uncivilized people.[46] That sad history is not new, and it must be revisited and remembered

---

43 Butler, "Sexual Politics," 3.
44 Tariq Modood, "Fuzzy Law and the Boundaries of Secularism," www.onelawforall.org.uk and www.religareproject.eu; also see Modood, *Multiculturalism*.
45 Cf. Charles Taylor's claim that the wrong definition of secularism can lead to fixation on religion as the problem, see "Why We Need a Radical Definition of Secularism," in Judith Butler, Jürgen Habermas, Charles Taylor & Cornel West (ed. Eduardo Mendieta & Jonathan VanAntwerpen), *The Power of Religion in the Public Sphere* (New York: University of Columbia, 2011), 48.
46 Jim F. Engel & William A. Dyrness, *Changing the Mind of Missions: Where Have We Gone Wrong?* (Downers Grove: InterVarsity Press, 2000), 45 ff; Lamin O. Sanneh, "Civilization and the Limits of Mission," in Lamin O. Sanneh, *Disciples of all Nations: Pillars of Christianity* (New York: Oxford University Press, 2008), 299, offers one of many examples when

by all workers involved in mission worldwide. What is new is the flow of "reverse mission"[47] referring to the missionary zeal and efforts of the formerly missionized peoples directed to the 'Christian West.' Often, this reverse mission is in the hands of marginalized people who perceive the Christian West as the center of power but no longer as the center of Christianity. In reverse mission, Europeans are sometimes viewed as Africans were in colonial times. The Dutch, including Dutch Christians, allow themselves and their children to drink alcohol, to dance, to enjoy modern music, to eat meat, to keep dirty pets in their homes, to smoke, to wear shorts in public, and some or all of these signs of 'uncivilized behavior' are abhorred by immigrant communities.[48] Moreover, the reputation of the Dutch as slave owners, their laxity regarding prostitution and human trafficking, their indifference to the fate of undocumented people, their disrespectful attitude toward the elderly are characteristics of their decline into paganism.

In all this mutual framing of secularists on the one side (believers are backward and need to be civilized through integration) and religious immigrants on the other (Dutch citizens are pagan and need to be civilized through conversion) we see that civilization has once again become an instrument of exclusion. The question is whether, and if so, how, the Protestant principle of refraining from giving any absolute authority to a relative reality might be of any help here.

Both secularist and Christian (and Muslim) civilization discourse creates boundaries. But all the emphasis on boundaries between civilizations, secular

---

he describes Roland Allen's critical questioning of his fellow missionaries: "When they spoke of 'Christian civilization', they had in mind, frankly, the civilization of Christian England: Western civilization. Allen objected that that was not Christian civilization. To a life devoid of Christian faith missionaries more willingly gave the name 'Christian' than to a life devoted to Christ and inspired by Christ under conditions the missionaries regarded as uncivilized."

47 For a broad look at reverse mission, see Afe Adogame & Shobana Shankar (eds.), *Religion on the Move! New Dynamics of Religious Expansion in a Globalizing World* (Leiden: Brill, 2013).

48 It would, however, be a misreading of the present situation if we were to look only at immigrants holding the Christian or Muslim fundamentalist view. Confining myself to the Christian immigrant churches, I find it hard to believe that the generalizations of reactionary southern Christianity, as they are pictured by Philip Jenkins, hold true for most of the immigrant Christian churches in the Netherlands; cf. Philip Jenkins, *God's Continent: Christianity, Islam, and Europe's Religious Crisis* (New York: Oxford University, 2007), 87 ff, 274 f; and Werner Ustorf, *Robinson Crusoe Tries Again: Missiology and European Constructions of "Self" and "Other" in a Global World 1789–2010* (Göttingen: Vandenhoeck & Ruprecht, 2010), 207 ff.

and religious outlooks, and differences cannot wipe out the deeply human longing for interconnectedness, which politicians and missionaries alike should take seriously. This longing for interconnectedness is quite compatible with ongoing conversations between people and even conversions. Real conversation requires more than good manners. It requires the courage to test convictions and the trust put in them: do they really provide helpful insights into reality? Do they provoke social justice and the survival of humanity?[49]

A commitment to a religious tradition may instill a sense of freedom to look outwards, to consider others, to embrace others, and to engage with others.[50] Perhaps this runs contrary to the fear of those designers of integration courses who expect these commitments to cause nothing but isolation and self-enclosure. They overlook the potential of all exhortations in religions to shape an attitude of seeing others with imagination and empathy.

Conclusions

Against the backdrop of social and political developments, the design of Dutch Civic Integration shows the imprint of the assumption that secularism is the route to integration. This is because the idea has gained ground that only secularism can create a critical attitude toward dogmatism, fanaticism, and violence. Conflicts on clothing, blasphemy, gender, sexuality, and other hot issues are explained by the division into two groups: the religious people attacking freedom versus the secularists defending freedom. Civilizing immigrants in a liberal democratic society can only be achieved if newcomers, suspected to be religious, turn to secularism. The language of secularism assumes that the secular worldview is more mature than religious worldviews. Islam especially, but other religious traditions as well, are portrayed as immature. Religion is a pre-adult stage of cultural development, and truly civilized people will leave that stage of development behind them because that stage is 'old-fashioned.' Secular civilization is accustomed to putting the backward religious state of mind and religious ways of living at a distance. Here, to civilize immigrant believers means to train and discipline them to turn them into modern people.

I have juxtaposed Christian mission efforts to civilize non-Europeans and the new heralding of liberal secularism from a missiological viewpoint and

---

49   Cf. the test questions that Walter Hollenweger put to his own religiosity in Ustorf, *Robinson Crusoe*, 244.
50   See David Cheetham, *Ways of Meeting and the Theology of Religions* (Farnham: Ashgate, 2013), 200.

suggested that they work with analogous concepts of civilizing 'the other.' European Christianity and post-Christian secularism mark their outsiders as uncivilized people of the past (out of time) and people of the wilderness (out of place). Both Christian mission and post-Christian democracies are being challenged to design formative education that binds discipline to the broader aim of fostering imagination, creativity, and empathy.

The current debates about the 'amount of religion' that can be tolerated in a democratic society pit religious and non-religious worldviews against each other in an atmosphere of political negotiation. The language of negotiation entails give and take, winning some and losing some, and in the end trying to sell the outcome as the best deal to one's supporters. The language of negotiation, however, does not fit the field of religions and worldviews. This field of convictions, traditions, practices, and beliefs—many of which are non-negotiable in the eyes of believers—requires a language of solidarity in hope. It is not that believers, religious or non-religious, are dogmatic and stubborn by nature but that their worldview is part of who they are. The language of negotiation still assumes that religions and non-religious worldviews are fixed packages of beliefs, whereas in real life people have made up and constantly are making up their life stories. In these stories, complex patterns of multiple modernities, religious affiliations, and secularisms are found. A language of solidarity in hope means strengthening one another's hope for a peaceful and just society. Such language can be spoken between adherents of different religions and between religious and secularist groups in society as long as both recognize that neither language as such is purer, holier, more mature, or more sensible. It is exactly the nature of *faith* (hope, trust, truth that can be confirmed by caring practices) that is kept alive by religions and that is desperately needed in societies that want to tackle extremist and violent absolutisms of secular and religious nature alike. The Protestant principle is 'civilizing' exactly in its desacralizing power over nationalism, ethnicism, state control, political, and religious absolutisms.

Today's life stories mirror the complex Christian-Secular mix of many identity formations in Europe. The framing of believers as backward often features in this complex Christian-secular mix, of which the Civic Integration Courses are but one example. Both governments and churches need to overcome the traditional division between the 'religious' and the 'secular' to gain a more adequate view of the people's spiritual quests that do not seem to be tolerated by political institutions nor properly welcomed and answered by ecclesial institutions. As a consequence, our civilization risks robbing itself, not only of religious newcomers but also of its long-standing tradition of loyal inhabitants wanting to give the best of their religious inspiration to that civilization.

Bibliography

Adogame, Afe & Shobana Shankar (eds.), *Religion on the Move! New Dynamics of Religious Expansion in a Globalizing World* (Leiden: Brill, 2013).

Baalen, Inge van & Wim Coumou, *Denkend aan Holland: Een programma Maatschappij-oriëntatie voor nieuwkomers (Thinking of Holland: Orientation on Dutch Society Textbook for Newcomers)* (Utrecht: NCB, 2004).

Berger, Peter; Grace Davie & Effie Fokas, *Religious America, Secular Europe: A Theme and Variations* (Farnham: Ashgate, 2008).

Borgman, Erik, *Metamorfosen: Over religie en moderne cultuur (Metamorphoses: On Religion and Modern Culture)* (Kampen: Klement, 2006).

Borgman, Erik & Anton van Harskamp, "Tussen secularisering en hernieuwde sacralisering" (Between Secularization and Renewed Sacralization), in Meerten ter Borg et al., *Handboek Religie in Nederland* (Zoetermeer: Meinema, 2008), 14–25.

Bosch, David, *Transforming Mission: Paradigm Shifts in Theology of Mission* (Maryknoll: Orbis, 1991).

Brown, Wendy, "Introduction," in Talal Asad, Wendy Brown, Judith Butler & Saba Mahmood (eds.), *Is Critique Secular? Blasphemy, Injury, and Free Speech* (Berkeley: University of California, 2009), 7–19.

———, "Why We Are Civilized and They Are the Barbarians," in Wendy Brown, *Regulating Aversion: Tolerance in an Age of Identity and Empire* (Princeton: Princeton University Press, 2006), 149–175.

Brueggemann, Walter, "Evangelism and Discipleship: The God who Calls, the God who Sends," *Word and World* 24:2 (2004), 121–135.

Bruquetas-Callejo, María; Blanca Garcés-Mascareñas; Rinus Penninx & Peter Scholten, "Policymaking Related to Immigration and Integration: The Dutch Case," *IMISCOE Working Paper 15*, Country Report Amsterdam (2007).

Butler, Judith, "Sexual Politics, Torture, and Secular Time," *British Journal of Sociology* 59:1 (2008), 1–23.

Carrera, Sergio, "A Comparison of Integration Programmes in the EU: Trends and Weaknesses," *CEPS CHALLENGE Papers No. 1* (2006).

———, *In Search of the Perfect Citizen? The Intersection between Integration, Immigration and Nationality in the EU* (Leiden: Brill, 2009).

———, "Integration as a Process of Inclusion for Migrants? The Case of Long-term Residents in the EU," in H. Schneider (ed.), *Migration, Integration and Citizenship: A Challenge for Europe's Future* (Maastricht: Maastricht University, 2005), 109–138.

Casanova, José, "Religion, European Secular Identities and European Integration," in Timothy A. Byrnes & Peter J. Katzenstein (eds.), *Religion in an Expanding Europe* (Cambridge: Cambridge University Press, 2006), 65–92.

Cheetham, David, *Ways of Meeting and the Theology of Religions* (Farnham: Ashgate, 2013).

Dallmayer, Fred, *Dialogue Among Civilizations: Some Exemplary Voices* (New York: Palgrave Macmillan, 2002).

Dronkers, Pieter, "Loyal to the Tricolour: Changing Regimes of Belonging in the Netherlands," http://www.raison-publique.fr/IMG/pdf/Dronkers_-_Loyal_to_the_tricolouri.pdf.

Engel, Jim F. & William A. Dyrness, *Changing the Mind of Missions: Where Have We Gone Wrong?* (Downers Grove: InterVarsity Press, 2000).

Etzioni, Amitai, "Citizenship Tests: A Comparative, Communitarian Perspective," *Political Quarterly* 78:3 (2007), 353–363.

Habermas, Jürgen, "Notes on Post-Secular Society," *New Perspectives Quarterly* 25 (2008), 17–29.

Hanciles, Jehu J., "Migration and Mission: The Religious Significance of the North-South Divide," in Andrew Walls & Cathy Ross (eds.), *Mission in the 21st Century: Exploring the Five Marks of Global Mission* (Maryknoll: Orbis, 2008), 118–129.

Herbst, Michael, "Bildsame Mission—Missionarische Bildung?" in Michael Herbst, Roland Rosenstock & Frank Bothe (eds.), *Zeitumstände: Bildung und Mission* (Frankfurt am Main: Peter Lang, 2009), 153–178.

Hiebert, Paul, *Anthropological Reflections on Missiological Issues* (Grand Rapids: Baker, 1994).

Jansen, Mechteld, *Inter Related Stories: Intercultural Pastoral Theology* (Zürich/Berlin: LiT Verlag, 2011).

Jenkins, Philip, *God's Continent: Christianity, Islam, and Europe's Religious Crisis* (New York: Oxford University, 2007).

Joppke, Christian, "Beyond National Models: Civic Integration Policies for Immigrants in Western Europe," *West-European Politics* 30:1 (2007), 1–22.

Kirk, J. Andrew, *Civilizations in Conflict? Islam, the West and Christian Faith* (Oxford: Regnum, 2011).

Koolen, Ben, "Godsdienst en levensovertuiging in het integratiebeleid etnische minderheden" (Religion and Philosophy of Life in Integration Policy for Ethnic Minorities), *Tijdschrift voor Religie, Recht en Beleid* 1:1 (2010), 5–27.

Ma, Wonsuk & Kenneth Ross (eds.), *Mission Spirituality and Authentic Discipleship* (Oxford: Regnum Books, 2013).

Modood, Tariq, "Fuzzy Law and the Boundaries of Secularism," www.onelawforall.org.uk.

———, *Multiculturalism* (London: Polity Press, 2007).

Pels, Dick, *Opium van het volk: Over religie en politiek in seculier Nederland* (*Opium of the People: On Religion and Politics in Secular Netherlands*) (Amsterdam: De Bezige Bij, 2008).

Robert, Dana L. (ed.), *Converting Colonialism: Visions and Realities in Mission History 1706–1914* (Grand Rapids: Eerdmans, 2008).

Sanneh, Lamin O., *Disciples of all Nations: Pillars of Christianity* (New York: Oxford University Press, 2008).

Scheffer, Paul, "Het multiculturele drama," NRC *Handelsblad* (29 January 2000).

Schuh, Cora; Marian Burchardt & Monika Wohlrab-Sahr, "Contested Secularities: Religious Minorities and Secular Progressivism in the Netherlands," *Journal of Religion in Europe* 5:3 (2012), 349–383.

Taylor, Charles, *A Secular Age* (Cambridge: Harvard University Press, 2007).

———, "Why We Need a Radical Definition of Secularism," in Judith Butler, Jürgen Habermas, Charles Taylor & Cornel West (ed. Eduardo Mendieta & Jonathan VanAntwerpen), *The Power of Religion in the Public Sphere* (New York: University of Columbia, 2011).

Tillich, Paul, *Systematic Theology* (Chicago: University of Chicago Press, 1967, 3 Vols. in 1).

———, *The Protestant Era* (Chicago: University of Chicago Press, 1948).

Ustorf, Werner, *Robinson Crusoe Tries Again: Missiology and European Constructions of "Self" and "Other" in a Global World 1789–2010* (Göttingen: Vandenhoeck & Ruprecht, 2010).

Verkaaik, Oscar, *Ritueel Burgerschap: Een essay over nationalisme en secularisme in Nederland (Ritual Citizenship: An Essay on Nationalism and Secularism in the Netherlands)* (Amsterdam: Amsterdam University Press, 2009).

Wijsen, Frans, "Global Christianity: A European Perspective," *Exchange* 38 (2009), 147–160.

Zimmermann, Johannes (ed.), *Darf Bildung missionarisch sein? Beiträge zum Verhältnis von Bildung und Mission* (Neukirchen-Vluyn: Neukirchener Verlag, 2010).

Prophecy and Democracy?
Some Arguments in Favor of Prophetic Discourse in Civilizing Democratic Societies

Nico Koopman

On the continent of Africa religion, both as religiosity in the sense of reverence for transcendence, and as adherence to institutional faith, is growing. Christianity enjoys its fastest growth on this continent. The question is whether Christianity, and other religions for that matter, would be healthy religion. The criteria for good or healthy religion can be phrased in the form of the following questions. Does religion enhance an honoring of God that is manifested in the commitment to acknowledging, affirming, advancing and actualizing dignity, freedom and justice for all? Does religion support intellectual practices that advance love of God with your mind, and does it oppose oversimplified, naïve and inadequate intellectual responses to complex public challenges in today's highly sophisticated societies? Does religion advance an ethos of tolerance and embrace in modern-postmodern societies where a plurality of often incommensurable moral, religious and secular comprehensive meaning-giving frameworks and life views co-exist and where consensus is hard to achieve, and does religion therefore free us from the violence of both absolutism and demonization of the other, on the one hand, and apathetic relativism and nihilism, on the other hand?

Building upon and extending earlier research this essay offers a discussion of the appeal for the healthy prophetic presence of religion in society. The argument is offered that the prophetic presence of Christian faith in democracies is crucial for the quest of democratic societies to build a life of civility and worth, dignity, freedom and justice for all. The notion of civil, civilizing and civilization in this essay is used to refer to the aim of a democracy to bring into being a society where everyone experiences a life of worth and dignity, freedom and justice. A civilized society is a society of dignity, justice and freedom for all. In this essay the view is rejected that the notion of civil, civilizing and civilization implies that some nations, ethnic groups or socio-economic groups are by nature uncivilized or less civil, or religiously, ethically and even aesthetically less developed than others. These notions rather refer to the quest of all societies of the world and of all ethnic and other groups for a life of dignity for all.

The calling of churches can be described in terms of a threefold calling, namely the prophetic calling, the priestly calling and the royal-servant calling. In the years of the struggle against apartheid the prophetic calling of churches was emphasized. The two other callings, namely the priestly and royal-servant callings, were also fulfilled, but the prophetic calling enjoyed prominence. In contemporary South Africa, where we celebrate twenty years of inclusive democracy, the pleas are heard from within and outside churches that the prophetic voice of churches be heard more clearly, that it be heard as clearly as was the case in apartheid South Africa. This plea comes from people in various other spheres of public life, including the media and political world, as well as from various church members.

During a visit to Stellenbosch University in 2014 minister Trevor Manuel, senior cabinet minister in the presidency and chairperson of the National Planning Commission, which drafted the National Development Plan, challenged various faculties of the university to contribute to the implementation of this plan. He specifically challenged the Faculty of Theology to view it as its first task to keep the vision alive of a civilized society where everyone enjoys a life of dignity, freedom and justice. Various political leaders in the governing African National Congress consistently challenge churches to offer courageous criticism to the government. Western Cape premier, Helen Zille, appeals to churches to bring the so-called unintended consequences of policies to the attention of government, especially the impact of policies upon vulnerable groups. The media in South Africa consistently view churches as too quiet about public affairs. They are convinced that the prophetic voices of churches and other religious bodies can make an indispensable contribution to the building of a new and civilized society.

Within the churches too various pastors and congregants hunger for a vibrant prophetic voice from their churches. They are frustrated by what they view as a lack of courage to speak out, and an anxiety to be politically correct and in good relationships with former comrades in the liberation struggle who now constitute the government, and who may view prophetic discourse as prophetic criticism.

There is also strong resistance to the idea of prophetic speaking in a democracy. The Dutch theologian Gerrit de Kruijf argued that there is no need for prophetic speaking in the context of a democracy.[1] The democratic ethos, democratic institutions and democratic practices make room for engagements other than the prophetic. Only where a democracy becomes oppressive does

---

1   See Gerrit de Kruijf, *Waakzaam en nuchter: Over christelijke ethiek in een democratie* (*Alert and Sober: About Christian Ethics in a Democracy*) (Baarn: Ten Have, 1993), 236–241.

prophetic speaking become necessary. This essay argues that prophetic speaking is essential even in societies with well-established democratic institutions and practices. As long as not all people in a society enjoy a life of civility and dignity, and as long as ecocide takes place, we need prophetic voices and practices. The type of prophetic discourse pleaded for in this essay might be broader than De Kruijf's definition of prophecy allows. But before we discuss the potential modes of prophecy in a democracy, let us tabulate the various objections to prophetic speaking in a democracy. These objections are not made in scientific publications, but mostly in informal discussions. Hence, they are articulated here on the basis of the author's observation of and participation in these discussions.

A first objection is that those engaged in prophetic speaking are dreamers who only spell out broad visions that do not really take realities into account, and who do not contribute to addressing the very complex challenges of democratic societies. They adhere to utopias and use unhelpful slogans, and alien and even alienating apocalyptic expressions.

A second objection suggests that prophetic discourse is not constructive. It only criticizes the various individual and institutional attempts to build a new society of civil and dignified living, but does not offer constructive proposals to build a new society. It does not acknowledge and appreciate the progress that is made, especially in a country like South Africa, where wrongs of centuries of colonialism and decades of apartheid need to be addressed.

The association of prophetic discourse with the plight of the poor and oppressed, the marginalized and vulnerable, is viewed as a way of causing division and alienation in societies. This objection is raised with a lot of emotion. Those who speak out on behalf of the marginalized are often severely criticized, and labeled as outdated Marxists, socialists and leftists, and also as troublemakers and instigators.

Fourthly, it is argued that prophetic discourse does not appreciate the extent, depth and complexity of challenges that we face in democracies. Prophetic discourse is unsophisticated with regard to the highly technical complexity of the manifold public challenges that democratic societies have to deal with. Prophetic discourse is therefore naïve and ill-informed. It cannot speak with the necessary nuances, authority and credibility.

Another objection to prophetic discourse that is expressed especially by Christians directly involved in politics, is the idea that we are now in a time of policy, and not prophecy. We need to be engaged in policy-making, policy-implementation and policy-monitoring processes. This policy discourse asks for compromises, for the openness to opt for what is less than ideal. Prophetic speaking, it is argued, is not open to compromises, to choosing that which is less than ideal. Prophetic speaking is also not open to the formation of partnerships and cooperation with various institutions in society, especially with government, which are indispensable for policy practices.

This essay attempts to address these objections. In addressing these objections we will develop the idea of various modes or forms of prophetic speaking: prophetic vision, criticism, story telling, analysis and policymaking successively. An awareness of the plurality of forms of prophetic discourse might assist us in overcoming the reduction of prophetic discourse to mere criticism. Where these manifold voices of prophetic speaking are acknowledged, greater hospitality to prophecy in democracy might also manifest. This attempt might show that a proper and nuanced employment of the prophetic discourse within democracies will advance a healthy impact of religion upon society. A thorough and appropriate prophetic voice in the context of democracies can assist discovering afresh the potential in the law of God for making distinct contributions to public discourses about various concrete challenges. The famous threefold function of the law (*triplex usus legis*) to identify and expose wrongs, to give guidelines for a life of gratitude, and to provide parameters for public policymaking processes can, for instance, be explored in prophetic discourse.

A Prophetic Vision that Undermines the Old

The Dutch theologian Harry Kuitert who is normally very reserved about the public role of religion, makes space for the visionary and inspiring role that religions can fulfill in public life.[2] The American theologian James Gustafson argues that the prophet has the twofold task of envisioning and criticizing.[3] Prophets as visionaries, according to Gustafson, portray an alluring vision of

---

2 Harry M. Kuitert, *'Dat moet ik van mijn geloof': Godsdienst als troublemaker in het publieke domein* (*'That Is What my Faith Requires': Religion as Troublemaker in the Public Domain*) (Kampen: Ten Have, 2008), 132–135.
3 In my work on prophetic discourses in a democracy I, with appreciation, draw upon, extend, amend and elaborate on the work of James Gustafson on the public speaking of the international ecumenical movement. The most important works in this regard are: James Gustafson, *Varieties of Moral Discourse: Prophetic, Narrative, Ethical, and Policy* (Stob lectures of Calvin College and Seminary, Grand Rapids: Calvin College, 1988). For an article in which Gustafson also discusses these discourses, see "An Analysis of Church and Society Social Ethical Writings," *Ecumenical Review* 40 (1988), 267–278. For an article in which Gustafson applies these discourses to medical questions, see "Moral Discourse about Medicine: A Variety of Forms," *Journal of Medicine and Philosophy* 15:2 (1990), 125–142.

the future.[4] They see a new world in which the strife and suffering that we currently experience, are overcome. This vision may indict the contemporary broken reality, but its main function is to allure and attract people to act concretely and to attempt to approximate the vision. Prophets as visionaries use utopian language, symbols, analogies, similes, and metaphors that move us. Their speeches are not technical moral arguments or policy statements. Hearers are moved by aspects like the passion of the speaker's voice, the cadences and figures of speech, many drawn from the Bible, that are employed, and also the moral authenticity of the speaker. Such visionary language moves us from indignation with the present to aspiration for the future.

The South African theologian John de Gruchy argues that democracy cannot flourish without a vision of a new society.[5] What occurred in ancient Athens was only the first step into an unknown future in pursuit of a vision of a transformed society in which all people are equal and their differences respected, free and responsible as citizens, but also liberated from oppression and poverty and therefore living in a society where justice prevails. This vision derives as much, if not far more, from the prophets of ancient Israel as it does from Athens, the Enlightenment, or the French Revolution.

Brazilian Reformed social scientist and theologian Rubem Alves offers a strong plea for prophecy as envisioning, especially in so-called postliberation societies.[6] He refers to societies that have struggled against oppression, but do not fulfill the vision of an alternative society years after the victory from oppression has been achieved. He speaks, in fact, of societies that had become democracies, but had forgotten the vision of a liberated society, the vision that had strengthened them during their struggle for liberation. This amnesia regarding the vision of a new society might even happen in older democracies like The Netherlands.

Alves states that the vision of hope and imagination is nurtured amongst those who suffer under our local and global democratic arrangements. He pleads for the restoration and revival of creative imagination and renewing hope. This vision of hope is born among people who suffer, and not among people who enjoy prosperity and well-being and are more easily tempted to view this as the best possible world. Hope and suffering function together, as Alves argues:

---

4 Gustafson, *Varieties*, 13 f.
5 John W. de Gruchy, *Christianity and Democracy: A Theology for a Just World Order* (Cape Town & Johannesburg: David Philip, 1995), 38 f.
6 Rubem Alves, *Tomorrow's Child: Imagination, Creativity, and the Rebirth of Culture* (New York, Evanston, San Francisco & London: Harper & Row Publishers, 1972), 183.

Those who live in the pain-delivering sectors of our society, however, even before they can articulate in speech the evil of this world, are already doing it by means of their inarticulate groans (Rom. 8:26). And this is the raw material the spirit takes unto Himself. In other words: this is the emotional matrix, which is the beginning of the creative event. Suffering prepares the soul for vision. Personality refuses to take things as they are. It spreads its wings and the heart emigrates to the horizons of the future.[7]

For creation to take place, suffering and hope cannot be separated. Suffering is the thorn that makes it impossible for us to forget that there is a political task still unfinished—still to be accomplished. And hope is the star that tells the direction to follow. The two, suffering and hope, live from each other. Suffering without hope produces resentment and despair. Hope without suffering creates illusions, naiveté, and drunkenness.[8]

This hope and creative imagination bring forth a new, surprising creative event, which cannot be scientifically analyzed, cognitively dissected and eventually duplicated.[9] This hope is religious hope. It is Trinitarian hope. It looks forward and it looks back. It rests upon what happened in the past and what is happening in the present, specifically in God's acts of creation, and of re-creation in Christ and renewal in the Spirit.[10]

This vision of the new is formed in Christian worship and prayer. The Dutch theologian Bram van de Beek demonstrates how the prayer for the coming of the kingdom helps us to see the new reality, and to work obediently for the realization of that reality.

> Where humans sacrifice themselves for others in his name, there one sees rays of the dawn of the kingdom. People who show compassion towards society's outcasts are following Jesus. People who devote their energies to the healing of the sick are erecting signs of the kingdom where there is no sickness. People who search for peace among the nations are followers of the peaceable kingdom. People who in the name of Jesus refuse to bow before this world's powers are erecting a visible

---

[7] Alves, *Tomorrow's Child*, 200 f.
[8] Alves, *Tomorrow's Child*, 203.
[9] Alves, *Tomorrow's Child*, 197 f.
[10] Alves, *Tomorrow's Child*, 198.

sign that Christ is Lord—even though they themselves are thrown to the lions.[11]

All these authors argue that the vision of a new society should be spelled out as long as that society is not fully actualized for all people and all of creation. And it is especially remarkable how they argue that the vision of the new requires no justification where people suffer, and, may I add, where there is solidarity with those who suffer. They also clearly show that envisioning does not imply a flight from the world, but rather a commitment to be empathically involved in the affairs of the world. This brief discussion also indicates that the notion of vision mobilizes people, nurtures hope, and prompts action.

Prophetic Criticism that Calls the New into Being

According to Gustafson the second dimension of prophetic speaking is that of courageous criticism. Besides annunciation, prophets have the task of denunciation. Besides the task of announcing the vision of a new society, prophets perform the task of denouncing the reality, which is in conflict with the vision of a new society. The prophet as critic, according to Gustafson, addresses what is perceived as the root of the problem.[12] The problem is not merely viewed as a matter of policies that are inadequate and wrong, but as a matter of religious, moral and social waywardness. The critic names the devil, who presumably underlies the various wrongs in society. Prophetic criticism gets to the roots of problems that pervade institutions and cultures, or that pervade the actions and behavior of individual persons. On the basis of statistical indicators and social analysis they expose the causes and roots of social and personal wrongs. Prophets as critics do not engage in detailed policy recommendations, and matters of strategy and tactics. The indictments of the prophet as critic construe the human condition in deep and broad proportions. And these prophetic indictments lead to conviction of guilt, and constitute a call to a fundamental repentance and a radical turn from unfaithfulness to faithfulness.

During apartheid the notion of apartheid as a heresy was employed to expose the theological causes and roots of what went wrong in our society. The notion of empire is currently employed to express what is wrong in contemporary societies in local, regional and global contexts.

---

11   Bram van de Beek, *Why? On Suffering, Guilt and God* (Grand Rapids: Eerdmans, 1990), 332 f.
12   Gustafson, *Varieties*, 7–11.

In various discourses about globalization the notion of prophetic speaking surface regularly. The globalization research initiative of the *Evangelisch Reformierte Kirche* in Germany and the Uniting Reformed Church in Southern Africa offers a helpful definition of empire. This research collaboration, which is hosted by the Beyers Naudé Centre for Public Theology, is one attempt amongst many to advance the reception of the Accra Declaration on global justice by so-called northern and southern churches:

> We speak of empire, because we discern a coming together of economic, cultural, political and military power in our world today, that constitutes a reality and a spirit of lordless domination, created by humankind yet enslaving simultaneously; an all-encompassing global reality serving, protecting and defending the interests of powerful corporations, nations, elites and privileged people, while imperiously excluding, even sacrificing humanity and exploiting creation; a pervasive spirit of destructive self-interest, even greed—the worship of money, goods and possessions; the gospel of consumerism, proclaimed through powerful propaganda and religiously justified, believed and followed; the colonization of consciousness, values and notions of human life by the imperial logic; a spirit lacking compassionate justice and showing contemptuous disregard for the gifts of creation and the household of life.[13]

The definition of these churches focuses on empire not only as specific nations, corporations, or institutions. This definition is deeper, wider and more inclusive than attempts to attribute the notion of empire only to such clearly definable institutions. It implies these institutions, but also unmasks the spirit, gospel and ethos that it is constituted and nurtured by, and that it in turn reinforces.

This definition of empire helps to unmask the spirit of empire in the practices, policies, and institutions in all walks of life, on local, regional and global level. Moreover it helps to unmask the spirit of empire in the hearts of humans and in the life of churches as well. Notions like empire are controversial. One often feels that it might be better to avoid such controversial and potentially divisive concepts. On the other hand, concepts like these enable us to notice what is happening around us and in us. These concepts shock in order to

---

[13] Allan Boesak et al. (eds.), *Dreaming a Different World: Globalisation and Justice for Humanity and the Earth: The Challenge of the Accra Confession for the Churches* (A Publication of the Uniting Reformed Church in Southern Africa and the *Evangelisch Reformierte Kirche* in Germany, 2010), 7.

restore. And prophets are called upon to, among other things, shock in order to restore.

Prophetic discourse as prophetic criticism also entails self-criticism. For various reasons churches should engage in constructive self-criticism. We should, however, guard against a form of self-criticism that has pacifying effects, a self-criticism that serves as excuse to terminate public involvement, because we ourselves are so very imperfect. What is required is a self-criticism that shows that we are aware of our sinfulness and fallibility as human beings. That we realize that because we are imperfect, sinful beings, even our best efforts as churches might be contaminated. Without constructive self-criticism we cannot speak legitimately in the world.

Racially and socio-economically divided churches in South Africa need to voice public self-criticism. Without such honesty our prophetic message to the public domain will be met with skepticism and rejection. The so-called Dutch Reformed Churches in South Africa are still divided racially and socio-economically. Even churches that are structurally one, still experience racial and class prejudice and stereotyping. If we want to speak prophetically about racism and classism in our world, we need to criticize these evils in our own bosoms even louder.

The mainly white Dutch Reformed Church (DRC) should unmask the unwillingness and fear of the other that prevents its members from uniting with the mainly black Uniting Reformed Church in Southern Africa (URCSA). The URCSA should practice self-criticism for its inability as church to fulfill the wonderful prophetic vision of the Confession of Belhar 1986. The URCSA that presented this confession to churches in the world should be more critical of its own role in embodying unity with especially the DRC, reconciliation and justice. Perhaps prophetic speaking as prophetic self-criticism might reveal to us as URCSA members that the church of the Belhar Confession has a bigger responsibility than its white so-called sister church to achieve unification. Such a prophetic, self-critical stance might enable us to work harder to actualize the unity within URCSA amid the diversity of URCSA members. This prophetic stance of self-criticism might also open our eyes wider for the voices of brothers and sisters who want to unite, to join hands, and to form a strong unstoppable coalition across church borders of people who are committed to unity, reconciliation and justice. Maybe the formation of such coalitions that do not function in exclusive mode, but aim to include the currently unwilling ones, is the prophetic thing to do now for DRC and URCSA members.

Besides the self-criticism with regard to justice in racial and class matters, churches need to practice prophetic self-criticism with regard to various other justice matters, like sexism, misogyny, heterosexism, patriarchalism, homophobia, nationalism, handicappism, ageism, ecocide, exclusion and exploitation. These evils are still tolerated too often in our own ranks.

Hopefully this brief discussion makes it clear that the practice of prophetic criticism is not destructive and negative. On the contrary, it is informed and inspired by the vision of a new reality. This focus upon the vision of the new prompts a stance of courageous and constructive criticism and self-criticism that opposes negativity and self-withdrawal, and that seeks the new in individuals and institutions, in churches and in broader society, including the natural environment.

Civilizing Prophetic Narratives from the Margin

Gustafson identifies three functions of stories in communities, especially Christian communities. Stories form the ethos and identity of a community and its members. Furthermore, stories inform and guide the moral choices of people. Stories, finally, perform a prophetic function.

Stories form moral identity by rehearsing the community's history and traditional meanings as they are portrayed in Scripture and other sources. The living tradition and truth transmitted through narratives, liturgies, rites, and other concrete terms and symbols, shape the ethos, vision, virtue and character, the values and outlooks as well as the moral interests and determining moral convictions of the moral and religious community.[14]

By referring to the ethical methods of Jesus and the rabbis, Gustafson argues that narratives can illuminate casuistic moral argumentation.[15] They do not provide single, clear and argued answers to specific moral cases, but they do provide nuanced and subtle illumination of the challenges that are faced and of possible outcomes. They show us features of life that are somehow excluded from technical abstract casuistry. Narratives do not offer distinctions and arguments, but they evoke imagination and stimulate our moral sensibilities and affections. And although they do not give clear and decisive conclusions, they do enlarge one's vision of what is going on. Where casuistic moral arguments call us to act in conformity with it, narratives invite us to act in the light of the vision they convey.

Stories are not only derived from biblical or theological material, but also from oral traditions. They do not offer theories of justice or injustice, but they

---

14 Gustafson, *Varieties*, 19 f, 22 ff.
15 Gustafson, *Varieties*, 20 ff.

do have a moving prophetic effect.[16] African theologian John Mbiti uses African prayers, poems, idioms and sayings to narrate how African people deal prophetically, hopefully and with resilience with the various plights that they face, especially the plight of poverty.[17] These narratives are also conveyed through songs. South African theologian Ferdinand Deist quotes a narrative in a song of a dehumanized and oppressed black person who bemoans his internalization of oppression in apartheid South Africa:

> I did the world great wrong
> with my kindness of a dog
> my heart like a dog's tongue
> licking too many hands, boots and bums
> even after they kicked my arse
> voetsek voetsek
> shit. I still wagged my tail
> I ran away still looking back
> with eyes saying please.[18]

Stories specifically reveal the plight of people living at the margins of our societies. The level of civility and dignity of a society is measured by how we care for the poor and vulnerable, the marginalized and vulnerable. The narratives of vulnerable people are determinative for the type of society we strive to be. Their stories provide the epistemologies and knowledge without which civilizing democracies cannot flourish.

The focus upon these stories from the margin does not take place in an exclusive manner. South African theologian John De Gruchy argues that the conviction of God's special identification with the poor and the marginalized is a Reformed notion, which, sadly, has been neglected,[19] although liberation theologies have helped us to re-value the importance of this conviction for faithful

---

16   Gustafson, *Varieties*, 20.

17   See amongst others John Mbiti, *The Prayers of African Religion* (Maryknoll: Orbis Books, 1975).

18   Ferdinand Deist, "Prophet and Society in Transition," in J. Mouton, A. van Aarde & W. Vorster (eds.), *Paradigms and Progress in Theology* (Pretoria: Human Sciences Research Council, 1988), 342.

19   John de Gruchy, *Liberating Reformed Theology: A South African Contribution to an Ecumenical Debate* (Grand Rapids: Eerdmans, 1991); "Towards a Reformed Theology of Liberation? Can we Retrieve the Reformed Symbols in the Struggle for Justice?" in W.A. Boesak & P.J.A. Fourie, *Vraagtekens oor Gereformeerdheid* (*Question Marks on Being Reformed*) (Belhar: LUS Publishers, 1998), 71–93.

living. This notion was prominent at the birth of the Reformed tradition, because many of the earliest Reformed theologians and pastors, as well as congregations, were persecuted, and much Reformed theology was conceived in exile, in poverty, amidst adversity and in the struggle against social and ecclesiastical tyranny. He cites the famous address of John Calvin to King Francis I of France in which he describes his fellow refugees as the "offscouring and refuse of the world."[20] De Gruchy's explanation about how this notion influenced the Reformation is worth quoting.

> The original impulse which led to the Reformation and to Calvin's interpretation of it, was a rejection of human tyranny of all kinds and the proclamation of the liberating power of the gospel of Jesus Christ. It was this which first led to Calvin's break with Rome, and it was this that motivated his attempt to create a new, just and equitable (if not egalitarian) society. Likewise, this has been the motivation of all those prophetic Calvinists who have taken the side of the oppressed, whether in the past or in the present.[21]

According to De Gruchy this theologizing from the perspective of the destitute faded, as Reformed Christians became part of the so-called middle and upper classes, where the dominant political power also resided.[22] It regained prominence in Reformed theology as a result of the challenge posed by Liberation theology about God's preferential option for the poor. Liberation theology's challenge to Reformed theology was to rediscover and to re-value the notion, which was so central at the birth of Reformed theology, namely to express its commitment to a civilized, dignified and humane society from the perspective and in the interest of the victims of oppressive power.

This analysis affirms that the practice of storytelling from the margin is indispensable for the building of democracies that bring a life of civility and honor, dignity and wellbeing for all. The wellbeing of the marginalized constitutes the acid test for the level of dignity and civility of our societies.

---

20   John Calvin, *Institutes of the Christian Religion*, 2 Vols., trans. Ford Lewis Battles, ed. John T. McNeill, Vol. 1 (Louisville: Westminster John Knox Press, 1960), 12.
21   De Gruchy, "Towards Liberation," 76.
22   De Gruchy, "Towards Liberation," 78.

Prophetic Analysis

After discussing the first three modes of prophetic speaking we now turn to the fourth mode, namely prophetic analysis. Gustafson describes ethical or philosophical moral discourse as follows:

> Ethical discourse provides the concepts, the modes of appropriate argumentation, and important distinctions which lead to greater precision and stronger backing for what Christians and other religious communities think is the right thing to do, the good thing to do.[23]

Gustafson admires the constant attention to the ethical moral discourse in the Roman Catholic tradition.[24] He argues that in the second part of the twentieth century Protestant ethicists started to give attention to the ethical, or philosophical moral discourse. He notes that the ethical writings of his teachers and of his pupils differ significantly in this regard. Ethical discourse, under the influence of especially Anglo-American moral philosophy, encourages a more precise use of concepts like justice, virtue, rights and duties. It offers more careful distinctions between concepts and classes of moral issues. It requires stronger logical arguments in support of moral prescriptions or moral condemnations.

Gustafson states that protestant theologians who engage in this 'technical,' prophetic discourse have to draw upon philosophical ethical discourses, as well as from their colleagues in the Jewish, Catholic and, to some extent, Anglican, traditions regarding the practice of constructive casuistry that is informed by philosophical insights and that employs a variety of ethical theories.

Drawing upon the work of James Gustafson, American theologian Bernard V. Brady mentions that the ethical discourse is drier and less exciting than the narrative and prophetic discourses.[25] Ethics can be tedious. Wording must be painstakingly accurate. Concepts need to be defined in a clear, comprehensive and concise manner. Clear thinking, precise use of words, and compelling reasoning facilitate the engagement of theology with public life. The ethical discourse helps to make narratives public and to translate the passionate pleas of the prophet into rationally defensible public positions. And by assisting these discourses to be more vocal and public in credible and constructive ways, an

---

23   Gustafson, *Varieties*, 42.
24   Gustafson, *Varieties*, 31 f.
25   Bernard V. Brady, *The Moral Bond of Community: Justice and Discourse in Christian Morality* (Washington: Georgetown University Press, 1998), 146 f.

impact is made on the formation of public opinion, public ethos, public *Zeitgeist/* thinking and eventually on public policy.

Accompanied by such thorough ethical analysis of various public challenges the prophetic task can be accomplished with intellectual sophistication, authority and credibility.

Prophetic Policy-making

To impact on public life and to affect the course of events, churches need to participate in policy discourse.[26] According to Gustafson the policy mode distinguishes itself from the other discourses in two ways. The first is that people who have the responsibility to make choices and to carry out the actions that are required by those choices conduct this discourse. Visionaries, critics, storytellers, technical analysts can all function with the external perspective of an observer, but policymakers function with the internal perspective of persons and agents who are responsible for making choices in quite complex and specific circumstances that constrain their possible actions.[27]

Gustafson refers to a second distinguishing characteristic of policy discourse. Policy is developed in particular conditions that both limit and enable the possibilities of action.

> The first question of the policymaker is likely to be "What is going on?" and not "What ought we to do?" Or, at least, both of these questions have to be kept in mind in a tandem and finally integrated way. The policymaker has to know what is possible, as well as what is the right thing to do, or what the most desirable outcomes are. What is desirable is always related to what is possible; it is always under the constraints of the possible. And a critical factor of judgment is precisely *what is possible*.[28]

The ethical should give direction to policy, but more is required for final decisions and policies: estimates and assessments of what is possible with the help of sociological, economic and other concepts; information on how to move the institution with efficiency from where it currently is to where it could be and ought to be within a specific time frame. For the policymaker the ethical is not

---

26 Gustafson, *Varieties*, 52.
27 Gustafson, *Varieties*, 43, 46.
28 Gustafson, *Varieties*, 47.

the only consideration, it is just a dimension of the economic, social, personal and historical.[29]

Within the framework of limited space, time, information and possibilities policymakers are challenged to make compromises, and even decisions that might seem morally wrong or morally inadequate to the storytellers, critics and visionaries.[30] Brady's elaboration on and application of the work of Gustafson is helpful. He argues that in policymaking the variety of vulnerable people need to be given priority, amongst others children, women, oppressed racial groups, poor people and exploited workers. This notion of the priority of the most vulnerable will help ensure that the unavoidable compromises do not impact negatively on them. This notion of the option of the most vulnerable serves as benchmark with regard to policymaking and especially the adoption of compromises.[31]

The enabling dimension of policy discourse resides in the fact that policymakers have sufficient power to implement decisions and policies.[32]

About two years ago the church leader's forum in the Western Cape and the provincial government of the Western Cape adopted a document that will serve as basis for the collaboration of churches with regard to policymaking, policy-implementation and policy-monitoring processes. This document reveals the commitment of churches to partnership, collaboration, and to practicing a policy discourse that is informed by the vision of a civilizing democracy, on the one hand, and that is open to making compromises without betraying the aim of the vision of a new society, especially the aim of civil and dignified living for the marginalized, on the other. This document also showed openness to narratives of the unintended negative consequences upon vulnerable people. The prophetic nature of policy discourse is demonstrated in this openness of the discourse to the insights derived from prophetic envisioning, prophetic criticism and prophetic story-telling.[33]

---

29   Gustafson, *Varieties*, 49 ff. For a discussion of the potential of Christian realism and middle axioms for policy discourses, see my recent still unpublished paper, titled "Churches and Public Policy Discourses in South Africa."
30   Gustafson, *Varieties*, 51.
31   Brady, *Moral Bond*, 48–153.
32   Gustafson, *Varieties*, 51.
33   For a reflection on this collaboration see Nico Koopman, "Churches in collaboration with Government: A Western Cape Story," in Heinrich Bedford-Strohm, Florian Hohne & Tobias ReitMayer (eds.), *Contextuality and Intercontextuality in Public Theology: Proceedings from the Bamberg Conference 23–25 June 2011* (Münster: Lit Verlag, 2013), 107–119.

Conclusion

It might be concluded that prophetic religion can advance the quest of civilizing democracies to build a society of worth and dignity, freedom and justice for all. This can be achieved if our understanding of the prophetic discourse is widened and deepened. A widened and broader understanding of prophecy acknowledges that prophecy has various interdependent and complementary modes in which it is practiced, namely envisioning, criticism, storytelling, ethical analysis and policymaking. A deepened and sympathetic understanding of prophecy acknowledges that envisioning is not day-dreaming and utopianism; criticism is not destructive and uncooperative; storytelling is not divisive and alienating; ethical analysis is not resisted or under-appreciated; policymaking is not viewed as alien to the prophetic task. Hopefully this essay stimulates some consideration of this acknowledgement in our ongoing quest for religion that fulfills a civilizing, dignifying and humanizing role in public life.

Bibliography

Alves, Rubem, *Tomorrow's Child: Imagination, Creativity, and the Rebirth of Culture* (New York, Evanston, San Francisco & London: Harper & Row Publishers, 1972).

Beek, Bram van de, *Why? On Suffering, Guilt and God* (Grand Rapids: Eerdmans, 1990).

Boesak, Allan, et al. (eds.), *Dreaming a Different World: Globalisation and Justice for Humanity and the Earth: The Challenge of the Accra Confession for the Churches* (A Publication of the Uniting Reformed Church in Southern Africa and the *Evangelisch Reformierte Kirche* in Germany, 2010).

Brady, Bernard V., *The Moral Bond of Community: Justice and Discourse in Christian Morality* (Washington: Georgetown University Press, 1998).

Calvin, John, *Institutes of the Christian Religion*, 2 Vols., trans. Ford Lewis Battles, ed. John T. McNeill (Louisville: Westminster John Knox Press, 1960).

De Gruchy, John W., *Christianity and Democracy: A Theology for a Just World Order* (Cape Town & Johannesburg: David Philip, 1995).

———, *Liberating Reformed Theology: A South African Contribution to an Ecumenical Debate* (Grand Rapids: Eerdmans, 1991).

———, "Towards a Reformed Theology of Liberation? Can we Retrieve the Reformed Symbols in the Struggle for Justice?" in W.A. Boesak & P.J.A. Fourie, *Vraagtekens oor Gereformeerdheid (Question Marks on Being Reformed)* (Belhar: LUS Publishers, 1998), 71–93.

Deist, Ferdinand, "Prophet and Society in Transition," in J. Mouton, A. van Aarde & W. Vorster (eds.), *Paradigms and Progress in Theology* (Pretoria: Human Sciences Research Council, 1988).

Gustafson, James, "An Analysis of Church and Society Social Ethical Writings," *Ecumenical Review* 40 (1988), 267–278.

———, "Moral Discourse about Medicine: A Variety of Forms," *Journal of Medicine and Philosophy* 15:2 (1990), 125–142.

———, *Varieties of Moral Discourse: Prophetic, Narrative, Ethical, and Policy* (Stob lectures of Calvin College and Seminary, Grand Rapids: Calvin College, 1988).

Koopman, Nico, "Churches and Public Policy Discourses in South Africa" (unpublished paper).

———, "Churches in collaboration with Government: A Western Cape Story," in Heinrich Bedford-Strohm, Florian Hohne & Tobias ReitMayer (eds.), *Contextuality and Intercontextuality in Public Theology: Proceedings from the Bamberg Conference 23–25 June 2011* (Münster: Lit Verlag, 2013), 107–119.

Kruijf, Gerrit de, *Waakzaam en nuchter: Over christelijke ethiek in een democratie (Alert and Sober: About Christian Ethics in a Democracy)* (Baarn: Ten Have, 1993).

Kuitert, Harry M., *'Dat moet ik van mijn geloof': Godsdienst als troublemaker in het publieke domein ('That Is What my Faith Requires': Religion as Troublemaker in the Public Domain)* (Kampen: Ten Have, 2008).

Mbiti, John, *The Prayers of African Religion* (Maryknoll: Orbis Books, 1975).

Mapping the Christian Character
Calvin and Schleiermacher on Virtue, Law and Sanctification

Heleen Zorgdrager

The New Testament scholar N.T. Wright has a talent for choosing appealing titles. I was drawn to his book *After You Believe: Why Christian Character Matters*.[1] In this book he asks the question: what happens, not only individually but also corporately, *after you believe*? Imagine a river. On this bank you declare your faith in Christ; the opposite bank is the ultimate result, final salvation. But what are you supposed to do in the meantime? In his book Wright points to an "old bridge" that joins the two banks of the river. One of its most obvious names is character.[2] He defines character as "the transforming, shaping, and marking of a life and its habits" and claims that this is what Jesus himself and the early Christian writers repeatedly were speaking about.[3]

Wright's thought-provoking account of Christian character, which I will describe in more detail below, converges to a large extent with my own desire to revise the Protestant, more specifically the Reformed, doctrine of sanctification both in light of the feminist affirmation and re-appreciation of the embodied self and a revival of the early Christian notion of deification as the goal and practice of Christian life.[4]

In this article I explore how Christians actually contribute to building human civilization. What does the moral subject look like *after she believes* and how does she enhance the good life for all? Inspired by Wright, I would like to explore and assess the notion of character in the context of the doctrine of sanctification. The doctrine of sanctification expresses a concern to affirm that a real change has taken place in the believer. It aims to articulate how the salvation in Christ is effective. However, Reformed theologians have been hesitant to specify that change in terms of the transformation of the person. Either they treat the new life in Christ as a mysterious change—a new qualification of the nature of the self the growth of which is hardly possible to spell out (John Calvin)—, or it is specified as a moral program with rules to follow and duties to

---

[1] Nicholas T. Wright, *After You Believe: Why Christian Character Matters* (New York: HarperOne, 2010).
[2] Wright, *After*, 4.
[3] Wright, *After*, 7.
[4] See Heleen Zorgdrager, "On the Fullness of Salvation: Tracking *theosis* in Reformed Theology," forthcoming in *Journal of Reformed Theology* in 2014.

fulfill (John Wesley). My suggestion is that the notion of character helps to overcome certain dead ends in the Reformed doctrine of sanctification. An important one of these dead ends is the overemphasis on an ethics of obligation and duty. Is the concept of character perhaps a better way to portray the new life in Christ? How would this character take shape, in our embodied lives both individually and communally?

Structure

In my exploration I will move from the discourse of contemporary theologians to inspiring ideas presented in subsequent lectures at Berlin University between 1809 and 1831 by the father of modern theology, Friedrich Schleiermacher.

First, I will seek in the discourse of contemporary scholars the motives behind the late modern quest to define a Christian character. N.T. Wright, Stanley Hauerwas and Nonna Verna Harrison are theologians who explicitly argue for a rehabilitation of Christian character ethics in today's world. I will highlight central concerns they bring to the fore and point to a certain affinity to the heritage of early Eastern theology. Second, I will turn to the Protestant tension between a virtue-based ethics (or character ethics) and a law-based ethics. Wright and Hauerwas, in particular, are aware of this tension and they attempt to overcome it in their revision of sanctification. Recently, Pieter Vos contributed to the discussion with a profound analysis of law and virtue in Calvin's theology. He reveals some unresolved issues in Calvin's ethics itself, and makes a thoughtful plea for a rehabilitation of the concept of virtue as *habitus* in Reformed ethics. Third, against the backdrop of Vos' argument for Calvin's basically positive attitude towards virtue, I will turn to Friedrich Schleiermacher who, in my opinion, continued the task that Calvin only partially fulfilled. Schleiermacher appears to be a most beneficial and promising theologian for providing a constructive and substantial theoretical framework for a present-day Protestant ethics of character. At the end of his lectures on Christian ethics, where he speaks about the witness of the faithful in daily life—a section of his ethics hardly noticed in scholarly discussions—, I detect a description of Christian life primarily embedded in the language of the cultivation of a virtuous character. Schleiermacher gives a theological twist here to the classical quartet of virtues, which might be best encapsulated by the term 'transfiguration.' The features of the Christian character that he analyzes and reconstructs seem as lifelike as they are Christlike. Moreover, they are as particularly embodied as they are open to the future, and as relevant and challenging to the individual as to the community.

Finally, I will evaluate how Schleiermacher's theory of the formation of a virtuous Christian character relates to the notion of the law of God, and in what sense Schleiermacher's theological ethics takes a different direction here than Calvin's. Could Schleiermacher's account of Christian character help us today in designing theories and practices of sanctified life that are actively supportive and formative for the kind of moral agents our late modern societies need and for the highly complex and embodied struggles of their moral and spiritual lives?

The Quest for a Christian Character: N.T. Wright and Nonna Verna Harrison

What are the motives behind the contemporary quest for a Christian character? N.T. Wright analyzes how Western culture has become law bound, rule bound, and regulation bound. It is believed that huge problems, like those in the financial world, can be solved by increased regulation. Wright approvingly quotes a phrase from a banker: "... the real problem in the last generation is that we've lost the sense that character matters; that integrity matters."[5] Wright argues that like the rich young man in the parable of Mark 10:17–31 our first question ought to be: "How should I behave?" This question concerns the content and the means of one's behavior. To both sides of the question Jesus seems to give the same answer: "Follow me!" He challenges the young man to make a transformation of character. Jesus calls on him to play a role within a story where there is one supreme Character whose life is to be followed.[6]

Besides the tendency towards legalism and over-regulation, Wright criticizes a second aspect of Western culture, namely the tendency towards emotivism. The latter reduces all moral discourse to statements of likes and dislikes. The ultimate truth is 'how you feel about it,' and if you are 'being true to yourself.' As an alternative to this massive presumption of authenticity and spontaneity, as well as to a rule-based mentality, Wright argues for recapturing the biblical vision of a genuinely good human life as a life of character formed by God's promised future.[7] What we need today is people of character.

---

5   Wright, *After*, 10.
6   Wright, *After*, 17.
7   Wright, *After*, 57.

Wright illustrates his argument by referring to the emergency landing of Captain Sullenberger on the Hudson River in 2009. You could attribute it to the power of good habits, or the result of many years of training and experience. You could attribute it to character and virtue. For Captain Sullenberger the wise and courageous choices had become 'second nature.' Human character is such a second nature; it is the pattern of thinking and acting that runs right through someone, and enables that person to make the right decision in the situation. After you believe, Wright asserts, you have to develop a Christian character by practicing the specific Christian virtues.[8] Believers have their character renewed, transformed and molded by Jesus Christ. Indeed, Jesus is more than an example of virtue,[9] yet Wright insists that it makes sense to think of Jesus going through the same laborious learning process, in terms of moral struggle, that we have to face. His way of 'learning obedience' can be understood in terms of pursuing virtue, and the result was that he became *teleios*, perfect, complete. This process is character formation in a completely new way. Jesus presents a way of being human that nobody had ever imagined before.[10] The apostle Paul teaches that the transformation of the believer begins with the renewal of the mind and involves practicing the virtues of patience, humility, and generous, self-giving love that spring from Christ as the source.[11] Sanctification means that we learn in the present the habits that anticipate the ultimate future.[12]

Wright's ethics of character is rooted in a theological anthropology with a surprisingly Eastern touch. Wright sees human beings as called to be a kind of mediator, a microcosm or living Temple. Their vocation is to reflect the glory of God into the world and to reflect the world back to God. This idea of royal priesthood, for example, echoes the thoughts of the Greek Church father Maximus the Confessor (c. 580–662). Humans fulfill this work of mediation by worshipping and reigning, as priests and rulers.[13] The community is the place where the "New Human" becomes manifest.[14] "This is what royal priesthood looks like in the present time: a community that together learns the lessons of holiness (Eph. 4:17–5:20), and that learns as well what it means to reflect God's character and actions to one another."[15]

---

8   Wright, *After*, 25.
9   Wright, *After*, 129.
10 Wright, *After*, 131.
11 Wright, *After*, 48.
12 Wright, *After*, 94.
13 Wright, *After*, 78.
14 Wright, *After*, 213.
15 Wright, *After*, 217.

Wright's account of sanctification resembles that of the patristic scholar Nonna Verna Harrison, who explicitly adheres to Eastern Orthodox Christianity. She also advances the idea of human reflection of God's character and the vocation to royal priesthood.[16] Harrison draws on Church fathers like Gregory of Nyssa (c. 335–395), who emphasizes human freedom as being central to the divine image,[17] and Maximus Confessor with his comprehensive vision of cosmic priesthood.[18] Virtues, according to Harrison, are originally aspects of God's own character and way of acting. They compose the most important dimension of the divine likeness to which every human being is called. Harrison writes that we are invited by grace to participate in God's virtues, which are actually divine attributes, such as justice, wisdom, compassion, love, mercy, kindness, and humility. Together these virtues shape God's splendid character. Humans are called to reflect God's character and to become many-splendored images of the divine. God's splendid character becomes manifest in the diversity and the mutual giving and receiving in community.

According to Harrison, both God and we, in a lifetime of sanctification, are engaged in the task of producing our character, as a result of a "happy synergy" between God's creativity and our freedom.[19] Along with Basil of Caesarea (c. 330–379) and Gregory of Nyssa, Harrison confirms that Christ is the living source of all virtues because he restored the distorted image in human nature. In character formation we always remain joined to him.[20]

Shaping our Character within Truthful Stories: Stanley Hauerwas

Wright is indebted to the moral theory of Alasdair MacIntyre (*After Virtue: A Study in Moral Theory*)[21] and to the work of Stanley Hauerwas. With the latter Wright shares an eschatologically driven ethics of character. I will specify the way Hauerwas draws on Calvin and also goes *beyond* Calvin in his account of sanctification, and how he introduces a narrative and communal understanding of character formation.

16　Nonna Verna Harrison, *God's Many-Splendored Image: Theological Anthropology for Christian Formation* (Grand Rapids: Baker Academic, 2010).
17　Harrison, *Image*, 97 f.
18　Harrison, *Image*, 131–137.
19　Harrison, *Image*, 27, 71.
20　Harrison, *Image*, 69 f.
21　Alasdair MacIntyre, *After Virtue: A Study in Moral Theory*, Second Edition (Notre Dame: University of Notre Dame Press, 1984).

Already in his doctoral dissertation, *Moral Character as a Problem for Theological Ethics* (1968),[22] subsequently published as *Character and the Christian Life* (1975),[23] Hauerwas wrote: "My thesis is that the idea of *character* can provide a way of explicating the kind of determination of the believer in Christ without necessarily destroying the tension between the 'already but not yet' quality of the Christian life."[24] Therefore we have to understand the nature of the self that is graced.[25] Hauerwas believes that Calvin laid a solid foundation for this undertaking with his concept of *unio cum Christo*, in which justification and sanctification are held together. The effect of Christ's work is never separated from its source. Hauerwas asks: how can we explain this in terms of character? Character is the orientation we give to our lives, the qualification of our agency acquired through our beliefs and actions in the past and affirmed by our actual choices in the present. Hauerwas proposes to reinterpret sanctification as the formation of our character. To be sanctified is to have one's character formed in a definite kind of way, namely in adherence to Christ. Calvin calls the outcome "rondeur et integrité" and "rondeur et syncérité," while Wesley calls it "perfection" and Jonathan Edwards "sincerity."[26]

Calvin assumes a real growth, a progress, which is intimately bound up with the sanctified life. What is the nature of this growth? Calvin concedes that restoration of the image of God in us takes place through continual and sometimes slow advances. The practice of repentance/mortification (dying to the law) marks the process of renewal. The closer humans come to the likeness of God, the more the image of God shines in them.[27] The goal of the process is to fully reflect the glory of God, "to render us eventually conformable to God, and,

---

[22] Stanley Hauerwas, *Moral Character as a Problem for Theological Ethics* (New Haven: Yale University Press, 1968).

[23] Stanley Hauerwas, *Character and the Christian Life: A Study in Theological Ethics* (San Antonio: Trinity University Press, 1975).

[24] Hauerwas, *Character*, 183. Italics mine, HZ.

[25] Hauerwas, *Character*, 193.

[26] Hauerwas, *Character*, 195–201. For "rondeur et integrité," see Jean Calvin, *Sermons sur le livre de Job, recueillis fidèlement de sa bouche selon qu'il les preschoit* (Genève, 1569), 4. For "rondeur et syncérité," see Jean Calvin, *Commentaires de Jehan Calvin sur le Nouveau Testament: Le tout reveu diligemment et comme traduit de nouveau tant le texte que la glose* (Paris: C. Meyrueis, 1854–1855), Vol. 2, 31.

[27] Hauerwas, *Character*, 216 f. He cites John Calvin, *Institutes of the Christian Religion*, 2 Vols., trans. Ford Lewis Battles, ed. John T. McNeill (Louisville: Westminster John Knox Press, 1960), III.3.9.

if we may so speak, to deify us,"[28] a terminus which lies beyond history. Calvin thus expresses the idea that the full reality that is Christ is to be increasingly worked out in our life and conduct, but he lacks the concepts to articulate this growth. Hauerwas argues that the notion of character may be helpful here. Our character grows because our present acts draw our past determinations of moral behavior into a new synthesis of possibilities. Hauerwas describes character as a narrative construction. We are only capable of moral action and moral growth by finding our particular role, our "character," within truthful stories.[29] To have one's character formed in Christ, by the story of Christ, is to always have one's life directed toward a fuller realization of that formation.[30] The significance of the inherence in Christ must be constantly deepened and enriched through our experience. In our lives this significance can only be partially embodied.[31] The character description of the Christian remains fundamentally open.

In his later work Hauerwas strongly emphasizes the role of the church as a "community of character."[32] This community is formed by the story of Christ. Central to the narrative is the cross, which determines the meaning of history and characterizes the social and prophetic life of the church.[33] Our individual characters are shaped by the language, rituals, and moral practices of these particular, historic church communities. In sum, the survey of these present-day theologians offers us the following insights. Biblical character ethics helps to develop an alternative to superficial legalism and self-centered emotivism. Character formation is primarily presented as a narrative construction, strongly related to the community, and a process in which our whole embodied existence is engaged. The process of sanctification can be conceived of as a Christlike character formation. Finally, the following significant concepts for Christian character formation are offered by the patristic tradition: the image of God, likeness to God, attributes of God, and the vocation to royal priesthood.

---

28   *Calvin's Commentaries* (Edinburgh: Calvin Translation Society, 1846–51), see Calvin's comments on 2 Pt. 1:4.
29   See Ariaan Baan, *The Necessity of Witness: Stanley Hauerwas' Contribution to Systematic Theology* ('s-Hertogenbosch: Uitgeverij BOXPress, 2014), 39.
30   Hauerwas, *Character*, 221.
31   Hauerwas, *Character*, 215.
32   Stanley Hauerwas, *A Community of Character: Toward a Constructive Christian Social Ethic* (Notre Dame: University of Notre Dame Press, 1981).
33   Hauerwas, *Community*, 12.

Tension between Ethics of Law and Ethics of Virtue in Calvinism

Hauerwas already touched on the fact that Calvin is unable to articulate the growth of Christian life within the framework of his theology. I will now address the underlying tension between law and virtue in Calvin in more detail.

So far we have used the terms character ethics and virtue ethics almost interchangeably. They are indeed closely interconnected. According to Lisa Sole Cahill, two models of character ethics can be distinguished that are nevertheless intertwined and interdependent.[34] The first is an ethics of character that holds that the basic moral dispositions (virtues) of the agent are more important than individual acts. 'Character' refers to the long-term formation and moral self-expression of the person. This model relies on the Thomistic account of virtues and is perhaps more rooted in the Catholic tradition.[35] A second model is the narrative approach of Hauerwas and others, according to which individual moral agency is situated within a community of formation. Writers in the first category often choose the term 'pursuing virtue' to describe their enterprise. However, we found that 'pursuing virtue' is also part of the character formation as envisioned by the second model. The meaning of the Greek word χαρακτήρ is 'engraved or stamped mark' on coins or seals.[36] Virtue is a stable disposition, a *habitus*. Virtues are carvings that become a track, through which a lasting character trait is developed. These traits become part of our attitude and determine our actions and choices.[37] Virtue can be both a means and an optimum, the best possible quality. For the 'virtues of character,' as Aristotle and Thomas Aquinas call them, virtue is primarily conceived of as a means.

The ethicist Pieter Vos addresses the problematic place of a virtue ethics in Protestant theology.[38] In the words of Eilert Herms, the aspect of duty has

---

[34] See Lisa Sowle Cahill, "Christian Character, Biblical Community, and Human Values," in William P. Brown (ed.), *Character & Scripture: Moral Formation, Community, and Biblical Interpretation* (Grand Rapids: Eerdmans, 2002), 3–17: 4 ff.

[35] MacIntyre would question this distinction; according to him, medieval thought already adds the notion of the narrative or the historic (life as a quest, a journey) to the Aristotelian account of virtue (*After Virtue*, 176). I thank Pieter Vos for this comment.

[36] Werner Brändle, lemma "Character," in Hans Dieter Betz et al. (eds.), *Religion in Geschichte und Gegenwart: Handwörterbuch für Theologie und Religionswissenschaft*, Band 2 (Tübingen: Mohr Siebeck, 1999), 109 ff.

[37] Gilbert C. Meilaender, *The Theory and Practice of Virtue* (Notre Dame: University of Notre Dame Press, 1984), 10 f.

[38] Pieter Vos, "After Duty: The Need for Virtue Ethics in Moral Formation," in Bram de Muynck, Johan Hegeman & Pieter Vos (eds.), *Bridging the Gap: Connecting Christian Faith*

come to outweigh that of virtue.[39] Vos, however, argues that Calvin himself did not reject the good gift of the virtues. From his concept of the *primus usus legis* Calvin values them as belonging to the domain of natural law, as "special graces [here understood as gifts, PV] of God, which he bestows variously and in certain measure upon men otherwise wicked."[40] The virtues bridle the perversity of nature but the natural or civic virtues can never undo the *corruptio totalis* of human beings. To attain justification, a complete renewal of the human will is needed. Virtues receive their proper place and quality when the human life is entirely re-directed *coram Deo*, that is, when the human being has truly become obedient and responsible to God.

Calvin at this point chooses to outline the features of the Christian moral life from the perspective of law (*tertius usus legis*). This choice, as Vos comments, is not by principle but motivated by practical reasons.[41] Calvin suggests that he could also have taken the virtues as his starting point. In his account of the sanctified Christian life (book III, chapter 6 of the *Institutes*) he gracefully refers to the Church fathers, who in their homilies wrote so well and profoundly about the various virtues. He himself does not deal with the virtues in detail because he does not want to digress into exhortations. He turns instead to the explanation of the Ten Commandments, to show "the godly man how he may be directed to a rightly ordered life," and to set down "some universal rule with which to determine his duties."[42]

The unintended effect of this rather pragmatic choice of Calvin, as Vos notes, was that in later Calvinism the law of God increasingly became the sole and final measure of morality. This happened despite the fact that for Calvin it was not God's law as such that was the core of Christian life, but the dedication of our lives to God in order that we may mediate his glory (which involves the free and joyful inner appropriation of the law and thus somehow the cultivation of virtues). Reformed ethics, after Calvin, developed into an ethics of obligation deriving ethical rules and precepts solely from God's revealed commandments. As Vos concludes, "… Protestant ethics has landed too much in the waters of an ethics of obligation (or of a halfhearted kind of virtue

---

        and Professional Practice in a Pluralistic Society (Sioux Center: Dorth Press, 2011), 143–158, and "Breakdown of the Teleological View of Life? Investigating Law, *Telos* and Virtue in Calvinistic Ethics," (unpublished paper IRTI-conference Sarospatak 2013).

39   Eilert Herms, "Virtue: A Neglected Concept in Protestant Ethics," *Scottish Journal of Theology* 35 (1982), 481–495: 485.

40   Vos, "Breakdown," with reference to Calvin, *Institutes*, II.3.4.

41   Vos, "Breakdown"; "After Duty," 150.

42   Calvin, *Institutes*, III.6.1.

ethics), in which general laws, external rules, regulations and duties prevail." He argues for a rehabilitation of the concept of virtue as *habitus* in Reformed ethics, for which Calvin himself has laid the foundation. In particular, he regards Calvin's emphasis on Christian life as mediating God's glory and Calvin's notion of Christ as the 'true fountain for the virtues' as promising starting points for a reintroduction of virtue ethics into Protestant theology and into the practice of moral character formation. There is enough room for a sanctification of human life, in the sense that a Christian, as a sinner, receives the moral good from God, but at the same time receives this truly so that it becomes the believer's *habitus* as being in Christ.[43]

This interpretation corresponds with the new approach to Calvin, as practiced by theologians such as J. Todd Billings, Julie Canlis, and Michael S. Horton.[44] These theologians have identified Calvin's core concept as the 'union with Christ' and subsequently see him valuing the aspects of real, ontological transformation and growth in believers. It prompts them to further explorations of the excitant themes of participation, ascension, and deification in Calvin's theology.

As for the place of the law, Vos argues for more interconnection of virtue and law. He believes that there is an ongoing need for precepts and law in ethics. According to Calvin's ethics, human nature is not inclined to (the highest good of) a flourishing life and therefore it not only needs to be transformed but also restrained by norms and laws. "Commandments are the necessary, complementary external precepts in relation to virtues as dispositional traits of character."[45]

I strongly concur with Vos that the reality of the transformed Christian life could be very well described in terms of an ethics of virtue or character, without immediately neglecting or downplaying the ongoing power of sin in human life. I suggest that in Schleiermacher, who is also rooted in the Reformed tradition but, so to speak, seasoned with the flavors of Moravian pietism and Enlightenment, we find a fine example of how this challenging task might be

---

43   Vos, "After Duty," 153.
44   E.g. J. Todd Billings, *Calvin, Participation, and the Gift: The Activity of Believers in Union with Christ* (New York: Oxford, 2007); Julie Canlis, *Calvin's Ladder: A Spiritual Theology of Ascent and Ascension* (Grand Rapids: Eerdmans, 2010); J. Todd Billings, "Union with Christ and the Double Grace: Calvin's Theology and Its Early Reception" and Michael S. Horton, "Calvin's Theology of Union with Christ and the Double Grace: Modern Reception and Contemporary Possibilities," in J. Todd Billings & I. John Hesselink (eds.), *Calvin's Theology and Its Reception: Disputes, Developments, and New Possibilities* (Louisville: Westminster John Knox Press, 2012), 49–71; 72–94.
45   Vos, "Breakdown."

performed. I divide the following section on Schleiermacher into three parts: 1) the account of the 'cultivation of the self' in his early Romantic writings; 2) the account of virtue and Christian virtue in his philosophical ethics; and 3) a construction of the virtuous Christian character in Christian ethics.

Friedrich Schleiermacher: Cultivation of the Self and the Concept of Individuality

Already in his youth manuscripts on ethical-philosophical questions, written between the years 1789–1792, Schleiermacher promoted an ethics that favored the idea of the cultivation of a character. Discussing the practical philosophy of Immanuel Kant, Schleiermacher profoundly criticizes the incongruence in Kant's system between the moral law and the sensory-conditioned motives of the moral agent.[46] Schleiermacher's aim is to base ethics on the reality of the embodied self. Inspired by his teacher in Halle, Johann August Eberhard (1739–1809), and by Lord Shaftesbury (1671–1730), Schleiermacher formulated a theory of the moral sense. The moral law affects our will through a moral sense that is matured by life experience. The human being should strengthen the practical influence of this moral sense in a lifelong process of moral cultivation, by way of character formation. The ideal he envisions is a character of "dispassionate meekness" (*leidenschaftsloser Sanftmuth*) in which the cooperation of reason and nature has elevated the faculty of sensual desire to a higher moral level.[47] Fully in line with this, Schleiermacher contests Kant's notion of transcendental freedom and, inspired by Spinoza, defends an understanding of freedom within the framework of a moral determinism that respects the finitude of human beings.[48] The self-consciousness or 'inner feeling' of the moral subject is capable of evaluating whether a possible act will contribute to strengthen the moral sense or not. For Schleiermacher, freedom is not autonomy to act in spite of natural causes or personal desires. His imagery is more organic. Human freedom is the freedom to express and develop oneself according to a higher necessity, conceived of as the presupposed unity and ultimate integration of the sensual and the intelligible world.

---

46 "Über das höchste Gut," (1789) in Friedrich Schleiermacher, *Kritische Gesamtausgabe: Jugendschriften 1787–1796*, Abt. I, Band 1 (*KGA* I.1), ed. Günter Meckenstock (Berlin/New York: Walter de Gruyter, 1984), 81–125.
47 "Über das höchste Gut," 124.
48 "Über die Freiheit" (between 1790–1792), in *KGA* I.1, 217–356.

In Schleiermacher's famous work *On Religion: Speeches to Its Cultured Despisers* (1799) and in the *Soliloquies* (*Monologen*, 1800) the term 'character' is not frequently used.[49] But its meaning is incorporated into Schleiermacher's key concept of individuality. This concept is considered to be his most original contribution to philosophy and theology. He expresses his joy at discovering this 'highest intuition' of human individuality and calls the principle of individuality the 'most mystical' in the field of philosophy.[50] Each person should develop and unify her powers in a manner characteristic of that person.[51] Each individual is a manifestation of the divine and has an infinite value as this unique and distinctive person. "It became clear to me that each person should represent humanity in his or her own way, with a particular mixture of its elements, so that humanity reveals itself in each way and all becomes realized in the fullness of space and time."[52]

Schleiermacher states that one of the aims of ethics is to encourage the development of this qualitative individuality. The ongoing process of self-cultivation (*Selbstbildung*) can best be described in artistic metaphors. The "humanity in me" is the substance out of which I mold the unique design of my individuality. Freedom is the self-expression towards that image. The cultivation of the self is driven both by self-knowledge that is experientially gained ('what I am') and by a prophetic-visionary image of the goal ('what I can be and become').[53] However, Schleiermacher rejects a solipsistic or egotistic understanding of the cultivation of the self. The process of moral cultivation, as he envisions it, takes place in a dialogue with and commitment to the social community in which humanity expresses itself in its whole diversity.[54]

---

49 "Über die Religion: Reden an die Gebildeten unter ihren Verächtern," in Friedrich Schleiermacher, *Kritische Gesamtausgabe: Schriften aus der Berliner Zeit 1796–1799*, Abt. I, Band 2 (*KGA* I.2), ed. Günter Meckenstock (Berlin/New York: Walter de Gruyter, 1984), 185–326; "Monologen," in Friedrich Schleiermacher, *Kritische Gesamtausgabe: Schriften aus der Berliner Zeit 1800–1802*, Abt. I, Band 3 (*KGA* I.3), ed. Günter Meckenstock (Berlin/New York: Walter De Gruyter, 1988), 1–62.

50 "Das principium individui ist das Mystischste im Gebiet der Philosophie …" Letter to Brinckmann, in Ludwig Jonas & Wilhelm Dilthey (eds.), *Aus Schleiermacher's Leben: In Briefen*, Band 4 (Berlin 1858–1863, Reprint: Berlin/New York, 1974), 59.

51 Frederick C. Beiser, "Schleiermacher's Ethics," in Jacqueline Mariña (ed.), *The Cambridge Companion to Friedrich Schleiermacher* (Cambridge: Cambridge University Press, 2005), 53–72: 61.

52 "Monologen," *KGA* I.3. Translation by Theodore Vial, *Schleiermacher: A Guide for the Perplexed* (London: Bloomsbury T&T Clark, 2013), 56.

53 Eilert Herms, *Herkunft, Entfaltung und erste Gestalt des Systems der Wissenschaften bei Schleiermacher* (Gütersloh: Gütersloher Verlagshaus Gerd Mohn, 1974), 203 ff.

54 "Monologen," *KGA* I.3, 43.

Schleiermacher can rightly be called a creator and promulgator of the Romantic expressivist anthropology in the way Charles Taylor has defined it.[55]

For Schleiermacher, the concept of individuality is religiously inspired. It emerges from being personally and irreducibly affected by the universe, by the living richness of the infinite world that in particular reveals itself in loving communication between humans. In the ungraspable moment of being religiously affected the person becomes aware of her unique relation to the divine universe. It seeks to express itself in the individual, as in everything else, in an utterly unique way.[56]

Virtue in Schleiermacher's *Philosophical Ethics*

Schleiermacher's approach to philosophical ethics is descriptive and historical. It is best conceived of as a theory of culture. There is no aspect of human activity and human community that does not fall under the domain of ethics. He derives the structure of his philosophical ethics from an analysis of the concept of human action in which he finds three constitutive elements.[57] If we think of human action we must think of a *rule* which such an action follows, of a *deed* which is performed by that action, and, thirdly, of a *responsible agent* who is able to perform that action. Therefore, ethics can be developed in three forms: as an ethics of duty, of the good, and of virtue. None of these concepts is reducible to the others. Each concept focuses on one aspect of human action respectively: the norm that governs the action, the good as the result of action, and the power to produce the good. Hence Schleiermacher's lectures on philosophical ethics[58] are divided into a doctrine of duty (*Pflichtlehre*), a doctrine of the good (*Güterlehre*) and a doctrine of virtue (*Tugendlehre*). Yet, as Friedrich Beiser comments, it is one of the noteworthy features of Schleiermacher's eth-

---

[55] Brent W. Sockness made this case in "Schleiermacher and the Ethics of Authenticity: The *Monologen* of 1800," *Journal of Religious Ethics* 32:3 (2004), 477–517. Charles Taylor describes the Romantic expressivist anthropology in *Sources of the Self: The Making of the Modern Identity* (Cambridge: Harvard University Press, 1989).

[56] In "Über die Religion": "... (die Religion) will im Menschen nicht weniger als in allen andern Einzelnen und Endlichen das Unendliche sehen, dessen Abdruck, dessen Darstellung" (*KGA* I.2, 211 f).

[57] Herms, "Virtue," 484 f.

[58] The English edition contains materials from the lectures 1812/13 and 1816/17. Friedrich Schleiermacher, *Lectures on Philosophical Ethics* (Cambridge: Cambridge University Press, 2002).

ics that he gives primacy to the concept of the highest good.[59] For him, the highest good is the central question of ethics, and it has the most immediate bearing on the conduct of life. He defines the highest good in a teleological way as the full integration of reason and nature.[60]

Nevertheless, Schleiermacher also pays ample attention to virtue, as C.J. Dickson recently demonstrated in a rich paper delivered at the American Academy of Religion.[61] Dickson shows that Schleiermacher not only extensively discusses the matter of virtue, but he also appears to be utterly interested in the notion of Christian virtue and how to give a proper account of Christian virtues in a moral theory. Against Hermann Peiter, who holds that the (assumed) lack of the concept of virtue in *Christian Ethics* supports the claim that Schleiermacher's system of Christian ethics is completely independent of his philosophical ethics,[62] Dickson argues that there is a significant interrelation between both, and that this can be demonstrated by Schleiermacher's multifaceted and coherent account of virtue.

Schleiermacher defines virtue as that morality which indwells the individual[63] and as a capacity that enables the individual to understand and to act upon the concrete implications of the moral law.[64] The first basic distinction is that between virtue as disposition (*Gesinnung*) and virtue as skill (*Talent, Fertigkeit*).[65] Given the fact that human life is an interconnection of reason and sensuality, we can speak about disposition as the ideal content of human activity, as "the *principle* of actual action."[66] And in the same human activity

---

59 Beiser, "Schleiermacher's Ethics," 69.
60 "Tugendlehre 1804/05," in *Schleiermachers Werke*, ed. Otto Braun & Johannes Bauer (Leipzig: Scientia Verlag Aalen, 1927, 1981), 3–74: 3. English translation: "Notes on the Theory of Virtue" (1804/05) in Friedrich Schleiermacher, *Brouillon zur Ethik (Notes on Ethics) (1805/1806); Notes on the Theory of Virtue (1804/1805)*, trans. John Wallhauser and Terrence N. Tice (Edwin Mellen Press, 2003).
61 C.J. Dickson, "Schleiermacher on Christian Virtue," unpublished paper, delivered in the Schleiermacher Group at the Annual Meeting of the American Academy of Religion, November 2013, Baltimore.
62 In discussion with Herrmann Peiter, "The Autonomy of Theological Ethics in Contrast with Philosophical Ethics Owing to the Fruitful Relation between Theological Ethics and Scriptural Exegesis," in Terrence N. Tice (ed.), *Christian Ethics According to Schleiermacher: Collected Essays and Reviews* (Eugene: Pickwick Publications, 2010), 213.
63 "Tugendlehre," 3.
64 Jean Porter, "Virtue ethics," in Robin Gill (ed.), *Cambridge Companion to Christian Ethics* (Cambridge: Cambridge University Press, 2006), 87–102: 96.
65 "Tugendlehre," 39. See also *Brouillon zur Ethik (1805/06)* (Hamburg: Felix Meiner Verlag, 1981), 125–155.
66 "Tugendlehre," 42.

we can look at how the right principle is carried out, how the person's understanding of the principle is made *manifest* in what she does. This is skill or proficiency. In the form of disposition, virtue is an "inspiring power" (*belebende Tugend*). Virtue as manifest in action is a "struggling power" (*bekämpfende Tugend*).[67] The moral task entails the development of virtue as both disposition and skill.

The second distinction introduced by Schleiermacher is that between the *cognitive* (symbolizing) activity of reason and its *depicting* (organizing) activity. In the symbolizing activity reason takes what is outside and brings it to oneself (reason shapes nature to its symbol). In the depicting activity, reason takes what is inside and makes it effective in the external world (nature becomes an organ for reason).

This analysis of a fourfold structure of the moral act, which attempts to reflect in theory the dynamics of real life, is very important, for it provides Schleiermacher with an original framework for mapping the virtues in a scientific, systematic way. He uses the fourfold distinction of the difference between skill and disposition on the one hand and between cognition and depiction on the other hand to arrive at an account of human excellence in all its various forms.[68] Four different forms come to the fore, which are in tune with the four classical virtues in Greek tradition.[69] Schleiermacher defines them as wisdom, *Weisheit* (disposition in cognition); love, *Liebe* (disposition in depiction, the inspiring power manifest in its external form); temperance in mind, restraint, *Besonnenheit* (the struggling power or skill in cognition); and fortitude, steadfastness, *Beharrlichkeit, Tapferkeit*[70] (the struggling power or skill in depiction).[71]

Of this quartet of virtues, three closely resemble the classical cardinal virtues—prudence/practical wisdom, temperance and fortitude—yet one is different. Love has replaced the virtue of justice. Schleiermacher argues that for the ancient Greek philosophers the state was everything. His own philosophical ethics, based on the presupposition of the kingdom of God as its highest

---

67   Friedrich Schleiermacher, "Über die wissenschaftliche Behandlung des Tugendbegriffes (1819)," in *Schleiermachers Werke*, Band 1, ed. Otto Braun & Johannes Bauer (Leipzig: Scientia Verlag Aalen, 1928, 1981), 349–377: 360; Herms, "Virtue," 484 f.
68   Dickson, "Christian Virtue."
69   "Unsere Darstellung ist dem wesentlichen nach schon in der hellenischen Quadruplicität enthalten, die aus der reinen Anschauung des Lebens in die philosophische Construction übergegangen war" (*Brouillon*, 154).
70   The particular names of the virtues change over the years in Schleiermacher's writings and lectures.
71   "Tugendbegriffes," 362; Herms, "Virtue," 485.

good, strives for a higher form of community.[72] Love is the virtue that articulates this power for an all-encompassing community. Moreover, Schleiermacher's concept of wisdom is more comprehensive than the rather one-sided Hellenistic rationalistic understanding of *phronesis*.[73] Notably Schleiermacher's *Christian Faith* presents the same pair love and wisdom as the distinctive attributes of God.[74]

The human virtues obviously represent the likeness to God. The resemblance to God (*imago Dei*) serves as the theological criterion for the theory of virtue, its transcendental presupposition. Schleiermacher concludes with a frank reference to the early Church fathers and their notion of deification:

> Not only is the basic principle of Christian ethics resemblance to God ... The ancients also said that the end of humankind is becoming like God to the extent it is possible. ... If the virtues we have presented are the *epitome* of human perfection, then each proposition proves itself on these terms: in these virtues the resemblance to God must be represented.[75]

Schleiermacher also points to an analogy between the so-called theological virtues of faith, hope and love and the philosophical virtues of wisdom, steadfastness, and love.[76] With this theological speculation we are leaving the domain of philosophical ethics and crossing the border into Christian ethics.

Schleiermacher's *Christian Ethics*: Christian Character in a Liturgical Framework

Already in *Notes on the Theory of Virtue* Schleiermacher underscores the need to keep in mind that there is a vision of transformation found in Christianity that goes beyond the manufacturability of a virtuous character. There is something about the acquisition of virtue and the possession of an exemplary character that exceeds instruction, teaching, and moral *Bildung*.

---

72 "Tugendbegriffes," 373 f.
73 "Tugendbegriffes," 363 f.
74 *Der Christliche Glaube 1821/22*, in Friedrich Schleiermacher *Kritische Gesamtausgabe*, Abt. 1, Band 7.2, (Berlin/New York: Walter de Gruyter, 1980), §§ 182–185 (hereafter CG 1821/22).
75 "Tugendbegriffes," 376.
76 "Tugendbegriffes," 375 f. He calls them the "christlichen Trias der Tugenden."

Now this feature [the vision of transformation, HZ] is the most completely expressed in Christianity through the doctrine of *grace*. If one asks why the disposition to virtue indwells one person but not another, there is no other way to answer this question than to say 'through the free grace of God.' If one asks how it is that a person awakens to the higher level of morality, there is no other way to respond than to say 'through the illumination of the Holy Spirit.'[77]

Christian Ethics[78] reflects on Christian piety as an incentive (*Antrieb*) for shaping the communal life and action of the church.[79] According to Schleiermacher, the discipline of *Christian Ethics* seeks to critically analyze and describe empirical Christian piety from the perspective of providing motives for action, in order to find general rules (*Formeln*) for ecclesial action. In short, Schleiermacher holds that Christian ethics is nothing more than the description of Christian life.[80] That life is a communal life in which the new God-consciousness of Christ the Redeemer brings people together.[81] *Christian Ethics* is fully an ecclesial ethics: an ethics of, for, and by the church. The action of the church in the

---

77 "Tugendlehre 1804/05," in *Schleiermachers Werke*, ed. Otto Braun & Johannes Bauer (Leipzig: Scientia Verlag Aalen, 1927, 1981), 3–74: 74. "Notes on the Theory of Virtue," 222. In gratitude to C.J. Dickson.
78 The lectures on Christian ethics were edited posthumously by Schleiermacher's student Ludwig Jonas under the title *Die Christliche Sitte nach den Grundsätzen der evangelischen Kirche im Zusammenhange dargestellt von Dr. Friedrich Schleiermacher*, in *Friedrich Schleiermacher's Sämmtliche Werke*, Abt. I, Bd. 12 (Berlin: G. Reimer, 1843), hereafter CS/Jonas. In 2011, a new text critical edition of the lectures appeared, edited by Hermann Peiter, *F.D.E. Schleiermacher, Christliche Sittenlehre* (*Vorlesung im Wintersemester 1826/27*), *nach größtenteils unveröffentlichten Hörernachschriften und nach teilweisen unveröffentlichten Manuskripten Schleiermachers*, ed. Hermann Peiter (Berlin/Münster: LIT Verlag, 2011), hereafter CS/Peiter.
79 CG 1821/22, § 112.5. See for an outstanding introduction to the structure of *Christian Ethics*: Eilert Herms, "Schleiermacher's Christian Ethics," in Jacqueline Mariña (ed.), *The Cambridge Companion to Friedrich Schleiermacher* (Cambridge: Cambridge University Press, 2005), 209–228, and James M. Brandt, "Translator's Introduction" to *Selections from Friedrich Schleiermacher's Christian Ethics* (Louisville: Westminster John Knox Press 2010) 1–19.
80 CS/Peiter, 20: "daß die christliche Sittenlehre nichts seyn soll als die Darstellung des christlichen Lebens."
81 CS/Jonas, 32: "Das spezifisch christliche aber ist, dass alle Gemeinschaft mit Gott angesehen wird als bedingt durch den Act der Erlösung durch Christum."

present is the ongoing redemptive action of Christ.[82] The Spirit, as the common spirit of the church (*Gemeingeist*), continuously transforms human life into its organ. Schleiermacher calls the completion of this process the "kingdom of God on earth."[83] The kingdom of God is the highest good in theological terms, and for Schleiermacher this is also the goal of human civilization. Ultimately, all will be included in Christ's perfection, as this is God's original intention for humanity. The vision is included in Schleiermacher's doctrine of election, which holds that there is one single divine decree, namely that all humans are predestined to the blessedness in Christ.[84]

Although he could construct Christian ethics from the threefold perspective of duty, virtue and the good, Schleiermacher's primary focus is clearly on the highest good (the kingdom of God, the reign of God-consciousness). He rather openly disapproves of starting from the perspective of duty, as he writes in the section on sanctification in *Christian Faith*: "Christian ethics will be far better in accordance with its relation to the doctrine of Christian faith, as well as with its own definiteness, when it abandons the imperative mode and merely describes the life in the reign of God in all relations."[85]

While the perspective of duty is rejected, the perspective of virtue comes to the fore in *Christian Ethics*. It finds its place at the very end, in the third part of *Christian Ethics* where Schleiermacher analyzes the activity of worship as a form of representational activity. Basically, the following actions of the church are distinguished: "broadening action" (*erweiterndes Handeln* with the focus on extending the reign of the Spirit over the flesh: cultivation of society, education, mission), "purifying action" (*wiederherstellendes Handeln*, for example, ecclesial discipline and reform, and criminal justice), and "representational action" (*darstellendes Handeln*, for example, worship, the arts, social relations).

The representational action can be distinguished in worship in the narrow and in the broader sense, or as "public and home worship" and "worship in daily life."[86] In its liturgy, either in the church or in the household, the Christian community expresses the pure joy of the self-consciousness that is entirely determined by the God-relation and the feeling of blessedness. Here, there is no stimulation from outside that affects the moral subject in the form

---

82 James M. Brandt, *All Things New: Reform of Church and Society in Schleiermacher's* Christian Ethics (Louisville: Westminster John Knox Press, 2001), 91.
83 CS/Jonas, 12 f; Brandt, *All Things New*, 7.
84 CG 1821/22, §§ 136–139.
85 *Der Christliche Glaube nach den Grundsätzen der Evangelischen Kirche im Zusammenhange darsgestellt (1830/31)*, ed. Martin Redeker (Berlin: Walter de Gruyter, 1960), Band II, § 112, 206 (hereafter CG 1830/31).
86 CS/Jonas, 534–619.

of sensuous pleasure or pain. These sensuous affects, however, are still present in the "worship in daily life" where the faithful live their lives. Daily worship, Schleiermacher explains, is the lived practice of Christian virtue in which the degree and progress of the reign of the Spirit over the flesh is demonstrated.[87] It is actual Christian witness in the world. A further differentiation between public worship and everyday witness is that the former never aims at an external result, but the latter does. However, this result is not intentional but coincidental, since according to Schleiermacher the motivation for Christian witness lies only in the desire for pure expression.[88]

Thus in daily worship believers are cultivating certain virtues. The source of these virtues is Christ. Schleiermacher conceives the whole process of sanctification from its core, the union with Christ. Like that of Calvin, Schleiermacher's theology is centered on *unio cum Christo*. In *Christian Faith* Schleiermacher defines sanctification as: "Through the incorporation/adoption as children of God a new power arises in the reborn person, that increasingly appropriates all his activities in order to cultivate a life that is akin to the sinless and blessed state of Christ."[89]

In every activity of the believer the inner motivation stems from Christ's power, and through his/her actions the communion with Christ will grow stronger. Christ is the prototype (*Urbild*) of which the believers are the images or representations (*Abbild*).[90] For the reconstruction of Christian virtue, this implies that the reign of the Spirit over the flesh must be characterized by easiness (*Leichtigkeit*), for Jesus performed the reign of God-consciousness with absolute *Leichtigkeit*. In *Christian Faith* easiness is the proper equivalent to grace.[91] The easiness of Jesus' performance only partially applies to his followers.[92] Christians will always be exposed to a certain amount of temptation that limits the absolute reign of the Spirit over the flesh. In traditional theological terms we can call Schleiermacher's view of the Spirit that permeates all aspects of human existence not only *sanctification* but also *transfiguration*, a spiritual transformation that (re)directs the will, the mind, the reason, the affections, and the senses of the person towards their truthful destination. This transfiguration or sanctification is as much a position (a graced position, not man-made but offered "by the free grace of God," as Schleiermacher writes in

---

87   CS/Jonas, 599 f.
88   CS/Jonas, 603.
89   CG 1821/22, § 131, 135.
90   CG 1821/22, § 144.
91   CG 1821/22, § 80, Anmerkung a, 256.
92   CS/Jonas, 606.

the *Notes on the Theory of Virtue*[93]) as a progressive process in time discernible as a moral character that shows an increasing likeness to Christ.[94]

Schleiermacher's theological theory of virtue, like his philosophical account, is built in a scientific way and structured by two oppositional pairs.[95] The first is that of the sensuous affects of *pleasure* or *pain* that continue to be produced in the Christian because of the ongoing influence of the outer world, the society that is "not yet church."[96] The second pair is based on the fact that the Christian can act more as an *individual* or more as a *member of the community*. Within this fourfold scheme Schleiermacher is now able to map the Christian virtues.

Chastity (*Keuschheit, agneia*) is the virtue in which the individual is affected by sensual pleasure but it does not lead to lust (*epithumia*), because the Spirit transfigures the receptiveness to pleasure in the proper way so that it does not start to dominate or enslave the individual.[97]

Steadfastness (*Geduld, Beharrlichkeit*) is the virtue in which the individual is affected from the outer world by pain. The person is able to endure the unpleasant affect without reacting to it by engaging in a sensuous activity. Schleiermacher hastens to add that this should not be confused with *apatheia*, which is understood as imperviousness to pain or social disturbances. In such *apatheia* the sensuous receptiveness is zero. In the Christian life, however, there is plenty of room for the feeling of pain but it becomes embedded in and softened by the joy and serenity (*Heiterkeit*) that are the keynotes of Christian life.[98]

Patience, tolerance (*Langmuth, makrothumia*) is the virtue related to a felt pain that crushes the sense of community. The pain is caused by moral failures and the imperfection of fellow members in the community. With patience, the Christian does not react in a sensuous way to this feeling of being hurt, but continues in solidarity to express the fraternal love that is the unifying principle of the Christian community.

Humility (*Demuth*), finally, is the virtue related to the felt pleasure that arouses the sense of community. Here, fellow members in the Christian community turn in their receptiveness to the one who is more spiritually and

---

[93] "Virtue," 222.
[94] I borrow this distinction of sanctification as position and process from Wim van Vlastuin, *Word vernieuwd: Een theologie van persoonlijke vernieuwing* (*Be Renewed: A Theology of Personal Renewal*) (Kampen: Kok, 2011), 244–262.
[95] CS/Jonas, 608.
[96] Brandt, *All Things New*, 53.
[97] CS/Jonas, 609 ff.
[98] CS/Jonas, 611 f.

morally advanced. This may easily lead to arrogance in that person. The virtue of humility ensures that one's self-evaluation is never the outcome of such a sensuous impression, but always subsumes the individual under the totality of the Christian community and its common spiritual calling.[99] Here we have the four virtues that structure the moral character of the members of the Christian community. In social life, these virtues are the basis of the Christian's social behavior. They are included in the other forms of the Christian's moral activity: the broadening action and the purifying action. Thus Schleiermacher can speak about a "worship in action" (*werkthätiger Gottesdienst*),[100] by which he means the representational action that has become the core of the broadening action. The process of civilizing the world is led by the increasing reign of God-consciousness. All four virtues are united, he adds, by the principle of fraternal love that governs the moral agency of the Christian in every aspect of life.[101] In this redeeming and unifying love we are truly united with Christ.

Conclusions

Much remains fragmentary and unfinished in Schleiermacher's *Christian Ethics*, and he keeps struggling with the question of how the representational and broadening activities precisely relate to each other. Nonetheless we may conclude, first of all, that Schleiermacher has developed a refined and positive theological virtue ethics. He draws the contours of the Christian as a moral agent in the modern world. In the virtuous Christian character he includes many aspects that colored his early notion of individuality, such as the understanding of freedom as the peaceful relation with nature, and the task of self-cultivation that is an imaginative and creative project of religiously inspired people.

Second, it is fascinating that he situates his account of Christian virtues in the framework of worship. Liturgy, more explicitly in the church or more implicitly in daily witness, is the context in which the virtues are nourished and strengthened and in which the Christian character flourishes. Liturgy, as he claims, has no purpose. In the church, communal worship is a pure expression of blessedness. Likewise, in daily witness, liturgical performance does not pursue any determined goal except the expression of an increasing likeness to the Savior. This embedment of the cultivation of character in what is most basically the act of liturgy is a very original contribution of Schleiermacher to the

---

99   CS/Jonas, 615 f.
100 CS/Peiter, 597 ff, from the lectures of 1826/27.
101 CS/Jonas, 619.

contemporary ethical discourse and it deserves to be investigated further. There may be fruitful intersections with the narrative (performative) approach to character as present in the work of Hauerwas and Wright, and with the patristic idea of cosmic priesthood as revitalized by Harrison and Wright.

Third, it remains unresolved how the Christian virtues (chastity, steadfastness, patience, humility) precisely relate to the philosophical virtues (wisdom, love, temperance in mind, steadfastness). The quartets do not easily match. Sometimes it looks like Schleiermacher tries to effectuate some kind of harmony by bridging the gap with the help of the theological virtues faith, hope and love.[102] However, this effort seems forced. Later, in constructing the Christian virtues in *Christian Ethics* he does not explicitly relate these to the *trias* of faith, hope and love, except when he comments on fraternal love as the unifying principle. Is he then constructing two different types of character, a philosophical (civic) one and a Christian one? Such a duality goes against the grain of Schleiermacher's thought. From the spirit of his whole work, I would suggest that the quartets find their unity in the highest good, which is defined philosophically as the integration of reason and nature, and in Christian terms like the kingdom of God. If this is the case, we can distinguish an account of moral formation from an inner perspective (the community of the faithful) and one from an outer perspective (the world, the *civitas*), both of which approach the same goal. The moral character in the Christian community is directly colored and impregnated by the story of Christ in a way the virtuous civic character never can be. Perhaps it is the challenge for the Christian in the secular world to combine the two character drafts in a personal and productive way, in a dynamic interplay. Perhaps we find in the twofold account of civic and Christian virtues Schleiermacher's version of the doctrine of the two kingdoms.

Finally, I note that in his account of the excellence of Christian character Schleiermacher pays no discernible attention to the function of the law of God. In his doctrine of sanctification he is of one accord with Calvin, whose theology also centers on the living 'union with Christ.' However, where Calvin then chooses to explain the Ten Commandments in the form of the *tertius usus legis* to show the direction to a 'rightly ordered life,' Schleiermacher bypasses the law because he profoundly believes that "propositions that refer to a disposition (fraternal love) cannot be called commandments"[103] and that the imperative form is not suitable for Christian ethics.[104] He adds: "today it is not desirable to begin catechetical education in the church with the Decalogue

---

102 E.g. "Tugendbegriff," 375 f. This is the proposed solution by Dickson, paper "Virtue."
103 CG 1830/31, 205.
104 CG 1830/31, 206.

because it leads to immature and superficial perceptions."[105] He does not reject the triplex function of the law,[106] but he does not deem it necessary to construct Christian ethics in terms of law, rules, and precepts. The only thing a systematic ethics needs is a scientific deduction of the *Formeln*, the general patterns of action of the Christian sanctified life.[107] These *Formeln* are always more or less descriptions of the manifestation in real life of the increasing communion with Christ. Instead of unfolding the doctrine of sanctification in the language of law (*tertius usus legis*) like Calvin, Schleiermacher unequivocally chooses the language of relation and participation in the divine life of Christ. He thus presents a powerful alternative to the legalistic 'dead ends' of the Reformed doctrine of sanctification.

Bibliography

Baan, Ariaan, *The Necessity of Witness: Stanley Hauerwas' Contribution to Systematic Theology* ('s-Hertogenbosch: Uitgeverij BOXPress, 2014).

Beiser, Frederick C., "Schleiermacher's Ethics," in Jacqueline Mariña (ed.), *The Cambridge Companion to Friedrich Schleiermacher* (Cambridge: Cambridge University Press, 2005), 53–72.

Billings, J. Todd, *Calvin, Participation, and the Gift: The Activity of Believers in Union with Christ* (New York: Oxford, 2007).

———. "Union with Christ and the Double Grace: Calvin's Theology and Its Early Reception," in J. Todd Billings & I. John Hesselink (eds.), *Calvin's Theology and Its Reception: Disputes, Developments, and New Possibilities* (Louisville: Westminster John Knox Press, 2012), 49–71.

Brändle, Werner, "Character," in Hans Dieter Betz et al. (eds.), *Religion in Geschichte und Gegenwart: Handwörterbuch für Theologie und Religionswissenschaft*, Band 2 (Tübingen: Mohr Siebeck, 1999), 109–111.

Brandt, James M., *All Things New: Reform of Church and Society in Schleiermacher's Christian Ethics* (Louisville: Westminster John Knox Press, 2001).

———. "Translator's Introduction" to *Selections from Friedrich Schleiermacher's Christian Ethics* (Louisville: Westminster John Knox Press, 2010), 1–19.

---

105   CG 1830/31, 206.
106   CG 1821/22, 151. Schleiermacher refers positively to the statements on the *tertius usus legis* in the Formula of Concord 1577, article VI.
107   CG 18301/31, 206.

Cahill, Lisa Sowle, "Christian Character, Biblical Community, and Human Values," in William P. Brown (ed.), *Character & Scripture: Moral Formation, Community, and Biblical Interpretation* (Grand Rapids: Eerdmans, 2002), 3–17.

Calvin, Jean, *Commentaires de Jehan Calvin sur le Nouveau Testament: Le tout reveu diligemment et comme traduit de nouveau tant le texte que la glose* (Paris: C. Meyrueis, 1854–1855), Vol. 2.

——. *Sermons sur le livre de Job, recueillis fidèlement de sa bouche selon qu'il les preschoit* (Genève, 1569).

——. *Institutes of the Christian Religion*, 2 Vols., trans. Ford Lewis Battles, ed. John T. McNeill (Louisville: Westminster John Knox Press, 1960).

Calvin's Commentaries (Edinburgh: Calvin Translation Society, 1846–51).

Canlis, Julie, *Calvin's Ladder: A Spiritual Theology of Ascent and Ascension* (Grand Rapids: Eerdmans, 2010).

Dickson, C.J., "Schleiermacher on Christian Virtue," unpublished paper, delivered in the Schleiermacher Group at the Annual Meeting of the American Academy of Religion, November 2013, Baltimore.

Harrison, Nonna Verna, *God's Many-Splendored Image: Theological Anthropology for Christian Formation* (Grand Rapids: Baker Academic, 2010).

Hauerwas, Stanley, *A Community of Character: Toward a Constructive Christian Social Ethic* (Notre Dame: University of Notre Dame Press, 1981).

——. *Character and the Christian Life: A Study in Theological Ethics* (San Antonio: Trinity University Press, 1975).

——. *Moral Character as a Problem for Theological Ethics* (New Haven: Yale University Press, 1968).

Herms, Eilert, *Herkunft, Entfaltung und erste Gestalt des Systems der Wissenschaften bei Schleiermacher* (Gütersloh: Gütersloher Verlagshaus Gerd Mohn, 1974).

——. "Schleiermacher's Christian Ethics," in Jacqueline Mariña (ed.), *The Cambridge Companion to Friedrich Schleiermacher* (Cambridge: Cambridge University Press, 2005), 209–228.

——. "Virtue: A Neglected Concept in Protestant Ethics," *Scottish Journal of Theology* 35 (1982), 481–495.

Horton, Michael S., "Calvin's Theology of Union with Christ and the Double Grace: Modern Reception and Contemporary Possibilities," in J. Todd Billings & I. John Hesselink (eds.), *Calvin's Theology and Its Reception: Disputes, Developments, and New Possibilities* (Louisville: Westminster John Knox Press, 2012), 72–94.

Jonas, Ludwig & Wilhelm Dilthey (eds.), *Aus Schleiermacher's Leben: In Briefen*, Band 4 (Berlin 1858–1863, Reprint: Berlin/New York, 1974).

MacIntyre, Alasdair, *After Virtue: A Study in Moral Theory*, Second Edition (Notre Dame: University of Notre Dame Press, 1984).

Meilaender, Gilbert C., *The Theory and Practice of Virtue* (Notre Dame: University of Notre Dame Press, 1984).

Peiter, Herrmann, "The Autonomy of Theological Ethics in Contrast with Philosophical Ethics Owing to the Fruitful Relation between Theological Ethics and Scriptural Exegesis," in Terrence N. Tice (ed.), *Christian Ethics According to Schleiermacher: Collected Essays and Reviews* (Eugene: Pickwick Publications, 2010), 210–297.

Porter, Jean, "Virtue ethics," in Robin Gill (ed.), *Cambridge Companion to Christian Ethics* (Cambridge: Cambridge University Press, 2006), 87–102.

Schleiermacher, Friedrich, *Brouillon zur Ethik (1805/06)* (Hamburg: Felix Meiner Verlag, 1981).

———. *Brouillon zur Ethik (Notes on Ethics) (1805/1806); Notes on the Theory of Virtue (1804/1805)*, trans. John Wallhauser and Terrence N. Tice (Edwin Mellen Press, 2003).

———. *Christliche Sittenlehre (Vorlesung im Wintersemester 1826/27), nach größtenteils unveröffentlichten Hörernachschriften und nach teilweisen unveröffentlichten Manuskripten Schleiermachers*, ed. Hermann Peiter (Berlin/Münster: LIT Verlag, 2011).

———. *Der Christliche Glaube nach den Grundsätzen der Evangelischen Kirche im Zusammenhange darsgestellt (1830/31)*, ed. Martin Redeker (Berlin: Walter de Gruyter, 1960).

———. *Kritische Gesamtausgabe*, Abt. I, Band 1, Jugendschriften 1787–1796, ed. Günter Meckenstock (Berlin/New York: Walter de Gruyter, 1984).

———. *Kritische Gesamtausgabe*, Abt. I, Band 2, Schriften aus der Berliner Zeit 1796–1799, ed. Günter Meckenstock (Berlin/New York: Walter de Gruyter, 1984).

———. *Kritische Gesamtausgabe*, Abt. I, Band 3, Schriften aus der Berliner Zeit 1800–1802, ed. Günter Meckenstock (Berlin/New York: Walter De Gruyter, 1988).

———. *Kritische Gesamtausgabe*, Abt. 1, Band 7.2 (Berlin/New York: Walter de Gruyter, 1980).

———. *Lectures on Philosophical Ethics* (Cambridge: Cambridge University Press, 2002).

———. *Sämmtliche Werke*, Abt. I, Bd. 12 (Berlin: G. Reimer, 1843).

Schleiermacher: A Guide for the Perplexed, trans. Theodore Vial (London: Bloomsbury T&T Clark, 2013).

Schleiermachers Werke, Band. 1, ed. Otto Braun & Johannes Bauer (Leipzig: Scientia Verlag Aalen, 1927, 1981).

Sockness, Brent W., "Schleiermacher and the Ethics of Authenticity: The *Monologen* of 1800," *Journal of Religious Ethics* 32:3 (2004), 477–517.

Taylor, Charles, *Sources of the Self: The Making of the Modern Identity* (Cambridge: Harvard University Press, 1989).

Vlastuin, Wim van, *Word vernieuwd: Een theologie van persoonlijke vernieuwing (Be Renewed: A Theology of Personal Renewal)* (Kampen: Kok, 2011).

Vos, Pieter, "After Duty: The Need for Virtue Ethics in Moral Formation," in Bram de Muynck, Johan Hegeman & Pieter Vos (eds.), *Bridging the Gap: Connecting Christian Faith and Professional Practice in a Pluralistic Society* (Sioux Center: Dorth Press, 2011), 143–158.

———. "Breakdown of the Teleological View of Life? Investigating Law, *Telos* and Virtue in Calvinistic Ethics," (unpublished paper IRTI-conference Sarospatak 2013).

Wright, Nicholas T., *After You Believe: Why Christian Character Matters* (New York: HarperOne, 2010).

Zorgdrager, Heleen, "On the Fullness of Salvation: Tracking *theosis* in Reformed Theology," *Journal of Reformed Theology* 8 (2014, forthcoming).

In Defense of Authenticity
On Art, Religion and the Authentic Self

Onno Zijlstra

In the seventies of the twentieth century authenticity became a criterion for judging people, their products and institutions in Western Europe and North America. But the last two decades have seen mounting criticism of the idea of individual authenticity. In the nineties it was increasingly held that 'authenticity' is a subjectivist and egocentric ideal and that its requirement has led to the moral crisis we find ourselves in nowadays.

The critics certainly do have a point, but tend to underestimate the importance of authenticity because of the factual derailment of the ideal in 'the culture of narcissism,' the consumer society, the culture of greed.[1] Besides critics, there are those who have worked at consolidation and repair of the ideal.[2] In support of this last group, this paper starts from the idea that 'authenticity' pays attention to everyone's unique individuality, and that the moral crisis we find ourselves in may well point to a loss of self and a lack of authenticity,[3] rather than to an overestimation of their value.

The Canadian philosopher Charles Taylor has reacted to the critics of authenticity as well as to the corruption of 'authenticity' in his *The Culture of Authenticity*, his *Sources of the Self*, and, to a lesser degree, in *A Secular Age*. Taylor admits that individualization and 'authenticity' have led to lapses, but maintains the idea of the authentic individual as an ideal. He makes a plea for self-realization that does not forget one's own sources and backgrounds, something the adherents of the ideal of authenticity have so often been accused of.[4]

Taylor ascribes a special role to the arts in the realization of authenticity: we discover and become who we are in what we create. Since Romanticism, thus

---

1 To name some in the USA: Daniel Bell, Allan Bloom and Christopher Lasch (*The Culture of Narcissism* (New York: Warner Books, 1979)), and in the Netherlands: Maarten Doorman and Ad Verbrugge.
2 For instance Charles Taylor, Alessandro Ferrara and Bas van Stokkom.
3 Cf. Bas van Stokkom, "Sensitief kapitaal: De revisie van het authenticiteitsideaal" (Sensitive Capital: The Revision of the Ideal of Authenticity), *Krisis* 76:3 (1999), 65–77.
4 See for instance Ad Verbrugge's criticism of Enlightenment individualism in his philippic against the individualist spirit of our times. Ad Verbrugge, *Tijd van onbehagen: Filosofische essays over een cultuur op drift* (*Time of Discontent: Philosophical Essays on a Culture Adrift*) (Amsterdam: SUN, 2004), 202–223.

Taylor, creativity and expression of one's unique self have become a mission because they enable everybody to supply his or her unique contribution to reality. This happens in language too, but for Taylor the work of art is paradigmatic.

Charles Taylor sees 'authenticity' as "powered by Christianity." In *A Secular Age* he argues in favor of 'the return of religion,' and ends the book with a chapter on conversions and "self-authenticating" religious experiences, thus relating his treatment of authenticity to his religious conviction in an encompassing critique of our culture.[5]

In this contribution I shall follow Taylor in his defense of 'authenticity' in relation to religion, but also in the importance he attaches to the arts. I shall try to sharpen Taylor's ideas on authenticity, religion and the role of the arts in Western civilization. First an idea of authenticity will be stipulated, if only to forestall a few standard critiques of 'authenticity.' (To be sure: the suggestion is not that authenticity is the highest value, let alone that it is the only one. Moreover, it will be put forward as a critical concept, the way it in fact functioned since being introduced by Jean-Jacques Rousseau.[6]) Next, I will go into the religious dimension of authenticity and the relation of the arts to the ideal of authenticity: the arts as being paradigmatic of authenticity (but not necessarily its only or even ultimate representative).

A prominent position will be given here to the oeuvre of Søren Aabye Kierkegaard, nineteenth-century Danish Protestant philosopher-theologian-author—conspicuously absent in Taylor's voluminous *A Secular Age*. Kierkegaard published his *Fear and Trembling: A Dialectical Lyric* in 1843 under the pseudonym Johannes *de silentio*.[7] The little book is about Abraham's willingness to sacrifice his son Isaac and Abraham's faith that he will receive his son back. *Fear and Trembling* will function here as a source of ideas on authenticity. At the end of this contribution Kierkegaard's oeuvre as a whole will be put forward as an instance of religious art in a culture of authenticity.

---

5   Charles Taylor, *A Secular Age* (Cambridge: The Belknap Press of Cambridge University Press, 2007), 158, Ch. 20.
6   Cf. Lionel Trilling, *Sincerity and Authenticity: The Charles Eliot Norton Lectures, 1969–1970* (Cambridge: Harvard University Press, 1972), 94.
7   Søren A. Kierkegaard, *Fear and Trembling & Repetition, Kierkegaard's Writings*, Vol. VI, trans. Howard V. Hong & Edna H. Hong (Princeton: Princeton University Press, 1983).

Authenticity Revisited

Central to the neo-conservative critique of 'authenticity' is that it gives in to trends of ego-culture. Authenticity as I see it does not imply self-sufficiency or even autonomy, let alone 'ego-culture.'[8] By authenticity I will understand being oneself by assuming, after reflection, one's commitments—including a commitment to the search for truth—and by acting accordingly.

Commitments keep us far from 'ego-culture.' Luc Ferry has pointed to the fact that in postmodern times "the very idea of limit seems to fade away, delegitimized as it is by the imperious demands made by individual self-cultivation and by the right to difference" as one of the "dead ends the culture of authenticity often ... leads into."[9] Over against this postmodern tendency Ferry holds up the moderns, who, despite the disappearance of the hierarchical cosmos and ancient virtue, remained "attached to the idea of law's transcendence."[10] The authentic individual does not act according to whatever comes into his mind, because it 'feels good,' or because in this way he 'stays close to himself.' Like Ferry I would underscore the subject's responsibility to some transcendence.

Commitments keep us far from 'ego-culture' and so does truth. Supporters of the ideal of authenticity have been accused of devaluating truth in favor of authenticity. One can begin to defend the ideal against these accusations by pointing to its roots in religious traditions that direct us "to look inward and make contact with an inner truth in order to gain guidance for our lives."[11] Bernard Williams writes about the modern ideal of authenticity that it "involves a demand of truthfulness between people which certainly transcends mere narcissism or self-concern" and goes so far as to directly relate authenticity to truth. "The pursuit of authenticity as a reflective ideal seems to turn on a notion of honesty that links sincerity and a courageous confrontation with the truth ..."[12]

---

8   Cf. Trilling, *Sincerity*, 99 f.
9   Luc Ferry, *Homo Aestheticus: The Invention of Taste in the Democratic Age*, trans. Robert de Loaiza (Chicago: Chicago University Press, 1993), 258.
10 Ferry, *Homo*, 257.
11 Charles Guignon, *On Being Authentic* (London: Routledge, 2004), x.
12 Bernard Williams, *Truth and Truthfulness: An Essay in Genealogy* (Princeton: Princeton University Press, 2004), 184 f. As is always the case with truth commitments, one may find oneself mistaken, in religion as well as in science. But, thus Williams, the presumed discovery always "is related to the need to resist fantasy in making sense of my beliefs ..." (204).

In an essentialist mindset authenticity means to become what we already 'really' are, to coincide with our deeper, hidden selves that have been there all along but have become overgrown by influences of others, social roles and conventions, etcetera.[13] The idea of authenticity as proposed here, however, is future-directed. By committing ourselves to a cause, we always move beyond the present. Bernard Williams sees our truthful acknowledgements connected to truth by "an element of hope or prediction."[14] Abraham, "the knight of faith" of Kierkegaard's pseudonym Johannes *de silentio* in his *Fear and Trembling*, is a telling paradigm of authenticity. In his decision and commitment after the call from God to sacrifice his son Isaac, Abraham anticipates a future that is uncertain and open. Abraham renounces his claim to the love that is the substance of his life, but at the same time holds fast to it, "... for it is great to give up on one's desire, but it is greater to hold fast to it after giving it up ..."[15]

In accordance with the biblical conception of unexpected life-changing events, Abraham is in a crisis and he goes on "from here."[16] Now another pitfall must be avoided: to see authenticity as an original immediacy—something said to be proper to animals and small children. One of the founders of the ideal, Jean-Jacques Rousseau, fell blindly into this pit: "The man who meditates is a depraved animal."[17] *De silentio* carefully marks off his 'knight of faith' from Rousseau's longing for immediacy. God's covenant with Abraham is renewed.

---

13   One can think here of Paul Ricoeur's distinction between selfhood (*ipse*-identity) and sameness (*idem*-identity) and his idea of faithfulness to oneself (*ipse*) in keeping one's word (Paul Ricoeur, *Oneself as Another,* trans. Kathleen Blamey (Chicago: The University of Chicago Press, 1994), 3, 116 ff). Kierkegaard will work out theoretically the idea of the self as a relation in his *The Sickness unto Death, Kierkegaard's Writings,* Vol. XIX, trans. Howard V. Hong & Edna H. Hong (Princeton: Princeton University Press, 1983).

14   Williams, *Truth,* 204.

15   Kierkegaard, *Fear and Trembling,* 18.

16   "From here" I borrow from Bernard Williams, who uses the phrase in his critique of Rawls' idea of a life plan: "the perspective of deliberative choice on one's life is constitutively *from here*" (*Moral Luck* (Cambridge: Cambridge University Press, 1981), 35). Charles Larmore quotes this in his *The Practices of the Self,* trans. Sharon Bowman (Chicago: The University of Chicago Press, 2010), 193. Writing about authenticity Larmore brings forward that today's wisdom might not suffice to assess what will happen: "our good itself is continually evolving ... and until the day we die it can always take an unexpected turn" (189).

17   Jean-Jacques Rousseau, quoted in Guignon, *Authentic,* 56; cf. the criticism of Charles Larmore on Sartre's "When I deliberate the chips are down" (Larmore, *Practices,* 169). The typically nineteenth-century way of expressing the ideal, 'become who you are,' puts into words, if not understood in an essentialist sense, the valuable intuition that everybody, born inauthentic, has the possibility to interpret his experiences from his own perspec-

Abraham can be called authentic in that he responds to his calling, makes it his own and goes his way to Moriah. He cannot be spontaneously his old self; the call makes that impossible. For *De silentio*, longing for an original, organic, immediate unity is no option. He never tires of specifying Abraham's spontaneity as a "later immediacy,"[18] a "new interiority."[19] This spontaneity is not without or before reflection, but after it. Neither does it remain suspended in reflection. One has to make a choice and commit oneself to one's calling.

Let us once more consider the critique. Narcissism and egocentrism, these 'malaises of modernity,' were supposed to be direct and unqualified consequences of the ideal of authenticity. Authenticity was played off against morality and awareness of one's place and role in society. However, 'authenticity' as stipulated above does not have to suffer from the flaws many critics have noted in it. Reflection does not take place in a void, but is always embedded in and related to given horizons or frameworks of meaning and significance.[20] Self-reflection is critical in relating one to moral standards. Authenticity 'after reflection' implies this critical stance as well as "openness and wonder."[21]

Another point of criticism is that the ideal of authenticity takes leave of the social sphere. However, the ideal does not necessarily deny that an individual is a social being, that the individual should relate to others, that he or she is part of and takes part in civilization, nor does it deny the importance of civil society. Charles Larmore refers to a telling statement of Jean de la Bruyère to illustrate that authenticity does not depend on freeing oneself of social bonds, the influence of others, social conventions, etc. Confronted with the possible reproach that his ideas are not new, de la Bruyère writes: "Horace or Boileau said it before you.—I take your word for that; but I said it as my own." De la Bruyère's statement is nicely ambiguous: he leaves open whether or not he knew about Horace saying the same before him.[22] De la Bruyère in his authenticity does not invite the response: 'How original!' *De silentio*'s underlining of

---

tive and in a future-directed way. This presupposes an a priori, counterfactual authenticity. Cf. Bas van Stokkom, "Sensitief," 71.

18   Kierkegaard, *Fear and Trembling*, 82.
19   Kierkegaard, *Fear and Trembling*, 69.
20   Charles Taylor, *Sources of the Self* (Cambridge: Cambridge University Press, 1989), Ch. 1 and 2.
21   Bas van Stokkom, "Sensitief," 71 (my translation, OZ). The idea of a second *immediacy* is, I think, slightly exaggerated. The human is never literally immediate. Elsewhere I have gone into the epistemology of Kierkegaard's pseudonym Climacus that belief is beyond science; it is not supposed to be 'meshugga,' *Kierkegaard in discussie (Kierkegaard in Discussion)* (Budel: Damon, 2012), Ch. 5.
22   Larmore, *Practices*, 58, 139 f.

the importance of man's inner life is not meant to close us off from the outer world and others or to celebrate the inner in itself.[23] We have to master language, culture, rules, and conventions. *De silentio* merely expands the element of the 'proprius,' that it is one's own. The inner can never be completely expressed in the universal.[24]

However, the ideal of authenticity does stress the value and responsibility of the individual beyond his/her role as a member of society and a link in the chain of tradition.[25] For Johannes *de silentio* the inner can never be expressed exhaustibly in the outer, or, as the old dictum goes: 'individuum ineffabile est.'

But, critics might ask, is this the message we need in our time? Should we not prefer an antidote to individualism? Kierkegaard thought his time needed correction and made a plea for individual authenticity.[26] Through his authorship he wanted to make a contribution. His pseudonym Johannes *de silentio* emphasizes the public character of the ethics he suspends to "save" Abraham. The target of his criticism is the prevalent philosophy, Hegel's philosophy, in fact Hegel's Danish followers, who ruled supreme in Copenhagen.[27] "In

---

23 In an early work Mark C. Taylor has criticized Kierkegaard in favor of Hegel. Kierkegaard presupposed an "isolated individuality" as "requisite for a proper relation between the believer and God." Hegel, thus Taylor, is right in pointing to the necessity for the individual to appropriate the universal to become a self. Taylor seems to forget that Kierkegaard does not deny the element of appropriation. See Mark C. Taylor, "Sounds of Silence," in Robert L. Perkins (ed.), *Kierkegaard's* Fear and Trembling: *Critical Appraisals* (Tuscaloosa: University of Alabama Press, 1981), 165–188: 188.

24 The socially fully adapted William in Kierkegaard's *Either/Or* seems called to order by the sermon, added by him at the end of the book, on the text that *vis à vis* God all stand 'in the wrong.' William remains immanent in the social world. Ultimately 'guilt' makes this position an impossibility for Kierkegaard. In the end reconciliation is only possible in faith— beyond the mediation of institutions and rules. That is why Johannes *de silentio* comes up with the extreme case of Abraham on his way to Moriah. In his relation to a transcendence the individual finds reconciliation and meaning.

25 In a modern civilization it is not enough to know the rules, to act 'by the book.' It is not enough, to use an image of Wittgenstein's, to be able to play the game well, because the question might be which game to play. Individuals get responsibilities and chances. C.A. van Peursen points to the phenomenon of triggering: the action of one individual can cause a series of reactions and thus considerable social changes—think of Rosa Parks in 1955 (C.A. van Peursen, *Strategie van de cultuur* (*The Strategy of Culture*) (Amsterdam: Elsevier, 1970), 147, 195).

26 Søren A. Kierkegaard, *The Point of View, Kierkegaard's Writings*, Vol. XXII, trans. Howard V. Hong & Edna H. Hong (Princeton: Princeton University Press, 1998), 205.

27 Jon Stewart has dedicated many pages to showing that where Kierkegaard has been read as a critic of Hegel, Kierkegaard in fact reacts against contemporaries and fellow-countrymen, but also that where Kierkegaard thinks that he is reacting against Hegel, he is in fact

Hegelian philosophy *das Äussere* (*die Entäusserung*) (the outer (the externalization)) is higher than *das Innere* (the inner)."[28] In Hegel the inner always appears under a negative sign: it needs to be mediated towards the outer.[29] To Hegel the inner becomes real and concrete in the outer. This gives a special position to *Sittlichkeit*, the institutions that realize what remains abstract and inner in Kant's ethics of conscience (*Moralität*). To be sure, Hegel leaves room for exceptional individuals in history. Noah and Abraham, because of their covenant with the infinite, were strangers on earth and to men, illustrations of the "unhappy consciousness."[30] In a developed, civilized society, however, where the estrangement of individual and society has been overcome, *Sittlichkeit* is mandatory. Over against this line of thought *de silentio* goes for the primacy of the inner. The more so because he does not believe in a Hegelian world history, in an end of history as the end of all estrangement. Abraham, called to an exceptional action, has to make a decision, without knowledge of the end of the story. Johannes *de silentio* stands up for the single individual.

In notes where he prides himself on helping to familiarize his age with hearing a personal *I* speak, Kierkegaard expresses his conviction that the time will come that someone stands up who speaks in the first person. Is not our time the opposite extreme with all these egos speaking up? It seems a fair point. On a more abstract level, however, we can see these lapses as a dimension of what Anton C. Zijderveld has called "the abstract society," a society where human existence is reduced to the pole of exteriority at the expense of interiority. Zijderveld writes in 1970:

> In summary, industrial society, losing more and more of its reality and meaning in the experience of man, tends to reduce him to a specialized expert and dehumanized functionary. If we interpret human life as extended between two balancing poles of exteriority and interiority, we

---

targeting the professor and bishop Martensen or the author Heiberg (Jon Stewart, *Kierkegaard's Relations to Hegel Reconsidered* (Cambridge: Cambridge University Press, 2003)).

28 Kierkegaard, *Fear and Trembling*, 69.
29 Renate von Heydebrand, "Innerlichkeit" (Interiority), in Gerhard Ritter & Karlfried Günder, *Historisches Wörterbuch der Philosophie*, Band 4 (Basel/Stuttgart: Schwabe & Co Verlag, 1976), 386 ff.
30 Mark C. Taylor, *Journeys to Selfhood: Hegel and Kierkegaard* (Berkeley: University of California Press, 1980), 38 ff.

may conclude that abstract society reduces human existence to just one pole, that of exteriority.[31]

Zijderveld's image is still recognizable; these egos speaking up, how much 'spontaneity after reflection,' how much interiority and real individuality do we find there?

Authenticity and Religion

In *A Secular Age* Taylor stresses that we cannot live without 'codes', but "we should find the center of our spiritual lives beyond the code ..."[32] Following Ivan Illich, Taylor refers to the parable of the Samaritan who "cuts across the boundaries of the permitted 'we's' in his world."[33] It is an act of his 'I.' The freedom of the Samaritan is not something he simply generates out of himself, though. In responding to the traveler, robbed and beaten and left by the road, he frees himself from the bounds of the 'we'—thus creating new kinds of belonging together. These again run the risk of institutionalization. "Something new emerges out of all this: modern bureaucracies, based on rationality, and rules. Rules prescribe treatments for categories of people ..."[34]

Taylor sees the gap between 'the city of God' and "the established order of civilization as we live it" being wrongly narrowed in the nineteenth century "as the sense of civilizational superiority, which grew with Western colonial power, became interwoven with a sense of Christendom as the bearer of this civilization."[35]

We can underscore the tension pointed out by Taylor by referring to Abraham in *Fear and Trembling*. Kierkegaard, living in the nineteenth century, was one of the first who keenly spotted the dangers of being 'civilized.' *Fear and Trembling* is directed against the spirit of the age that values knowledge more highly than faith and sees in the bourgeois ethics of Danish society an ultimate normativity. For Hegel the ethical task of the individual is "to get his own particular will to conform to the universal will" as realized in society.[36] Abraham

---

31 Anton C. Zijderveld, *The Abstract Society: A Cultural Analysis of Our Time* (New York: Doubleday & Company, 1971), 88.
32 Taylor, *Secular Age*, 743.
33 Taylor, *Secular Age*, 738.
34 Taylor, *Secular Age*, 738 f.
35 Taylor, *Secular Age*, 736 f.
36 The quoted expression is Lippitt's (John Lippitt, *Kierkegaard and 'Fear and Trembling'* (London: Routledge, 2003), 86).

is Johannes *de silentio*'s hero of faith—his book is a 'lyric.' However, Johannes repeatedly declares that he cannot understand Abraham: his dialectic comes up against a limit. Abraham is addressed by a transcendence that is strange to others—if not to himself. Abraham is open to a voice that calls him from outside, to "what no human mind has conceived."[37]

The critical dimension of Johannes *de silentio*'s eulogy on Abraham might come out well in our time when we compare it to Luc Ferry's argumentation in his *Learning to Live*. Ferry argues in favor of the individual and of "immanent transcendence."[38] Central in Ferry's philosophy is the idea that there is no closure to our knowledge, we have to accept certain mysteries, human freedom for instance.[39] Ferry describes this freedom as "transcendence within immanence."[40] It is, like love and beauty, transcendent in the sense that it is "in excess of nature and history."[41] Ferry argues for an "enlarged thought."[42] "It's exhorting us to come out of ourselves the better to find ourselves—which is Hegel's dialectical definition of 'experience'—enables us to better know and love others."[43] Compared to *de silentio*'s God and Abraham, this "transcendence within immanence" and the Hegelian notion of enlarged thinking appear self-consciously self-centered ("to find ourselves"). The Samaritan however, did not ask for the man along the road. Johannes *de silentio* might open our eyes to a Hegelianism that has been embraced by 'our kind of people' because it provides us with an ideology that excludes those who don't fit the story. *De silentio*'s Abraham thus deserves my attention, however much he challenges my comprehension. His authenticity breaks through all possible complacency and shows something of that single individual that remains ineffable.

De silentio underscores Abraham's commitment and spontaneity in order to forestall the Hegelian critique that this religiousness keeps the individual estranged. In *Fear and Trembling* the critical discussion of Abraham's willingness to sacrifice Isaac is preceded by a 'tuning' that offers four variations of the

---

37   1 Cor. 2: 9. With these words of Paul, quoted by Kierkegaard's pseudonym Climacus, van Riessen indicates very precisely what is meant here by transcendence (Renée D.N. van Riessen, *Verder gaan dan Socrates? Over onderwijs, bezieling en innerlijkheid bij Kierkegaard en Levinas* (*Going Further than Socrates? On Education, Animation and Interiority in Kierkegaard and Levinas*) (Leiden: Universiteit Leiden, 2012), 9).
38   Luc Ferry, *Learning to Live: A User's Manual* (Edinburgh: Canongate, 2010).
39   Ferry, *Learning*, 230.
40   Ferry, *Learning*, 236 f.
41   Ferry, *Learning*, 227.
42   Ferry, *Learning*, 248.
43   Ferry, *Learning*, 250.

biblical story. The tuning shows what faith is not. Faith is not a matter of believing that God exists and accepting his authority, but rather of entering heart and soul into the relation to the absolute *and* returning to the universal and social in a "second spontaneity," the spontaneity after reflection.

For a moment this might suggest that by taking one's point of departure from *de silentio*'s Abraham, one argues for the authenticity of blind obedience. But that would be contrary to Kierkegaard's intentions. The view that the point of *Fear and Trembling* is not blind obedience but rather devotion to what is greater than us is supported by the role of Job in Kierkegaard's book *Repetition*, published on the same day as *Fear and Trembling*. Job features in *Repetition* as the paradigm of the religious individual, as Abraham does in Johannes' dialectical lyric, and Job becomes an outsider in a group of friends by venturing to start an argument with God. An ideology may narrow life, religion makes life larger.[44]

Art and Authenticity

In the history of 'authenticity' art has played a significant role. To Jean-Jacques Rousseau the arts are a threat to authenticity—for novels he made an exception. But Rousseau's idea of authenticity, over against ours, is essentialist and implies a self-sufficiency that can indeed only be threatened by cultural impulses from outside.[45] Distrust towards the arts in relation to authenticity is found in Søren Kierkegaard too—in his case without being connected to an essentialist idea of authenticity. Kierkegaard was confronted with an effect of the autonomy art had gained in modern times: the possibility to shy away from life and hide in aesthetics. Especially the work of art as a completed object may seduce us away from our lives, which to Kierkegaard are by definition incomplete.[46] Art then becomes the opposite of commitment: entertainment. And the spectator becomes a consumer. Kierkegaard needed to resist and criticize this tempting possibility very explicitly. Here I want to look at the option that the arts may be a stimulus to authenticity. This option is part of the history of

---

44   Cf. Ludwig Wittgenstein, *Tractatus Logico-Philosophicus, Werkausgabe*, Band 1 (Frankfurt a.M: Suhrkamp, 1984), 6.43.
45   Cf. Trilling, *Sincerity*, 61, 67 ff.
46   Cf. Pieter Vos, "Self," in Steven Emmanuel, William McDonald & Jon Stewart (eds.), *Kierkegaard's Concepts* (Kierkegaard Research: Sources, Reception, and Resources, Vol. 15, Tome VI) (Aldershot: Ashgate, forthcoming).

the idea of authenticity as individual self-sufficiency as well,[47] but here we will consider it in its connection with authenticity as consciously embedded in society and history—Kierkegaard's version.

In the process of individualization the arts play an important role—especially in our 'fluid modernity' (Zygmunt Bauman), characterized by changing individual preferences and choices. The artist is the personification of an attitude of openness and wonder. Thus artists contribute to our continuing endeavor to make sense of new thoughts and feelings, to make them our own.

Originality and authenticity have become prominent in the arts and the arts have become paradigmatic in a culture that values innovation and authenticity. From the nineteenth century on this tendency has only become stronger. The artist is regarded as a special individual and we have come to expect personal products from him or her. That in postmodernism we reach out for traditions, conventions and figurative images does not mean that this tendency has come to a stop. The application is still a very personal one. Artists work from private fascinations. Jan Hoet writes, under the heading "Authenticiteit": "Earlier we had much more mentally and pictorially closed movements in art … and within that frame artists were working who were inspired by the same conviction … today we have more idiosyncrasy, artists working out of individually defined peculiarities."[48] In modern times the public is stimulated to attach its own meanings to the work of art. The work of art does not have a fixed meaning. As Immanuel Kant expresses it, the work of art gives us much to think about, but does not impose one meaning on us.[49]

In art too authenticity is not linked to an abstract, asocial and ahistorical, individualism. Being the individual he or she is, the authentic artist is not a solipsist. Originality is not a question of isolation, but of a freedom of imagination that may not be possible in other areas. It is the artist's competence to be at the same time very individual *and* to communicate with a public, to be idiosyncratic but not an idiot. The work of art addresses a public. And an original work always reacts to its own times as well as to other works and the tradition. Milan Kundera:

> To my mind, great works can only be born within the history of their art and as *participants* in that history. It is only inside history that we can see

---

47   Trilling, *Sincerity*, 100 ff.
48   Jan Hoet, *In de wereld van Jan Hoet* (*In the World of Jan Hoet*) (Gent: Borgerhoff & Lamberigts, 2008), 17 (my translation).
49   Immanuel Kant, *Critique of Judgement*, trans. James Creed Meredith (Oxford: Oxford University Press, 2007 (1952)), AA 315/ B 194–195.

what is new and what is repetitive, what is discovery and what is imitation; in other words, only inside history can a work exist as a *value* capable of being discerned and judged. Nothing seems to me worse for art than to fall outside its own history, for it is a fall into the chaos where aesthetic values can no longer be perceived.[50]

Exactly because artists are so interwoven in tradition and context, they can express themselves in such a layered and yet accessible way.

Charles Taylor points to the contribution of art, since Romanticism, to the development of a civilization through the design of "subtler languages."[51] New events and new experiences ask for imagination to articulate new visions. The artist makes his or her unique contribution to society by creating subtler languages, beyond accepted conventions, to give expression to our thoughts and feelings. This asks for a personal reaction from the viewer.

The philosopher Herman van Gunsteren points to the paradox in our culture that the individual is publicly applauded while real individuality seems to be disappearing from our culture, dominated as it is by mass media and consumerism. According to Van Gunsteren this is happening because it is a difficult task to be an individual—individuality is a venerable cultural product—, and there is little private space to foster individuality.[52] We most of all become the individuals we are in communication with others, in personal relations and discussions.[53] When the discussion touches on our deepest convictions, it might become what Karl Jaspers has called a "loving struggle."[54] Art's relative autonomy allows experimentation with thoughts and images without real blood being drawn. That is why art offers an excellent chance to keep the struggle loving: the matter may touch us deeply but the discussion is mediated by the work.

---

50 Milan Kundera, "Testaments Betrayed," trans. Lida Asher (London: Faber and Faber, 1995), 18, quoted in *Contemporary South African Art 1985–1995* (Cape Town: SANG, 1997), 11.

51 Taylor, *Sources*, 381.

52 "Het verdwijnende individu," *De Volkskrant*, 2 January 2010.

53 As Kierkegaard's pseudonym Vigilius Haufniensis says: "Appropriation is precisely the secret of conversation" (*The Concept of Anxiety: A Simple Psychologically Orienting Deliberation on the Dogmatic Issue of Hereditary Sin, Kierkegaard's Writings*, Vol. VIII, trans. Reidar Thomte & Albert D. Anderson (Princeton: Princeton University Press, 1980), 16).

54 In Jasper's philosophy "loving struggle" is a highlight of/between cultures of individualization that started in what he called the 'Aksenzeit,' around 500 B.C., the time when the world religions and philosophies were born that share a breaking away from collectivistic tribal thinking and the discovery of the individual and humanity. See Karl Jaspers, *Vom Ursprung und Ziel der Geschichte* (München: Piper, 1983).

Art offers a place to foster individual authenticity. Throughout the history of aesthetics the thought has been that art combines the private and concrete with universal intent.[55] However much the artist is preoccupied with his own feelings, thoughts, ideas, via the work he or she speaks to a public. Kierkegaard paid a great deal of attention to this question. He was aware that, to address his reader, he had to transform personal experiences, his "actuality" into "ideality," the sphere of concrete possibilities that are real for everyone.[56]

Civilization, Authenticity, Religion

Above I broke a lance for the arts as a private-public place where individuality can flourish. I also paid attention to the religious dimension of the plea for authenticity in Kierkegaard and Taylor. In the final part of my essay I would like to reflect shortly on Kierkegaard's oeuvre as part of the quest for authenticity, also in its religious dimension.

From the outset our author struggles with the problem of how to combine trying to be a Christian and being an author. Thomas Mann sums up the problem nicely in his *Doctor Faustus* where the Devil describes Kierkegaard as "the Christian in love with aesthetics." Kierkegaard's oeuvre is colored and informed by this problem. A remark of Johannes *de silentio* in a footnote in *Fear and Trembling* points at the direction in which Kierkegaard was looking for a solution: "Generally, if poetry becomes aware of the religious and of the inward-

---

55   Aristotle already claimed poetry to be more general and therefore more philosophical and of graver import than history, because poetry describes what might be, what such or such a kind of man will probably or necessarily do or say—though it fixes proper names to the characters. Thus poetry searches for the general and tries to express it. In the eighteenth century Immanuel Kant claims for the aesthetic judgment of taste a generality that seems to contradict the subjectivity he attributes to it (Immanuel Kant, *Critique of Judgement*, AA 211–212 / B 16–17). In the nineteenth century Hegel speaks, in relation to art, of the "concrete universal" (Georg W.F. Hegel, *Hegel's Aesthetics*, Vol. I, trans. T.M. Knox (Oxford: Clarendon, 1975), 51 f). And in the twentieth century Ludwig Wittgenstein wonders about the artist's competence to show us the value of contemplating everyday things that would otherwise not interest us because they are too much a personal matter (Ludwig Wittgenstein, *Culture and Value*, trans. Peter Winch (Oxford: Blackwell, 1980), 4). We can think here of the difference between photography as art and the pictures one takes during vacation.

56   Cf. Howard V. Hong & Edna H. Hong in their "Historical Introduction" to *Fear and Trembling & Repetition*.

ness of individuality, it will acquire far more meaningful tasks than those with which it busies itself now."[57]

In his writing, Kierkegaard tried to move "that single individual whom I with joy and gratitude call *my* reader"[58] towards an authenticity after reflection. Seeing the necessity of art in the quest for individual authenticity, he groped for a strategy and style to make his contribution. Kierkegaard experienced his new commitment as a religious calling. He became an author with a religious mission. In realizing this mission he found himself.

Pieter Vos hits the nail on the head: "... the problem of the self touches on the core of Kierkegaard's authorship as directed to existential meaning requiring personal involvement."[59] The individual's task is always to give a concrete expression to the universal 'being human.' "'Self' signifies ... the contradiction of positing the universal as the particular."[60] Kierkegaard was aware that his task as an artist is parallel to that of each individual. The interwovenness of the singular and the universal is part and parcel of how art works. It colors the way art contributes to individual authenticity. To address his reader, Kierkegaard had to transform personal experiences, his "actuality," into "ideality," the sphere of concrete possibilities that are real for everyone.[61]

The work is directed at "that single individual" and tries to bring that individual to herself. To this end the reader is every now and then personally addressed, as for instance in the first line of *Either/Or*: "It may at times have occurred to you, dear reader ..."[62] The use of "poetized personalities" contributes to making the work personal too. In notes for a lecture on communication Kierkegaard writes: "... I regard it as my service that by bringing poetized personalities who say *I* (my pseudonyms) into the center of life's actuality I have contributed, if possible, to familiarizing the contemporary age again to hearing an *I*, a personal *I* speak ..."[63]

---

57   Kierkegaard, *Fear and Trembling*, 91 note. Joachim Garff rightly calls this remark "programmatic" (Joachim Garff, *Søren Kierkegaard: A Biography* (Princeton: Princeton University Press, 2005), 252).

58   Kierkegaard dedicated every collection of upbuilding discourses to "that single individual whom I with joy and gratitude call *my* reader."

59   Vos, "Self."

60   Kierkegaard, *The Concept of Anxiety*, 78.

61   Cf. Howard V. Hong & Edna H. Hong in their "Historical Introduction" to *Fear and Trembling & Repetition*.

62   Søren A. Kierkegaard, *Either/Or, Part I, Kierkegaard's Writings*, Vol. III, trans. Howard V. Hong and Edna H. Hong (Princeton: Princeton University Press, 1987), 3.

63   Søren A. Kierkegaard, *Journals and Papers* (Bloomington: Indiana University Press, 1967–1979), Vol. I, no. 656.

The pseudonymous character of his writings gives Kierkegaard extra space to create a world for that single individual he may call his reader. While his theoretical constructions are oriented towards truth, there too we find the openness of a diversity of pseudonyms and genres. As reader one enters a world of values. In that world a great deal of deliberation takes place and one is invited, if not pressed, to take a stand. Kierkegaard's oeuvre is a private-public space where individuality can flourish and where a 'loving struggle' can take place mitigated by the mediation of an oeuvre that, like all great literature, lets one feel and live with the other.

In the case of Kierkegaard it is important that the work is not detached from reality. It is not given in isolation from tradition and society. Kierkegaard draws deeply on tradition. He refers to, quotes from, alludes to and varies on biblical stories and texts, folk-tales, world literature, national literature. Names mentioned include Job, Abraham, Antigone, Agnete, the woman who was a sinner, Richard III, Elvira, Prometheus, Thor, Loki, David, Don Quixote, Scheherazade, Valvorg, Zacharias, Bluebeard, Agamemnon, Iphigeneia, Jephthah, etc., etc.. In this way Kierkegaard evokes within the microcosm of his oeuvre a world of meanings and values. It is only within a tradition that one can criticize tradition. 'Kierkegaard' does not arise *ex nihilo*, apart from society and tradition. In his criticism of the established church Kierkegaard refers to original Christianity, as he understood it. Thus he develops his own voices, becomes who he is.

His extreme reflectiveness compels him to think about the exceptionality of the human individual *vis à vis* God. The oeuvre is the result of this reflectiveness. Romanticism and Hegelianism both fall short through their premature reconciliation of the contradictions of life in an attractive or grand story. When, at the end of his life, Kierkegaard reflects on his work as an author, he feels reconciled—not with his oeuvre as the product of an autonomous creator, but with his oeuvre as the result of "strange" influences and interactions as well as divine guidance.[64] The oeuvre is deployed to keep history and society open—in favor of the individual who, with no helpers in the ring, has to make his/her own decisions. Transcendence—God, "with whom everything is possible"—keeps the oeuvre itself open.

Conclusion

Kierkegaard has become part of our civilization, adored by some, despised by others, read, translated, edited, commented upon and written about by many.

---

64   Kierkegaard, *The Point of View*, 12.

But in his work is a restlessness: we cannot fall asleep there, as in *Fear and Trembling* the preacher takes a nap just before his sermon on Abraham and the congregation takes its nap during the sermon. In the service of civilization we have to keep our eyes and ears wide open. We can still profit from Kierkegaard's critique of church and civilization, given the threats to authenticity we are confronted with, ranging from consumerism and the empire of public opinion to the temptations of scientific and religious fundamentalisms.

However difficult it is to digest the obedience of Johannes *de silentio*'s Abraham, 'Abraham' helps us to stay self-critical in our reasonableness and civilization. I think this essential, if only to keep alive the ideal of love—the only real standard of civilization, according to the Dutch historian Johan Huizinga at the end of his life.[65] Thus Kierkegaard's work can be seen as a welcome contribution to our civilization in inviting the reader to a responsive and responsible authenticity.

Bibliography

Contemporary South African Art 1985–1995 (Cape Town: SANG, 1997).
Ferry, Luc, *Homo Aestheticus: The Invention of Taste in the Democratic Age*, trans. Robert de Loaiza (Chicago: Chicago University Press, 1993).
———. *Learning to Live: A User's Manual* (Edinburgh: Canongate, 2010).
Garff, Joachim, *Søren Kierkegaard: A Biography* (Princeton: Princeton University Press, 2005).
Guignon, Charles, *On Being Authentic* (London: Routledge, 2004).
Gunsteren, Herman van, "Het verdwijnende individu" (The Disappearing Individual), *De Volkskrant*, 2 January 2010.
Hegel, Georg W.F., *Hegel's Aesthetics*, Vol. I, trans. T.M. Knox (Oxford: Clarendon, 1975).
Heydebrand, Renate von, "Innerlichkeit," in Gerhard Ritter & Karlfried Gründer, *Historisches Wörterbuch der Philosophie*, Band 4 (Basel/Stuttgart: Schwabe & Co Verlag, 1976), 386–388.
Hoet, Jan, *In de wereld van Jan Hoet (In the World of Jan Hoet)* (Gent: Borgerhoff & Lamberigts, 2008).
Huizinga, Johan, *Geschonden wereld (Damaged World)* (Haarlem: Tjeenk Willink, 1945).
Jaspers, Karl, *Vom Ursprung und Ziel der Geschichte* (München: Piper, 1983).
Kant, Immanuel, *Critique of Judgement*, trans. James Creed Meredith (Oxford: Oxford University Press, 2007 (1952)).

---

65   Johan Huizinga, *Geschonden wereld (Damaged World)* (Haarlem: Tjeenk Willink, 1945), 181.

Kierkegaard, Søren A., *Either/Or, Part I, Kierkegaard's Writings*, Vol. III, trans. Howard V. Hong and Edna H. Hong (Princeton: Princeton University Press, 1987).

―――. *Fear and Trembling & Repetition, Kierkegaard's Writings*, Vol. VI, trans. Howard V. Hong & Edna H. Hong (Princeton: Princeton University Press, 1983).

―――. *Journals and Papers* (Bloomington: Indiana University Press, 1967–1979), Vol. I.

―――. *The Concept of Anxiety: A Simple Psychologically Orienting Deliberation on the Dogmatic Issue of Hereditary Sin, Kierkegaard's Writings*, Vol. VIII, trans. Reidar Thomte & Albert D. Anderson (Princeton: Princeton University Press, 1980).

―――. *The Point of View, Kierkegaard's Writings*, Vol. XXII, trans. Howard V. Hong & Edna H. Hong (Princeton: Princeton University Press, 1998.

―――. *The Sickness unto Death, Kierkegaard's Writings*, Vol. XIX, trans. Howard V. Hong & Edna H. Hong (Princeton: Princeton University Press, 1983).

Kundera, Milan, *Testaments Betrayed*, trans. Lida Asher (London: Faber and Faber, 1995).

Larmore, Charles, *The Practices of the Self*, trans. Sharon Bowman (Chicago: The University of Chicago Press, 2010).

Lasch, Christopher, *The Culture of Narcissism* (New York: Warner Books, 1979).

Lippitt, John, *Kierkegaard and 'Fear and Tembling'* (London: Routledge, 2003).

Peursen, C.A. van, *Strategie van de cultuur (The Strategy of Culture)* (Amsterdam: Elsevier, 1970).

Ricoeur, Paul, *Oneself as Another*, trans. Kathleen Blamey (Chicago: The University of Chicago Press, 1994).

Riessen, Renée D.N. van, *Verder gaan dan Socrates? Over onderwijs, bezieling en innerlijkheid bij Kierkegaard en Levinas (Going Further than Socrates? On Education, Animation and Interiority in Kierkegaard and Levinas)* (Leiden: Universiteit Leiden, 2012).

Stewart, Jon, *Kierkegaard's Relations to Hegel Reconsidered* (Cambridge: Cambridge University Press, 2003).

Stokkom, Bas van, "Sensitief kapitaal: De revisie van het authenticiteitsideaal" (Sensitive Capital: The Revision of the Ideal of Authenticity), *Krisis* 76:3 (1999), 65–77.

Taylor, Charles, *A Secular Age* (Cambridge: The Belknap Press of Cambridge University Press, 2007).

―――. *Sources of the Self* (Cambridge: Cambridge University Press, 1989).

Taylor, Mark C., *Journeys to Selfhood: Hegel and Kierkegaard* (Berkeley: University of California Press, 1980).

―――. "Sounds of Silence," in Robert L. Perkins (ed.), *Kierkegaard's* Fear and Trembling: *Critical Appraisals* (Tuscaloosa: University of Alabama Press, 1981), 165–188.

Trilling, Lionel, *Sincerity and Authenticity: The Charles Eliot Norton Lectures, 1969–1970* (Cambridge: Harvard University Press, 1972).

Verbrugge, Ad, *Tijd van onbehagen: Filosofische essays over een cultuur op drift (Time of Discontent: Philosophical Essays on a Culture Adrift)* (Amsterdam: SUN, 2004).

Vos, Pieter, "Self," in Steven Emmanuel, William McDonald & Jon Stewart (eds.), *Kierkegaard's Concepts* (Kierkegaard Research: Sources, Reception, and Resources, Vol. 15, Tome VI) (Aldershot: Ashgate, forthcoming).

Williams, Bernard, *Moral Luck* (Cambridge: Cambridge University Press, 1981).

———. *Truth and Truthfulness: An Essay in Genealogy* (Princeton: Princeton University Press, 2004).

Wittgenstein, Ludwig, *Culture and Value*, trans. Peter Winch (Oxford: Blackwell, 1980).

———. *Tractatus Logico-Philosophicus, Werkausgabe*, Band 1 (Frankfurt a.M: Suhrkamp, 1984), 7–86.

Zijderveld, Anton C., *The Abstract Society: A Cultural Analysis of Our Time* (New York: Doubleday & Company, 1971).

Zijlstra, Onno K., *Kierkegaard in discussie (Kierkegaard in Discussion)* (Budel: Damon, 2012).

Religious Transformations within Modernity
Religion and the Modern Discourse about Human Dignity and Human Rights

Wilhelm Gräb

Interpreters of religion are continuously updating secularization theory. One of the consequences of the secularization thesis is that religious belief has turned into one of many options for individuals today. Hence, for many prominent interpreters, religion is not a constitutive factor of modernity with normative influence on human development. For them, belief seems to be one possible mode for understanding life and gaining orientation in life. In their opinion belief is driven by an irrational obedience to a God who is understood as a heteronomous factor in the life of believers. Believing is merely one option that exists alongside the option of not believing. Not believing means understanding life as something immanent, without religious reference point but with the challenge of autonomy and rational self-determination.

There are various religions and options for belief as well as different ways of non-believing. This situation of ideological pluralism is even more confusing than secularization theory itself. For the secular differentiation between, on the one hand, 'the religious,' regardless of specific orientation, and 'the secular' on the other, remains attractive and is used by prominent interpreters of religion to support a theory of religion that frames religion as an orientation to a transcendent dimension and obedience to God's law. Dominant throughout is the secular opinion that sees the world within an immanent framework and proclaims the rationality of ethics and of civil society.

This view of the modern cultural situation may seem convincing, but it is based on a highly problematic differentiation between a religious and a secular sphere: between faith and rationality, between believers and non-believers, between God's law and civil law. The aim of this article is to demonstrate *why* this secular differentiation creates problems for understanding modernity and the transformed presence of religion.

The Secular Differentiation

Well-known diagnosticians of the 'Zeitgeist' repeatedly propose secular differentiation theories, which are positively received. This is clear when we consider Charles Taylor, the Canadian social philosopher, who proclaims the "Secular Age,"[1] or for example Jürgen Habermas, who refers to a post-secular society.[2] Or consider Hans Joas, who recently presented Christian belief as 'one' possible option for the interpretation of individual life in his book *Zukunftsmöglichkeiten des Christentums*.[3] In fact, these definitions of religion are put forward with very different intentions. Habermas, arguing for a post-secular late Modernity, tries to present religion as a possible resource for moral motivation. Taylor's secularization thesis describes secularization as a loss for modern society because people leave their religions and churches and as a religious-ideological individualism. In contrast, Joas wants to assure religious people that they should be afraid neither of other religious orientations nor of secular alternatives. He claims that the optional character of belief and membership liberated from strong social pressure adapts and reinforces personal faith certainty. He refers to a contingent certainty of faith, no longer based on absolute truths or communal plausibility supported by society's majority, but becoming stronger and more stable in personal confession.

Despite the different interests pursued by these prominent contemporary diagnosticians in their discourse about religion, they have one aspect in common. For all of them, modern societies place religion and religions in a precarious position. Modernity's modes of power, set free by enlightenment—modes such as the separation of religion and politics, inexorable progress in science and technology and the all-determining authority of economy—have driven religion into private realms and turned it into a matter of personal decision. Religions nevertheless do reach the public's attention; they become assigned in the secular differentiation as phenomena of an anti-modernist modernity. They can be understood as a protest movement against modernity's achievements which intends to reverse those achievements. At the same time, they are accused of losing the increased freedom that modernity achieved against authoritative social formations. In these prominent contemporary diagnoses religion is in no way a normative factor, constitutive either of modernity or of further human development.

Non-believing became the most popular option in contemporary society for the contemporary diagnosticians mentioned above. This should not merely be an observation of sociological facts. It is combined with the proposal that there

---

1   Charles Taylor, *A Secular Age* (Cambridge: Harvard University Press, 2007).
2   Jürgen Habermas, *Nachmetaphysisches Denken II: Aufsätze und Repliken* (Berlin: Suhrkamp, 2012).
3   Hans Joas, *Glaube als Option: Die Zukunftsmöglichkeiten des Christentums* (Freiburg i. Br.: Herder, 2012).

are good reasons for not believing. Living without religion turns into a life option which supposedly has entirely reasonable grounds and motives. In this way, prominent contemporary diagnosticians like Taylor, Habermas and Joas continue to perpetuate the secularization thesis, even if post-secularism deals with optionalization of belief and new forms of religion. They understand secularization not merely as the church's social loss of power and the separation of politics and religion, but precisely as the widespread decline of church and religion, which they equate with the loss of religious belief in society. The evidence for this kind of secularization thesis is underlined by sociological data, which show a decline in regular church attendance and church membership. But at the same time it becomes clear, as Charles Taylor in particular notes, that modern pluralism and modernism throw up a variety of new forms of the religious and that in no way is it only the strongly institutionalized religions that provide space for religious experiences and communication. These new forms of lived religion that are not linked to a certain church or denomination are often accused of revering an asocial individualism as well as a superficial culture of authenticity. In a rough and dismissive manner, Charles Taylor sets "the new forms of the religious"[4] against the old Catholic belief that is bound to the church. Alongside the purported secular decline in religion, the only categories left for interpreting what is now leading to new forms of religious organization are aesthetic expressionism and again the emphasis on individual subjectivity, which, in a framework like Taylor's, has lost sight of serious decisions concerning religious questions and the divine demand for an absolute.

Hence, the proclamation of a secular age and the optionalization of belief legitimize each other. They degrade religious belief into a particular concern, something that is only relevant for people who practice religion actively. In this way they degrade dynamic forms of belief that are sociologically difficult to identify.

In this essay, I give a different view on religious development in modernity, a view that is opposed to the discourse of the optionalization of belief and the secularization of society.[5] With the help of the human rights discourse I want

---

4   Cf. Charles Taylor, *Varieties of Religion Today: William James Revisited* (Institute for Human Sciences Vienna Lecture) (Cambridge: Harvard University Press, 2003).

5   Cf. Wilhelm Gräb & Lars Charbonnier (eds.), *Secularization Theories, Religious Identity and Practical Theology: Developing International Practical Theology for the 21st century*, International Academy of Practical Theology Berlin 2007 (Wien/Berlin: Lit, 2009); Wilhelm Gräb, "The Transformation of Religious Culture within Modern Societies: From Secularization to Postsecularism," in Arie L. Molendijk, Justin Beaumont & Christoph Jedan, (eds.), *Exploring the Postsecular: The Religious, the Political and the Urban* (Leiden/Boston: Brill, 2010), 113–131; Wilhelm Gräb, "Each One Is a Particular Case: Aspects of the

to show that secular differentiation cannot be maintained anymore. Modernity neither leads to nor has it caused a decline in religion. On the contrary, modernity's modes of power like the separation of religion and politics, continuous development in science and technology and the all-determining authority of media and economy are at the same time religious forces. To see this, one must understand religion in the context of modernity and take into consideration religion's transformation in modernity. If one looks closely at these new forms of religion, one can recognize religion's presence and liveliness and its necessity in human culture as a normative power to protect humanity's humanness. Human rights discourse, for me, seems to be one of these 'new faces' of religion.

In contemporary societies it seems totally inappropriate to talk about a "Secular Age." Such talk is not due to the Enlightenment. The view that modernity has developed into a secular alternative to traditional belief ignores the fact that religion develops new modes of power in this allegedly secular modernity that does not trust in belief anymore. Tendencies to withdraw and signs of deterioration are most observable in Christian churches, in particular in Roman Catholicism. The proclamation of a secular age equates religion with church and its rules of faith. Furthermore, talk about post-secular circumstances ascribes to religion only a limited impact in a still (more fundamentally) secularizing society. However, belief deserves acknowledgement from secular people because it should be understood as something that has tremendous motivational potential for life practice, something the secular citizen is often thought to lack. At the same time, secular people are supposed to be assured that religious speech, for example speech of God's creation, is only relevant if religious people succeed in explaining their religious belief rationally. The fact remains: belief is only a matter for believers. Secular people cannot be expected to feel that belief might concern them as well. Moreover, secular people have reason on their side, even if the thesis of post-secularization shows that there is awareness of the fact that reason might be limited as well.

Today's spokespersons in questions concerning the interpretation of religion perpetuate the thesis of secularization, even if they claim the contrary. For them, belief is not a topic for all people. It is a topic for religious, for believing people. It is for people belonging, for whatever reason, to a church or to one of the institutionalized, large or small, old or young, religious denominations. No attention is paid to the fact that the European Enlightenment developed a way of thinking about religion which located religion in the concrete human

---

Transformation of Christianity in Global Modernity," in Tadeusz Buksinski (ed.), *Religions in the Public Spheres* (Frankfurt a. M./ Berlin etc.: Peter Lang, 2011), 35–50.

being and his implicit claim to human dignity. Human rights are founded on the basis of this inalienable human dignity. In a way, they are based on the person's sacralization and on the belief in the divinity of each single individual. In the spirit of the Enlightenment this belief belongs to each single person.

Religious thinkers of the Enlightenment thus found a completely new way of thinking about the question of religion's universality, and their attention to inalienable human dignity illustrates the point. These thinkers took a position on religion and church from which they placed religion and church in a critical process of transformation, proclaiming the universally human character of religion in its historical forms of realization. Without a doubt, they often understood Christianity as the absolute religion, claiming the highest value for it. They believed that religion found its fullest realization in Christianity. Today we look back critically at this conclusion. However, that should in no way imply that the Enlightenment's transformation of the study of religion writ large made no important contributions. In particular human rights discourse is one such contribution. This discourse has had an enormous impact on the self-understanding of religions. But in fact, this impact should be examined carefully in each of the different religions, for one finds that it happens in very different and even contradictory ways. I myself am only able to discuss it with regard to Christianity. It is important to say right at the beginning that churches and formal church theology denied much of the Enlightenment's analysis of religion and refused to acknowledge human rights for a long time. In regard to Christianity it will furthermore be important to pay attention to those transformations which triggered the Enlightenment's human rights thinking and which keep it dynamically going to this day. These preconditions make secularization theory untenable and show rather a religion of humanity through the historical persistence and ongoing transformation of empirical religions.

To show that the historical movement towards a religion of humanity has not passed by concrete religions and churches but passes through them, I want to present the example of South Africa and its human rights discourse with reference to the continuing debate on the history of apartheid.

A South African Example

Desmond Tutu's book *God is not a Christian* is a collection of sermons, speeches and statements from the former Anglican bishop of Cape Town.[6] "God is clearly not a Christian. His concern is for all his children," insisted Tutu in a

---

6   Desmond Mpilo Tutu, *God Is Not a Christian*, ed. John Allen (New York: Harper One, 2012).

sermon in the church of St. Martin-in-the-Fields near Trafalgar Square in London, after the fall of the Berlin Wall and at the end of apartheid in South Africa.[7]

For Tutu, there is no conflict between human rights' universal validity and the obligation of Christians to speak up for human rights out of their Christian belief. This is not because Christianity invented human rights and their worldwide distribution would be more successful under the Christian banner. Such a cultural-imperialist interpretation of the relationship between human rights and Christianity was far from what Tutu had in mind. It was rather his deep concern to win all religions for a universal enforcement of human rights in all his sermons and speeches, which he has delivered all over the globe since the 1980s.

Tutu confesses his Christian faith in strong terms. He often underlines that it is essential to take his own faith seriously. But taking his own religion seriously does not mean devaluing other religions or refusing the idea of a natural universal religion that is inherent in nature of human beings from the beginning. Religions are different, the Gods in whom they believe are different. Nevertheless they have something in common: they reveal a transcendent element in humanity.

God is not a Christian. "God is clearly not a Christian. His concern is for all his children." Christians do not have an exclusive relationship with God, and God has no exclusive relationship with Christians. He is the God of all human beings and they have their different relations to him. This also is important to Tutu: religions are not identical, "the" God can be understood in many different ways. As God is never without the individual relation, "we must hold to our particular and peculiar beliefs tenaciously."[8] Tutu combines these confessions into a religious individuality, holding that God generally can only be thought and believed in the different relationships people have with him. God only is God in the plurality of the individual religious perspectives on him. For relations among religions, Tutu stresses, this means that "we must be ready to learn from another, not claiming that we alone possess all truth and that somehow we have a corner on God."[9]

By acting in this way we will discover many things we have in common. What we actually have in common depends on what we are searching for. For Tutu the direction is clear. All religions he mentions have a transcendent referent that is compassionate and concerned; all see human beings as "creatures of

---

7   Tutu, *God Is Not a Christian*, 12.
8   Tutu, *God Is Not a Christian*, 6.
9   Tutu, *God Is Not a Christian*, 6.

this supreme, supra-mundane reality, with a high destiny that hopes for an everlasting life lived in close association with the divine."[10] This distinction of human beings as "creatures" of a higher holy reality and their being this in "close association with the divine" is what Tutu hopes to find as the common denominator of the different religions. Each human being is holy, a taboo for everyone who wants to hurt him.

Tutu is delighted that he finds this holiness of human beings in the Christian tradition as well. "Surely, it is good to know that God (in the Christian tradition) created us all (not just Christians) in his image, thus investing us all with infinite worth."[11] It is equally important for Tutu to emphasize that, like Christianity, other religious traditions regard human beings with holiness as well:

> Surely we can rejoice that the eternal word, the Logos of God, enlightens everyone—not just Christians, but everyone who comes into the world; that what we call the Spirit of God is not a Christian preserve, for the Spirit of God existed long before there were Christians, inspiring and nurturing women and men in the ways of holiness, bringing them to fruition, bringing them to fruition what was best in all. We do scant justice and honor to our God if we want, for instance, to deny that Mahatma Gandhi was a truly great soul, a holy man who walks closely with God. Our God would be too small if he was not also the God of Gandhi.[12]

Christianity is neither allowed to claim to be the religion that discovered the holiness of human beings (which would be a historical mistake in any case) nor is it allowed to claim that Christianity alone is the best and only condition for promoting human holiness. Access to the sanctity of human beings and work towards the preservation of this sanctity can be found in other religious convictions as well.

To clarify that he recognizes motifs of a universal religion of humanity in his own Christian belief, Tutu now avoids consciously the usage of Christian and uniquely biblical language while speaking about religion. This can be seen in particular when he describes his participation in the Truth and Reconciliation Commission. The Truth and Reconciliation Commission was actually founded after the end of apartheid as a compromise between those who argued for a general amnesty and those who advocated legal proceedings, similar to the

---

10   Tutu, *God Is Not a Christian*, 7.
11   Tutu, *God Is Not a Christian*, 7.
12   Tutu, *God Is Not a Christian*, 7.

Nuremberg trials, in which the offenders would be brought before court to get their just punishment. In contrast to this, Tutu recommended a concept not of retributive but of restorative justice. This was also the proposal which the parliament, after detailed consultations between the old and the new government, agreed on. The victims should have the opportunity to tell their stories and the offenders should have the possibility to admit their guilt. This path of restorative justice symbolized and expressed Tutu's Christian belief in reconciliation. In the divine justification of the sinner and the human force for reconciliation that results from the belief in God's righteousness, he saw a decisive contribution of the Christian religion to South Africa's democratic reconstruction. Nevertheless, Tutu avoids the use of language that is influenced by Christian belief. He often speaks about an outer perspective and about the Christian belief as one religious worldview among others.

It is obvious that Tutu tries to point out that religion—and thus the relation of a human to something transcendent—are expressed in various ways within different religions. Each religion has its own specific way of expressing this relation. Religions even respond to secular people and people who have no specific relation to any religion at all.

Religion is something that belongs to the human being. This can be seen in the way that religion resists all determining associations of individual human beings with their particular circumstances. Religion provocatively insists that one has dignity simply because one is a human being, regardless of one's characteristics or affiliations, independent of one's deeds or misdeeds. Religion shifts one's being into an unconditional horizon. One's right to exist derives from conditions that are independent of oneself. A human being is not able to and does not have to earn this right. One's right to exist is derived from something that is beyond oneself, it derives from God. In Christian discourse this means that a person is God's creature, his beloved child, and a justified sinner. But Tutu speaks only rarely and cautiously in this biblical language. Tutu counts on a transversal religious reason to which all humans with good will respond. This transversal religious reason is the truly religious matter in all religions: that is, religion sees the individual human being from the perspective of a self-transcended humanity founded in the Unconditional. Religion is a transcendent determination of human existence that then, in a surprising twist, revokes itself and gives humanity back to itself.

Tutu used such common religious language, compelling even for secular people, in referring to the "essential humanity of the perpetrator of even the most gruesome atrocity"[13] in his plea for a path of reconciliation. He could

---

13   Tutu, *God Is Not a Christian*, 42.

have spoken about the public-political force of Christian belief in reconciliation. But instead he alludes to "essential humanity," including that of "the perpetrator." He mentions the fact that no one should deny the human dignity of a person, however heinous his deed. This is a reformulation of a religious interpretation of human rights discourse from Tutu's Christian orientation. Tutu emphasizes that the evidence of what religion generally contributes to human life and society shows religion to be indispensable in the realization of humanity.

In this way the path of restorative justice should become passable for people who come from other non-Christian, religious worldviews too. Tutu specifically points to the African worldview of *Ubuntu*. *Ubuntu* is a Xhosa word that expresses the essential individual's affiliation to a community. *Ubuntu* also stands for the transcending of each individual human being in a larger, infinitely extending whole. For the community of *Ubuntu* that qualifies the being of an individual is not only the visible tribal community but also the chain that forms links to the ancestors. The African worldview of *Ubuntu*, together with the biblical idea that human beings are made in God's image and the Christian understanding of the sinner's unconditional justification, represents for Tutu an integral and universal religion of human rights. At the same time it is important for him to point out that, on the one hand, these three ideas are indispensable elements in the construction of this universal religion of human rights while, on the other hand, religion cannot be identified with them.[14]

Tutu is not interested in a historical independence of different religious traditions and worldviews. He is rather interested in "religion" as the plurality of religions, i.e. in an aspect that is undeniable in human beings. "Don't we have to be reminded too that the faith to which we belong is far more often a matter of the accidents of history and geography than personal choice?"[15] This is an allusion to Rousseau, who also held that the religion we belong to is a question of geography. But it is also a suggestion that religious belief belongs to the human condition. Tutu goes on to advance ideas of natural law and natural religion by referring to Paul's argument of a natural theology and to Kant and the Enlightenment.

> Everyone of God's human creatures has the capacity to know something about God from the evidence God leaves in his handiworks (Rom. 1:18–20); this is the basis for natural theology and natural law. Immanuel Kant spoke about categorical imperative. All human creatures have a sense

---

14   Tutu, *God Is Not a Christian*, 21–24.
15   Tutu, *God Is Not a Christian*, 16.

that some things ought to be done just as others not to be done. This is a universal phenomenon—what varies is the content of natural law. ... In his speech before the Areopagus, Paul speaks about how God created all human beings from one stock and given everyone the urge, the hunger, for divine things so that all will seek after God and perhaps find him, adding that God is not far from us since all (not just Christians) live and move and have their being in him (Act. 17: 22–31). Talking to pagans, Paul declares that all are God's offspring.[16]

The "universal phenomenon" is the phenomenon of a religious consciousness that was given initially to the human being. This religious consciousness becomes concrete in an openness to transcendence: searching for and questioning something that is beyond oneself. The particular religions are built on this natural religion. But they also presuppose this natural religion as the universal resonance chamber that outlives their own history. Natural religion exists in the particular religions. But not exclusively; pointing out this fact is very important for me. There is one universal religion in all concrete religions that acts through and beyond them, a religion which we should by all means call the religion of human rights.

Although Tutu has not articulated it in such an explicit way, this view is in my opinion implied by his argumentation in the way he describes the particular, concrete religions—and not only Christianity—by asking about their contribution to the enforcement of human rights. In doing this he tries to see the best in each of them as something that serves the humanity of human beings.

> We must not make the mistake of judging other faiths by their least attractive features and adherents: It is possible to demolish the case for Christianity by, for instance, quoting the Crusades, or the atrocities of the Holocaust, or the excess of apartheid. But we know that that would be unfair in the extreme, since we claim them to be aberrations, distortions and deviations. What about Francis of Assisi, Mother Teresa, Albert Schweitzer, and all the wonderful and beautiful people and things that belong to Christianity? We should want to deal with other faiths and their best and highest, as they define themselves, and not shoot down the caricatures that we want to put up.[17]

---

16   Tutu, *God Is Not a Christian*, 10.
17   Tutu, *God Is Not a Christian*, 16.

The Universal Declaration of Human Rights as a Confessional Basis of a Universal Religion

Human rights were initially formulated in the political revolutions of the 18th century. They can be traced back to the American Declaration of Independence as well as to the French Revolution. Finally they were laid down in international law in the UN Charter with The Universal Declaration of Human Rights. Let us take a brief look at the three preambles to those three declarations of human rights: none of the three contains any reference to a particular, concrete religion, not even to Christianity. There can be no talk of any explicit theological basis of human rights. Nevertheless one has to admit that religion is a topic in those declarations. Indeed, a confessional basis explicitly characterizes the American and French Declaration of Human Rights and this religious character was maintained in the UN Charter of 1948. The American Declaration of Independence from 1776 insists that "all men are created equal, that they are endowed by their Creator with certain inalienable Rights" and the French National Assembly explicitly claims that it "recognizes and declares" human and civil rights "in the presence and under the auspices of the Supreme Being." In The Universal Declaration of Human Rights from 1948 the explicit reference to God is absent. That human beings have inalienable rights is no longer directly connected to the authority and will of a God anymore. Instead there is talk about an "inherent dignity" which belongs to every human being. Because it belongs to "all members of the human family," all of them have "equal and inalienable rights."[18] It is obvious that talk of the "inherent dignity," which is first found in The Universal Declaration of Human Rights from 1948, is functionally equivalent to the reference to God from the Declaration of Human Rights of the 18th century.[19]

The fact that nations with different cultural and religious backgrounds would sign the Declaration of Human Rights from 1948 makes it easier to understand the omission of any reference to God. But the American and French human rights declarations already claimed a universal approach. Both combined this universal approach with a confessional base: because it is God who makes all human beings, no matter what their differences, as beings standing under God, the Supreme Being and their Creator, human beings should have equal rights. This religious meaning also becomes obvious in talk of "inherent

---

18   Cf. http://www.ohchr.org/EN/UDHR/Documents/UDHR_Translations/eng.pdf.
19   Cf. The Declaration of Independence, July 4, 1776: http://www.archives.gov/exhibits/charters/declaration_transcript.html; The French Declaration of the Rights of Man and the Citizen, August, 1789: http://www.historyguide.org/intellect/declaration.html.

dignity." The language of inherent dignity places human rights under conditions that are irrevocably given to every human being and which cannot be the subject of negotiation in the specific communities to which human beings belong. Human dignity belongs to every human being in an unconditional way. This is precisely what it means to see someone through the eyes of faith. At the end of the 18th century this faith could be easily pronounced faith in God, the Creator. In the UN Charter the confessional foundation of the universal approach of human rights had to change, if only semantically. Only with such a change could it be possible for so many different cultural and religious traditions to accept and adopt the Declaration.

This cultural transformation and adaptation is in fact what happened in the beginning and merged in the process of placing the Declaration of Human Rights in different cultural and religious traditions. The process is far from completed and, with regard to religion, is often controversially discussed because the role of religion in human rights discourse often becomes closely related to specific religions. And then, of course, one is often quickly involved in a very ambivalent history. It must be confessed that Christian churches accepted the idea of human rights quite late and even today are often accused of failing to make a strong stand for human rights. Religions have their own legal orders that can lead to conflicts with national law and even with human rights, especially in cases where human rights have entered into national legal orders. But that religion is necessary for the realization of humanity, that religion constitutively belongs to human beings: this is something that was registered in the declarations of human rights from their beginning and ultimately makes The Declaration of Human Rights from 1948 the confessional base of a universal religion.

Although there were already attempts during the French Revolution to found a practice of a new humanitarian Christianity on the basis of the Declaration of Independence, this universal approach contrasts with the particularized approach in specific religions, churches, and denominations. Consider the theophilanthropists, a humanistic religious group that held its services from 1794 to 1810 in France. Often these services took place in Catholic churches which were partly used for theophilanthropic and partly for Catholic services. One of these churches was Saint-Merri in the center of Paris. The services of the theophilanthropists were well attended but were then prohibited by Napoleon.

In our days it is very rarely the case that religions, let alone states and their legal apparatuses, can prohibit such free human-rights-based religious organizations or even desire to. Rather we are seeing the universal norms of human rights appear in traditional religious forms and cultures all over the world.

However, the negotiation of a universal religion of humanity in particularized forms of concrete religious traditions proves challenging. Wherever the idea of human rights enters, these rights change the constituted religions. What is more, the idea of human rights itself can become a religious movement or organization. It articulates itself as it is in reality: a belief in the human being, in the transcendent divine determination of the human, in an inventive creativity and hence in man's inviolable dignity.

How traditional religious cultures transformed under the impact of the human rights campaign can well be seen in the fact that the theology of the second part of the 20th century understood human dignity as an expression, if not almost as a consequence, of man's likeness to God. This shows how, for theology, the human-religious understanding of human dignity was enriched by the religion of human rights.

Like all other particular human living conditions, the particular, concrete religions are by no means rendered less important in the universal approach of human rights. The concrete religions face the challenge and possibility of accentuating their particularity in a way that connects to a common religious dimension. This can take place through re-examination of the practices and self-understandings of religious traditions. I am talking about a synchronization of people's concrete religious practices with humanity's actual, existential condition. The religions ought to further the universal humanity religion of human rights by means of their historical, ritual and ideological resources. People long to feel at home in the religion into which they are born and grow in the way that human beings always feel at home in the universal transcendence of their humanity.

The world is growing more and more together. We call this phenomenon globalization. Globalization is driven by information technologies and high-speed economy. But more than a billion people *do not* benefit from this technological and economical globalization. They do not have access to internet. They do not get a chance to participate in the wealth of their countries and regions. Their human rights to life, freedom, self-development and security are refused. Particular differences in sex and race, skin color and language, religion and nation place hard limits on the global realization of human rights. Especially the concrete religions are strict border guards against the enforcement of equal rights to freedom, justice and security for all human beings. They often prevent people from "act[ing] towards one another in a spirit of brotherhood."[20] There is no other time during the week in which the racial segregation can be

---

20   UN Declaration of Human Rights, Art. 1, http://www.ohchr.org/EN/UDHR/Documents/UDHR_Translations/eng.pdf.

felt so strongly as every Sunday morning between nine and eleven o'clock, while the white, the black, the colored and the Indian communities hold their services, each alone, apart from the others.

On the Way to a Universal Religion of Human Rights

The Declaration of Human Rights did not emerge from any concrete religion, not even from Christianity. Its starting point was the experience of pain and harm, the experience of brutal non-recognition, "barbarous acts,"[21] as it is called in the UN Charter's preamble from 1948. The screams of those deprived of their right to live by the totalitarian regimes of National Socialism and Stalinism, of those tormented, tortured, and killed because of racial, national, political or religious reasons or because of their sexuality, can still be heard in the declaration. To this day it is the experience of violations of human rights that underlies the appeal to maintain and enforce them. Yet, this is only possible because they have a global status as a universal valid norm under international law and have been turned into enforceable rights in the constitutions of many countries. If a blatant violation becomes public anywhere in the world, an appeal to human rights will be made immediately. Recent examples include the brutal rape and murder of young Indian women and the restrictions on same-sex relationships in Russia, to name only two. Such violations clearly indicate that human rights must prevail over (and at times be protected from) cultural traditions and the symbolic systems of religions—both of which are often associated with the political powers that use them for their needs.

For this reason the defense and enforcement of human rights is often suspected of a cultural-imperialist bias. When, in addition, wars are declared under the pretext that they are in support of human rights, although in reality the main interest is rights to oil production, these suspicions are clearly confirmed. Hence, human rights are often understood as a continuation of Western colonialism. Nevertheless, it must be said that only through an intervention, legitimized by international law, in the affairs of a state that either threatens the security of its citizens or is not able to ensure it, is it possible to prevent further violations (as for example currently in Mali).

The question is whether international interventions for the enforcement of human rights, especially if they create a military conflict that causes additional harm, have cultural-imperialist features, even if the intention was good. This

---

[21] UN Declaration of Human Rights, Preamble, http://www.ohchr.org/EN/UDHR/Documents/UDHR_Translations/eng.pdf.

question actually raises a difficult issue. For the intention behind these interventions to enforce human rights is their claim to a universal normativity and thus ultimately to a universal religion of the human. The idea of human rights is not something invented behind a desk. They exist in a concrete manner in the heads and hearts of numerous people, who stand up for them as they constitute their value orientation and religious belief.

Thus, it must be generally accepted that on the one hand human rights require self-determined values and on the other they support certain values that are not equally appreciated and practiced in all cultures and religions around the world. Alongside this universal religion of human rights, cultural and also religious differences will indeed continue to exist. Religious ties and affiliations supply these values with a strong potential of motivation for daily living. All religious cultures are different in what they consider law and rights to be and in how they appreciate individual choice with regard to sexual orientation and choice of partner, profession and residence. You can find many different cultural opinions about the relation between the individual and community, about the idea of physical integrity, about who takes precedence in the relation of individual and community and about the hierarchy of individual and community (e.g. family, clan, and nation). They might all be different, but at the same time they all have a religious foundation. Likewise, you will find different but always religiously founded opinions about the idea of equality of men and women, about religious tolerance or about the value of democratic participation.

The UN commission already knew, in the constituting phase of The Universal Declaration of Human Rights, that there is a high tension between a universal normativity of human rights and the pluralism of all the different religious cultures. In his book on the genealogy of human rights Hans Joas offers a good insight into the work of the UN commission, in which delegates from 18 nations participated.[22] He especially points to two delegates, namely Charles Malik, the Lebanese representative, and Peng-Chun Chang, the Chinese representative. Charles Malik, speaker for the Arab world, was an orthodox Christian whereas, according to Joas, Pen-Chun Chang often referred to his Confucian background during the drafting process of the Declaration. Yet Pen-Chun Chang was also the person who warned on the one hand against a foundation

---

22 Hans Joas, *Die Sakralität der Person: Eine neue Genealogie der Menschenrechte* (Berlin: Suhrkamp, 2012), 251–281, esp. 273 f. English translation: *The Sacredness of the Person: A New Genealogy of Human Rights* (George Town: George Town University Press, 2013). See more at: http://press.georgetown.edu/book/georgetown/sacredness-person#sthash.tDnPcFHh.dpuf.

for the human rights that is limited to reason and on the other against a special emphasis on one single religious tradition. He was interested in a synthesis of all the different religious traditions of vindication into one common value system. This is consistent with the fact that there is no reference to a universal *ratio* of humans but to a universal "faith"[23] in a human religious conviction in the preamble to the documents of the constitution: "the faith in fundamental human rights, in the dignity and worth of the human person."[24] It proclaims the human rights movement to be a religious movement, a movement that is based on a faith, faith in the possibility of creating conditions around the world that gives every human being access to certain rights, as Hanna Arendt interpreted the fundamental claim of The Declaration of Human Rights.

The faith that is apparent in the United Nations' founding documents as well as in their declaration of human rights was a result of the work of people coming from different cultures, religions and parts of the world. What becomes evident is that this faith never would have gained such popularity if it was not to a large extent compatible with the concrete, positive religious faith that is practiced in the different religions and cultures in so many different ways. Still, what remains important is the question who will take charge when the concrete religions and cultural traditions merge into one universal religion of human rights. Is it the normative universality of human rights with the attempt to find recognition as official rights? Or will it be the particular religious traditions that only want to assign human rights to their own believers, thinking that in this way the rights will be maintained according to their own norms of faith?[25]

Conclusions

There is no doubt that the validity of universal human rights has to be transmitted in accordance with the self-understanding of particular and regional religious cultures. To a certain extent, human rights have to incarnate in the

---

23   UN Declaration of Human Rights, Preamble.
24   UN Declaration of Human Rights, Preamble.
25   The person, who was responsible for the drafting of the United Nations Charter's preamble, was Jan Smuts. He wrote the impressive words about "the faith in fundamental human rights, in the dignity and worth of the human person" that I just quoted (Preamble, UN Declaration of Human Rights). Smuts was head of the South African government several times in the 1930s and the early 1940s, although he was not directly responsible for the policy of racial apartheid, enacted in 1948, the same year The Declaration of Human Rights was enacted.

minds and hearts of people during their acquisition process in different cultures and religions. Therefore, human rights discourse talks about a necessary cultural synthesis and value generalization. But in this process of synthesis and generalization it has to be ensured that human rights remain intact and inviolable and that states and societies follow their requirements. Cultural synthesis and value generalization will only be of any help if they support the enforcement of human rights within historical religions, if the universal religion of human rights finds recognition in the particular religions and in the cultures that are merged with them. This will have practical consequences for religious as well as for judicial practice in the countries in which human rights claim validity.

First of all this means that religious cultures have to legitimize themselves to human rights and not vice versa. Religions, their practices and legal interpretations have to prove themselves to be compatible with human rights. Secondly, this means that one has to insist on the validity of human rights, in particular on the right to self-determination, even if they are opposed to religious ideas of morality. If the human right for self-determination, for justice and security is valid in a state, this right has to be valid for all people, independently of their religious denomination or ethnicity, even if this right might contradict the norms of a religious community, for instance regarding freedom of sexual orientation.

Therefore, the universal religion of human rights can hardly be enforced without conflicts with religious and political powers. Hence, this religion will be all the more vigorous the more states incorporate human rights into their constitutions and the more people are committed to human rights. People may come from concrete religions, they may stay in contact with them or just pass them by, but they are all connected in a worldwide community with the same spirit of the universal religion of human rights. But it is also clear that faith in the holiness of every human being, confessed by the universal religion of human rights, will gradually change the religions. It is a faith in the holiness of the human being—not of a human being formed and acting in such and such a way, but of the human being just the way he or she already exists. This faith alone will change the world. It changes the world through the way that love, mercy and forgiveness are practiced, that there will be help where people are victimized by violence and state terror, where hungry people suffer from starvation and are forced to flee their home countries.

Indeed, many things need to be done along these lines. Without the incorporation of human rights into the constitutions of states and the enforcement of their validity under international law, much less would have been achieved in the pursuit of a more human world. Yet, all this effort is based on the faith in the holiness of the human being. It is this faith, in the end, that encourages people to fight for adherence to and enforcement of human rights, whether they are members of a religious community or not.

However, it should be highlighted that people with a religious background, like Desmond Tutu, do fight for human rights worldwide, that religious moral values lead to an active cooperation in NGOs and that churches and parishes offer room and financial help to human right groups.

Bibliography

Gräb, Wilhelm, "Each One Is a Particular Case: Aspects of the Transformation of Christianity in Global Modernity," in Tadeusz Buksinski (ed.), *Religions in the Public Spheres* (Frankfurt a. M./ Berlin etc.: Peter Lang, 2011), 35–50.

Gräb, Wilhelm, "The Transformation of Religious Culture within Modern Societies: From Secularization to Postsecularism," in Arie L. Molendijk, Justin Beaumont & Christoph Jedan, (eds.), *Exploring the Postsecular: The Religious, the Political and the Urban* (Leiden/ Boston: Brill, 2010), 113–131.

Gräb, Wilhelm & Lars Charbonnier (eds.), *Secularization Theories, Religious Identity and Practical Theology: Developing International Practical Theology for the 21st century*, International Academy of Practical Theology Berlin 2007 (Wien/Berlin: Lit, 2009).

Habermas, Jürgen, *Nachmetaphysisches Denken II: Aufsätze und Repliken* (Berlin: Suhrkamp, 2012).

Joas, Hans, *Die Sakralität der Person: Eine neue Genealogie der Menschenrechte* (Berlin: Suhrkamp, 2012).

———. *Glaube als Option: Die Zukunftsmöglichkeiten des Christentums* (Freiburg i. Br.: Herder, 2012).

———. *The Sacredness of the Person: A New Genealogy of Human Rights* (George Town: George Town University Press, 2013).

Taylor, Charles, *A Secular Age* (Cambridge: Harvard University Press, 2007).

———. *Varieties of Religion Today: William James Revisited* (Institute for Human Sciences Vienna Lecture) (Cambridge: Harvard University Press, 2003).

Tutu, Desmond Mpilo, *God Is Not a Christian*, ed. John Allen (New York: Harper One, 2012).

List of Contributors

Alfons Brüning
received his PhD at Berlin Free University. Between 2005 and 2007 he was Assistant Professor at the Theological Faculty of Münster University (Germany). In 2007 he became Lecturer of Christianity in Eastern Europe at the Institute of Eastern Christian Studies at Radboud University Nijmegen (the Netherlands). Since 2012 he is Professor of Orthodoxy, Peace Studies, Human Rights at VU University Amsterdam and the Protestant Theological University (Amsterdam/Groningen). His recent publications include *Orthodox Christianity and Human Rights* (co-editor) (Leuven 2012); "Different Humans and Different Rights? On Human Dignity from Western and Eastern Orthodox Perspectives," *Studies in Interreligious Dialogue* (2013).

Jaeseung Cha
holds a PhD from VU University Amsterdam. He is Associate Professor at New Brunswick Theological Seminary in New Jersey. His publications include *Doctrine of the Atonement in Seven Theologians: The Cross as Such and the Cross Overflowing* (Seoul 2014); "A Dialog between Patristic Christology and the Yin-Yang Perspective on the Relationship of Christ with his Person," *Journal of Reformed Theology* (2013); "The Cross: Love Revealed by Death" in *How to Preach Love* (Seoul 2013); *The Mystery and Paradox of the Cross: Jesus' Proclamation of the Crucifixion in his Five Statements* (Seoul 2013).

Jonathan Chaplin
received his PhD from the University of London. He is Director of the Kirby Laing Institute for Christian Ethics, Cambridge. His publications include *Herman Dooyeweerd: Christian Philosopher of State and Civil Society* (Notre Dame 2011); *Multiculturalism: A Christian Retrieval* (Theos 2011); *God and Global Order* (co-editor) (Baylor 2010) and *Living Lightly, Living Faithfully: Religious Faiths and the Future of Sustainability* (co-editor) (KLICE/Faraday Institute 2013). His recent articles include "Law, Religion and Public Reasoning," *Oxford Journal of Law and Religion* (2012) and "Subsidiarity and Social Pluralism" in Michelle Evans & Augusto Zimmermann (eds.), *Global Perspectives on Subsidiarity* (2014).

Wilhelm Gräb
received his PhD in Göttingen (Germany), was minister of the Lutheran Church and Professor of Practical Theology at Ruhr-Universität Bochum.

Since 1999 he is Professor of Practical Theology at Humboldt-Universität Berlin and since 2011 Extraordinary Professor at the Theological Faculty of the University of Stellenbosch (SA). Publications: *Sinn fürs Unendliche: Religion in der Mediengesellschaft* (Gütersloh 2002); *Sinnfragen: Transformationen des Religiösen in der modernen Kultur* (Gütersloh 2006); *Religion als Deutung des Lebens: Perspektiven einer Praktischen Theologie gelebter Religion* (Gütersloh 2006); *Predigtlehre: über religiöse Rede* (Göttingen 2013).

Mechteld M. Jansen
holds a PhD from the VU University Amsterdam. She is currently Professor of Missiology at the Protestant Theological University (Amsterdam/Groningen). Her main research areas are migration and theology, new concepts of mission in the context of secularity, world Christianity and boundaries, postcolonial studies. Publications: *Talen naar God: wegwijzers bij Paul Ricoeur* (Gorinchem 2002); *A New Day Dawning: African Christians Living the Gospel* (co-editor) (Zoetermeer 2004); *A Moving God: Immigrant Churches in the Netherlands* (co-editor) (Zürich/Berlin 2008); *Wie zijn wij dan? Over erkenning en verbondenheid tussen mensen die alles, bijna niets, een beetje of heel veel geloven* (Zoetermeer 2008); *Interrelated Stories: Intercultural Pastoral Theology* (Zürich/Münster 2011).

Nico N. Koopman
is Professor of Systematic Theology, Director of the Beyers Naudé Centre for Public Theology and Dean of the Faculty of Theology at Stellenbosch University in South Africa. He completed his doctoral dissertation at the University of the Western Cape. During his doctoral studies he also undertook research at VU University Amsterdam. His research focuses on the public content, public rationality and public meaning of Christian faith. For *Die ligtheid van die lig: morele oriëntasie in 'n postmoderne tyd* (with Robert Vosloo) (Cape Town 2002) he won the Andrew Murray Prize for Theological Literature.

Ábrahám Kovács
is Associate Professor at Debrecen Reformed University (Hungary). He received his PhD from the University of Edinburgh and published *In Academia for the Church: Eastern and Central European Theological Perspectives* (co-editor) (Carlisle 2014); "The First Hungarian Handbook on Comparative Religion" in James L. Cox & Ábrahám Kovács (eds.), *New Trends and Recurring Issues in the Study of Religion* (Budapest 2014); "The Challenge of post Christendom Era" in Stephen R. Goodwin (ed.), *World Christianity in Local Context: Essays in Memory of David A. Kerr* (London/New York 2009). His research

focuses on Christian theology, comparative theologies, mission studies, Jewish-Christian relations and Scottish and Hungarian ecclesiastical, social and intellectual history. Currently he is guest professor at PUTS, Seoul, Korea.

Renée D.N. van Riessen
holds a PhD from VU University Amsterdam. She is Senior Lecturer of Philosophy at the Protestant Theological University (Amsterdam/Groningen) and Professor Extraordinary of Christian Philosophy at Leiden University. Her works include *Man as a Place of God: Levinas' Hermeneutics of Kenosis* (Dordrecht 2007) and *De ziel opnieuw: Over innerlijkheid, inspiratie en onderwijs* (Amsterdam 2013).

Emanuel Gerrit Singgih
is Professor of Biblical Hermeneutics and Indonesian Contextual Theologies at Duta Wacana Christian University, Yogyakarta, Indonesia. He took his PhD from Glasgow University and an honorary doctorate from the Protestant Theological University (Amsterdam/Groningen). He has written commentaries on Ecclesiastes and Genesis 1–11 in Indonesian, and a commentary on Isaiah 40–55 is forthcoming this year. He sits in the Advisory Board of *Exchange*.

Gé M. Speelman
is Lecturer in Religious Studies at the Protestant Theological University (Amsterdam/Groningen). She is interested in interreligious hermeneutics and women's dialogue. Recent publications are: "Interreligious Reading Strategies: A Case Study From the Netherlands" in Volker Küster and Robert Setio (eds.), *Muslim Christian Relations Observed* (Leipzig 2014); *Een kleine Koran* (co-author) (Gorinchem 2011); *Claiming Space for Women: Women Reading Scripture in Critical Dialogue* (forthcoming, Amsterdam 2014).

David VanDrunen
is Robert B. Strimple Professor of Systematic Theology and Christian Ethics at Westminster Seminary California. He earned the J.D. from Northwestern University School of Law and the Ph.D. from Loyola University Chicago. His research interests include natural law, the two kingdoms doctrine, and bioethics. Among his recent books are *Natural Law and the Two Kingdoms: A Study in the Development of Reformed Social Thought* (Grand Rapids 2010) and *Divine Covenants and Moral Order: A Biblical Theology of Natural Law* (Grand Rapids 2014).

Pieter H. Vos
is Lecturer in Ethics at the Protestant Theological University (Amsterdam/ Groningen) and Vice Director of the International Reformed Theological Institute (IRTI). He received his PhD from the Protestant Theological University (Amsterdam/Groningen). In his research Vos concentrates on virtue ethics, moral formation and professional practices, existential ethics, and Kierkegaard. His publications include *De troost van het ogenblik: Kierkegaard over God en het lijden* (Baarn 2002); *Søren Kierkegaard lezen* (Kampen 2010); "After Duty: The Need for Virtue Ethics in Moral Formation", in Bram de Muyck, Johan Hegeman & Pieter Vos (eds.), *Bridging the Gap: Proceedings of the IAPCHE-Europe Conference* (Sioux Center 2011), 143–158; "Self" in Steven M. Emmanuel, William McDonald & Jon Stewart (eds.), *Kierkegaard's Concepts* (KRSRR Vol. 15, Tome VI) (Aldershot, forthcoming).

Onno K. Zijlstra
holds a PhD from VU University Amsterdam and has taught philosophy at VU University, the Protestant Theological University (Amsterdam/Groningen) and ArtEZ Institute of the Arts. In his research Zijlstra focuses on the relations of aesthetics and ethics/religion. His works include *Dilemma's: Een kortere inleiding in de filosofie* (Budel 2003); *Language, Image and Silence: Kierkegaard and Wittgenstein on Ethics and Aesthetics* (Budel 2006); *Wat doet die rode vlek daar linksboven? Inleiding in de esthetica* (Arnhem 2007); *Kierkegaard in discussie* (Budel 2012). He is co-editor of *Als ik job niet had: Tien denkers over God en het lijden* (Zoetermeer 1997) and editor of *Letting Go: Rethinking Kenosis* (Bern 2002).

Heleen E. Zorgdrager
received her PhD from the Protestant Theological University (Amsterdam/ Groningen), where she is Professor of Systematic Theology and Gender Studies. Zorgdrager's research concentrates on gender, *theosis*, sanctification and the Protestant-Orthodox dialogue. Her publications include: "On the Fullness of Salvation," *Journal of Reformed Theology* (2014); "Homosexuality and Hypermasculinity in the Public Discourse of the Russian Orthodox Church," *International Journal of Philosophy and Theology* (2013); "Homemade Mission, Universal Civilization: Friedrich Schleiermacher's Theology of Mission," *Mission Studies* (2013); "A Practice of Love: Myrrha Lot-Borodine and the Modern Revival of the Doctrine of Deification," *The Journal of Eastern Christian Studies* (2012). She is Visiting Professor at the Ukrainian Catholic University in Lviv.

Index

Abraham   10, 12, 175, 178, 182–184, 188–191, 195–204, 207–209, 283, 285–291, 296–297
   Abraham's trial   175, 188–189 *see also* Aqedah
Accra Declaration   246
Ackerman, Bruce A.   68, 74n
Aesthetic(s)   209, 291, 293–294, 302
Africa   15–16, 124–125, 173, 239–254, 304–309
Akhenaten   139–148, 186n
Alves, Rubem   243, 244n
Amarna complex   141
Ancient Near East   140, 142, 145
Aniconic God   135–149
An-Na'im, Abdullahi Ahmad   6, 14, 33–36, 39, 41
Apartheid   15, 125, 240–241, 245, 249, 304–309, 315n
Aqedah   12, 178, 187, 189, 195, 197, 204, 212
Aquinas, Thomas/ Thomistic   66–70, 77, 158n39, 263
Arendt, Hannah   315
Argumentation   77, 80, 120, 248, 251
Aristocracy/ aristocratic   105–111
Aristotle   67–68, 263, 294n
Art/ the arts/ artist   14, 17, 282–283, 291–295
Asad, Muhammad   32
Asad, Talal   6, 24, 28–34, 41
Assmann, Jan   10, 136, 139–149, 174n4, 175, 185–188, 190
Audi, Robert   80
Authenticity/ authentic   5, 13–17, 23, 54, 113, 209, 243, 258, 282–297, 302
Autonomy   29, 65n, 80, 173, 184, 195, 266, 300
   of art   291–293
   of morality   12, 195, 200–205
   of cultural groups   53, 60

Backward   87, 217, 227, 231, 234–235
Babylonian Exile   136, 138
Bal, Rasit   23, 41, 42n
Bánffy, Dezső   106–107

Barbarism/ barbarian   2, 9, 87, 173–174, 211, 227n, 236
Barr, James   71n
Bartha, Tibor   114–115, 120–122, 129n
Basil of Caesarea   260
Bavinck, Herman   5, 81n, 82n
Beek, Bram van de   162n, 171n, 244, 245n, 254n
Beeldenstorm   135, 146, 149
Beer, Paul de   25–27, 42n
Beiser, Friedrich   267–269, 278n
Bereczky, Albert   114, 116, 129n
Bible
   1 Corinthians 1:28   109
   1 Corinthians 2:9   290n37
   2 Corinthians 3:18   229
   1 Kings 20   143
   2 Kings 1   143
   2 Kings 3   143
   Acts 17:22–31   309
   Colossians 1:20   170n
   Deuteronomy 6:4   144
   Deuteronomy 32   144
   Ephesians 2:13–14   169n
   Ephesians 4:17–5:20   259
   Exodus 32:27   183
   Galatians 3:13–14   207
   Galatians 3:28   211n
   Genesis 8:20–9:17   8, 64, 70–77
   Genesis 9:6   73–76
   Genesis 22, *see also Aqedah*   10, 12, 178n, 179, 185–191, 195, 204n, 207
   Genesis 31:43–53   143
   Hebrews 11:17–19   207
   Hosea 11:8   168
   Isaiah 40–55   136–138
   Isaiah 43:10   10, 136–138, 148
   Isaiah 55: 8–9   151
   James 1:17–22   210n
   John 12:32   169n, 170n
   John 19:30   170n
   Judges 3:20   143
   Judges 7:12–15   143
   Judges 11:23–24   143, 178

Bible (cont.)
  Luke 10:17–20   229
  Mark 10:17–31   258
  Mark 10:45   170n
  Mark 14:22–24   170n
  Mark 15:34   170n
  Matthew 22:37–39   126
  Matthew 28:19   113
  Numbers 23–24   143
  Numbers 25   178
  Philippians 2:12–13   195n
  Romans 1:18–20   308
  Romans 8:26   244
  Romans 13:1–7   75–76
Bickel, Alexander M.   65n
Biezeveld, Kune   145
Bildung   2, 12–13, 194, 196, 207–214, 225–227, 229–230, 236–238, 267, 271
Billings, J. Todd   265, 278
Binding of Isaac, *see Aqedah*
Blair, Tony   45
Boesak, Allan   246n, 249n
Bogárdi, Szabó István   115–120, 124n
Bosch, David   224, 236
Brady, Bernard V.   251, 253
Brandt, James M.   272n, 273n, 275n
Britain/Great Britain   46, 107
Bruyère, Jean de la   286
Burney, Charles F.   143
Butler, Judith   219n, 231, 232n
Byzantium   8, 90, 92, 95, 98

Calling of the church   240
Cahill, Lisa Sole   263
Calvin, John   109–111, 250, 256–258, 260–265, 174, 277–278
  'new approach to Calvin'   265
Calvinism   9, 105–116, 123, 136, 149, 180n, 250, 263–264
  Neo-calvinism   5, 46
Canlis, Julie   265
Cantwell Smith, Wilfred   147
Carrol, Robert   147, 149
Casanova, José   221 222
Character   16, 177–178, 180, 256–278, 296, 301
  Christian character   16, 156–178
  Character ethics, *see also* virtue   202, 248, 257, 259

Chemosh   143
Christendom   3, 8–9, 29, 107, 112–113, 121, 126
Christian life   113, 121, 126, 128, 231, 256, 257, 261–165, 272, 275
Christology   118–119, 151–171, 207
Church   6, 15, 25, 52, 54, 220, 221, 226, 229–230, 233n, 235, 240, 246–253, 262, 272–278, 302–305
  Church and civilization   84–101
  Dutch Reformed Church (DRC)   16, 247
  Reformed church   4, 106
  Reformed Church of Hungary (RHC)   6, 9, 16, 105–127
  Uniting Reformed Church in Southern Africa (URCSA)   16, 246–247
Citizenship   1, 37, 57–62, 219, 226
Civic reason   35–36
Civil   25, 31, 34, 50, 54–58, 75–77, 108–110, 126, 253, 300, 310
  Civil society   53, 57
  Civil religion   61
  Civil order   110
Civilisation   2–3, 180, 194n
Civilization   1–19, 45–46, 84–101, 106, 111, 113, 123, 127, 136, 173–176, 180–185, 194–212, 217–219, 224–235, 239, 256, 286, 287n, 289, 293–394, 297
  Anti-civilization   91–92
  Christian civilization   3–5, 90, 92, 197, 211, 233
  Civilized society   1, 15, 239, 240, 288
  Clash of civilizations   4, 86, 174
  Eurasian civilization   93
  God and civilization   1, 4–6, 13, 18, 176, 197–198, 217–218
  Human civilization   3, 11, 17, 99, 121, 128, 151, 171, 185, 256, 273
  Orthodox civilization   8, 85–86, 96, 101
  Western civilization   7–8, 64–81, 90, 195, 198, 218–219, 224, 229, 233n, 283
Civilizing   1, 13–15, 18, 194, 198, 212, 221, 224, 227–235, 239–254, 276
Cliteur, Paul   11–12, 175–180, 184–186, 190, 195, 196, 210
Commitment   4, 34, 48, 71, 78, 234, 284–285, 290–291, 295
Common grace   71

INDEX

Communism 6, 9, 99, 105, 111–115, 117–126
Community 6, 23–27, 37–41, 49, 54, 58, 67, 135, 139, 225, 248, 257–278
   Christian community 248, 273, 275–277
   Community and character 262–268
   Migrant community 41, 49, 58, 233
   Muslim community 6, 23, 39–41
   Religious community 23–27, 35, 37, 39–41, 49, 52, 54, 58, 248, 251
Confession of Belhar 16, 247
Constitutional monarchy 105–106, 109–111
Consumerism 61, 246, 293, 297
Corporatism 55–56
Cosmotheism 145–148
Covenant 8, 64, 70–81, 285

Daley, Janet 45
Danilevsky, Nikolai 93
Deist, Ferdinand 249
Democracy 9–10, 14, 18, 31, 45–48, 58, 107–111, 123, 128, 196, 232, 239, 243
   Liberal democracy/ democratic 6, 9, 15, 18, 45–46, 52, 59, 66n, 69–70, 105, 107–111, 128, 219, 226, 234–235, 239–243, 307, 314
Deneen, Patrick 65n, 68, 69n
Derrida, Jacques 180
Deutero-Isaiah 10, 137, 140, 144, 148
Diakonia 114, 118–119
Dialogue 9, 10, 12, 54, 74n, 102, 128, 153, 177, 196, 267
Diaspora 8, 88
Dickson, C.J. 269, 270n, 272n, 277n
Dignity, human 6, 14, 65n2, 74, 126, 304, 308, 311–312
Dionysius the Areopagite (Pseudo-Dionysius) 11, 151–161, 165, 169–170
Discipline 13, 16, 28, 40–41, 45, 52, 84–85, 122, 207, 219, 230–231, 234–235, 272–273
Discipling 228–230
Diversity 23, 34, 36, 38, 40, 58, 66, 247, 267, 296
   Cultural 7, 44n, 47, 88
   Religious 7, 47, 88, 224
Divine certainty 301
Divine Command Theory 10, 178–179, 190, 195–196
   Divine Command Ethics 5, 12, 196, 200

Doctrine 6, 28–30, 32–33, 45, 68n, 70, 80, 81n, 120, 122, 180n, 219n, 256–257, 268, 272–273, 277–278
Dooyeweerd, Herman 5, 46, 47n, 50, 55n
Duncan, Forrester 125

Eastern Orthodox tradition/ theology 5, 8, 19, 84–89, 91, 93–102, 260
Eagleton, Terry 173–174
Eckhart, Master John 183
Education 59–61, 87nn1 194, 208, 226, 228–230, 235, 273, 277
   Civic/ citizenship education 59, 226
Edwards, Jonathan 261
El/ Elohim 136, 143–144
Eliot, T.S. 2, 13–14
Ego-culture 284
Egypt 10, 138–143, 146–147
Emotivism 258, 262
Empire 8, 90–93, 98, 245–246
Enlightenment 3, 17, 100, 181, 184–185, 194, 208, 221, 243, 265, 282n4, 301, 303–304, 308
Eschatology 101, 118, 120–121, 128, 260
Ethics 30, 178–180, 188–189, 196–197, 200–207, 211–212, 251–252, 266–278, 287–289
   Ethics of law/ obligation 257, 263–266, 276–278, 288
   Ethics of virtue/ character 16, 257, 259–278
   Rationalistic ethics 201, 204, 211, 300
   Religious ethics 10–12, 195, 200–207, 211–212
   Reformed ethics 257, 263–266
Euthyphro-dilemma 195, 204
Evans, C. Stephen 200
Exclusivism 8, 98

Faith 9, 12–15, 18–19, 29, 49, 99–101, 119–121, 175–178, 181, 188–191, 195–202, 204–205, 208–212, 230, 235, 239, 256, 283, 285, 287n24, 289–291, 300–301, 305, 308–309, 311, 315–317
   Moral faith 206
   Virtue of 271, 277
Ferry, Luc 284, 290
Fiqh 33
Florovsky, Georges 8–9, 88–102

Freedom   6, 45, 59, 106, 123, 128, 226, 231–232, 234, 239–240, 260, 266–267, 290, 312
　Freedom of religion   9, 25–28, 33, 40–41, 51, 91
French Revolution   243, 310–311
Freud, Sigmund   10, 142, 144–145, 147, 184

Gift   181, 207, 209–210, 212, 225, 246, 264
'Gothic space'   6, 39
Grace   5, 71, 117, 119, 205, 207, 210, 260, 264, 272, 274
Grayling, A.C.   173
Green, Ronald M.   196n10, 198, 204
Gregory of Nyssa   260
Gregory of Palamas   95
Griffioen, Sander   49
Gruchy, John de   243, 249–250
Guilt   205–207, 211, 224, 245, 287n24, 307
Gunsteren, Herman van   293
Gustafson, James   15, 242, 245, 248, 251–253

Habermas, Jürgen   17, 35, 301–302
Habitus   257, 263, 265
Hare, John E.   205
Harrison, Nonna Verna   257–258, 260, 277
Hauerwas, Stanley   257, 260–263, 277
Hayek, Friedrich A.   66n4
Hegel, Georg W.F.   12, 183, 189, 196, 201–204, 208–211, 287–290, 294n55, 296
Hegelianism/ Hegelian   197, 200, 287, 288, 290
Hellenism   86, 89–90, 92, 95, 97, 141n20, 270n69, 271
Hennes Plasschaert, Jeanine   25
Henotheism   144, 148, 182n29
Herms, Eilert   263–264
Heschel, Abraham J.   191
Hesychasm   95, 96n34
History   92–93, 100, 120, 208–209, 248, 262, 288, 290, 292–294, 296
　'Mnemohistory'   139–140, 142, 147
Hoet, Jan   292
Hope   7–8, 15, 64, 81, 128, 179, 218, 235, 243–245, 285, 306
　Virtue of   271, 277

Human being   5, 68, 72–79, 100, 118, 121, 126, 151, 158, 161–164, 166–168, 176, 184, 206, 208, 210, 212, 247, 259–260, 264, 305–309, 311, 315
Humane, humanness   2, 10, 286n21, 225–226, 250, 303, 314
Human rights   13–14, 17, 33, 36, 51–52, 96, 302, 304–317
Humanity   1, 11, 17, 72, 75, 156–161, 169–170, 182, 246, 267, 273, 295, 304, 306–307, 312
Humanism   123, 126, 187
Huizinga, Johan   297
Hungary   9, 105–129
Hume, David   174, 177
Huntington, Samuel   4, 8, 86, 87n12, 174

Iconoclasm   11, 135–136, 148–149 see also Idols/ idolatry, *Beeldenstorm*
Identity   8, 44, 49–51, 53, 151, 155–156, 159, 197, 217, 219–221, 248
Ideology   8, 9, 88, 92–94, 101, 121–123, 127, 290–291, 300–301
　Atheist ideology   112–113, 119
　Calvinist ideology   114–115
Idols/ Idolatry   137–138, 142, 147–149 see also iconoclasm
Image of God (*imago Dei*)   12, 73, 126, 147n44, 155, 184, 189, 194, 210–212, 261–262, 271
Immediacy   209, 285–286
Immigration   14, 46, 231–232
　Dutch immigration   219–220
Incarnation   97, 100, 151–163, 165, 169–170
Individuality/ individual   2, 8, 13–14, 17, 25–27, 33, 38, 48–61, 66–68, 74–77, 80, 90, 117, 120, 155, 201–202, 204, 207–211, 225–226, 230, 256–258, 262–263, 266–269, 275–278, 282, 284–297, 300–309, 314
Individualization   292–293
Indonesia   11, 135–136, 138, 147, 149
Integration/ societal integration   7, 14–15, 44, 47, 57–58, 60, 217–235
　Civic integration exam/ course   222–223, 226–231, 234–235
　Dutch Civic Integration   222–235
Interiority/ the inner   90, 95, 264, 266, 286–290

INDEX

Intolerance   146, 174, 222
Isaac   10, 12, 183, 188–189, 195, 198–199, 201, 204, 283, 285, 290
   Binding of, *see Aqedah*
Islam   5–6, 8, 11, 17, 29–42, 54, 58, 135–136, 173, 176, 178, 195, 220, 232, 234
Israel   10, 55, 71, 136–138, 142–148, 177–178

János, Győri   116
Jánosi, Zoltán   9, 108–111, 123
Jaspers, Karl   293
Joas, Hans   17, 301–302, 314
Job   161, 291, 296
Josephus, Flavius   140–141
Jural interests   7, 48, 50, 53, 54
Justice   7, 30, 48, 53, 68–69, 72–75, 78, 126, 239–240, 246–248, 307–308
   Public justice   7, 46–50, 52, 55–58
   Social justice   116, 120, 122
   Virtue of   270

Kant, Immanuel   65n4, 184, 188–189, 196, 200–201, 203–206, 211, 266, 288, 292
Károli, Gáspár   116
Kenessey, Béla   9, 106–109, 111
Kierkegaard, Søren A.   12–13, 17, 179, 184n34, 185, 188–191, 194–212, 225, 283, 285, 287–292, 294–297
Kingdom of God   81, 91, 106–108, 111, 113, 118, 120, 122, 128, 244, 270, 273, 277
Kirill, Patriarch   84–85
Knott, Kim   37
Koyzis, David   49
Kruijf, Gerrit de   240–241
Kuitert, Harry   242
Kultur   2–3, 87nn1, 65n4, 194n1
Kuyper, Abraham   5, 7, 46
Kymlicka, Will   50

Larmore, Charles   286
Law   2, 14, 26–27, 31, 45–49, 51, 55–57, 59, 108–109, 219, 232, 258, 263–266, 300, 310–311
   God's law/Law of God   4–6, 12, 18–19, 24, 33–34, 36–37, 39–41, 68, 105, 112–113, 123, 125–126, 128, 195, 218, 242, 264–266, 277–278, 300
   Moral law   196, 201, 205–206, 269

Secular law   7, 45
Ten commandments   264, 277
Lee, Seung-Goo   200
Levinas, Emmanuel   184–185
Liberalism   7–8, 10, 18, 25, 50–51, 64–71, 74–81, 111, 222, 225
   Neo-liberalism   9, 105, 107, 123–127
Liberation theology   249–250
Liturgy   92, 100, 271, 273, 276
Lloyd, Vincent   38–39

MacIntyre, Alasdair   7, 68, 260, 263n35
Mann, Thomas   182
Manuel, Trevor   240
Marx, Karl   112
Marxism   112, 118–119, 122, 241
Maximus the Confessor   259–260
Mbiti, John   249
McConnell, Michael W.   70
Middle space (broken middle)   24, 38–41
Milbank, John   6, 38–39
Missiology / missiological   217, 224, 225, 228–230, 234
Mission   1–2, 15, 87, 88, 93, 113, 119, 121–125, 218, 220, 222, 224–225, 228–235, 273
   Mission civilisatrice   224
Modernity/ modern   2, 10, 14–18, 23–24, 26, 28–29, 68–69, 93n, 96, 101, 128, 175, 181, 185, 198, 217–218, 221–222, 225, 231–232, 239, 257, 276, 284, 286, 291–292, 300–303
   Modern nation state   24, 27, 31–38, 40–41, 45, 106
Modood, Tariq   46, 232
Monasticism/ monks   90–92, 94–95
Monolatry   148, 182
Monotheism   10–13, 18, 135–137, 139–142, 144–149, 151–153, 173–180, 182–191, 195
Morals/ morality   2, 10, 12, 29n, 35, 61, 108, 178, 195–198, 201–207, 210–211, 251, 258
   Moral gap   205–207, 211
   Moral obligation   67, 73, 206
   Moral order   67–68, 72, 79, 205
Mosaic distinction   139–145, 148, 186–188
Moses   10, 136, 139–144, 186
Mouw, Richard   49
Multiculturalism/ multicultural   7, 18, 44–50, 53, 56–59, 177, 219–220
Müller, Max   144, 182n29

Muslim   6, 23–41, 49, 56, 58, 116, 135, 149, 173, 220–222, 226–227, 231, 233
Mysticism   11, 95, 151n4, 152–153, 168–170
 Dionysian mysticism   153–161
 Taoistic mysticism   165, 168

Napel, Hans-Martien ten   47, 55
Narrative   15, 46, 151, 196, 212, 248–249, 251, 253, 260–263, 277
Natural law   7–8, 64–81, 174n4, 264, 308–309
 Natural law liberalism   65, 67–71, 77–81
Negotiation   15, 30, 39–40, 235, 311–312
Netherlands, the   3n4, 37–38, 46, 217, 220–223, 225–228, 232–233
Neutrality   6, 25, 37, 68, 70, 81, 228
Nietzsche, Friedrich   14, 184–185
Noahic covenant   8, 70–78, 80–81
Noll, Rüdiger   128
Noort, Ed   179–180n, 189

Obedience   45, 200, 210, 230, 259, 291, 297, 300
Osarsiph   141
Other/ otherness   4–5, 9–10, 13, 15, 18, 87, 126–128, 181, 194, 204, 211, 221, 235, 296
Overlapping consensus   30, 37, 78

Pagan/ paganism   116, 174n7, 140, 187, 224, 233, 309
Participation   41, 57
 Political   47, 59–61, 314
 Societal   57, 62
 in/of God   19, 265, 278
Passion/ *pathos*   174, 188, 190–191, 208–210, 243
Peiter, Hermann   269
Peursen, C.A. van   287n25
Pluralism   47, 56, 74n, 123, 148, 300, 314
 Legal pluralism   49, 55–59
Policy discourse   241–242, 252–254
Politics/ political   34–35, 38, 61, 69, 75, 78–80, 84, 101, 110
Polytheism   139, 142, 145–148, 174–175, 177, 186
Postmodernity/ postmodern   38, 284, 292
Private-public   35, 38, 56, 293–294, 296

Prophecy/ prophetic   115–116, 120–121, 125, 136–137, 191, 239–243, 245–254
Protestantism/ protestant   4–5, 19, 46, 67, 70, 256–257, 264–265
 Protestant principle   4–5, 13, 101, 218, 226, 233, 235
Pseudo-Dionysius, *see* Dionysius the Areopagite
Public, the   292–294
Public domain/ public sphere   23–26, 34–41, 44–61, 80–81, 125, 135, 176, 184, 222, 233, 242, 247, 251–252
Public good   48, 53–55, 58
Public theology   125, 242, 246, 251

Rad, Gerhard von   147
Ratzinger, Joseph   145
Ravasz, László   121–122
Rawls, John   30, 35, 68–69, 78–80, 285n16
Reconciliation   71, 95, 124–125, 203, 247, 287n24, 296, 306–308
Reformed   4–5, 8, 11, 46–48, 55, 66, 70–71, 78, 120, 126, 200, 243, 249–250, 256–257, 264–265
 Dutch Reformed Church (DRC), *see* Church
 Hungarian Reformed   9, 105–128
 Reformed Church of Hungary (RHC), *see* Church
 Reformed (covenant) theology   64, 70–77
 Uniting Reformed Church in Southern Africa (URCSA), *see* Church
Responsibility   5, 27, 57, 76, 198–199, 201, 206–207, 252, 284
Revelation   67, 80n39, 81, 118, 120, 181
Rights   26–27, 49–60, 65, 69, 74n27, 76, 110–111, 125–127, 226n32, 228, 307, 310, 312, 316
 Constitutional rights   59
 Cultural/ religious rights   49–55, 220, 232
 Natural rights   69–70
Robinson, Marilynne   185
Romanticism   209, 282, 293, 296
Rosenblum, Nancy   53
Rousseau, Jean-Jacques   283, 285, 291, 308
Rule of Law   45, 61, 65n2
Russia   8, 84–86, 89, 93–94, 96n, 98, 313

INDEX

Russian orthodox tradition   84–85, 94–98
Russian revolution   88, 93

Sacks, Jonathan   44
Samaritan, the   289–290
Sanctification   5, 13, 16, 19, 256–257, 259–262, 265, 273–278
Schleiermacher, Friedrich   16, 256–258, 265–278
Schwartz, Regina M.   145, 151
Schmemann, Alexander   9, 97–101
Secular/ secularity   3–10, 18, 24, 28–31, 36–41, 45, 62, 80–81, 92, 105, 125, 177, 181, 217, 221–222, 224–225, 231, 234–235, 300–303
Secularism   13, 15, 24, 29–31, 35n44, 37, 96, 194–195, 219, 221–225, 230–235
Secularization   17, 29, 35, 112–113, 146, 194, 217–219, 300–303
   Post-secularization   16–17, 181, 219n7, 301–303
Selbstbildung   267–268
Self   13, 17, 207–211, 230, 234, 256, 261, 263, 266–267, 270, 276, 282–287, 290–292, 295
   Self-criticism   9, 16, 105, 125–126, 247–248, 297
Separation church-state   17, 25, 29, 220, 301–303
Setio, Robert   148–149
Shari'a   6, 24, 27, 29n, 31–41, 47, 56
Sittlichkeit   201, 288
Skillen, James   47
Sloterdijk, Peter   12, 175–176, 180–186, 188, 190
Smith, Mark S.   142–145, 147–149
Social order   9, 66, 69n14, 74, 77, 105–109
South Africa   6, 15–16, 124–125, 240–241, 243, 247, 249, 304–305, 307, 315n
Spencer, John   142
Sphere sovereignty   7, 55
Spengler, Oswald   3, 8, 86, 93–94
Spinoza, Benedict   183, 266
State   6–7, 9, 23–27, 30–41, 45–51, 53–61, 68, 70, 74–77, 84, 91, 99, 105–106, 109–115, 119–121, 128, 202–203, 220–221, 313, 316
Stewart, Jon   287–288n
Suffering   11, 16, 112, 118–119, 122, 151–153, 156, 160–161, 169–171, 197, 243–244

Summotheism   182–183
Swinburne, Richard   174

Tao/ Taoism   11, 152–154, 161–170
Taylor, Charles   17, 30, 232n45, 268, 268n55, 282–283, 289, 293–294
Taylor, Mark C.   287n23
Terrorism   178–179, 194, 196, 231
Tildy, Zoltán   111, 123
Tillich, Paul   4–5, 13, 101, 177, 226
Tolerance   14, 44, 126, 128, 221, 227, 239, 275, 314
Toynbee, Arnold   8, 86
Tradition   2, 293, 296, 312, 315
Transcendence/ transcendent   2, 11, 152–157, 161, 168, 181, 184–185, 201–202, 209–210, 284, 290, 296, 300, 305, 307, 309
Transfiguration   257, 274
Transformation   5, 13–14, 17, 256, 258–259, 265, 271–272, 274, 302n, 304–305, 311
Translatability   139–140, 142–144, 148–149
Tutu, Desmond   304–309, 317

Ubuntu   308
Unio cum Christo   261, 274
Universal/Universalism   4, 8, 10–11, 19, 36, 71–72, 75, 79, 81, 88, 92, 95, 97, 117–118, 173–174, 200–204, 209–211, 264, 287, 289, 291, 294–295, 304–306, 308–316
Universal Declaration of Human Rights   310–311, 314

Verbrugge, Ad   282n4
Victor, János   117–118
Violence   4–5, 10–12, 30, 45, 74, 135, 145–146, 151–153, 161, 168, 170–171, 175–180, 186–191, 194, 234, 239, 316
Voegelin, Eric   144
Vos, Pieter H.   257, 263–265, 295
Virtue   7, 16, 48, 52, 55, 61, 67n8, 68, 76, 162n, 165–166, 257, 259–260, 263–277, 284

Weber, Max   146–147
Wesley, John   257, 261
Wildberger, Hans   137
Williams, Bernard   284–285
Williams, Rowan   38, 45, 56n

Wittgenstein, Ludwig   287n25, 291, 294n
Woldring, Hendrik   57
Wolterstorff, Nicholas   69–70, 76, 80
Worship   10–11, 16, 92, 136–137, 139, 141, 146–148, 174–175, 177, 185, 190, 210, 229, 244, 259, 273–274, 276
Worldview   8, 15, 77–78, 105, 107–113, 121–123, 127–128, 146–147, 223, 234–235, 307–308

Wright, Nicholas T.   256–260, 277

Yahweh   137–138, 143–144, 147n44, 148
Yannaras, Christos   86, 95–96

Zeal   12, 174, 180–185, 190
Zijderveld, Anton   288–289
Zille, Helen   240
Žižek, Slavoj   175